Road Atlas of AUSTRALIA

YOUR ESSENTIAL TRAVEL COMPANION

• ALL STATES AND TERRITORIES • CAPITAL CITIES • MAJOR TOURIST REGIONS

1st edition

Published in Australia by Gregory's Publishing Company
(A division of Universal Press Pty Ltd)
ABN 83 000 087 132

Marketed and distributed by Universal Press (Publisher) Pty Ltd

New South Wales: 1 Waterloo Road,
Macquarie Park 2113
Ph: (02) 9857 3700 Fax: (02) 9888 9850

Queensland: 1 Manning Street,
South Brisbane 4101
Ph: (07) 3844 1051 Fax: (07) 3844 4637

South Australia:
Freecall: 1800 636 1972

Victoria: 585 Burwood Road,
Hawthorn 3122
Ph: (03) 9818 4455 Fax: (03) 9818 6123

Western Australia: 38a Walters Drive,
Osborne Park 6017
Ph: (08) 9244 2488 Fax: (08) 9244 2554

International distribution
Ph: (02) 9857 3700 Fax: (02) 9888 9850

The Publisher would be pleased to receive additional or updated material, or suggestions for future editions. Please address these to the Publishing Manager at Universal Press Pty Ltd.
If you would like to use any of the maps in this book please contact the CMS Manager at Universal Press Pty Ltd.

1st edition published 2000
Reprinted 2001

National Library of Australia Cataloguing-in-Publication data

Gregory's Road Atlas of Australia
1st Ed.
Includes index
ISBN 0 7319 0966 6 (pbk.)

1. Australia – Guidebooks. 2. Australia – Road Maps
I. Gregory's Publishing Co. II. Title: Robinson's road atlas
of Australia

912.94

Publishing Manager: Greg Reid
Production Manager: Harold Yates
Design Manager: Bronwynne Davis
Researcher/Writer: Kathleen Gandy
Editor: Sarah Baker
Editorial Assistant: Germaine Joffe
Internal Design: Bronwynne Davis

DTP/Layout: Graphic Skills
Illustrator, State Emblems: Brian Johnston
Photographic Researcher: Grant Nichol
Cartography: Universal Press &
                   Laurie Whiddon, Map Illustrations
Reproduction by: Graphic Skills
Printed by: Craft Print International Ltd

Photographic Acknowledgments

The publisher would like to gratefully acknowledge the following individuals and organisations for their generosity in supply photographs and images, and for their permission to reproduce photographic material used in this book.

Bunbury Tourism p. 192 (T & B)

Coolangatta Estate p. 62 (T)

Flinders Island Tourism p. 246 (B)

Geoff Higgins pp. 4 (T, MT & MB), 5 (T, MT, MB & B) 8, 10, 13, 16 (T & B), 18 (T & B), 49 (B), 52 (B), 54 (T&B), 58 (B), 70 (M), 91 (T & B), 96 (B), 100 (T & B), 102 (B), 104 (T & B), 126 (T), 128 (T), 140 (B), 142 (T & B), 144 (T), 160 (B), 162, 163, 164 (T & B), 166 (T), 168 (B), 170 (T & B), 172 (M), 194 (T & B), 199, 200 (T & B), 202 (T & M), 224 (T & B), 226, 228 (T & B), 230 (T & B), 232 (T & B), 244 (T), 248 (T & B)

Grant Nichol pp. 12, 58 (T), 59, 64 (B), 144 (M), 160 (T), 166 (B), 168 (T), 172 (T), 196 197, 222 (T & B), 225, 227, 229, 244 (B)

Gregory's Automotive Guides p. 9

King Island Tourism p. 246 (T)

Milawa Cheese Company p. 103

Port Stephens Tourism p. 61

Tom Eaton © Universal Press p.198

Tourism New South Wales pp. 22 (B), 48, 49 (T), 52 (T), 56 (T & B), 60 (T & B), 62 (B), 64 (T), 66 (T)

Tourism Queensland pp. 4 (B), 106 (T), 108 (T), 126 (B), 128 (B), 132 (T & B),134 (T), 136 (T & B), 137, 138 (T & B), 140 (T)

Tourism South Australia pp. 165, 169

Tourism Victoria pp. 68 (T & B), 90, 94, 95, 96 (T), 98 (T & B) 99, 102 (T)

Viewfinder Library pp. 22 (T), 24 (T & M), 66 (B), 106 (B), 108 (M), 130 (T & B), 134 (B)

FRONT COVER
Main Photograph: NOAA satellite image provided by the Australian Centre for Remote Sensing (ACRES), a business unit of the Australian Surveying and Land Information (AUSLIG), Australia's national mapping agency. www.auslig.com.au
Small Photographs: Geoff Higgins

CAPTIONS
Page 4: Floriade Festival, Canberra, ACT (T), Bondi Beach, Sydney, NSW (MT), 12 Apostles, Great Ocean Rd, Vic (MB), Scuba Diving, Great Barrier Reef, Qld (B)
Page 5: Lyndoch, Barossa Valley, SA (T), Lake Cave, near Margaret River, WA (MT), Devils Marbles, Sth of Tennant Creek, NT (MB), Cradle Mountain, Cradle Mt-Lake St Clair NP, Tas (B)

Contents

Acknowledgements — 3
State and Region Map Symbols — 6
Australia Key Map & City Map Symbols — 7
Planning a Trip — 8
Preparing for a Trip — 9
Motoring Hints — 10
Motoring Survival — 11
Useful Addresses — 12
Accident Checklist — 13
Intercity Distance Chart — 14

Australian Capital Territory — 16

Canberra — 18
Canberra Suburbs Map — 20
Australian Capital Territory Map — 21

New South Wales — 22

Sydney — 24
Sydney Suburbs Map — 26
New South Wales Maps — 30
Ballina to Byron Bay — 48
Blue Mountains — 49
Central Coast — 52
Coffs Harbour — 54
Hunter Valley, Lower — 56
Hunter Valley, Upper — 58
Myall Lakes and Nelson Bay — 60
Nowra and Jervis Bay — 62
Snowy Mountains — 64
The Illawarra & Southern Highlands — 66

Victoria — 68

Melbourne — 70
Melbourne Suburbs Maps — 72
Victoria Maps — 76
Gippsland Lakes — 90
Great Ocean Rd — 91
Macedon Ranges & Sunbury Wineries — 94
Phillip Island — 95
The Dandenongs — 96
The Goldfields — 98
The Grampians — 100
Victorian Alps — 102
Wilsons Promontory — 104

Queensland — 106

Brisbane — 108
Brisbane Suburbs Maps — 110
Queensland Maps — 114

Cairns 126
Fraser Coast 128
Gold Coast 130
Rockhampton & Capricorn Coast 132
Sunshine Coast 134
The Scenic Rim 136
Toowoomba & Eastern Downs 138
Whitsunday Islands 140

South Australia 142
Adelaide 144
Adelaide Suburbs Maps 146
South Australia Maps 150
Barossa Valley 160
Fleurieu Peninsula 162
Flinders Ranges 163
Kangaroo Island 164
Mt Gambier District 166
Riverland 168

Western Australia 170
Perth 172
Perth Suburbs Maps 174
Western Australia Maps 178
Bunbury District 192
Caves District 194
Fremantle 196
Mandurah-Pinjarra 197
Rottnest Island 198
Stirling Range NP to Albany 199

Northern Territory 200
Darwin 202
Darwin Suburbs Map 204
Northern Territory Maps 206
Alice Springs 222
Kakadu NP 224
Katherine Gorge (Nitmiluk NP) 226
Litchfield NP 227
Uluru-Kata Tjuta NP to Alice Springs 228

Tasmania 230
Hobart 232
Hobart Suburbs Map 234
Tasmania Maps 236
Cradle Mountain-Lake St Clair NP 244
Flinders Island & King Island 246
Tasman Peninsula 248

Index and Gazetteer 250

Explanation of Map Symbols

City Maps

MOTORWAY	Dual Carriageway	🏛	Museum
HIGHWAY	Metroad	①	Metroad
HIGHWAY	Through Route	32	National Route Marker
MORT ST	Major Road	→	One Way Street
LAWSON RD	Minor Road	P	Parking Area
LEURA ST	Other Road		Picnic Area
	Railway line & station	5	Place of Interest
	Walking Track	■	Point of Interest
	Ferry Route	○	Roundabout
	Ambulance	20	State Route Marker
	Boat Ramp		Toilets
	Camping Ground		Beach
	Caravan Park		Building
	Golf Course		National Park Recreation Reserve
	Hospital		Mall
	Information Centre		School
	Lookout 360°, 180°		Other Areas

Suburban Maps

FEDERAL HIGHWAY	Dual Carriageway	✈	Airport
BELCONNEN WAY ①	Metroad & Route Marker		Aerodrome
BARTON HIGHWAY 23 A1 A1	Through Route, National Route Marker		Hospital
MAJURA ROAD 20 C1	Main Road, State Route Marker	■ Casino	Point of Interest
KURINGA DR	Other Road	+ Glebe Hill 135	Mountain, height in Metres
	Railway and Station		National Park, Reserve, Recreation area
	Ferry Route		State Forest
N.S.W. A.C.T.	State Boundary		Educational Institution
CANBERRA	Major Centre		Other Areas
Gungahlin	Main Centre		Sand
Franklin	Suburb		

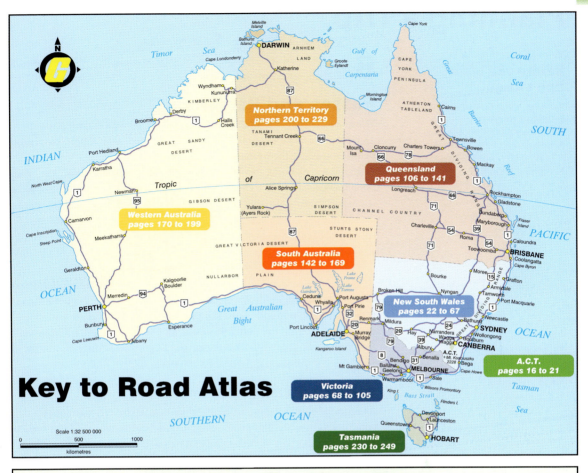

Key to Road Atlas

Northern Territory pages 200 to 229

Queensland pages 106 to 141

Western Australia pages 170 to 199

South Australia pages 142 to 169

New South Wales pages 22 to 67

A.C.T. pages 16 to 21

Victoria pages 68 to 105

Tasmania pages 230 to 249

Scale 1:32 500 000

0   500   1000
kilometres

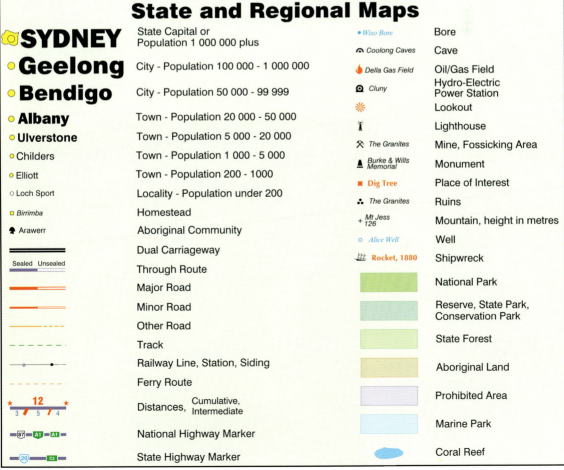

State and Regional Maps

Symbol	Description
SYDNEY	State Capital or Population 1 000 000 plus
Geelong	City - Population 100 000 - 1 000 000
Bendigo	City - Population 50 000 - 99 999
Albany	Town - Population 20 000 - 50 000
Ulverstone	Town - Population 5 000 - 20 000
Childers	Town - Population 1 000 - 5 000
Elliott	Town - Population 200 - 1000
Loch Sport	Locality - Population under 200
Birrimba	Homestead
Arawerr	Aboriginal Community
	Dual Carriageway
	Through Route
	Major Road
	Minor Road
	Other Road
	Track
	Railway Line, Station, Siding
	Ferry Route
Sealed Unsealed	
12 3 5 4	Distances, Cumulative, Intermediate
87 A1 A1	National Highway Marker
20 C3	State Highway Marker

Symbol	Description
• Wiso Bore	Bore
Coolong Caves	Cave
Della Gas Field	Oil/Gas Field
Cluny	Hydro-Electric Power Station
	Lookout
	Lighthouse
The Granites	Mine, Fossicking Area
Burke & Wills Memorial	Monument
Dig Tree	Place of Interest
The Granites	Ruins
+ Mt Jess 126	Mountain, height in metres
○ Alice Well	Well
Rocket, 1880	Shipwreck
	National Park
	Reserve, State Park, Conservation Park
	State Forest
	Aboriginal Land
	Prohibited Area
	Marine Park
	Coral Reef

Planning a Trip

Before any road trip, either short or long, it is important to be prepared. Following are a few tips to help you have a successful trip.

Passes and Permits

Passes and permits are necessary for travelling through certain parts of Northern Australia and South Australia. If needed, they should be organised before you begin the journey.

If you are planning to visit or travel through Aboriginal land, you must obtain a special permit. There are two types of permit. A transit permit will allow you to drive through Aboriginal land but you cannot stop or leave the designated road. An entry permit will allow you to enter a certain area for a specific reason and period of time. Permits are obtained from the relevant Lands Council. You should allow 3 weeks for processing your application. See page 12 for Land Council addresses around Australia.

You will need to obtain a Desert Parks Pass if travelling into the desert parks of northern South Australia. They are issued by the National Parks and Wildlife Service of South Australia and replace the usual daily camping permit for entering the parks. Passes include detailed maps, information on first aid and survival skills. Telephone the Department for Environment, Heritage and Aboriginal Affairs, Ph: 1800 816 078.

What to take

As much of your holiday will be spent driving in the car, take lots of comfortable clothes. Even if travelling throughout summer, take at least one set of warm clothing as nights can still be cool. Also, take more changes of clothes if the area you will be exploring is cold and wet. Soft baggage is ideal for car journeys as they can be squashed into tight spaces in the vehicle.

Commonly forgotten items that you should pack include hats, walking shoes, sunblock, sunglasses, insect repellent and a camera. It is a good idea to keep tissues, extra water and snacks, maps and a compass in the car, within easy reach. The glovebox can be used to keep important papers that you may need during your trip. Vehicle registration, the number of your insurance policy and medical prescriptions should be included.

First aid kit

You must always keep a first aid kit in your car. If you are driving to remote areas it is advisable to do a certified first aid course. Commercially prepared kits are available from chemists and camping equipment shops. Alternatively, you can make up your own kit in a clean, waterproof container.

Listed are recommendations of what you should include in your kit:

- Absorbent gauze
- Antihistamine (for bee stings)
- Asprin or paracetamol
- Bandaids and assortment of adhesive dressings
- Conforming bandages
- Crepe bandages
- Eye bath
- Pen torch
- Saline eyewash
- Sterile dressings
- Stingose
- Triangular bandages
- Alcohol swabs
- Antiseptic cream and swabs (eg Betadine)
- Car-sickness tablets
- Clinical thermometer
- Cotton wool
- Current first aid book
- Latex gloves
- Safety pins
- Scissors
- Sticking plaster
- Tongue depressor
- Tweezers

Car Preparation

Nowadays many of Australia's roads are sealed or well-graded, so most cars can drive on them without any problems. However, if venturing off the beaten track is more to your liking, you should investigate hiring or buying a 4WD. If planning to tow a caravan or trailer, stay on the sealed roads, regardless of whether you are travelling in a 4WD.

Before you leave home

Make sure that your car has been checked by a qualified mechanic. If you are towing a caravan or trailer, get them serviced as well - particularly the tyres, lights, blinkers and general condition of their working parts.

Some things that need checking, both before and during the trip are:
- Battery and mountings
- Tyre condition and pressure (remember the spare!)
- Wheel balance and alignment
- Wheel bearings
- Windscreen wipers — blades and reservoir
- Brake system
- Exhaust system
- Cooling system — radiator, hoses and thermostat
- Engine drive belts
- Automatic transmission
- Heater and demister
- Air conditioning
- Lights
- Filters — air, oil and fuel
- Suspension
- Oil and coolant

Extras to take

Carry a spare set a keys, set of spanners and screwdrivers, jumper leads, WD lubricant, spare engine drive belt(s), radiator hoses, light globes and fuses, fire extinguisher, a jack and tools for changing tyres.

Motoring Hints

T his practical information is designed to make your trip more comfortable and enjoyable.

Beating fatigue

Today, 7 per cent of all accidents are due to driver fatigue. In country areas it accounts for 30 per cent of fatal accidents. Here are some tips to help combat driver fatigue:

- Take a break from driving every 2 hours
- Change drivers at this point
- Pull over and stop when drowsiness or discomfort occurs
- Wear comfortable clothes and sit upright with good back support
- Keep the windscreen clean and clear
- Avoid alcohol and eating a heavy meal before driving
- Get a good nights sleep before a long drive

Packing the car

Don't overload your car or 4WD as it will cause suspension problems. Have the suspension strengthened if you think you may have to overload the car.

Pack heavy items in cabin, boot or trailer. The weight of heavy items on the roof could easily throw the car off balance. When packing lighter items on a roof rack, make the load lower at the front and higher at the back so there is little wind resistance.

If carrying tools and equipment inside the car, make sure they are tightly secured. It is sensible to install a cargo barrier for this purpose. Emergency equipment, such as a fire extinguisher, must be easily accessible. Keep close at hand the things you may want or need during the journey.

Fuel Economy

Fuel consumption is affected by both the condition of the car and where it is driven. Here are some ways to help conserve your petrol:

- Avoid delays (peak hour traffic or scheduled bridge closures)
- Distribute weight through the car evenly
- Service the car regularly
- If held up in traffic turn off engine if safe to do so
- Drive as smoothly as possible
- Ensure tyres are inflated to ideal pressure and wheel alignment and balance are correct
- Make sure handbrake is fully released when car is mobile, and foot operated brakes are not dragging
- If using roof racks, keep load as low as possible to avoid excess drag
- Avoid driving at high speeds
- Use air conditioner only when absolutely necessary

When covering long distances on remote roads, you must know your car's fuel consumption. Here is a basic formula for working out fuel consumption:

FORMULA FOR WORKING OUT FUEL CONSUMPTION

$$\text{Total litres} \div \frac{\text{total km}}{100} = \text{litres per 100km}$$

OR

$$100 \times \text{total litres} \div \text{total km} = \text{litres per 100km}$$

Example

$$60 \text{ litres} \div \frac{300 \text{ km}}{100} = 20 \text{ litres per 100km}$$

Travelling with children

To prevent boredom and fighting after the novelty of travelling wears off, try the following:

- Bring child's favourite toys
- Play music and sing together
- Play family car games (there are books available on these)
- Stop for frequent breaks

Car sickness is very common in children. To lessen the symptoms you should:

- Drive as smoothly as possible
- Keep windows down
- Don't let children read or write while car is moving.
- Don't let children watch things flashing past — encourage them to watch things in distance

Motoring Survival

There are many weather conditions that can make driving hazardous. Some helpful hints for dealing with different conditions are outlined in this section.

Driving in fog

- Pull off road and wait for fog to lift if in zero or near-zero visability
- Put parking and hazard lights on
- Keep seat-belt fastened
- If driving in fog, go slowly and keep fog lights on
- Avoid crossing roads or busy highways when visibility is reduced

Survival Hints

- Don't panic — think of a course of action
- Stay with your vehicle – it provides shelter, increasing chances of survival spotting a car is easier than finding a person
- Conserve food and water — always carry enough food and water to keep you supplied for a few days (4 litres of water per person per day)
- Stay in the shade — keep clothes on to help protect against exposure
- Prepare adequate signals — if in a remote area use your flares or light a fire to attract attention

Surviving a Bushfire

If you get caught in a bushfire, it is important that you don't keep driving through the dense smoke. Follow the points below for survival. Also note that there is little risk of the petrol tank exploding in a bushfire.

- Pull to the side of the road away from the leading edge of the fire and stop
- Switch on headlights
- Stay in car
- Wind up windows and close air vents
- Crouch in car and shelter body
- Stay there until fire passes

Driving in Northern Australia

When travelling around northern Australia, the climate can dictate when to travel.

There are two distinct seasons experienced in northern Australia. The wet season (October to April) and the dry (May to October). Generally, the dry season consists of comfortable daytime temperatures and cool nights. It is the best time of year to explore the Northern Territory, far north Queensland and northern Western Australia. The wet season is characterised by monsoonal rainfall and it is not a pleasant time for a driving holiday. It is quite common with the heavy rainfall for roads to become impassable. The dangerous box jellyfish are also present in the ocean in the Northern Territory and far north Queensland at this time of year and it is advisable not to go swimming.

Driving in Alpine Regions

When driving through the alpine regions of Australia in winter, problems may occur. If you are prepared and aware of special driving techniques for these conditions, you will be able to avoid most problems.

Before leaving home:
- Have tyres and brakes checked, add anti-freeze to radiator
- Renew windscreen wiper blades
- Check heater and demister are working properly
- Take blankets and/or sleeping bags
- A torch, old piece of rug or plastic sheet and small shovel could be useful

Some techniques for driving in snow and ice worth learning are:
- Don't put handbrake on when parking unless slope demands it
- Use brakes as little as possible to avoid skidding
- Carefully control speed — on downhill sections use low gear instead of brakes
- Going uphill use higher gears as over-revving can cause wheel slip
- When changing down gears, do it smoothly with engine speed the same as wheel speed
- Put lights on low beam and chains on tyres when it is snowing

Outback Motoring

When driving on unsealed roads there are special techniques that can be employed to avoid problems such as getting bogged.

- On sand keep 4WD in a straight line — if you have to make a turn, do it by turning wheel quickly, then back to the original position
- Drive carefully at a safe speed on dirt roads, even when road is badly corrugated.
- When making a creek crossing, check the underlying surface, depth and flow of water — drive slowly in centre of crossing, keep the wheels straight and do not change gear midstream
- When overtaking, beware of soft or loose verges and the dust caused from road trains — if behind a road train, pull over to the side of the road until the dust has settled.
- If stuck in sand, use floor mats to give support and traction — use hub caps as jack supports — lowering tyre pressure also assists traction

Useful Addresses

ACT

Canberra Visitor Information Centre
Ph: (02) 6205 0044
www.canberratourism.com.au

NRMA (National Roads
& Motorists Association)
Ph: 132 900
www.nrma.com.au

ACT Parks & Conservation Service
Ph: (02) 6207 2900
www.act.gov.au\environ

NEW SOUTH WALES

Tourism NSW
Ph: 132 077
www.tourism.nsw.gov.au

NRMA (National Roads
& Motorists Association)
Ph: 132 900
www.nrma.com.au

NSW National Parks & Wildlife
Service
Ph: (02) 9585 6333
www.npws.nsw.gov.au

VICTORIA

Tourism Victoria
Ph: 13 28 42
www.tourism.vic.gov.au

RACV (Royal Automobile Club of
Victoria)
Ph: 13 19 55
www.racv.com.au

Dept of Natural Resources &
Environment
Ph: 13 61 86
www.nre.vic.gov.au

QUEENSLAND

QLD Government Travel Centre
Ph: (07) 3874 2800
www.queensland-travel-centre.com.au

RACQ (Royal Automobile
Club of Queensland)
Ph: (07) 3361 2468
www.racq.com.au

Environmental Protection Agency
Ph: (07) 3227 8185
www.env.qld.gov.au

Dept of Aboriginal & Torres Strait
Lands Acts Branch
Ph: 1800 645 874

SOUTH AUSTRALIA

South Australian Travel Centre
Ph: 1300 655 276
www.visit-southaustralia.com.au

RAA (Royal Automobile
Association)
Ph: (08) 8202 4600
www.raa.net

Department of Environment
& Heritage
Environment Shop
Ph: (08) 8204 1910
www.environment.sa.gov.au

Anangu Pitjantjatjaraku
Yankuytjatjara Land Council
Ph: (08) 8950 1511

NORTHERN TERRITORY

Darwin Region Tourism
Association
Ph: (08) 8981 4300
www.ntholidays.com.au

AANT (Automobile Association
Northern Territory)
Ph: (08) 8981 3837

Parks and Wildlife Commission
Ph: (08) 8999 4454
www.nt.gov.au/paw

Northern Land Council – Darwin
(For Top End land permits)
Ph: (08) 8920 5100

Central Land Council
(For Central Aust Land Permits)
Ph: (08) 8951 6211

WESTERN AUSTRALIA

Western Australian Tourist Centre
Ph: 1300 361 351
www.westernaustralia.net

RACWA (Royal Automobile
Club WA)
Ph: 13 11 11
www.nrma.com.au

Department of Conservation
& Land Management
Ph: (08) 9334 0333
www.calm.wa.gov.au

WA Aboriginal Affairs Dept – Perth
Ph: (08) 9235 8000

TASMANIA

Tasmanian Travel
& Information Centre
Ph: (03) 6230 8235
www.tourism.tas.gov.au

RACT (Royal Automobile
Club of Tasmania)
Ph: (03) 6232 6300
www.ract.com.au

Department of Environment
& Land Management
Parks & Wildlife
Ph: (03) 6233 8011
www.parks.tas.gov.au

Accident Checklist

If you are involved in a road accident and you are not injured, it is worthwhile to record the facts while you are on the scene. You will need a record if reporting the accident to the police, filling in your insurance claim or taking other action to cover your repair costs.

Here is a checklist of facts to record:

Details of Accident
- Date, time and location of accident
- Was the road wet or dry?
- Width of road
- Was your car on correct side of road?
- Estimated speed of both cars at time of impact
- If after sunset, was accident site well lit?
- On cars involved, what lights were on?
- Sketch of accident scene
- Names, addresses and phone numbers of witnesses

Other Car(s)
- Driver's name, licence number, address and phone number
- If different, owner's name and address
- Make, model and rego number
- Extent of damage
- Was car already damaged before this accident?
- Name of insurance company, policy number and type
- Did other driver admit liability? Record exact words

Injured Persons
- Names and addresses of injured persons
- Degree of injuries

Damage to Property
- Details of damage to property other than cars
- Name and address of owner of damaged property

Towing
- Name of tow truck service
- Destination of towed car

Police Involvement

Police must be called to an accident if anyone is killed or injured, or if either of the drivers involved appears to be affected by alcohol or drugs. It must also be reported if either driver leaves the scene without exchanging details.

If police are called, record the following:

- Names of attending officers and their police station
- The reading obtained if other driver was breathalysed
- Whether the police laid blame or mentioned charges?

Note:

If the police are not called, report the accident to the police within 24 hrs.

Distance Chart

All distances in this chart have been measured over highways and major roads, not necessarily by the shortest route.

Tasmania has not been included.
Refer to page 231 for Tasmania distance chart.

Approximate Distance	Adelaide SA	Albany WA	Albury NSW	Alice Springs NT	Ayers Rock/Yulara NT	Bairnsdale VIC	Ballarat VIC	Bathurst NSW	Bega NSW	Bendigo VIC	Bordertown SA	Bourke NSW	Brisbane QLD	Broken Hill NSW	Broome WA	Bunbury WA	Cairns QLD	Canberra ACT	Carnarvon WA	Ceduna SA	Charleville QLD	Coober Pedy SA	Darwin NT	Dubbo NSW	Esperance WA	Eucla WA	Geraldton WA	Grafton NSW
Adelaide SA		2642	932	1526	1570	1006	611	1183	1329	770	267	1129	2054	514	4242	2855	2964	1153	3556	769	1583	837	3018	1175	2168	1256	3083	1815
Albany WA	2642		357	3558	3602	3648	3253	3664	3810	3251	2909	3366	4291	2751	2582	361	5201	3634	1292	1873	3820	2869	4375	3503	474	1386	819	4079
Albury NSW	932	357		2458	2502	310	372	443	426	297	665	847	1375	866	4905	3637	2650	346	4338	1551	918	1619	3662	531	2950	2038	3865	1162
Alice Springs NT	1526	3558	2458		442	2532	2137	2548	2694	2135	1793	2250	3004	1635	2735	3771	2293	2518	4128	1685	2332	689	1492	2387	3084	2172	3999	2963
Ayers Rock/Yulara NT	1570	3602	2502	442		2574	2181	2592	2738	2179	1837	2294	3219	1679	3177	3815	2735	2562	4516	1729	2748	733	1934	2431	3128	2216	404	3007
Bairnsdale VIC	1006	3648	310	2532	2574		395	878	326	432	739	1157	1691	1120	5215	3861	2960	450	4562	1775	1611	1843	3972	841	3174	2262	4089	1334
Ballarat VIC	611	3253	372	2137	2181	395		815	721	121	344	995	1655	753	5436	3466	2830	718	4167	1380	1449	1448	4193	882	2779	1867	3694	1522
Bathurst NSW	1183	3664	443	2548	2592	878	815		468	740	1093	574	1004	958	5015	3877	2325	274	4578	1791	1028	1859	3772	206	3190	2278	4105	735
Bega NSW	1329	3810	426	2694	2738	326	721	468		709	1065	965	1373	1292	5406	4023	2723	222	4724	1937	1419	2005	4163	604	3336	2424	4251	1034
Bendigo VIC	770	3251	297	2135	2179	432	121	740	709		368	874	1534	697	4851	3464	2795	643	4165	1378	1328	1446	3627	761	2777	1865	3692	1401
Bordertown SA	267	2909	665	1793	1837	739	344	1093	1065	368		1242	1929	781	4509	3122	3160	1011	3823	1036	1779	1104	3285	1085	2435	1523	3350	1725
Bourke NSW	1129	3366	847	2250	2294	1157	995	574	965	874	1242		924	615	4441	3579	1835	743	4280	1493	454	1561	3198	368	2892	1980	3807	813
Brisbane QLD	2054	4291	1375	3004	3219	1691	1655	1004	1373	1534	1929	924		1540	4659	4504	1701	1223	5205	2418	754	2486	3416	844	3817	2905	4732	339
Broken Hill NSW	514	2751	866	1635	1679	1120	753	958	1292	697	781	615	1540		4351	2964	2450	1080	3665	878	1069	946	3127	752	2277	1365	3192	1328
Broome WA	4242	2582	4905	2735	3177	5215	5436	5015	5406	4851	4509	4441	4659	4351		2538	3948	5184	1461	3569	3987	3405	1861	4809	912	3082	1934	4901
Bunbury WA	2855	361	3637	3771	3815	3861	3466	3877	4023	3464	3122	3579	4504	2964	2538		5414	3847	1069	2086	4033	3082	4183	3716	687	1599	596	4292
Cairns QLD	2964	5201	2650	2293	2735	2960	2830	2325	2723	2795	3160	1835	1701	2450	3948	5414		2435	5429	3328	1381	2982	2705	2119	4727	3815	5642	2048
Canberra ACT	1153	3634	346	2518	2562	450	718	274	222	643	1011	743	1223	1080	5184	3847	2435		4548	1761	1197	1829	3941	382	3160	2248	4075	884
Carnarvon WA	3556	1292	4338	4128	4516	4562	4167	4578	4724	4165	3823	4280	5205	3665	1461	1069	5429	4548		2787	4734	3783	3254	4417	1600	2300	473	4993
Ceduna SA	769	1873	1551	1685	1729	1775	1380	1791	1937	1378	1036	1493	2418	878	3569	2086	3328	1761	2787		1947	996	3177	1630	1399	487	2314	2206
Charleville QLD	1583	3820	918	2332	2748	1611	1449	1028	1419	1328	1779	454	754	1069	3987	4033	1381	1197	4734	1947		2015	2744	822	3346	2434	4261	997
Coober Pedy SA	837	2869	1619	689	733	1843	1448	1859	2005	1446	1104	1561	2486	946	3405	3082	2982	1829	3783	996	2015		2181	1698	2395	1483	3310	2274
Darwin NT	3018	4375	3662	1492	1934	3972	4193	3772	4163	3627	3285	3198	3416	3127	1861	4183	2705	3941	3254	3177	2744	2181		3566	4307	3664	3727	3658
Dubbo NSW	1175	3503	531	2387	2431	841	882	206	604	761	1085	368	844	752	4809	3716	2119	382	4417	1630	822	1698	3566		3029	2117	3944	640
Esperance WA	2168	474	2950	3084	3128	3174	2779	3190	3336	2777	2435	2892	3817	2277	912	687	4727	3160	1600	1399	3346	2395	4307	3029		912	1319	3605
Eucla WA	1256	1386	2038	2172	2216	2262	1867	2278	2424	1865	1523	1980	2905	1365	3082	1599	3815	2248	2300	487	2434	1483	3664	2117	912		1827	2693
Geraldton WA	3083	819	3865	3999	404	4089	3694	4105	4251	3692	3350	3807	4732	3192	1934	596	5642	4075	473	2314	4261	3310	3727	3944	1319	1827		4520
Grafton NSW	1815	4079	1162	2963	3007	1334	1522	735	1034	1401	1725	813	339	1328	4901	4292	2048	884	4993	2206	997	2274	3658	640	3605	2693	4520	
Horsham VIC	424	3066	508	1950	1994	582	187	951	908	211	157	1085	1745	609	4666	3279	3006	854	3980	1193	1539	1261	3442	972	2592	1680	3507	1612
Kalgoorlie/Boulder WA	2153	799	2935	3069	3113	3159	2764	3175	3321	2762	2420	2877	3802	2262	2185	764	4712	3145	1161	1384	3331	2380	3978	3014	389	897	988	3590
Katherine NT	2709	4066	3353	1183	1625	3663	3884	3463	3854	3318	2976	2889	3107	2818	1552	3874	2396	3632	2945	2868	2435	1872	309	3257	3998	3355	3418	3349
Kununurra WA	3202	3554	3865	1695	2137	4175	4396	3975	4366	3830	3488	3401	3619	3330	1040	3362	2908	4144	2433	3380	2947	2384	821	3769	3486	3867	2906	3861
Longreach QLD	2097	4334	1432	1818	2260	1671	1963	1542	1933	1842	2293	968	1186	1583	3473	4547	1053	1711	4954	2461	514	2507	2230	1336	3860	2948	4775	1428
Mackay QLD	2475	4712	2009	2396	2838	2319	2341	1684	2082	2220	2588	1346	980	1961	4051	7925	729	1860	5532	2839	892	2907	2808	1478	4238	3326	5153	1319
Meekatharra WA	2872	1116	3654	3788	3832	3837	3483	3894	4040	3481	3139	3596	4521	2981	1466	924	5344	3864	620	2103	4050	3099	3248	3733	1108	1616	540	4309
Melbourne VIC	723	3365	314	2249	2293	283	112	759	609	149	456	989	1658	837	4965	3578	2933	660	4279	1492	1443	1560	3741	814	2891	1979	3806	1476
Mildura VIC	372	2849	571	1733	1777	821	454	811	957	398	411	877	1647	299	449	3062	2749	781	3763	976	1368	1044	3225	803	2375	1463	3290	1443
Moree NSW	1548	3812	904	2696	2740	1214	1255	579	977	1134	1458	445	479	1061	4616	4025	1790	755	4726	1939	629	2007	3373	373	3338	2426	4253	368
Mt Gambier SA	435	3077	677	1961	2005	695	305	1120	1026	426	183	1300	1960	870	4677	3290	3135	1023	3991	1204	1754	1272	3453	1187	2603	1691	3518	1827
Mt Isa QLD	2702	4734	2074	1176	1618	2313	2605	2184	2575	2484	2852	1610	1828	2225	2831	4947	1117	2353	4312	5861	1156	1865	1588	1978	4279	3348	4697	2070
Newcastle NSW	1509	3884	693	2768	2812	865	1065	326	570	990	1358	749	818	1133	5099	4097	2339	415	4798	2011	1121	2079	3856	381	3410	2498	4325	479
Perth WA	2689	406	3471	3605	3649	3695	3300	3711	3857	3298	2956	3413	4338	2798	2372	182	5248	3681	903	1920	3867	2916	4017	3550	714	1433	430	4126
Port Augusta SA	305	2337	1087	1221	1265	1311	916	1327	1473	914	572	1029	1954	414	3937	2550	2864	1297	3251	464	1483	532	2713	1166	1863	951	2778	1742
Port Hedland WA	3744	1988	4526	3349	3791	4750	4355	4766	4912	4353	4011	4468	5205	3853	614	1796	4543	4736	867	2975	4533	3971	2407	4605	1980	2488	1340	5447
Port Lincoln SA	642	2277	1424	1558	1602	1648	1253	1664	1810	1251	909	1366	2291	751	3973	2490	3201	1634	3191	404	1820	869	3050	1503	1803	891	2718	2079
Renmark SA	247	2724	696	1608	1652	940	573	1714	1082	517	279	1039	1772	424	4324	2937	2874	906	3638	857	1493	919	3100	928	2250	1388	3165	1568
Rockhampton QLD	2268	4505	3255	3389	3433	1986	2027	1351	1749	1906	2230	1139	647	1754	4154	4718	1062	1527	5419	2632	780	2700	2911	1145	4031	3119	4946	986
Sydney NSW	1384	3865	562	2749	2793	734	934	201	418	859	1227	775	957	1159	5216	4078	2400	284	4779	1992	1229	2060	3973	407	3391	2479	4306	618
Tamworth NSW	1510	3774	866	2658	2702	1129	1217	430	813	1096	1420	584	574	1023	4879	3987	2062	704	4688	1901	901	1969	3636	335	3300	2388	4215	305
Tennant Creek NT	2040	4072	2736	514	956	2975	3267	2846	3237	2649	2307	2272	2490	2149	2221	4285	1779	3015	3614	2199	1818	1203	978	2640	3598	2686	4087	2732
Toowoomba QLD	1894	4158	1250	3042	3086	1560	1601	3148	1314	1480	1786	791	125	1407	4534	4371	1702	1205	5072	2285	629	2353	3291	719	3684	2772	4599	367
Townsville QLD	2617	4854	2303	2067	2509	2613	2483	1978	2420	2362	2813	1488	1376	2103	3722	5067	347	2088	5203	2981	1034	3049	2479	1772	4380	3468	5295	1701
Wagga Wagga NSW	936	3417	125	2301	2345	435	497	318	393	422	790	722	1250	863	5017	3630	2525	244	4331	1544	1176	1612	3793	406	2943	2031	3858	1046
Warrnambool VIC	617	3259	544	2143	2187	513	171	986	839	292	365	1162	1826	850	4859	3472	3001	889	4173	1386	1621	922	3635	1053	2785	1873	3700	1693
West Wyalong NSW	919	3400	278	2284	2328	588	626	264	501	505	829	572	1100	846	5000	3613	2375	271	4314	1527	1026	1595	3776	256	2926	2014	3841	896

Approximate Distance	Horsham VIC	Kalgoorlie/Boulder WA	Katherine NT	Kununurra WA	Longreach QLD	Mackay QLD	Meekatharra WA	Melbourne VIC	Mildura VIC	Moree NSW	Mt Gambier SA	Mt Isa QLD	Newcastle NSW	Perth WA	Port Augusta SA	Port Hedland WA	Port Lincoln SA	Renmark SA	Rockhampton QLD	Sydney NSW	Tamworth NSW	Tennant Creek NT	Toowoomba QLD	Townsville QLD	Wagga Wagga NSW	Warrnambool VIC	West Wyalong NSW
Adelaide SA	424	2153	2709	3202	2097	2475	2872	723	372	1548	435	2702	1509	2689	305	3744	642	247	2268	1384	1510	2040	1894	2617	936	617	919
Albany WA	3066	799	4066	3554	4334	4712	1116	3365	2849	3812	3077	4734	3884	406	2337	1988	2277	2724	4505	3865	3774	4072	4158	4854	3417	3259	3400
Albury NSW	508	2935	3353	3865	1432	2009	3654	314	571	904	677	2074	693	3471	1087	4526	1424	696	3255	562	866	2736	1250	2303	125	544	278
Alice Springs NT	1950	3069	1183	1695	1818	2396	3788	2249	1733	2696	1961	1176	2768	3605	1221	3349	1558	1608	3389	2749	2658	514	3042	2067	2301	2143	2284
Ayers Rock/Yulara NT	1994	3113	1625	2137	2260	2838	3832	2293	1777	2740	2005	1618	2812	3649	1265	3791	1602	1652	3433	2793	2702	956	3086	2509	2345	2187	2328
Bairnsdale VIC	582	3159	3663	4175	1671	2319	3837	283	821	1214	695	2313	865	3695	1311	4750	1648	940	1986	734	1129	2975	1560	2613	435	513	588
Ballarat VIC	187	2764	3884	4396	1963	2341	3483	112	454	1255	305	2605	1065	3300	916	4355	1253	573	2027	934	1217	3267	1601	2483	497	171	626
Bathurst NSW	951	3175	3463	3975	1542	1684	3894	759	811	579	1120	2184	326	3711	1327	4766	1664	1714	1351	201	430	2846	3148	1978	318	986	264
Bega NSW	908	3321	3854	4366	1933	2082	4040	609	957	977	1026	2575	570	3857	1473	4912	1810	1082	1749	418	813	3237	1314	2420	393	839	501
Bendigo VIC	211	2762	3318	3830	1842	2220	3481	149	398	1134	426	2484	990	3298	914	4353	1251	517	1906	859	1096	2649	1480	2362	422	292	505
Bordertown SA	157	2420	2976	3488	2293	2588	3139	456	411	1458	183	2852	1358	2956	572	4011	909	279	2230	1227	1420	2307	1786	2813	790	365	829
Bourke NSW	1085	2877	2889	3401	968	1346	3596	989	877	445	1300	1610	749	3413	1029	4468	1366	1039	1139	775	584	2272	791	1488	722	1162	572
Brisbane QLD	1745	3802	3107	3619	1186	980	4521	1658	1647	479	1960	1828	818	4338	1954	5205	2291	1772	647	957	574	2490	125	1376	1250	1826	1100
Broken Hill NSW	609	2262	2818	3330	1583	1961	2981	837	299	1061	870	2225	1133	2798	414	3853	751	424	1754	1159	1023	2149	1407	2103	863	850	846
Broome WA	4666	2185	1552	1040	3473	4051	1466	4965	449	4616	4677	2831	5099	2372	3937	614	3973	4324	4154	5216	4879	2221	4534	3722	5017	4859	5000
Bunbury WA	3279	764	3874	3362	4547	7925	924	3578	3062	4025	3290	4947	4097	182	2550	1796	2490	2937	4718	4078	3987	4285	4371	5067	3630	3472	3613
Cairns QLD	3006	4712	2396	2908	1053	729	5344	2933	2749	1790	3135	1117	2339	5248	2864	4543	3201	2874	1062	2400	2062	1779	1702	347	2525	3001	2375
Canberra ACT	854	3145	3632	4144	1711	1860	3864	660	781	755	1023	2353	415	3681	1297	4736	1634	906	1527	284	704	3015	1205	2088	244	889	271
Carnarvon WA	3980	1161	2945	2433	4954	5532	620	4279	3763	4726	3991	4312	4798	903	3251	867	3191	3638	5419	4779	4688	3614	5072	5203	4331	4173	4314
Ceduna SA	1193	1384	2868	3380	2461	2839	2103	1492	976	1939	1204	5861	2011	1920	464	2975	404	857	2632	1992	1901	2199	2285	2981	1544	1386	1527
Charleville QLD	1539	3331	2435	2947	514	892	4050	1443	1368	629	1754	1156	1121	3867	1483	4533	1820	1493	780	1229	901	1818	629	1034	1176	1621	1026
Coober Pedy SA	1261	2380	1872	2384	2507	2907	3099	1560	1044	2007	1272	1865	2079	2916	532	3971	869	919	2700	2060	1969	1203	2353	3049	1612	922	1595
Darwin NT	3442	3978	309	821	2230	2808	3248	3741	3225	3373	3453	1588	3856	4017	2713	2407	3050	3100	2911	3973	3636	978	3291	2479	3793	3635	3776
Dubbo NSW	972	3014	3257	3769	1336	1478	3733	814	803	373	1187	1978	381	3550	1166	4605	1503	928	1145	407	335	2640	719	1772	406	1053	256
Esperance WA	2592	389	3998	3486	3860	4238	1108	2891	2375	3338	2603	4279	3410	714	1863	1980	1803	2250	4031	3391	3300	3598	3684	4380	2943	2785	2926
Eucla WA	1680	897	3355	3867	2948	3326	1616	1979	1463	2426	1691	3348	2498	1433	951	2488	891	1388	3119	2479	2388	2686	2732	3468	2031	1873	2014
Geraldton WA	3507	908	3418	2906	4775	5153	540	3806	3290	4253	3518	4697	4325	430	2778	1340	2718	3165	4946	4306	4215	4087	4599	5295	3858	3700	3841
Grafton NSW	1612	3590	3349	3861	1428	1319	4309	1476	1443	368	1827	2070	479	4126	1742	5447	2079	1568	986	618	305	2732	367	1701	1046	1693	896
Horsham VIC		2577	3133	3645	2053	2431	3296	299	310	1345	261	2695	1201	3113	729	4168	1066	429	2117	1070	1307	2464	1691	2573	633	241	580
Kalgoorlie/Boulder WA	2577		3669	3157	3845	4223	719	2876	2360	3323	2588	4264	3395	594	1848	1591	1788	2235	4016	3376	3285	3583	3669	4365	2928	2770	2911
Katherine NT	3133	3669		512	1921	2499	2948	3432	2916	3064	3144	1279	3547	3708	2404	2098	2741	2791	2602	3664	3327	669	2982	2170	3484	3326	3467
Kununurra WA	3645	3157	512		2433	3011	2436	3944	3428	3576	3656	1791	4059	3196	2916	1586	3253	3303	3114	4176	3839	1181	3494	2682	3996	3838	3979
Longreach QLD	2053	3845	1921	2433		793	4564	1957	1845	1143	2268	642	1626	4381	1997	4068	2334	2007	681	1743	1406	1304	1061	706	1690	2134	1540
Mackay QLD	2431	4223	2499	3011	793		4942	2175	2223	1105	2624	1220	1764	4759	2375	4646	2712	2385	333	1715	1377	1882	973	382	1884	2512	1734
Meekatharra WA	3296	719	2948	2436	4564	4942		3595	3079	4042	3307	4227	4114	758	2567	872	2507	2954	4735	4095	4004	3617	4288	5094	3647	3489	3630
Melbourne VIC	299	2876	3432	3944	1957	2175	3595		538	1187	412	2599	1007	3412	1028	4467	1365	657	1959	876	1180	2763	1533	2477	439	230	558
Mildura VIC	310	2360	2916	3428	1845	2223	3079	538		1176	571	2524	1137	2896	512	3951	849	125	1948	1012	1138	2247	1522	2365	564	551	547
Moree NSW	1345	3323	3064	3576	1143	1105	4042	1187	1176		1560	1785	492	3859	1475	4914	1812	1301	772	610	272	2447	346	1443	779	1426	629
Mt Gambier SA	261	2588	3144	3656	2268	2624	3307	412	571	1560		2910	1370	3124	740	4179	1077	462	2332	2268	1522	2475	1906	2788	802	182	795
Mt Isa QLD	2695	4264	1279	1791	642	1220	4227	2599	2524	1785	2910		2268	4781	2397	3426	2734	2649	1323	2385	2048	662	1703	891	2332	2776	2182
Newcastle NSW	1201	3395	3547	4059	1626	1764	4114	1007	1137	492	1370	2268		3931	1547	4986	1884	1262	1264	152	277	2930	778	1992	591	1236	590
Perth WA	3113	594	3708	3196	4381	4759	758	3412	2896	3859	3124	4781	3931		2384	1630	2324	2771	4552	3912	3821	4119	4205	4901	3464	3306	3447
Port Augusta SA	729	1848	2404	2916	1997	2375	2567	1028	512	1475	740	2397	1547	2384		3439	337	387	2168	1528	1437	1735	1821	2517	1080	922	1063
Port Hedland WA	4168	1591	2098	1586	4068	4646	872	4467	3951	4914	4179	3426	4986	1630	3439		3776	3826	5607	4967	4876	2767	5080	4317	4519	4361	4502
Port Lincoln SA	1066	1788	2741	3253	2334	2712	2507	1365	849	1812	1077	2734	1884	2324	337	3776		724	2505	1865	1774	2072	2158	2854	1417	1259	1400
Renmark SA	429	2235	2791	3303	2007	2385	2954	657	125	1301	462	2649	1262	2771	387	3826	724		2073	1137	1263	2122	1647	2527	689	676	672
Rockhampton QLD	2117	4016	2602	3114	681	333	4735	1959	1948	772	2332	1323	1264	4552	2168	5607	2505	2073		1382	1044	1985	640	715	1554	2198	1401
Sydney NSW	1070	3376	3664	4176	1743	1715	4095	876	1012	610	1239	2385	152	3912	1528	4967	1865	1137	1382		395	3263	896	2053	470	1105	465
Tamworth NSW	1307	3285	3327	3839	1406	1377	4004	1180	1138	272	1522	2048	277	3821	1437	4876	1774	1263	1044	395		2710	501	1715	741	1388	591
Tennant Creek NT	2464	3583	669	1181	1304	1882	3617	2763	2247	2447	2475	662	2930	4119	1735	2767	2072	2122	1985	3263	2710		2365	1553	2815	2657	2798
Toowoomba QLD	1691	3669	2982	3494	1061	973	4288	1533	1522	346	1906	1703	778	4205	1821	5080	2158	1647	640	896	501	2365		1355	1125	1772	975
Townsville QLD	2573	4365	2170	2682	706	382	5094	2477	2365	1443	2788	891	1992	4901	2517	4317	2854	2527	715	2053	1715	1553	1355		2178	2654	2028
Wagga Wagga NSW	633	2928	3484	3996	1690	1884	3647	439	564	779	802	2332	591	3464	1080	4519	1417	689	1554	470	741	2815	1125	2178		668	153
Warrnambool VIC	241	2770	3326	3838	2134	2512	3489	230	551	1426	182	2776	1236	3306	922	4361	1259	676	2198	1105	1388	2657	1772	2654	668		661
West Wyalong NSW	580	2911	3467	3979	1540	1734	3630	558	547	629	795	2182	590	3447	1063	4502	1400	672	1401	465	591	2798	975	2028	153	661	

Australian Capital Territory

ACT: The Federal Capital

- Area = 2538sq km
- Covers 0.03% of Australia
- Canberra occupies 15% of the ACT

Royal Blue Bell   *Gang Gang Cockatoo*

The ACT is situated in the Southern Highlands, surrounded by the State of New South Wales. Canberra, the capital city of the ACT, is also the capital city of Australia. Bordered by the Boboyan, Tidbinbilla and Booth mountain ranges, the ACT is within close proximity to many national parks, including Kosciuszko NP in NSW.

Overlooking the city is the futuristic telecommunications tower on Black Mountain, situated NW of Canberra. From the public galleries on the tower, see panoramic views across the capital.

Although small in size, the ACT has much for visitors to see when they have exhausted the sight seeing opportunities in Canberra.

Cockington Green

ℹ Tourist Information

Canberra Visitors Centre
330 Northbourne Ave,
Dixon 2602
Ph: (02) 6205 0666

Main Attractions

★ **Brindabella Valley**
The childhood home of Australian writer, Miles Franklin.
★ **Canberra Deep Space Communication Complex**
This tracking station displays spacecraft and antenna models.
★ **Cockington Green**
Consists of perfect one-twelth size models of buildings from around the world. Colourful and beautifully manicured gardens surround the miniature buildings.
★ **Lanyon**
This colonial homestead was beautifully restored by the National Trust. It is set in landscaped gardens on the banks of the Murrumbidgee River. See the gallery of Sir Sidney Nolan's paintings.
★ **Namadgi NP**
This mountainous NP covers 45% of the ACT. It is ideal for bushwalking, picnicking and camping.
★ **Tidbinbilla Nature Reserve**
Features wetlands and large wildlife enclosures with koalas, red kangaroos and a waterfowl area.

Historical homestead, Lanyon

Australian Capital Territory Key Map

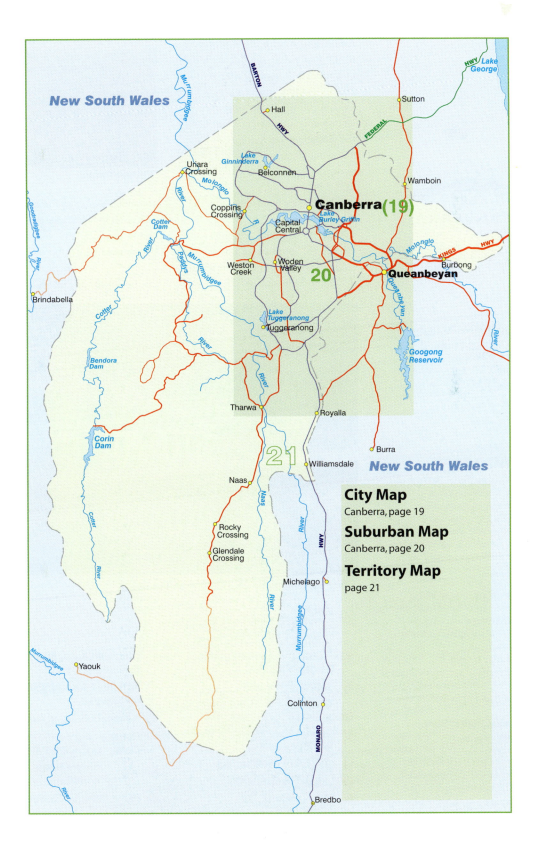

New South Wales

BARTON HWY

HWY Lake George

Sutton

Hall

FEDERAL

Murrumbidgee River

Lake Ginninderra

Uriara Crossing

Belconnen

Wamboin

Molonglo

Coppins Crossing

Canberra (19)

Lake Burley Griffin

Capital Central

Cotter Dam

Molonglo

KINGS HWY

Goodradigbee River

Paddys River

Murrumbidgee

Weston Creek

Woden Valley

Burbong

Queanbeyan

Queanbeyan River

20

Brindabella

Cotter

Lake Tuggeranong

River

Tuggeranong

Googong Reservoir

River

Bendora Dam

River

21

Tharwa

Royalla

Corin Dam

Burra

Williamsdale

New South Wales

Naas

City Map
Canberra, page 19

Cotter

Naas River

Rocky Crossing

Suburban Map
Canberra, page 20

Glendale Crossing

HWY

Territory Map
page 21

River

Michelago

River

Murrumbidgee

Murrumbidgee

Yaouk

Colinton

MONARO

River

Bredbo

Canberra

CANBERRA

The site for Canberra, the national and the ACT capital, was acquired by the Commonwealth Government in 1911, only after Sydney and Melbourne competed unsuccessfully to be chosen as Australia's premier city. Construction of the first public buildings started in 1913. The original Parliament House building was completed in 1927. Although it was only ever intended as a temporary home for the parliament, it was used for the following 60 years. Canberra occupies approximately 15% of the ACT land area.

The climate is quite severe, ranging from very hot and dry in summer to cold and frosty in winter. The distinct seasons add to the city's charm, especially in autumn when deciduous trees and shrubs provide a colourful display in the streets, parks and gardens. Floriade, the annual spring flower festival, is celebrated between 20 September and 17 October in Commonwealth Park on the shores of Lake Burley Griffin.

Floriade Festival

🛈 Tourist Information

Canberra Visitors Centre
330 Northbourne Ave,
Dickson 2602
Ph: (02) 6205 0666

Parliament House

Main Attractions

★ **Australian National Gallery**
Displays a fine collection of Australian and international art. There is also a sculpture garden.

★ **Australian War Memorial**
This shrine is the most visited building in Canberra. It honours all Australians who fought and died for their country.

★ **Diplomatic Missions**
Most of these are located in the suburban streets of Yarralumla and Red Hill and offer a marvellous variety of distinctive international architecture.

★ **Lake Burley Griffin**
Named after the American architect who won the international competition to design the city of Canberra.

★ **Parliament House (New)**
An excellent focal point for the city, it was designed to merge with and form part of Capital Hill. From its grassed roof there are magnificent views of Canberra's cityscape. The entire building is very impressive. A guided tour is recommended.

Places of Interest

❶ Australian National Botanic Gardens **A2**

❷ Australian National University **B2**

❸ Blundell's Farmhouse **D4**

❹ Captain Cook Memorial Water Jet **C4**

❺ Centenary Carillion **D5**

❻ City Hill Lookout **C2**

❼ Ferry Terminal **B3**

❽ High Court of Australia **D5**

❾ National Capital Planning Exhibition **C4**

❿ National Film and Sound Archive **B3**

⓫ National Library of Australia **C5**

⓬ National Science and Technology Centre (Questacon) **C5**

⓭ Old Parliament House, including the National Portrait Gallery **C6**

⓮ Prime Minister's Lodge **A7**

⓯ Royal Australian Mint **C5**

Scale 1:25 000

0   1
Kilometre

Scale 1:151 300

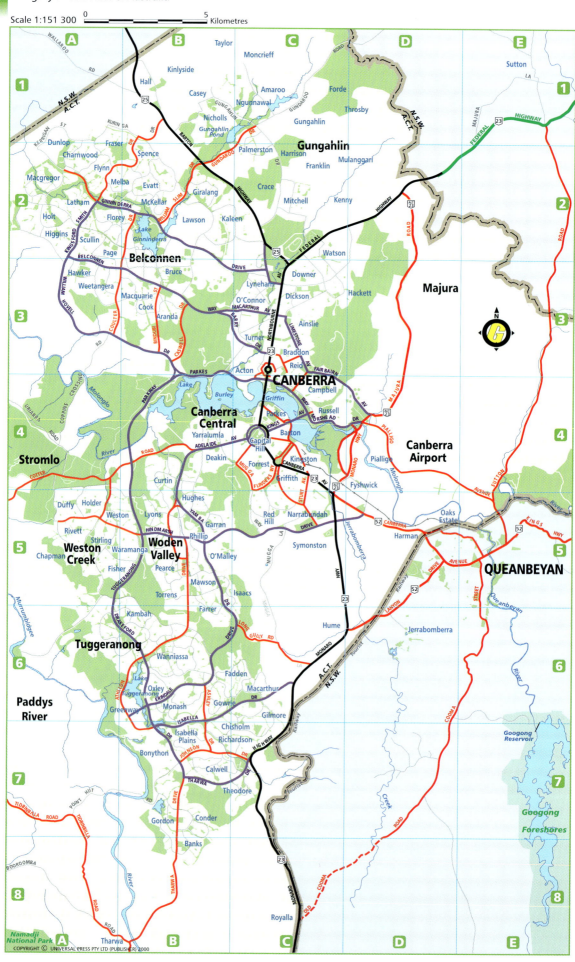

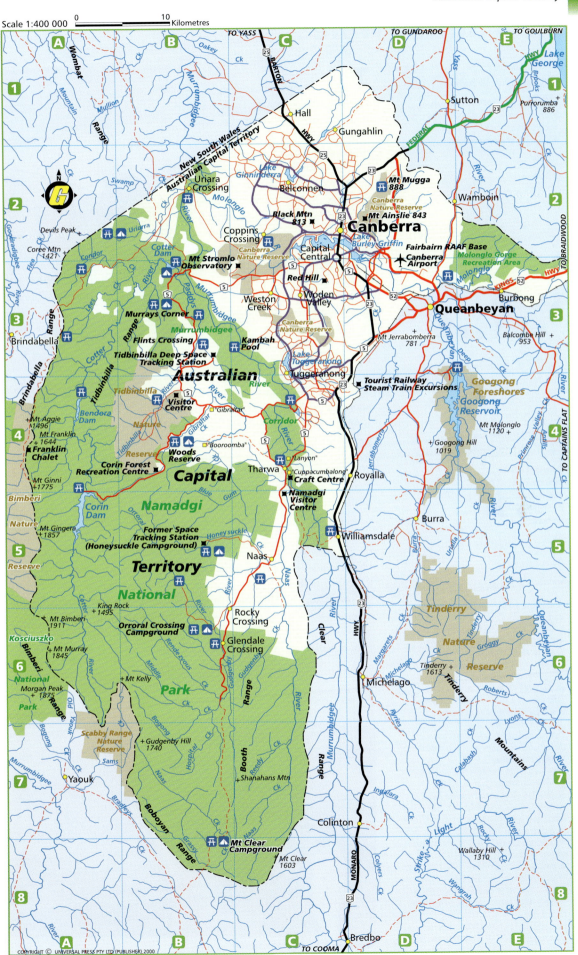

Scale 1:400 000

0   10 Kilometres

TO YASS
TO GUNDAROO
TO GOULBURN

Lake George
Purrorumba 886
Sutton
Hall
Gungahlin
Wamboin
Wombat

New South Wales
Australian Capital Territory

Mullion Range
Oakey Ck
Murrumbidgee River

Uriara Crossing
Lake Ginninderra
Belconnen
Canberra Nature Reserve
Mt Mugga 888
Mt Ainslie 843

Black Mtn 813
Canberra
Lake Burley Griffin
Fairbairn RAAF Base
Canberra Airport
Molonglo Gorge Recreation Area

Devils Peak
Coree Mtn 1421
Coppins Crossing
Canberra Nature Reserve
Capital Central
Red Hill

Murrays Corner
Cotter Dam
Mt Stromlo Observatory
Weston Creek
Woden Valley
Queanbeyan
Burbong
KINGS HWY 52
TO BRAIDWOOD

Flints Crossing
Kambah Pool
Canberra Nature Reserve
Mt Jerrabomberra 781
Balcombe Hill 953

Tidbinbilla Deep Space Tracking Station
Australian
Lake Tuggeranong
Tuggeranong
Googong Foreshores
Googong Reservoir

Brindabella
Tidbinbilla Nature Reserve
Visitor Centre
"Gibraltar"
Tourist Railway Steam Train Excursions
Mt Molonglo 1120

Mt Aggie 1496
Mt Franklin 1644
"Booroomba"
Googong Hill 1019
TO CAPTAINS FLAT

Franklin Chalet
Woods Reserve
Capital
"Lanyon"
Royalla

Corin Forest Recreation Centre
Tharwa
"Cuppacumbalong" Craft Centre

Mt Ginni 1775
Corin Dam
Namadgi
Namadgi Visitor Centre
Burra

Bimberi Nature Reserve
Mt Gingera 1857
Former Space Tracking Station (Honeysuckle Campground)
Williamsdale
Tinderry Nature Reserve

Territory
Naas
Tinderry 1613

Kosciuszko
Mt Murray 1845
King Rock 1495
National
Orroral Crossing Campground
Rocky Crossing
Michelago

Mt Kelly
Park
Glendale Crossing

Morgan Peak 1875
National
Park
Booth Range

Scabby Range Nature Reserve
Gudgenby Hill 1740
Mountains

Yaouk
Shanahans Mtn
Wallaby Hill 1310

Boboyan Range
Mt Clear Campground
Mt Clear 1603
Colinton

MONARO HWY
Bredbo

TO COOMA

New South Wales

NSW: The Premier State

- Total area = 801 431 sq km
- Occupies 10.4% of Australia
- Length of coast = 1099km
- Length of seaboard = 1459km

Waratah   *Platypus*

ℹ Tourist Information

Tourism NSW
Sydney Visitor Centre
106 George St, The Rocks 2000
Ph: 132 077
www.tourism.nsw.gov.au

Main Attractions

★ **Ballina to Byron Bay**
This area is part of a chain of golden beaches and coastal villages running up to the Qld border.
★ **Blue Mountains**
These ranges feature spectacular cliffs and wild valleys, dotted with villages.
★ **Central Coast**
This area is a playground of lakes, beaches and holiday retreats.
★ **Coffs Harbour**
This town is nestled between the Pacific Ocean and a sub-tropical hinterland.
★ **Hunter Valley**
This area is one of the finest wine-producing regions of Australia.
★ **Myall Lakes and Nelson Bay**
Watersports, whale and dolphin watching are popular activities here.
★ **Nowra and Jervis Bay**
The South Coast is full of charming towns and striking headlands.
★ **Snowy Mountains**
This alpine region takes in Kosciuszko NP, a haven for skiers.
★ **The Illawarra and the Southern Highlands**
This region is characterised by lovely countryside and seaside towns.

The State of NSW was named by Captain James Cook when he landed at Botany Bay in 1770. Seven times the size of England, it is a vast area. Its climate is diverse and ranges from sub-tropical temperatures (Northern Rivers region) to dry, desert-like conditions (Far West), to the ice and snowfalls of the South.

NSW has the largest population of any Australian state or territory. Sydney, the capital of NSW has the largest population of any capital city in Australia.

NSW could be described as the country in microcosm as the environment is a study in contrasts. Rainforests abound in the north, while the romance of the past is preserved along the historic Murray River. This river forms the southern boundary of the State. Sparkling surfing beaches dot the coast, all the way to the Qld border. NSW is also home to the popular alpine region of the Snowy Mountains. Completing the picture is the beauty of the harsh and rugged outback.

Major highways, all within easy reach of Sydney, will lead tourists to these diverse regions. The Pacific Highway goes north from Sydney, up the coast, all the way to Queensland. The New England Highway follows an inland route going north from Newcastle. It goes through the Hunter Valley, and the NSW towns

Opera House and Harbour Bridge

of Tamworth, Armidale and Tenterfield. The Great Western Highway goes inland from Sydney and follows the dramatic landscape of the wild cliffs and valleys that form the Blue Mountains. A couple of hours driving SW along the Hume Highway reveals the charming Southern Highlands, characterised by historic towns and national parks. The Princes Highway is a coastal road going south from Sydney. It goes through the NSW towns of Wollongong, Nowra, Batemans Bay and Bega.

Hanging Rock, Blue Mountains

New South Wales Key Map and Distance Chart

All distances shown in the chart below have been measured over highways and major roads, not necessarily by the shortest route.

City Map
Sydney, page 25

Suburban Maps
Sydney, pages 26 to 29

State Maps
pages 30 to 45

Region Maps
Ballina-Byron Bay, page 48

Blue Mountains, pages 50 and 51

Central Coast, page 53

Coffs Harbour, page 55

Lower Hunter, page 57

Upper Hunter, page 59

Nelson Bay-Myall Lakes, page 61

Nowra-Jervis Bay, page 63

Snowy Mountains, page 65

Southern Highlands -Illawarra, page 67

Approximate Distance	Albury	Bathurst	Bega	Bourke	Broken Hill	Canberra	Cooma	Dubbo	Goulburn	Grafton	Mildura VIC	Moree	Newcastle	Port Macquarie	Sydney	Tamworth	Tweed Heads	Wagga Wagga	West Wyalong	Wollongong
Albury		443	426	847	866	346	315	531	367	1162	567	904	693	935	562	866	1401	125	278	505
Bathurst	443		468	574	958	274	382	206	185	735	811	579	326	568	201	430	974	318	264	237
Bega	426	468		965	1292	222	111	604	283	1036	993	977	570	809	418	813	1275	393	501	336
Bourke	847	574	965		615	743	854	368	720	813	877	445	745	861	775	584	1052	722	572	811
Broken Hill	866	958	1292	615		1080	1181	752	1101	1328	299	1061	1129	1300	1159	1023	1567	863	846	1195
Canberra	346	274	222	743	1080		111	382	89	884	781	755	415	657	284	704	1123	244	271	227
Cooma	315	382	111	854	1181	111		493	197	992	882	866	523	765	392	815	1231	282	390	335
Dubbo	531	206	604	368	752	382	493		352	640	803	373	377	612	407	335	879	406	256	443
Goulburn	367	185	283	720	1101	89	197	352		795	802	725	326	568	195	569	1034	265	292	138
Grafton	1162	735	1036	813	1328	884	992	640	795		1513	368	479	249	618	305	239	1046	966	700
Mildura VIC	567	811	993	877	299	781	882	803	802	1513		1176	1137	1415	1012	1138	1682	564	547	940
Moree	904	579	977	445	1061	755	866	373	725	368	1176		490	498	610	272	568	779	629	692
Newcastle	693	326	570	745	1129	415	523	377	326	479	1137	490		252	152	275	718	591	590	234
Port Macquarie	935	568	809	861	1300	657	765	612	568	249	1415	498	252		391	277	488	833	868	473
Sydney	562	201	418	775	1159	284	392	407	195	618	1012	610	152	391		395	857	470	465	82
Tamworth	866	430	813	584	1023	704	815	335	569	305	1138	272	275	277	395		544	741	591	477
Tweed Heads	1401	974	1275	1052	1567	1123	1231	879	1034	239	1682	568	718	488	857	544		1299	1166	939
Wagga Wagga	125	318	393	722	863	244	282	406	265	1046	564	779	591	833	470	741	1299		153	403
West Wyalong	278	264	501	572	846	271	390	256	292	966	547	629	590	868	465	591	1166	153		430
Wollongong	505	237	336	811	1195	227	335	443	138	700	940	692	234	473	82	477	939	403	430	

Sydney

SYDNEY CONVENTION
& VISITORS BUREAU

One of Australia's most vibrant and dynamic cities, Sydney has flourished as a cosmopolitan cultural and financial centre. Although Sydney is not Australia's capital, it is the nation's oldest and largest city, occupying 3700km². Sydney's urban sprawl is an immense natural playground within close proximity to the city, which is bordered by the Pacific Ocean in the east, the Blue Mountains in the west and stunning national parks in both the north and south. With Sydney's temperate climate, it is possible to make the most of the city's striking surroundings in any season.

The major gateway to Australia, Sydney is undoubtedly a prime tourist destination in its own right, as it features many impressive attractions. Sightseeing is very easy,

Centrepoint Tower at Night

as the city centre is a manageable size, with many people preferring to see its attractions on foot. Alternatively, the bright red Sydney Explorer bus takes in almost all of the major tourist attractions on its 20km route. No one should visit Sydney without taking a ferry ride or cruise on the magnificent harbour. Cruises and regular harbour ferries all depart from Circular Quay.

Queen Victoria Arcade

ℹ Tourist Information

Sydney Visitor Centre
106 George St,
Sydney The Rocks 2000
Ph: 132 077
www.sydneycity.nsw.gov.au

Main Attractions

Chinatown
★ This area features Kam Fook, biggest Chinese restaurant in the Southern Hemisphere.
Darling Harbour
★ This is a waterside plaza with parks, shops, restaurants and nightclubs.
Macquarie St
★ This is an elegant street lined with many historic sandstone buildings.
Queen Victoria Building
★ Once the home of the city markets, this is now a stunning shopping centre.
Royal Botanic Gardens
★ Covering 30ha, these gardens include rare and exotic plantlife.
The Rocks
★ This historic area, Sydney's first seaport, now has galleries, shops, restaurants and Sydney's oldest pubs.
Sydney Harbour Bridge
★ The world's widest single span arch bridge links the city to the North Shore.
Sydney Opera House
★ This has been regarded as one of the architectural wonders of the world since it opened in 1973.

Places of Interest

❶ AMP Tower C5
❷ Anzac Memorial D6
❸ Archibald Fountain D5
❹ Art Gallery of NSW E4
❺ Australian Museum of Natural History D6
❻ Cadman's Cottage C2
❼ Chinese Garden B6
❽ Circular Quay D2
❾ Conservatorium of Music E3
❿ Cook and Phillip Park Aquatic Centre D5
⓫ Customs House D3
⓬ Entertainment Centre B7

⓭ Garrison Church C2
⓮ Great Synagogue D5
⓯ Hyde Park D5
⓰ Martin Pl D4
⓱ Museum of Contemporary Art C2
⓲ Museum of Sydney D3
⓳ National Trust Centre C3
⓴ St Andrew's Anglican Cathedral C6
㉑ St Mary's Catholic Cathedral D5
㉒ Strand Arcade C5
㉓ Sydney GPO C4
㉔ Sydney Observatory B2

Scale 1:15 000   0   500 Metres

A   **B**   **C**   **D**   **E**

Port Jackson

Dawes Point

Sydney Harbour Bridge

The Rocks

Port Jackson

Walsh Bay

Millers Point

Balmain East

Thornton Park

Illoura Reserve

Peacock Point

Darling Harbour

Johnstons Bay

Jones Bay

Pyrmont

Pyrmont Bay

Darling Harbour

Cockle Bay

Ultimo

Broadway

Chippendale

Haymarket

Chinatown

Central

Surry Hills

Darlinghurst

East Sydney

Sydney Cove

Sydney Opera House

Bennelong Point

Government House

Farm Cove

Royal Botanic Gardens

The Domain

Wynyard

Sydney

Martin Place

Town Hall

Museum

13 Garrison Church
6 Cadman's Cottage
17 Museum of Contemporary Art
8 Circular Quay
24 Sydney Observatory
19 National Trust Centre
11 Customs House
9 Conservatorium of Music
18 Museum of Sydney
16 Martin Place
23 GPO
22 Strand Arcade
1 AMP Tower
3 Archibald Fountain
15 Hyde Park
14 Great Synagogue
21 St Marys Catholic Cathedral
4 Art Gallery of N.S.W.
10 Cook & Phillip Park Aquatic Centre
20 St Andrews Anglican Cathedral
5 Australian Museum of Natural History
2 ANZAC War Memorial
7 Chinese Garden
12 Entertainment Centre

COPYRIGHT © UNIVERSAL PRESS PTY LTD (PUBLISHER) 2000

Scale 1:200 0

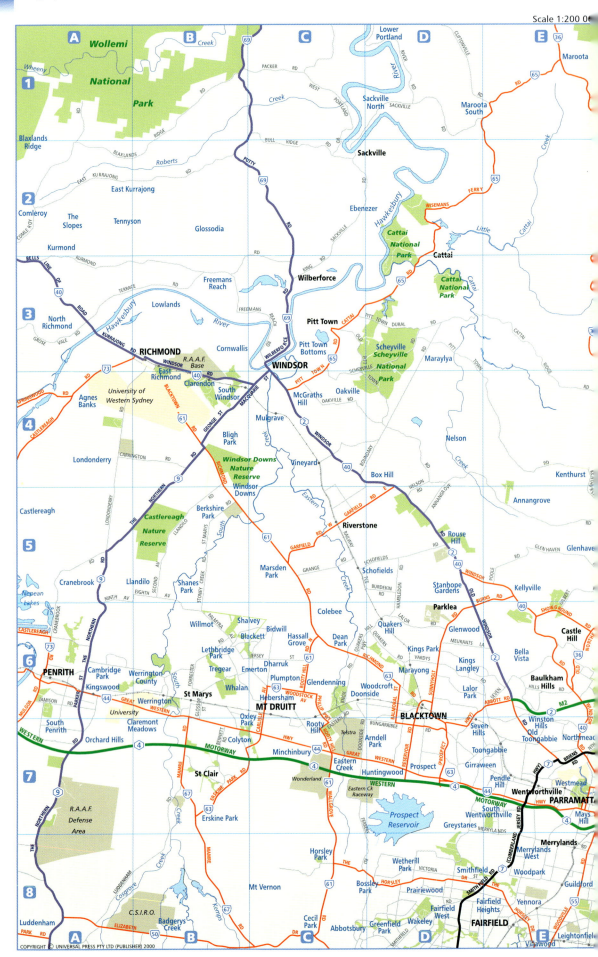

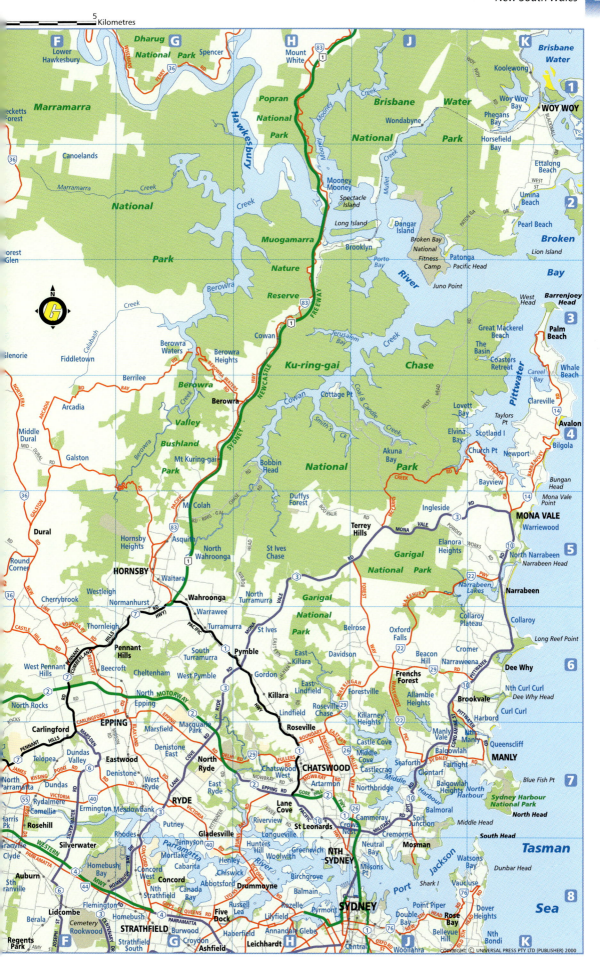

Scale 1:200 00

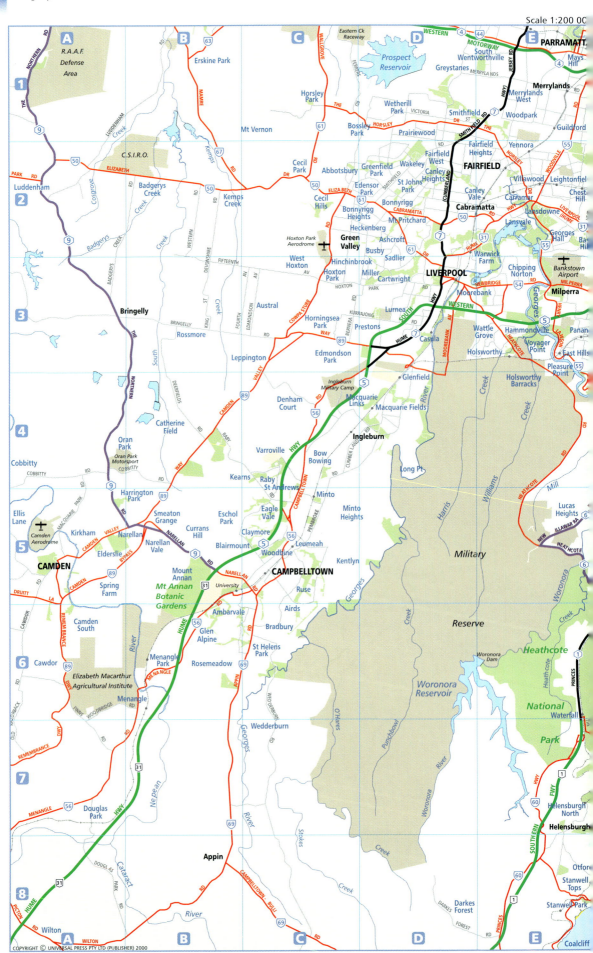

Scale 1:1 600 00

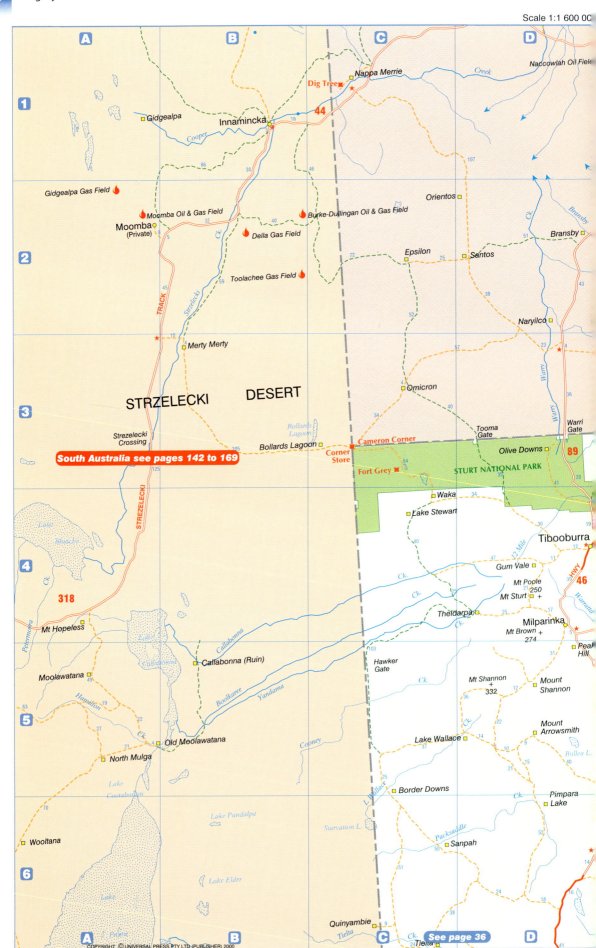

A   B   C   D

Naccowlah Oil Field

Nappa Merrie

Dig Tree

44

Creek

Gidgealpa

Innamincka

16

Cooper

86

38

46

107

Gidgealpa Gas Field

Moomba Oil & Gas Field

Moomba
(Private)

32

40

5

Della Gas Field

Burke-Dullingan Oil & Gas Field

Orientos

Bransby

Ck.

51

Bransby

72

Epsilon

25

Santos

43

TRACK

45

Strzelecki

59

Toolachee Gas Field

38

52

Naryilco

23

4

Warri

57

Omicron

36

10

Merty Merty

STRZELECKI   **DESERT**

34

40

Tooma
Gate

Warri
Gate

Strzelecki
Crossing

*Bollards
Lagoon*

105

Bollards Lagoon

Cameron Corner

Corner
Store

Olive Downs

89

STRZELECKI

125

54

Fort Grey

STURT NATIONAL PARK

41

28

35

Waka

34

30

19

STRZELECKI

Lake Stewart

40

Tibooburra

12

11

*Lake
Blanche*

47

Gum Vale

12 Mile

HWY

39

46

Ck.

Mt Poole
250

21

Mt Sturt +

Theldarpa

25

17

Milparinka

5

318

Mt Hopeless

Petermorra

Ck.

103

Mt Brown +
274

31

Peak
Hill

Callabonna (Ruin)

Hawker
Gate

Ck.

Mt Shannon
+
332

36

12

Mount
Shannon

Moolawatana

49

Hamilton

19

Boolkaree

Yandama

Copney

22

Mount
Arrowsmith

63

22

Lake Wallace

14

Bulloo L.

27

21

Old Moolawatana

37

10

9

40

15

North Mulga

21

*Lake
Cootabulka*

25

Border Downs

Pimpara
Lake

L. Wallace

52

70

Lake Pundalpa

Starvation L.

Packsaddle

50

Sanpah

Wooltana

51

Lake Elder

24

18

16

*Lake
Frome*

A   B   C   **See page 36**   D

Quinyambie

9

Tielta

Ck.

Tielta

24

41

South Australia see pages 142 to 169

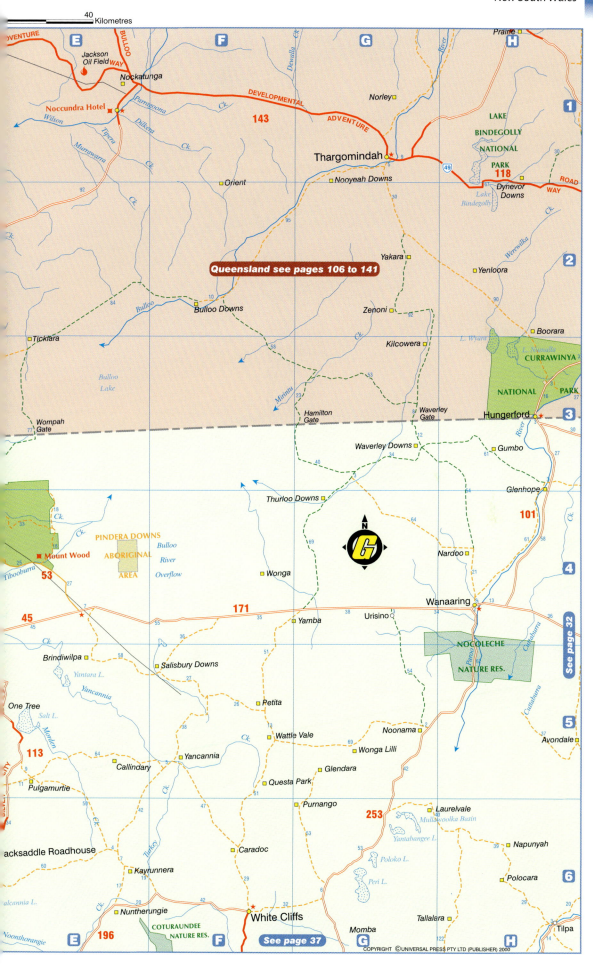

40 Kilometres

Queensland see pages 106 to 141

VENTURE

E
Jackson Oil Field
Nockatunga
Noccundra Hotel
Wilson
Murrawarra
Tibera
Dilkera
Purragoona
BULLOO WAY
DEVELOPMENTAL
ADVENTURE
143
Orient
Ticklara
Bulloo
84
Bulloo Downs
Bulloo Lake
Wompah Gate
77

F
Nockatunga
Norley
Nooyeah Downs
Yakara
Zenoni
Kilcowera
Minntu
Hamilton Gate
Waverley Gate

G
Praine
LAKE BINDEGOLLY NATIONAL PARK
Thargomindah
49
Lake Bindegolly
Yenloora
Boorara
L. Wyara
L. Numalla
CURRAWINYA
NATIONAL PARK
Hungerford
Werewilka

H
1
118
ROAD WAY
Dynevor Downs
2
3

Waverley Downs
Gumbo
Glenhope
101
Nardoo
Thurloo Downs
PINDERA DOWNS ABORIGINAL AREA
Bulloo River Overflow
Mount Wood
Tibooburra
53
Wonga
Wanaaring
See page 32
4

45
171
Yamba
Urisino
NOCOLECHE NATURE RES.
Brindiwilpa
Yantara L.
Yancannia
Salisbury Downs
Petita
One Tree
Salt L.
Morden
113
Wattle Vale
Noonama
Avondale
5
Callindary
Yancannia
Wonga Lilli
Pulgamurtie
Glendara
Questa Park
Purnango
253
Laurelvale
Mullowoolka Basin
Yantabangee L.
Napunyah
acksaddle Roadhouse
Caradoc
Poloko L.
Polocara
6
Kayrunnera
Peri L.
alcannia L.
Nuntherungie
COTURAUNDEE NATURE RES.
White Cliffs
Momba
Tallalara
Tilpa
Noonthorangie
196

E **196**   F See page 37   G   H

COPYRIGHT ©UNIVERSAL PRESS PTY LTD (PUBLISHER) 2000

Scale 1:1 600 000

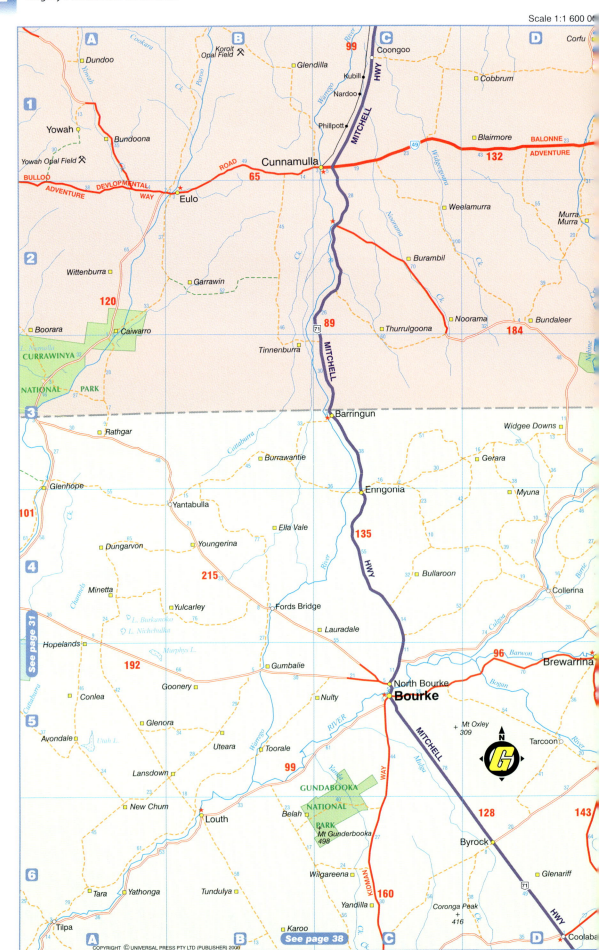

See page 38

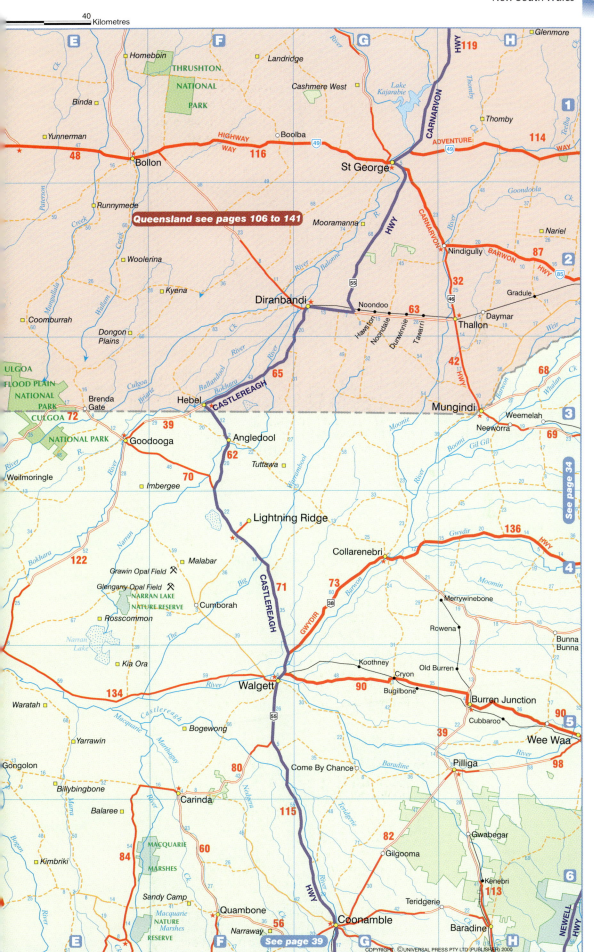

40 Kilometres

Queensland see pages 106 to 141

Glenmore

E | F | G | H

Homeboin
Landridge
Cashmere West
Lake Kajarabie
Thomby

CARNARVON HWY 119

1

Binda
THRUSHTON NATIONAL PARK

Yunnerman
Boolba
St George
114

HIGHWAY 48
Bollon
HIGHWAY 116
49
ADVENTURE WAY

CARNARVON HWY
Mooramanna
Nariel

Runnymede
Nindigully
BARWON HWY 87

2

Woolerina
32
Gradule
85

Kyena
Diranbandi
Noondoo
Daymar

Coomburrah
Hayston Noondale Dunwinnie Tamarri
Thallon

Dongon Plains
63

42

ULGOA FLOOD PLAIN NATIONAL PARK
65
CASTLEREAGH
68

CULGOA
Brenda Gate
Hebel
Mungindi
Weemelah

72
39
Goodooga
Angledool
Neeworra
69

3

NATIONAL PARK
62
Tuttawa

Weilmoringle
70
Imbergee

122
Lightning Ridge
136

Malabar
Collarenebri
14

4

Grawin Opal Field
Glengarry Opal Field
NARRAN LAKE NATURE RESERVE
Cumborah
71
73
GWYDIR
Merrywinebone

Rosscommon
38
Rowena

Narran Lake
Kia Ora
Koothney
Old Burren
Bunna Bunna

134
Walgett
Cryon
Bugilbone
90
Burren Junction

Waratah
55
39
90

5

Bogewong
Cubbaroo
Wee Waa

Yarrawin
80
Come By Chance
Pilliga
98

Gongolon
Carinda
115

Billybingbone
Baradine

Balaree
60
82
Gwabegar

Kimbriki
84
MACQUARIE MARSHES
Gilgooma

Sandy Camp
Kenebri

Macquarie NATURE MARSHES RESERVE
Quambone
56
113

6

Narraway
See page 39
Coonamble
Teridgerie
Baradine

NEWELL HWY

E | F | G | H

Scale 1:1 600 00

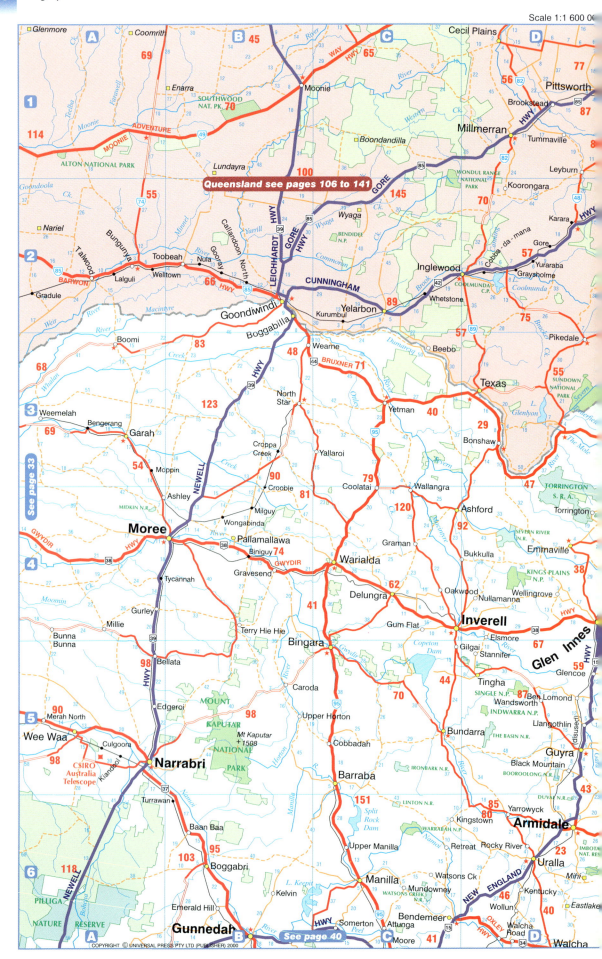

Queensland see pages 106 to 141

See page 33

See page 40

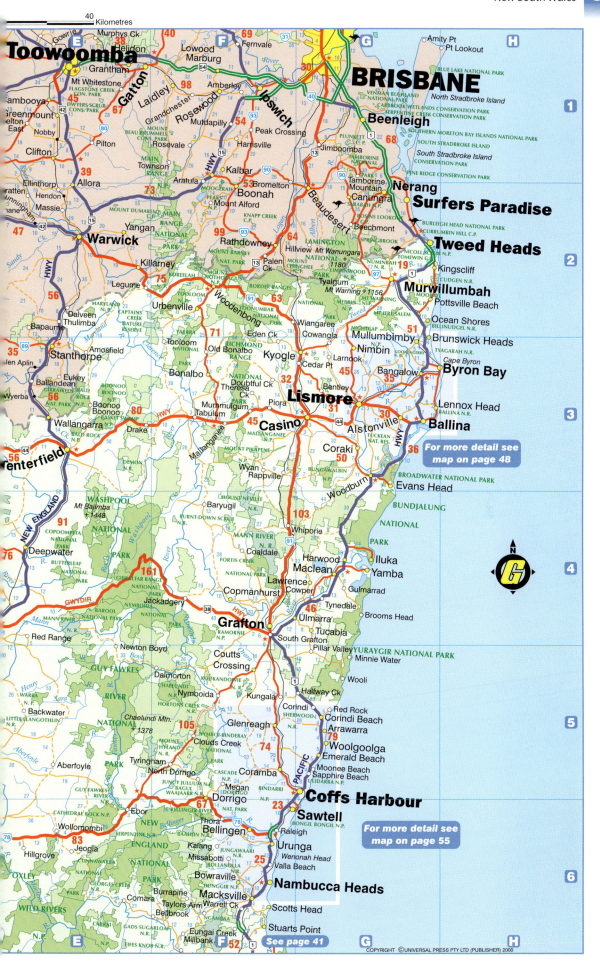

40 Kilometres

Toowoomba
Gowrie
Murphys Ck
Lowood
Marburg
Fernvale
Flagstone Creek
Grantham
Mt Whitestone
Heldon
FLAGSTONE CREEK CON. PARK
Gatton
Laidley
Grandchester
Rosewood
Ipswich
Amberley
DWYERS SCRUB CONS. PARK
Mutdapilly
Peak Crossing
BEAU BRUMMELL CONS. PARK
Harrisville
Jimboomba
BRISBANE
Amity Pt
Pt Lookout
BLUE LAKE NATIONAL PARK
North Stradbroke Island
VENMAN BUSHLAND NATIONAL PARK
CARBROOK WETLANDS NATIONAL PARK
SERPENTINE CREEK CONSERVATION PARK
Beenleigh
SOUTHERN MORETON BAY ISLANDS NATIONAL PARK
SOUTH STRADBROKE ISLAND CONSERVATION PARK
South Stradbroke Island
PINE RIDGE CONSERVATION PARK
Rosevale
MOUNT BEAU BRUMMELL CONS. PARK
MAIN HWY
Townson
Pilton
Clifton
Ellinthorp
Hendon
Massie
Allora
Yangan
MOUNT DUMARESQ MAIN RANGE NATIONAL PARK
Kalbar
Bromelton
Aratula
Boonah
Mount Alford
KNAPP CREEK C.P.
Beaudesert
Tamborine
TAMBORINE NATIONAL
Tamborine Mountain
Canungra
SARAH N.P.
Nerang
Surfers Paradise
BOSNS LOOKO
Beechmont
Beechmont
SPRINGBROOK
BURLEIGH HEAD NATIONAL PARK
CURRUMBIN HILL C.P.
Tweed Heads
NICOLL SCRUB N.P.
TOMEWIN GP.
Warwick
Rathdowney
Hillview
Mt Wanungara +1180
LAMINGTON NATIONAL PARK
Palen Ck
MOUNT CHINGHEE N.P.
LIMPINWOOD
NUMINBAH
Kingscliff
CUDGEN N.R.
Killarney
MOUNT CLUNIE NATIONAL PARK
MOUNT NOTHOFAGUS
BORDER RANGES
Tyalgum
Mt Warning +1156
Murwillumbah
MOOBALL N.P.
Pottsville Beach
Legume
KOREELAH N.P.
Urbenville
BONDUMBAR NATIONAL PARK
Woodenbong
MOUNT JERUSALEM N.P.
Ocean Shores
BILLINUDGEL N.R.
Eden Ck
Wiangaree
Cowangla
Mullumbimby
NIGHTCAP
Brunswick Heads
TYAGARAH N.R.
Tooloom
TOOLOOM NATIONAL PARK
Old Bonalbo
RICHMOND RANGE NATIONAL PARK
Kyogle
Nimbin
Larnook
GOONENGERRY
Bonalbo
Cedar Pt
Bangalow
Byron Bay
Cape Byron
Amosfield
Doubtful Ck
Theresa Ck
Bentley
Piora
Lismore
WILSONS R.
Lennox Head
BALLINA N.R.
Stanthorpe
GIRRAWEEN NATIONAL PARK
Boonoo Boonoo
BOONOO BOONOO NATIONAL PARK
Mummulgum
Tabulam
Casino
Ballina
Ballandean
Eukey
BALD ROCK NATIONAL PARK
Wallangarra
BASKET SWAMP N.P.
Drake
BALD ROCK N.P.
MALLANGANEE N.R.
Coraki
TUCKEAN NAT. RES.
For more detail see map on page 48
MOUNT PIKAPENE N.P.
Wyan
Rappville
BUNGAWALBIN N.P.
Woodburn
Evans Head
BROADWATER NATIONAL PARK
Tenterfield
DEMON N.R.
MOUNT NEVILLE N.P.
Baryugil
BURNT-DOWN SCRUB N.R.
Whiporie
BUNDJALUNG NATIONAL PARK
MOUNT BAJIMBA +1448
WASHPOOL NATIONAL PARK
NEW ENGLAND NATIONAL PARK
COPOOMPTA NATIONAL PARK
Coaldale
FORTIS CREEK NATIONAL PARK
Deepwater
BUTTERLEAF NATIONAL PARK
GIBRALTAR RANGE NATIONAL PARK
Lawrence
Cowper
Harwood
Iluka
Maclean
Yamba
Gulmarrad
GWYDIR HWY
NYMBOIDA NATIONAL PARK
BAROOL NATIONAL PARK
Jackadgery
Copmanhurst
Tynedale
Brooms Head
MANN RIVER N.R.
Red Range
Newton Boyd
Grafton
RAMORNIE N.P.
Ulmarra
Tucabia
South Grafton
Pillar Valley
YURAYGIR NATIONAL PARK
Minnie Water
GUY FAWKES RIVER NATIONAL PARK
Coutts Crossing
Dalmorton
KOUKANDOWIE N.R.
Wooli
CHAELUNDI N.R.
Nymboida
Kungala
Halfway Ck
Backwater
LITTLE LANGLOTHIN N.R.
HORTONS CREEK N.R.
Corindi
SHERWOOD S.F.
Red Rock
Chaelundi Mtn +1378
NYMBOI-BINDERAY NATIONAL PARK
Glenreagh
Corindi Beach
Arrawarra
Clouds Creek
Woolgoolga
Aberfoyle
MOUNT HYLAND NATIONAL PARK
Emerald Beach
Tyringham
CASCADE N.P.
Coramba
Moonee Beach
Sapphire Beach
ULIDARRA N.P.
North Dorrigo
Megan
BINDARRI N.P.
GUY FAWKES RIVER NATIONAL PARK
JUNUY JULUUM N.R.
BAGUL WAAJAARR N.R.
Dorrigo
DORRIGO NAT. PARK
Coffs Harbour
Ebor
CATHEDRAL ROCK N.P.
NEW ENGLAND NATIONAL PARK
Thora
BELLINGER RIVER NAT. PARK
Sawtell
BONGIL BONGIL N.P.
Wollomombi
SERPENTINE N.R.
Bellingen
Raleigh
For more detail see map on page 55
Hillgrove
Jeogla
CUNNAWARRA NATIONAL PARK
Kalang
JUNGAWARRA N.R.
Urunga
Wenonah Head
Missabotti
BOLLANOLLA N.R.
Valla Beach
OXLEY WILD RIVERS NATIONAL PARK
GEORGES CREEK N.R.
Bowraville
BUNGGIR N.R.
Comara
Burrapine
Macksville
Scotts Head
Taylors Arm
Warrell Ck
Bellbrook
NGAMBAA N.R.
Nambucca Heads
CARRAI N.P.
WILD RIVERS N.P.
GADS SUGARLOAF N.R.
Eungai Creek
Millbank
Stuarts Point
FIFES KNOB N.R.
See page 41
COPYRIGHT © UNIVERSAL PRESS PTY LTD (PUBLISHER) 2000

Scale 1:1 600 00

See page 30

121

SILVER CITY HWY

Mount Westwood

Fowlers Gap

McDougalls Well

Mount Woowoolahra

Kantappa

Corona

Acacia Downs

Bijerkerno

Wilangee

Paringa

Mount Gipps

Purnamoota

53 Yanco Glen

Glen Idol

Stephens Creek

Silverton

Broken Hill

HWY 32

Huonville

Cockburn

White Leeds

Quondong

79

Wompinie

Mingary

Tepco

Cultana

Corella

Ascot Vale

Pine Point

Aroona

Enmore

Langwell

Olary

Eringa Park

Burta

Wonga

125 SILVER CITY

Maldorkey

Mutooroo

Netley

Blackwell

Devonborough Downs

Middle Camp

Mannahill

Wadnaminga

Buckalow

Kudgee

Benda Park

Mazar

South Ita

Budgeree

Olorah Downs

Kimberley

Terrananya

Nagaela

Coombah Roadhouse

South Australia see pages 142 to 169

Oakvale

Twin Wells

79

Lilydale

Oakbank

Popiltah

Faraway Hill

Morgan Vale

DANGGALI

Windamingle

Bendigo

Sturt Vale

CONSERVATION PARK

TARAWI NATURE RESERVE

Pine Valley

Hog Back

141 Bunneringee

Canopus

Hypurna

Huntingfield

Canegrass

CHOWILLA REGIONAL RESERVE

Pine Camp

Lake Victoria

Redcliffe

Balah

Florieton

CHOWILLA GAME RESERVE

Warranangra

Chaffey

Renmark North

Cal Lal

Rufus River

Moorna

Morgan

43

Renmark

Paringa

Waikerie **STURT** 79

88 A20

Meringur North

Cullelleraine

A (top): Pauls Bore, Frome Downs, Woolshed, Erudina, Curnamona, Koonamore, Mt Victor, Plumbago, Bindyi, Four Brothers, Outalpa, Oopina, Morialpa, Waukaringa, Bonnie Brae, Melton, Old Wabricoola, Winnininnie, Yunta, Oulina Park, Paratoo, Tiverton, Manunda

B: Mooleulooloo, Yarramba, Kalkaroo, Bimbowrie, Bulloo Creek, Kalabity, Boolcoomta

BARRIER A32 150

B (bottom): Pulpara, Willara, Kia Ora, Fords Lagoon, Caroona, Glenora, Muckaby, Chalk Cliffs, Robertstown, Mount Mary, Bower, Qualco, Murbko, Ramco, Sutherland, King-On-Murray, **MURRAY RIVER**

Frome, Eurinilla, Pasmore

Quinyambie

Tielta

Morphetts

Mulyungarie

BARRIER RANGE

Umberumberka Resvr

Stephen Ck Resvr

Mount Gipps

COPYRIGHT © UNIVERSAL PRESS PTY LTD (PUBLISHER) 2000

Yamba

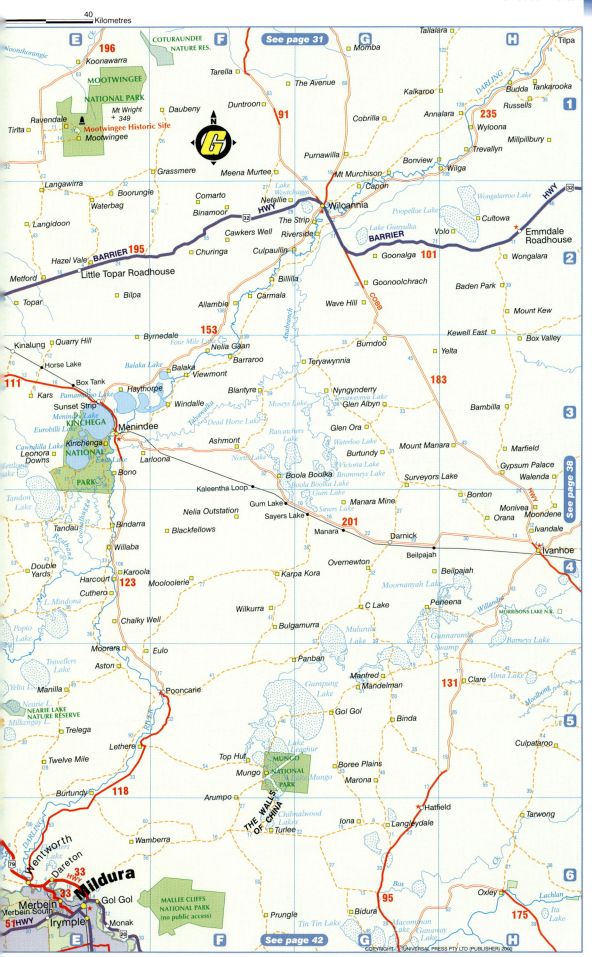

Scale 1:1 600 000

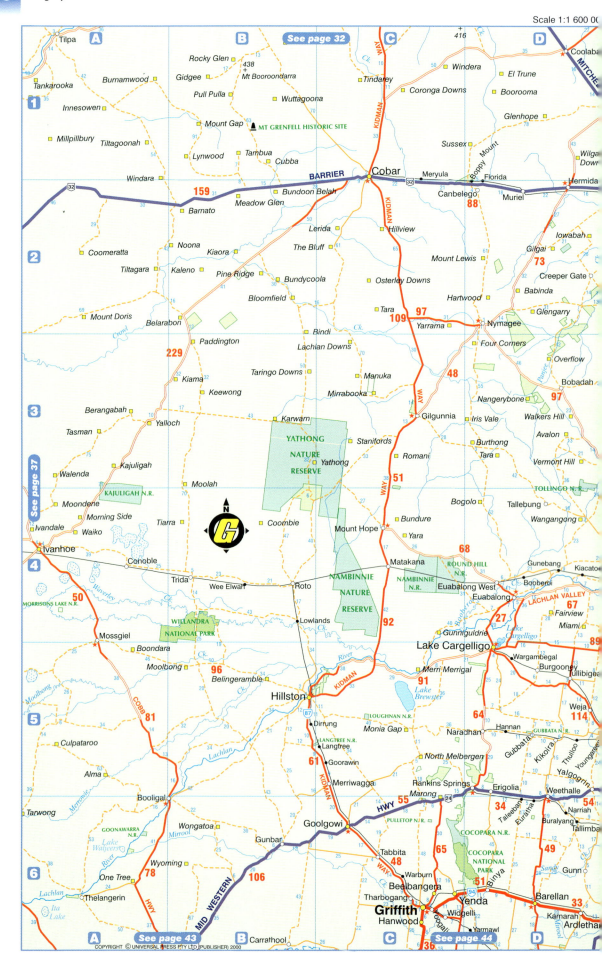

See page 32

See page 43   Carrathool   See page 44

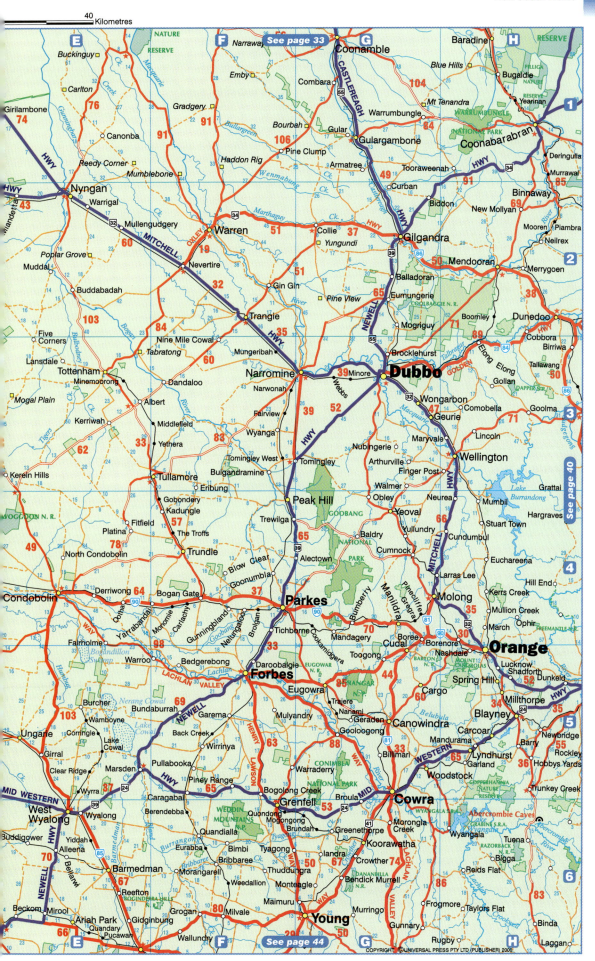

40 Kilometres

Scale 1:1 600 00

Scale 1:1 600 00

40 Kilometres

See page 38

E   F   G   H

Penarie
Nap Nap   Yerrinbool   Hay   Carrathool   Hanwood   Yoogali
Maude   57 STURT   Willbriggie   36
MURRUMBIDGEE RIVER   Whitton   Darlington Point
Ravensworth   57   HWY   20   Waddi   56
STURT HWY   Balranald
Yangalake   75   Elginbah   Coleambally
Yanga N.R.   Eurolie   KIDMAN HWY
Yanga Lake   62   94   110
77   Miranda   Booroorban   124   Willurah   137   The Yanko   Coonong
78   Windouran   Moonbria   LAKE URANA N.R.
Perekerten   58   Urana
Stony Crossing   69   Dhuragoon   107   Wanganella   Jerilderie   Bundure
Dilpurra   Niermur   Conargo   85   Coree Sth   66
70   Jimaringle   Morago   Mayrung   Nyora   53
Burraboi   122   Dahwilly   85   Osborne Well
Wakool   Deniliquin   34   Finley   22   Berrigan   56
Lake Boga   Ballbank   Yallakool   Blighty   58   Sangar
Gonn Crossing   Caldwell   Savernake   Warragoon   Renmie
Mystic Park   Murrabit   100   85   Gulpa   Moroco   34   Tocumwal   Koonoomoo   Barooga   61   Mulwala
Lake Charm   Myall   75   Mathoura   Strathmerton   Bundalong
27   Barham   Bunnaloo   15   Cobram   Yarrawonga
Kerang   Koondrook   Thyra   BARMAH STATE PARK   Katamatite   81   Tungamah   37
Quambatook   31   Womboota   Barmah   63   Nathalia   Numurkah   Lake Rowan
Kerang Sth   23   Cohuna   15   Gunbower   Wunghnu   Invergordon   WARBY RANGE S.P.
Leaghur   45   Leitchville   Patho   Torrumbarry   Moama   Wyuna   53   Congupna   Dookie   Glenrowan
Gredgwin   Loddon Vale   Echuca   32   Tongala   41   Tallygaroopna   Nalinga   45
Minmindie   50   Pyramid Hill   Wyuna   Kyabram   62   Koonda   Benalla   Winton
Boort   Durham Ox   Kotta   Nanneella   Mooroopna   Shepparton   MIDLAND HWY
Mysia   Mitiamo   Lockington   45   Girgarre   Tatura   77   A300
Borung   33   Jarklin   Rochester   Stanhope   Rushworth   Violet Town   45   Tatong
Korong Vale   Milloo Dingee   Hunter   Mathiesons   Murchison   81   Euroa   Swanpool   64
Wedderburn   Bears Lagoon   Summerfield   Goornong   Mt Black +318   Nagambie   Strathbogie   Mt Samaria
Wedderburn Junction   37   21   Serpentine   46   Avonmore   Graytown   47   Avenel   Merton   Barjarg
Inglewood   49   Elmore   52   Mitchellstown   HUME   31   Maindample
Logan   Bridgewater   38   Huntly   Heathcote   Puckapunyal   Mangalore   38   Mansfield
Kingower   Sebastian   Bendigo   Sutton Grange   Tooborac   Seymour   Bonnie Doon   27
Rheola   Arnold   Marong   Strathfieldsaye   Redesdale   50   Pyalong   Tallarook   Highlands   42   Alexandra   Goughs Bay
59   Llanelly   Lockwood   29   Sedgwick   Tooborac   39   Yea   33   Acheron   Eildon   Howqua
Moliagul   Dunolly   Ravenswood   Harcourt   Metcalfe   Broadford   54   Strath Creek   Taggerty   Jamieson
Bealiba   Natte Yallock Havelock   Maldon   Malmsbury   Kyneton   Lancefield   Flowerdale   Kevington
Maryborough   Castlemaine   Chewton   Carlsruhe   Kilmore   Strath Creek   69   Buxton   Mt Duffy
27   Moolort   47   Newstead   Woodend   18   Wandong   Glenburn   Lake Mountain 1402   +1029
Talbot   Clunes   Tylden   Macedon   40   Marysville
Lexton   Evansford   Smeaton   Hepburn Springs   Daylesford   Riddells Creek   Whittlesea   Toolangi   WARBY RANGES
72   Creswick   Trentham Newbury   Gisborne   Kinglake   KINGLAKE N.P.   CATHEDRAL RANGE S.P.
48   Learmonth   17   Blackwood   Craigieburn   Narbethong   YARRA RANGES
Ballarat   WESTERN   71   Sunbury   Hurstbridge   Yarra Glen   Healesville   Upper Yarra Reservoir
Smythesdale   Ballan   Melton   41   Lilydale   Coldstream   Warburton
Buninyong   Bacchus Marsh   Rockbank   MELBOURNE   Tooronga
Linton   Enfield   Kilmore   Sunshine   H
Cape Clear

COPYRIGHT © UNIVERSAL PRESS PTY LTD (PUBLISHER) 2000

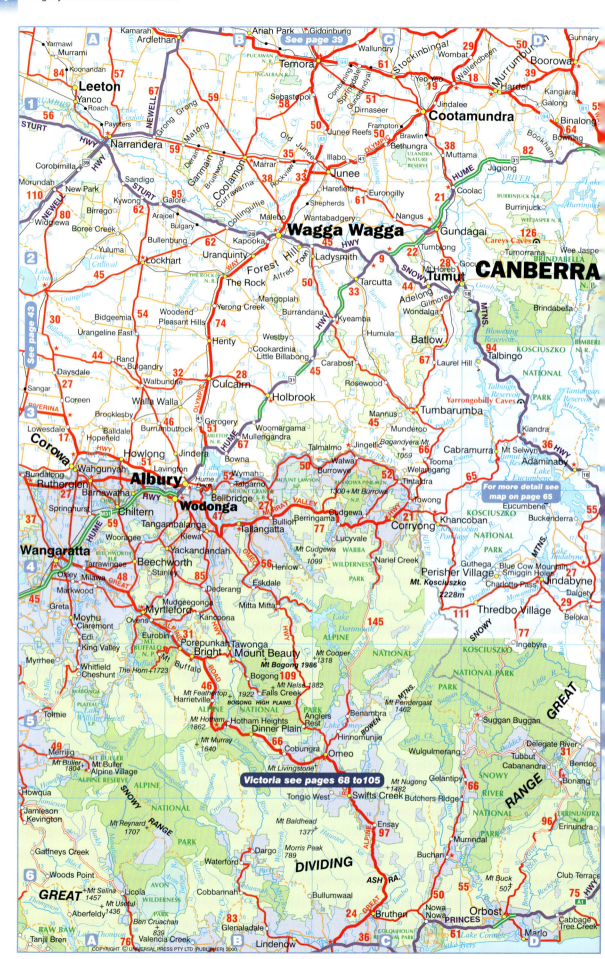

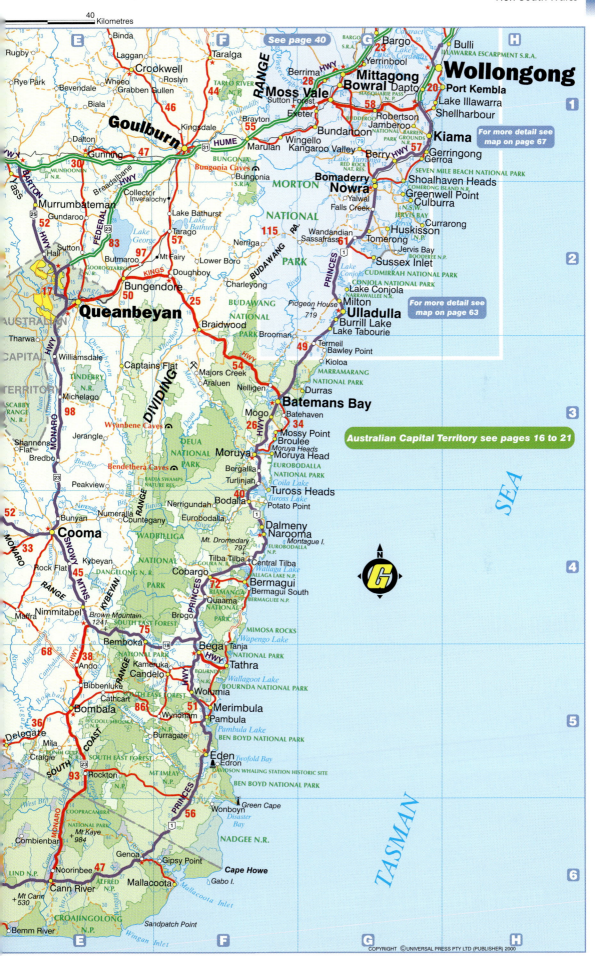

40 Kilometres

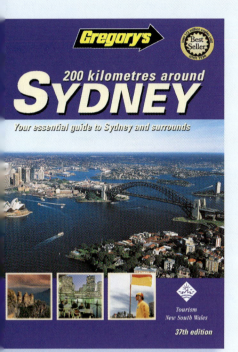
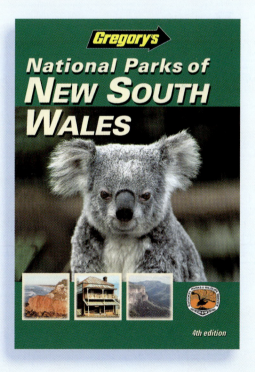

Ballina-Byron Bay

Situated on the Far North Coast of NSW, the stunning stretch of coastline between Ballina and Byron Bay boasts an excellent array of surf and swimming beaches. Although the two townships share a sunny sub-tropical climate and are both increasingly popular as holiday destinations, their histories betray a different past. Ballina was the site of a short-lived goldrush in the 1880s while Byron Bay, once filled with dilapidated weatherboard cottages, was known for its abattoir.

The charm of this picturesque area now attracts so many visitors that during the summer months the locals are outnumbered by tourists. It is still possible to find a private spot to enjoy the sun in this idyllic coastal retreat.

Must Visit

• Ballina Naval & Maritime Museum
• Byron Lighthouse
• Brunswick Heads
• Nightcap NP

ℹ Tourist Information

Ballina Visitor Information Centre
cnr River St & Las Balsas Plaza,
Ballina 2478
Ph: (02) 6686 3484
www.ballina.tropicalnsw.com.au
Byron Bay Visitor Information Centre
80 Johnson St, Byron Bay 2481
Ph: (02) 6685 8050
www.visitbyronbay.com.au

Cape Byron Lighthouse

Scale 1:320 000

Blue Mountains

Named the Blue Mountains due to the bluish haze that can be seen from Sydney, created by light interacting with the mist emanating from the millions of eucalypt trees, this rugged region features cliffs, rock formations, waterfalls and caves. Once seen as a barrier to the infant colony's expansion westwards, the Blue Mountains is now a popular holiday or weekend destination due to its close proximity to Sydney.

Located approximately 105km from Sydney, this spectacular mountain range can be enjoyed all year round. Seasonal changes here are more marked than in Sydney, and temperatures can plummet, especially in winter, so it is wise to always be prepared for the cold. This climate makes the Blue Mountains an ideal location for Yulefest, a mid-winter Christmas festival, held annually between June

Zig Zag Railway

and August. Many quaint villages dot the landscape, offering excellent restaurants, cafes, pubs, gardens, antique stores and other shops to entertain less energetic visitors.

The Three Sisters' Legend

To protect them from the bunyip, their father, a witchdoctor, turned the sisters to stone and himself into a lyrebird, but then lost his magic bone. He is still searching for it today, while the sisters silently wait.

ℹ️ Tourist Information

Blue Mountains Tourism Ltd
Echo Pt Visitor Information Centre
Echo Pt Rd, Echo Pt, Katoomba 2780
Freecall: 1300 653 408

Main Attractions

★ **Blue Mountains NP**
This is a popular park offering many walks.
★ **Echo Point Lookout**
This lookout provides breathtaking views from Jamison Valley to the Three Sisters.
★ **Hydro Majestic**
Built last century, this hotel remains a popular retreat.
★ **Jenolan Caves**
Limestone caverns lie underground, with icy rivers and impressive limestone formations.
★ **Leura**
A picturesque town classified by the National Trust.
★ **Megalong Valley**
This valley is the horseriding centre of the mountains.
★ **Norman Lindsay Gallery and Museum**
Formerly the home of the renegade artist, cartoonist and writer, it is now a gallery of Lindsay's works.
★ **Zig Zag Railway**
This railway was named in 1886, after a series of zig zags were constructed in the track enabling coal trains to descend into the valley.

Three Sisters

Scale 1:190 00

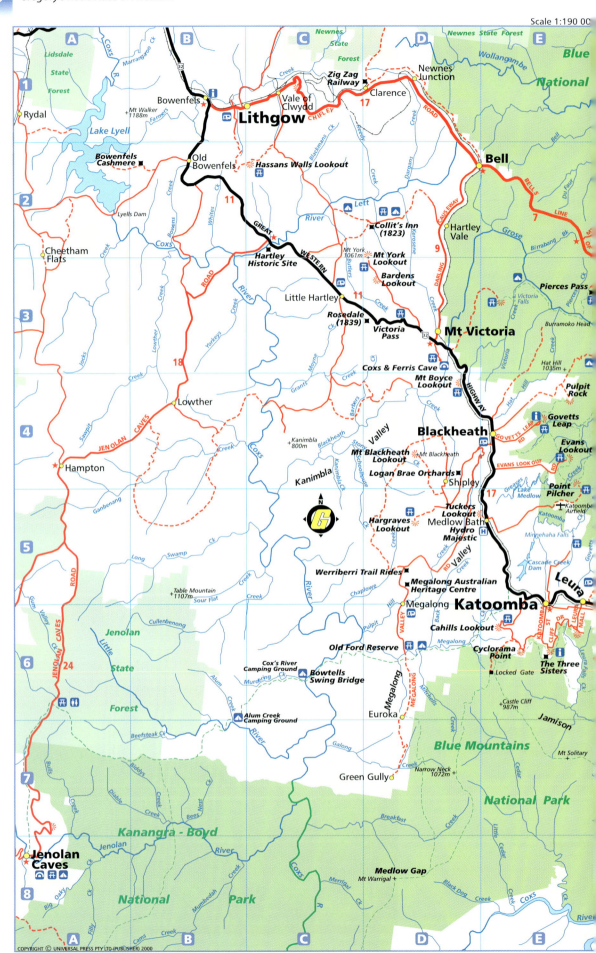

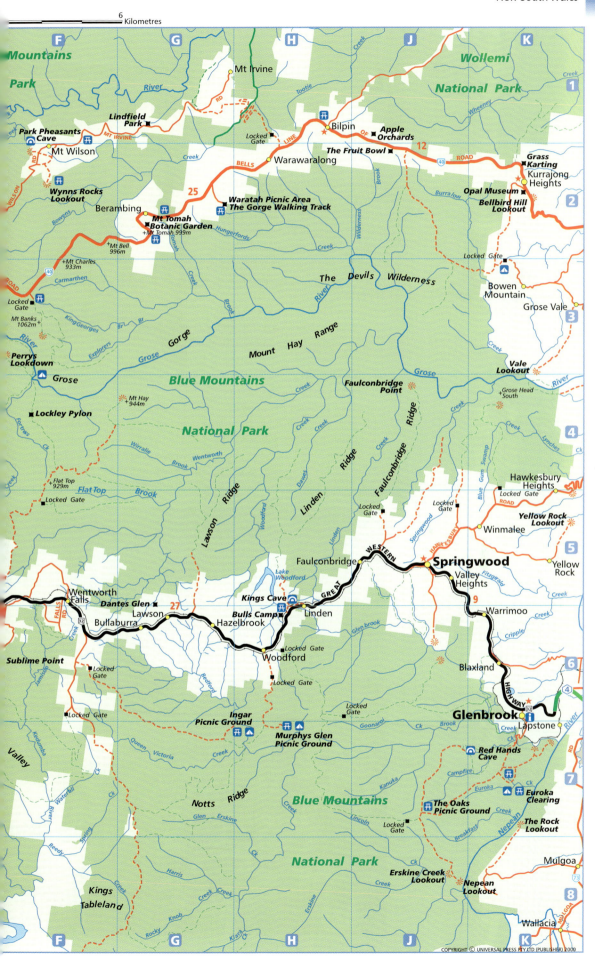

6 Kilometres

Central Coast

ℹ Tourist Information

Central Coast Tourism
Marine Pde, The Entrance 2261
Ph: (02) 4385 4430
Freecall: 1800 806 258
www.cctourism.com.au

Located barely an hour from Sydney, the Central Coast is a water playground on Sydney's northern fringe. Its close proximity to Sydney and easy accessibility via fast freeways has ensured this region's development as a prime holiday destination. Characterised by large saltwater lagoons, connected to the ocean via a number of small waterways, with an array of excellent beaches on the coastline, this area is a watersports haven. Fishing and surfing opportunities abound, charter cruises and hire boats are available on all major bodies of water, and it is also possible to rent a houseboat on Lake Macquarie, the region's largest lake.

Much of the Central Coast is covered by national parks, where bushwalking, camping and picnicking are popular pastimes. Gosford, the hub of the Central Coast, is about 80min drive from Sydney; while a number of smaller townships such as

Old Sydney Town

Patonga and Umina offer seaside retreats with a village-like atmosphere. At Ettalong Beach, the weekend undercover markets attract crowds of bargain hunters who come to explore the colourful stalls.

Main Attractions

★ **Australian Reptile Park**
A highlight is watching venomous snakes being milked of their poison.
★ **Avoca**
This tiny seaside village is a relaxing holiday spot.
★ **Bouddi NP**
See a diversity of habitats, bird and animal life.
★ **Forest of Tranquility**
Askania Park contains a pristine pocket of preserved original rainforest.
★ **Old Sydney Town**
This theme park recreates Sydney's colonial past.
★ **Terrigal**
Home to the Central Coast's most impressive hotel development, Terrigal is a top surfing spot.
★ **The Entrance**
Pelicans are fed at Memorial Park at 3.30pm daily.
★ **Watagan State Forest**
Walking tracks lead past giant cedar and turpentine trees to waterfalls and lookouts.

Pelican feeding – The Entrance

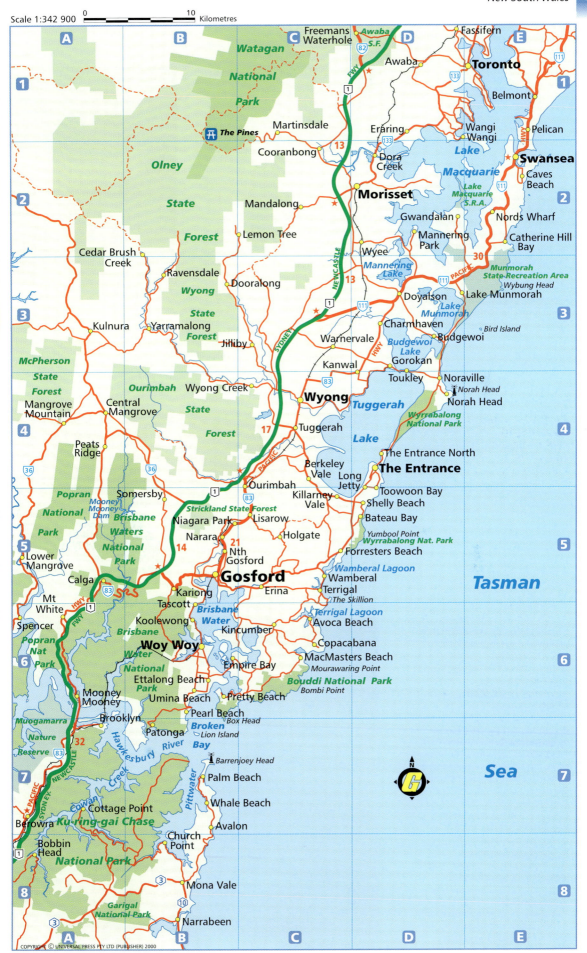

Scale 1:342 900   0   10   Kilometres

Coffs Harbour

Muttonbird Island

Spectacular coastal views abound from this nature reserve, which features Australia's most interesting migratory birds — muttonbirds. They return to the island in August after travelling thousands of kilometres from SE Asia. The tiny island is reached by walking along Coffs Harbour's northern sea wall.

Tourist Information

Coffs Harbour Visitor Information Centre
Cnr Rose Ave & Pacific Hwy,
Coffs Harbour 2450
Ph: (02) 6652 1522

Main Attractions

★ **Big Banana**
A Coffs Harbour icon - the Big Banana celebrates the banana, the mainstay of the local economy.
★ **Coffs Harbour**
Watersports can be enjoyed here at a myriad of beaches.
★ **George's Gold Mine**
Facilities include BBQ's, picnic grounds and walking trails through the surrounding ancient forest.
★ **Kingfisher Conservation Park**
This park has more than 400 animals, some threatened by extinction.
★ **North Coast Regional Botanic Gardens**
The sub-tropical gardens include a rainforest patch, a number of endangered species and a mangrove boardwalk.
★ **Storyland Gardens**
This theme park for small children features fairytale settings, a playground and animal nursery.
★ **Woolgoolga**
This town offers both an excellent surfing beach and swimming and boating on Woolgoolga Lake.

Between the two popular coastal resort towns of Port Macquarie and Coffs Harbour, on the NSW Mid-North Coast, lies a scenic sub-tropical retreat. From secluded beaches, tourist towns and luxury resorts to tranquil forests, tiny fishing villages and sleepy townships, this stretch of sun, sea and sand offers many holiday options.

The coastline is speckled with protected inlets, picturesque bays, rocky promontories and long, sandy beaches. In contrast, the parallel inland strip houses the rainforest-clad mountains of the Great Dividing Ra. Its lush, thickly wooded areas are protected as national parks or state forests. Fertile river valleys support sub-tropical agricultural ventures such as banana plantations.

The Big Banana

The moderate climate and relaxed lifestyle have attracted retirees from the cooler southern climes, while holidaymakers from a range of age groups find many activities to entertain them.

Sunrise near Sawtell

Scale 1:360 000

0   15
Kilometres

Tasman

Sea

Hunter Valley, Lower

Thanksgiving Festival

A perfect opportunity to experience wine country culture and tradition. After harvesting the grapes (mid-Apr), leading wineries toast their crop with a variety of banquets, lunches and dinners as well as more traditional activities like barrel tastings.

ℹ Tourist Information

Wine Country Visitors Information Centre
Turner Park
Aberdare Rd, Cessnock 2325
Ph: (02) 4990 4477
www.winecountry.com.au

Main Attractions

★ **Hunter Valley Gardens**
These gardens are the site of a wine theme village with a resort, restaurants and activities.
★ **Koolang Observatory**
Nestled in bushland, this observatory offers guided tours of the night sky.
★ **Morpeth**
One of the most unspoilt heritage towns in NSW, the entire village of Morpeth has been classified by the National Trust.
★ **Pokolbin**
Home to many wineries, both large and boutique, Pokolbin is home to the Hunter Valley Wine Society headquarters, a good starting point for a tour of the vineyards.
★ **Richmond Vale Railway and Mining Museum**
This museum brings the era of steam locomotives alive.
★ **Rusa Park Zoo**
See the only albino kangaroos in captivity, the white euro kangaroos, at Rusa Park Zoo.
★ **Wollombi**
Endeavour Museum showcases Wollombi's strong links to its colonial past.

A scenic 90min drive from Sydney, the Hunter Valley is one of Australia's premier wine-producing regions. The fertile flats of the Hunter River continue to nourish some of the nation's first vineyards. The first vines were planted as far back as 1832 and medals for Hunter wines were won as early as 1882.

A fabulous place for wine and food lovers, there are at least 50 wineries, large and boutique, and almost as many restaurants. Although only about five per cent of Australia's wine comes from here, the Hunter is home to some of the most respected wineries. These wineries include Drayton, Lindemans, Tyrrells and Tulloch, some of the best known names in Australian wine.

The region caters to the needs of wine lovers with cellar door sales, winery tours, restaurants, picnic areas and a diverse range of accommodation.

While the region is bursting with natural beauty, huge seams of high quality coal are found throughout the valley, and coal mining remains a pillar of the local economy. However, mining activity is localised to specific areas and does not impose on the tranquility of the valley. Cessnock is the region's main

Peppers Creek Winery, Pokolbin

coal-mining town. Maitland is another main centre for the region's coal industry. It also has a rich heritage as one of the early colonial Australia's most important towns. Maitland is home to the annual Hunter Valley Steamfest, a premier event for train buffs.

The lush river flats are home to dairy and beef cattle, fruit and vegetable crops and thoroughbred horses.

There is much to see and do in this region and while many may initially come to sample the fruits of the wine, it will not be just the wine that encourages their return.

Boy in vineyard

Scale 1:96 700

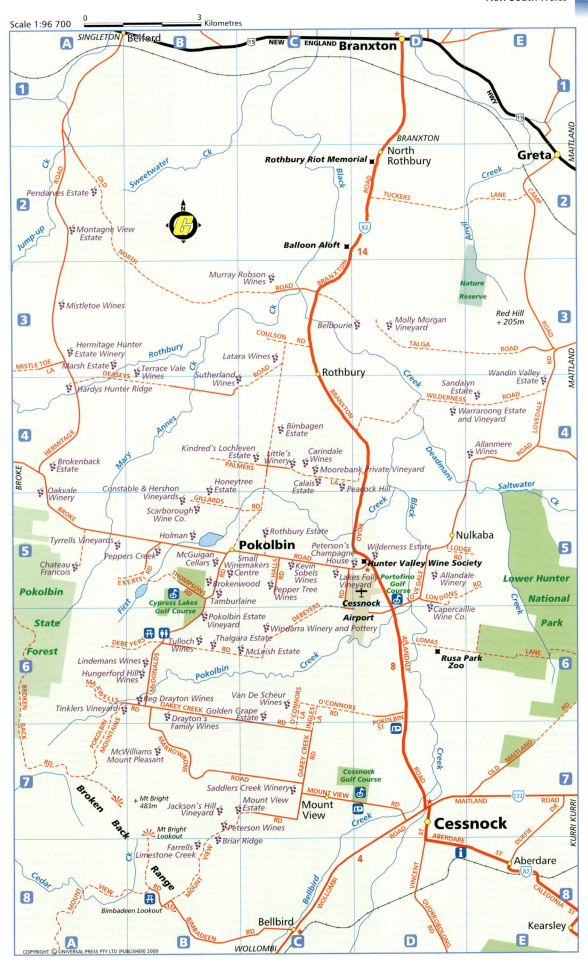

0   3 Kilometres

SINGLETON Belford   **B**   15   NEW **C** ENGLAND **Branxton**   **D**   HWY   **E**   MAITLAND

1

BRANXTON

Rothbury Riot Memorial ■   North
Rothbury   Creek   **Greta**   MAITLAND

Sweetwater   Ck   Black   TUCKERS   LANE   CAMP

2

Pendarves Estate

Jump-up   Montagne View
Estate   NORTH   82   **Balloon Aloft** ■   14   Anvil   Red Hill
+ 205m   ROAD   **3**

Murray Robson
Wines   ROAD   Molly Morgan
Vineyard   TALGA   ROAD

3   Mistletoe Wines   COULSON   RD   Belbourie   Creek

Hermitage Hunter
Estate Winery   Rothbury   Ck   Latara Wines   ROAD   **Rothbury**   Wandin Valley
Estate

MISTLETOE
LA   Marsh Estate   Terrace Vale
Wines   Sutherland
Wines   BRANXTON   Sandalyn
Estate   WILDERNESS   ROAD

DEASEYS   Hardys Hunter Ridge   Warraroong Estate
and Vineyard   LOVEDALE

HERMITAGE   Annes   Bimbagen
Estate   Carindale
Wines   Deadmans   Allanmere
Wines   ROAD   **4**

4   Mary   Kindred's Lochleven
Estate   Little's
Winery   Moorebank Private Vineyard   Black

BROKE   Brokenback
Estate   PALMERS   Honeytree
Estate   Calais
Estate   LA   Peacock Hill   Saltwater

Oakvale
Winery   Constable & Hershon
Vineyards   GILLARDS   Creek   Ck

BROKE   Scarborough
Wine Co.   RD   **Lower Hunter**

Tyrrells Vineyards   Holman   Rothbury Estate   ROAD   Wilderness Estate   LODGE   Nulkaba   **National**

5   Peppers Creek   McGuigan
Cellars   Small
Winemakers
Centre   Peterson's
Champagne
House   RD   Allandale
Winery   RD   **Park**

Chateau
Francois   EKERTS   RD   Kevin
Sobels
Wines   **Hunter Valley Wine Society**   LONDONS   Capercaillie
Wine Co.   **5**

Pokolbin   THOMPSONS   Brokenwood   Pepper Tree
Wines   Lakes Folly
Vineyard   **Portofino
Golf
Course**   LOVEDALE

State   Cypress Lakes
Golf Course   Tamburlaine   **Cessnock
Airport**   ATLANDALE   LOMAS   LANE

Forest   DEBEYERS   Tulloch
Wines   Pokolbin Estate
Vineyard   Thalgara Estate   RD   McLeish Estate   Wipdarra Winery and Pottery   DEBEYERS   **Rusa Park
Zoo**   **6**

6   Lindemans Wines   McDONALDS   Pokolbin   Creek   8

Hungerford Hill
Wines   MAXWELLS   Van De Scheur
Wines   O'CONNORS   LA   MAITLAND

BROKEN   Reg Drayton Wines   RD   OAKEY CREEK   Golden Grape
Estate   RD   O'CONNORS
LA   INGLES
LA   O'CONNORS
RD   POKOLBIN
ST   OLD

BACK   Tinklers Vineyard   Drayton's
Family Wines

POKOLBIN
MOUNTAINS   MARROWBONE   Creek   **7**

7   McWilliams
Mount Pleasant   ROAD   Cessnock
Golf Course   MAITLAND   132   ROAD   KURRI KURRI

Broken   Saddlers Creek Winery   MOUNT VIEW   RD   DUFFIE

+ Mt Bright
483m   Jackson's Hill
Vineyard   Mount View
Estate   **Mount
View**   **Cessnock**

Back   Mt Bright
Lookout   Peterson Wines   Creek   RD   **i**   ABERDARE
ST   **Aberdare**

Farrells
Limestone Creek   Briar Ridge   4   82   CALEDONIA ST

Cedar   **Range**   VINCENT   OLD   **8**

8   Bimbadeen Lookout   BIMBADEEN   Bellbird   WOLLOMBI   QUORROBOLONG   RD   **Kearsley**

A   **B**   **C**   **D**   **E**

Hunter Valley, Upper

The upper side of the Hunter Valley, surrounding the pretty little town of Scone, is widely regarded as Australia's premier thoroughbred and horse-breeding district. There are more than 30 studs located in this part of the Hunter, some offering personalised tours for those who book. In May, Scone hosts the annual Scone Horse Week, complete with rodeos – a must for equestrian types.

Wineries also characterise the Upper Hunter, as its history demonstrates. In the 19th century the region's wine growers stopped planting Cabernet Sauvignon vines – fortunately Max Lake of Lake's Folly reintroduced these grapes in the 1960s – and now Cabernet Sauvignon is one of Australia's most popular red wines. Many wineries,

Singleton sundial

including Rosemount Estate and Mount Arrow Wines, offer wine tasting and sales at the cellar door.

Prospering from coal mining, vineyards and horse studs, the Upper Hunter is also the site of some of Australia's oldest towns.

Tourist Information

**Muswellbrook Tourist
Information Centre**
87 Hill St, Muswellbrook 2333
Ph: (02) 6541 4050
www.musswellbrook.org.au

Main Attractions

★ **Barrington Tops NP**
About 85% of the park is declared wilderness. Part of Eastern Australia's World Heritage-listed rainforests.

★ **Denman**
This quaint township was traditionally known for its horse and cattle studs. Today wine is a feature and a number of vineyards are established there, including Rosemount Estate and Arrowfield.

★ **Recreation Area**
This water playground is ideal for watersports. Water from the dam is used to irrigate the valley.

★ **Muswellbrook**
Originally a government planned village, it has become a regional centre. Vineyards, including Reynolds Yarraman Estate, are clustered to the SW of the town.

★ **Singleton**
Singleton is the gateway to the Upper Hunter Valley. At Singleton you can see the largest sundial in the southern hemisphere.

★ **Upper Hunter Wine Centre**
This one-stop-shop showcases the Upper Hunter's wines.

Waterfall, Barrington Tops

Upper Hunter Wineries

NAME	MAP	ADDRESS	PHONE	OPEN
Arrowfield Wines	C3	Denman Rd, Jerry's Plains	(02) 6576 4041	*10am–5pm daily*
Barrington Estate	B1	Yarraman Rd, Wybong	(02) 6547 8118/ (02) 6547 8055	*Phone for appointment*
Birnam Wood Wines	D1	Turanville Rd, Scone	(02) 6545 3286	*11am–4pm weekdays*
Cruikshank Callatoota Estate	B1	2656 Wybong Rd, Wybong	(02) 6547 8149	*9am–5pm daily*
Horseshoe Vineyards	B3	Horseshoe Valley, Denman	(02) 6547 3528	*10am–4pm weekends and public holidays, other times by appointment*
Inglewood Vineyard	B2	Yarrawa Rd, Denman	(02) 6547 2556	*Phone for appointment*
James Estate Wines	A2	951 Rylstone Rd, Baerami	(02) 6547 5168	*10am–4pm daily*
London Lodge Estate	A1	Muswellbrook Rd, Gungal	(02) 6547 6122	*8am–9pm Sun–Thurs 8am–12am Fri & Sat*
Reynolds Yarraman Estate	B1	Yarraman Rd, Wybong	(02) 6547 8127	*10am–4pm Mon–Sat 11am–4pm Sun*
Rosemount Estate	B2	Rosemount Rd, Denman	(02) 6549 6400	*10am–4pm Mon–Sat 10:30am–4pm Sun*

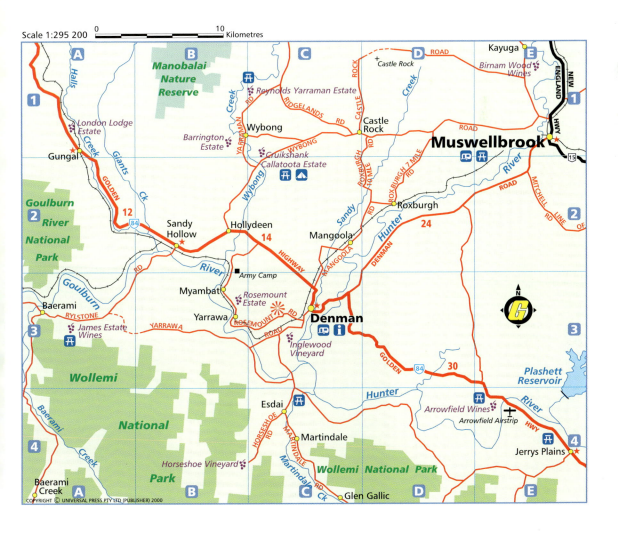

Scale 1:295 200

Myall Lakes and Nelson Bay

Features of Myall Lakes NP

Containing the largest coastal lake system in NSW. This NP is an important waterbird habitat. Walk through rainforest, hire a houseboat or go 4WD-beach driving. With an area of just over 44ha, this popular Park has something to offer everyone.

ℹ Tourist Information

Port Stephens Visitor Information Centre
Victoria Pde, Nelson Bay 2315
Freecall: 1800 808 900

Main Attractions

★ **Bulahdelah**
This tiny township is a convenient base for exploring the region.
★ **Myall Lakes NP**
A unique and very popular NP. Lakes are ideal for watersports and houseboating. Wildlife in the park includes kangaroos, swamp and red-necked wallabies, possums, bandicoots, gliders, spiny anteaters and marsupial mice.
★ **Nelson Bay**
Scenically located on a protective inlet surrounded by towering headlands. This is a great place for dolphin spotting.
★ **Seal Rocks**
This small and remote fishing village, popular with surfers and beachside campers, is a secluded spot offering excellent surfing opportunities. There is a blowhole and the lighthouse gives sweeping views off the coast.
★ **Tea Gardens and Hawks Nest**
These twin towns are connected by a single bridge. Hawks Nest boasts a 40km surf beach. At Tea Gardens, houseboats are available, as are dolphin-watching and adventure cruises.

Myall Lakes is a system of shallow waterways stretching along the coast of the Tasman Sea, 236km north of Sydney. The tranquility of this unique area is conserved in a very popular national park scattered with numerous camping retreats.

The eastern edges of the lakes can be accessed via numerous roads and trails leading through the forests from the Pacific Highway.

Also known as the Great Lakes district, the lakes are ideal for watersports and boating. Their banks are dotted with launching ramps and boats can be hired from Myall Shores and Tea Gardens. For a different sort of adventure, hire a houseboat from the nearby town, Bulahdelah. The name Bulahdelah originates from the Aboriginal word for 'meeting of two streams'. The Myall River forms the town's southern boundary.

On the other side of the narrow strip of sand dunes separating the lakes from the ocean, there are surfing beaches.

O'Sullivans Gap Flora Reserve is a great place to visit. Located in Wang Wauk Forest, past flooded giant gum trees known as The Grandis, this reserve has a creek-side walk that affords sightings of bandicoots, goannas, koalas, marsupial mice, gliders, possums and many bird species.

Nelson Bay is the main town on the Tomaree Peninsula. This resort

Port Stephens sunset

town boasts galleries, gardens and ocean-fresh fish to catch or buy. Nearby Nelson Head houses the Inner Lighthouse, carefully restored by the National Trust. It includes a teahouse, cottage, maritime museum and coastal patrol base. Nelson Bay is a good location from which to go on day cruises whale watching and dolphin spotting. Game fishing is popular and boats of various sizes can be chartered - there are several game fishing competitions throughout the year at Nelson Bay.

Nelson Bay and its nearby townships, including Shoal Bay, Fingal Bay and Salamander Bay, offer a wide range of accommodation and activities year round. The Tomaree NP is also worth visiting due to the koala colonies there.

Myall Lakes houseboat

Dolphin Watching

Pods of friendly bottlenose dolphins are one of this region's most noted attractions. During winter and spring, Tomaree Heads provides an excellent vantage point for sighting migrating whales from a number of lookouts dotting the headlands. Approximately 12 operators offer cruises from Port Stephens or Nelson Bay, providing opportunities for visitors to enjoy: dolphin and whale watching; cruising Broughton Island, Myall River and Lakes, and Tea Gardens; and viewing the area's dramatic sunsets.

Dawson's Scenic Cruises conducts a range of cruise options for exploring Port Stephens, with booking recommended for their luncheon cruises, which operate on most days.

Advance II, a sleek 17m yacht, provides sunset sailing and daily dolphin watch cruises from Nelson Bay between October and May.

Moonshadow Cruises offers whale watching cruises in season and dolphin watching cruises daily, plus dinner and Broughton Island cruises.

Tamboi Queen run daily dolphin watching cruises from Port Stephens, however, bookings are essential. A boom net allows observers closer encounters with the dolphins.

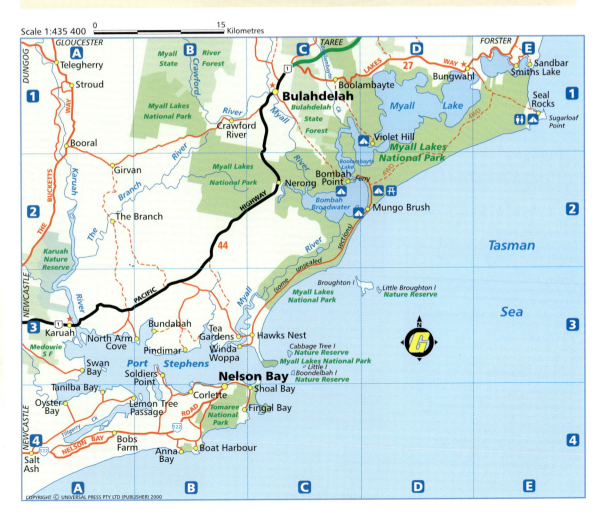

Nowra and Jervis Bay

Located approximately 163km south of Sydney's southern fringe, the area between Nowra and Jervis Bay is a study in contrasts.

The picturesque rich rolling hills surrounding the south coast town of Nowra support a thriving dairying industry, with many small farms selling fresh, seasonal produce from the farmhouse door. Heading to the coast, you will pass through quaint rural villages, featuring teahouses, antique shops, cosy bed and breakfast cottages and old-fashioned pubs.

Once at Jervis Bay, there is a wonderful ocean playground along the shores of this stunning sheltered inlet. Not surprisingly, fishing is one of the region's key industries and a pleasant pastime for amateurs.

Coolangatta Estate

A safe haven

Abraham's Bosom Beach, Jervis Bay, was the site where the shipwrecked passengers of the SS Merimbula found safety. It is named after the Bosom of Abraham described in the Old Testament, where children found shelter and safety.

ℹ️ Tourist Information

Booderee NP Visitors Centre
Jervis Bay Rd, Jervis Bay 2540
Ph: (02) 4443 0977
Shoalhaven Visitors Centre
Princes Hwy, Nowra 2541
Ph: (02) 4421 0778
www.shoalhaven@nsw.gov.au

Main Attractions

★ **Berry**
This pretty hamlet boasts many charming buildings classified by the National Trust.
★ **Bundanoon**
Visit famous painter Arthur Boyd's scenic property, now a gallery.
Coolangatta Historic Village
This historic village was the first European south coast settlement.
★ **Jervis Bay**
This is a beautiful inlet with a 50km shoreline of protected beaches.
★ **Jervis Bay NP**
This national park boasts an array of pristine beaches.
★ **Lady Denman**
Once a ferry, Lady Denman now houses a maritime museum.
★ **Nowra Animal Park**
Native fauna is on show in a rainforest setting at Nowra Animal Park.
★ **Nowra Historical Buildings**
St Andrews church, the old police station and Meroogal house are all historical buildings in Nowra.
★ **Seven Mile Beach NP**
This national park has a long expanse of white, sandy beach flanked by sand dunes.

On the beach at Jervis Bay

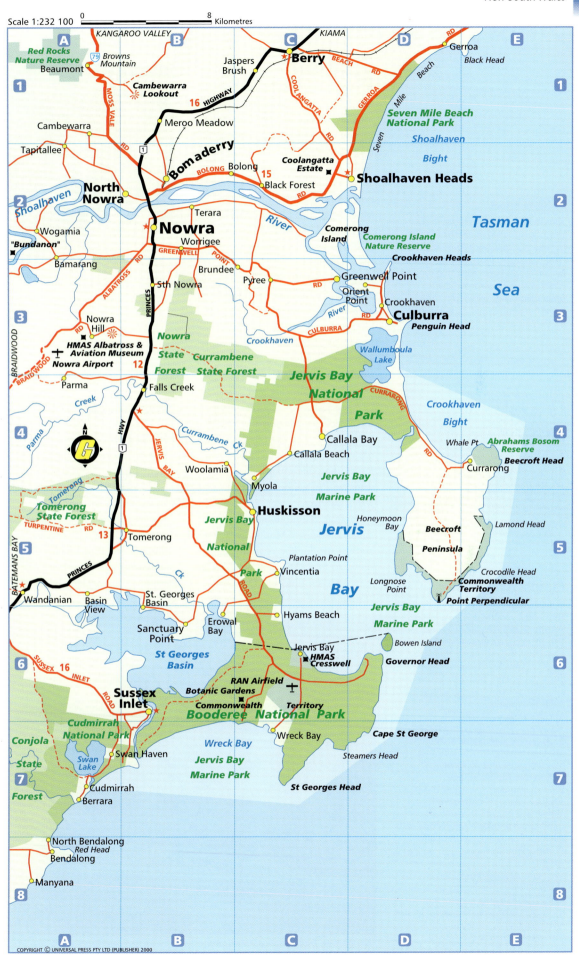

Scale 1:232 100   0   8 Kilometres

Snowy Mountains

Snowfields

Thredbo is a popular ski resort town, sandwiched in a small valley between Crackenback River and the road. Charlotte's Pass, Perisher Valley and Smiggins Holes lie within the Kosciuszko NP's borders. All offer great skiing and visitors can easily travel between some of the resorts on the Skitube.

ℹ Tourist Information

Snowy Region Visitors Centre
National Parks and Wildlife Service (NPWS),
Kosciuszko Rd, Jindabyne 2627
Ph: (02) 6450 5600
www.npws.nsw.gov.au

Main Attractions

★ **Jindabyne**
The gateway to the alpine ski resorts.
★ **Kosciuszko NP**
This NP occupies most of the Snowy Mountains region. Due to the heavy snowfall, vehicles inside the NP must carry chains between 1 June and 10 October.
★ **Mt Kosciuszko**
At 2228m above sea level, Mt Kosciuszko is Australia's highest point. An accessible walking trail crosses the flattened top of the mountain, providing breathtaking views.
★ **Thredbo Alpine Village**
Sandwiched in a small valley, this attractive village is dotted with Alpine-style chalets. This area offers some of the best skiing and is one of the most popular ski resort towns.
★ **Yarrangobilly Caves**
Surrounded by virgin bush, this limestone cave system features about 60 caves. The nearby walking trails, located by the edge of the rocky plateau next to the caves, offers panoramic views of Yarrangobilly Gorge.

Part of the NSW section of the Great Dividing Ra, the Snowy Mountains are approximately 160km long and 80km wide. Much of the rugged terrain is 900m or more above sea level, with the mountainous ridge rising to 2228m at Mt Kosciuszko, Australia's highest point. Although the Snowy Mountains are situated in NSW, they are close to the ACT and their southern boundary extends to the Victorian border.

To create Lake Jindabyne, the site of the old township was flooded as part of the Snowy Mountains Hydro Electric Scheme. The town of Jindabyne also offers many summer activities, including bush walking, trout fishing, sailing, sailboarding, waterskiing, canoeing and swimming.

Kosciuszko NP occupies most of this region, in fact it is the largest NP in NSW. The park has much to offer all year-round, including, golf, horseriding, mountain bike riding, trout fishing, canoeing and white-water rafting.

Despite the mountain range's name, the Snowy Mountains actually lie beneath the line of permanent snow, so heavy snowfall will only be seen between June and October. During the winter months skiers,

Skiing at Thredbo

both local and international, flock to the many ski resorts dotting the mountains.

Summer also has much to offer visitors. Lower prices and less crowds make the area a perfect destination for a bushwalking, trout fishing or a cycling holiday. The wildflowers and abundance of birdlife are particularly impressive during these months.

Khancoban Dam, Snowy Mountains

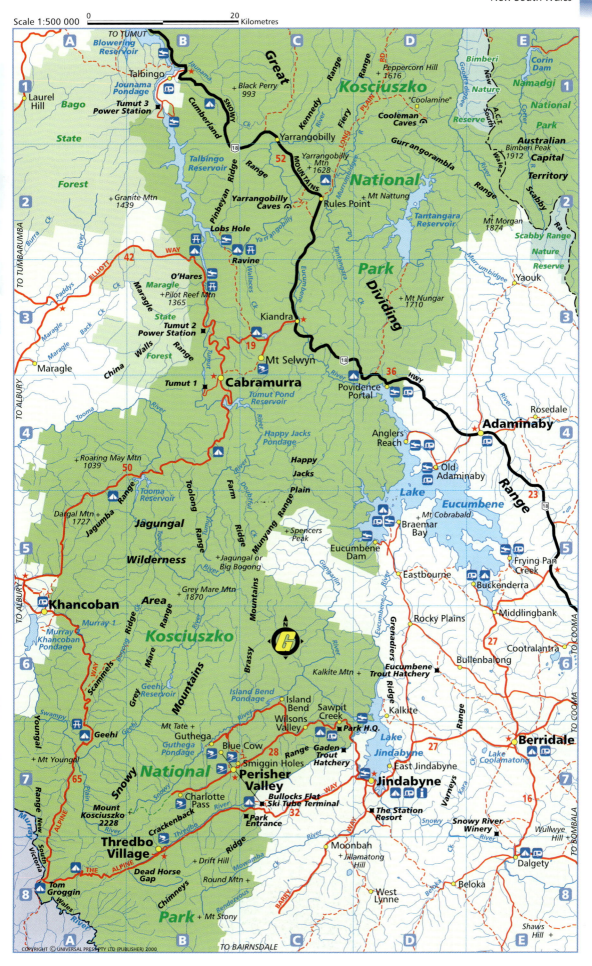

Scale 1:500 000

0   20 Kilometres

The Illawarra and Southern Highlands

Although the Illawarra and Southern Highlands are located on Sydney's SW fringes and they border each other, both have unique identities. The Illawarra — the name is a corruption of the Aboriginal word meaning 'between the high place and the sea' — has Wollongong as its centre.

Flanked by the Tasman Sea shores and the parallel mountainous terrain inland, this region is a study in contrasts. The Illawarra is a coastal haven for sun-worshippers and watersports fans. The neighbouring Southern Highlands have their own distinct character – the cooler climate and picturesque villages dotting the landscape lead to comparisons with rural England. In

Tulip time in Bowral

summer it is possible to experience the 4 seasons in a single day trip by touring the many attractions offered in this diverse region.

Best kept secret

Kiama's best kept secret is the Harbour Rock Pool at Blowhole Point, a fantastic place for a refreshing swim. The harbour is also a great spot for family fishing and has a boat ramp.

ℹ Tourist Information

Tourism Southern Highlands
62-70 Main St, Mittagong 2575
Ph: (02) 4871 2888
Freecall: 1300 657 559
Tourism Wollongong Visitors Centre
93 Crown St, Wollongong 2500
Ph: (02) 4227 5545

Main Attractions

★ **Berrima**
Several buildings in this town, founded in 1831, are listed on the National Estate. Visit the Surveyor-General Inn, Australia's oldest continuously licensed pub.
★ **Bowral**
Well-known for its annual Tulip Time Festival held each spring, Bowral is an idyllic country retreat. The Bradman museum pays tribute to one of Bowral's most famous residents, Sir Donald Bradman.
★ **Bundanoon**
Visit the Glow Worm Glen between September and May. After dark it becomes a fairyworld.
★ **Kiama**
See the Kiama Blowhole spray water 60m into the air.
★ **Minnamurra Rainforest**
This region's finest attraction has won many tourist awards.
★ **Nan Tien Temple**
This is the biggest Buddhist temple in the southern hemisphere.
★ **Stanwell Park**
To the park's north, sheer cliffs and panoramic vistas offer a great spot for hang-gliding.

Kiama Blowhole

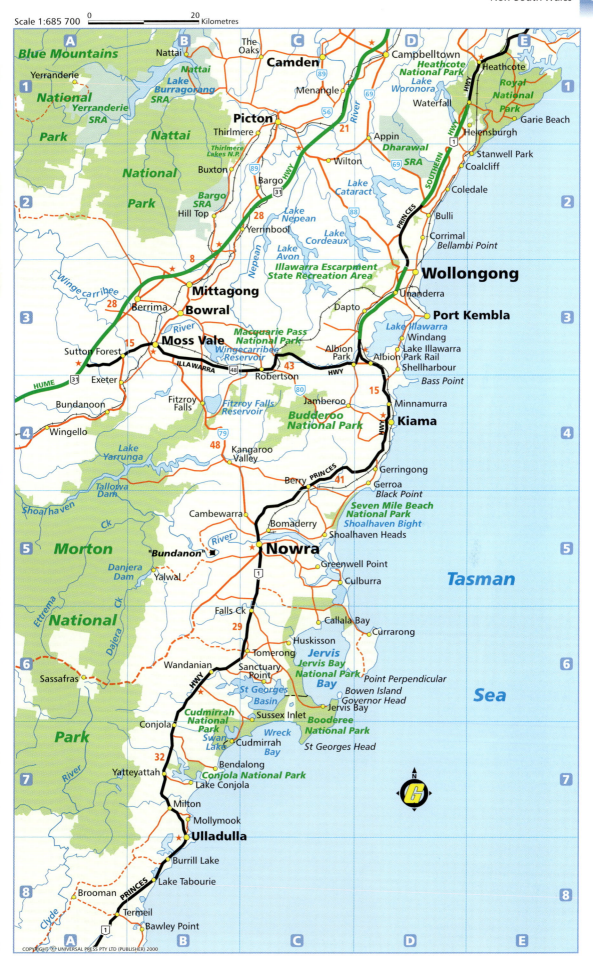

Scale 1:685 700

0   20 Kilometres

Victoria

VIC: The Garden State

- Area = 220 620 sq km
- Occupies 2.9% of Australia
- Length of coast = 1 577km
- Breadth of State = 467km

Pink Heath   *Leadbeaters Possum*

ℹ Tourist Information

Victoria Visitor Information Centre
Melbourne Town Hall
Cnr Swanston St and Little Collins St,
Melbourne 3000
Ph: 132 842
www.tourism.vic.gov.au

Main Attractions

★ **The Dandenongs**
The Dandenong Ranges feature a blue haze emitted by the gum trees.
★ **The Goldfields**
Ballarat, the capital of the Goldfields, was the site of a great goldrush during the 1850s.
★ **The Grampians NP**
This NP is famous for its rugged sandstone ranges, lakes, waterfalls and Aboriginal rock art.
★ **Great Ocean Rd**
The Twelve Apostles rock formation are a famous natural wonder.
★ **Macedon Ranges and Sunbury Wineries**
This region is known as the Spa Country. It has spa resorts, historic towns and established wineries.
★ **Phillip Island**
The renowned Penguin Parade is the drawcard for 50 000 visitors annually to Phillip Island.
★ **Victorian Alps**
The Victorian Alps include the premier skiing areas of Mt Buffalo, Mt Buller, Hotham Heights and Falls Creek.

Victoria occupies the south-eastern extremity of the Australian continent. It is Australia's second smallest state. Relatively compact, Vic has a well developed and efficient highway system which carries traffic quickly between destinations. Its greatest length from east to west is 793 km, its breadth is 467km, and its coastline is 1577km long. A diverse range of attractions are offered in this compact area, all within approximately a 5hr radius of the State's cultured and cosmopolitan capital city, Melbourne. Victoria is rich in colonial heritage, home to many of Australia's goldfields and commemorating the wild past of bushrangers and goldrushes through museums, recreational activities and tour routes.

It is also a huge natural playground as bushland covers a large proportion of the State, with over 30 national parks covering its varying landscape, which includes spectacular coastal stretches,

Mansfield Mountain Festival

mountain ranges, scenic rivers, stark deserts and lush forests. Aboriginal history is also evident, with many rock paintings and a rich cultural centre in the Wimmera region. The legacy of Vic's prosperous pastoral past is evident today. The western region is still wool country, while orchards and vineyards thrive in the oasis surrounding the Murray River, Australia's most important inland waterway.

Hepburn Spa Resort, autumn

Victoria Key Map and Distance Chart

All distances shown in the chart below have been measured over highways and major roads, not necessarily by the shortest route.

City Map
Melbourne, page 71

Suburban Maps
Melbourne, pages 72 to 75

State Maps
pages 76 to 87

Region Maps
Gippsland Lakes, page 90
Great Ocean Road, pages 92 and 93
Macedon Ranges, page 94
Phillip Island, page 95
The Dandenongs, page 97
The Goldfields, page 99
The Grampians, page 101
Victorian Alps, page 103
Wilsons Promontory, page 105

Approximate Distance	Albury NSW	Bairnsdale	Ballarat	Bega NSW	Bendigo	Bordertown SA	Cooma NSW	Geelong	Hamilton	Horsham	Melbourne	Mildura	Mount Gambier SA	Portland	Renmark SA	Shepparton	Swan Hill	Traralgon	Wangaratta	Warrnambool
Albury NSW		310	372	426	297	665	315	388	545	508	314	571	677	628	696	177	384	427	73	544
Bairnsdale	310		395	326	432	739	339	357	568	582	283	821	695	608	940	462	619	117	310	513
Ballarat	372	395		721	121	344	734	89	173	187	112	454	305	256	573	241	273	278	345	171
Bega NSW	426	326	721		709	1065	111	683	894	908	609	957	1026	934	1082	589	796	443	485	839
Bendigo	297	432	121	709		368	598	176	294	211	149	398	426	377	517	120	187	315	224	292
Bordertown SA	665	739	344	1065	368		966	433	259	157	456	411	183	281	279	488	396	622	592	365
Cooma NSW	315	339	734	111	598	966		696	907	921	622	1160	1039	947	1279	478	685	456	374	852
Geelong	388	357	89	683	176	433	696		238	276	74	543	338	251	662	253	362	240	315	156
Hamilton	545	568	173	894	294	259	907	238		129	285	439	132	83	558	414	368	451	526	112
Horsham	508	582	187	908	211	157	921	276	129		299	310	261	212	429	331	239	465	435	241
Melbourne	314	283	112	609	149	456	622	74	285	299		538	412	325	657	179	336	166	241	230
Mildura	571	821	454	957	398	411	1160	543	439	310	538		571	522	125	433	218	704	537	551
Mount Gambier SA	677	695	305	1026	426	183	1039	338	132	261	412	571		98	462	546	500	578	650	182
Portland	628	608	256	934	377	281	947	251	83	212	325	522	98		641	497	451	491	601	95
Renmark SA	696	940	573	1082	517	279	1279	662	558	429	657	125	462	641		558	343	657	662	676
Shepparton	177	462	241	589	120	488	478	253	414	331	179	433	546	497	558		215	345	104	412
Swan Hill	384	619	273	796	187	396	685	362	368	239	336	218	500	451	343	215		502	319	480
Traralgon	427	117	278	443	315	622	456	240	451	465	166	704	578	491	657	345	502		407	396
Wangaratta	73	310	345	485	224	592	374	315	526	435	241	537	650	601	662	104	319	407		471
Warrnambool	544	513	171	839	292	365	852	156	112	241	230	551	182	95	676	412	480	396	471	

Melbourne

Capital of the 'Garden State', Melbourne is by any standards a sophisticated and vibrant city, offering a wonderful variety of inviting activities and attractions. Located on Port Phillip Bay, with the picturesque Yarra River running through it, Melbourne is the actual centre point of Vic's coastline, with most of the State's attractions within a short 5hr radius. The grand-scale city architecture, wide streets, symmetrical grid design and formally landscaped parks are legacies of the goldrush in nearby Ballarat.

Melbourne's trams give the city a unique flavour – quiet and pollution free, they are an efficient and attractive means of transport, quickly carrying passengers up and down the main thoroughfares. The free city circle line transports visitors in a loop that takes in all the major CBD sights and stores.

The changeable climate is renowned, with the more marked seasonal changes helping give the city its more European feel. Large-scale immigration from Europe also adds to this atmosphere and, along with more recent immigration from South East Asia, contributes to the diverse mix of cultures, foods and people which make Melbourne the cosmopolitan, vibrant city that it is today.

ℹ Tourist Information

Victoria Visitor Information Centre
Melbourbe Town Hall
Cnr Swanston St and Little Collins St, Melbourne 3000
Ph: 132 842
www.tourism.vic.gov.au

Main Attractions

★ **AFL**
Aussie Rules is a Melbourne obsession during the winter months.
★ **Brunswick St**
This street is a vibrant shopping zone, also known for its cafes and restaurants.
★ **Lygon St**
Lygon St is one of the city's premier eat streets.
★ **Old Melbourne Gaol and Penal Museum**
The museum houses the gallows on which bushranger Ned Kelly was hanged.
★ **Royal Botanical Gardens**
See over 10 000 different plant species at the Botanical Gardens.
★ **Shopping in Melbourne**
On Collins St and the streets running west off Swanston St are most of the city's major stores.
★ **Southgate Centre**
This area features cafes, lively bars and boutiques on the river's edge.
★ **Yarra River Cruises**
Explore the country's seventh longest river on a short cruise.

City skyline at night

Places of Interest

1. Albert Park **D8**
2. Chinatown **C3**
3. Crown Casino **B5**
4. Exhibition Building **D1**
5. Flagstaff Gardens **A3**
6. Flinders St Station **C4**
7. GPO **B3**
8. Grand Prix **D8**
9. Melbourne Central Shopping Centre **B3**
10. Melbourne Cricket Ground **E4**
11. Melbourne Park **E4**
12. Myer Music Bowl **D5**
13. National Gallery of Victoria **C5**
14. Parliament House **D3**
15. Polly Woodside Maritime Museum **A5**
16. Queen Victoria Gardens **C5**
17. Queen Victoria Market **B2**
18. Rialto Towers Lookout **B4**
19. St Patrick's Catholic Cathedral **D3**
20. St Paul's Anglican Cathedral **C4**
21. Shrine of Remembrance **D6**
22. Town Hall **C3**
23. Treasury Building and Gardens **D3**
24. World Trade Centre **A5**

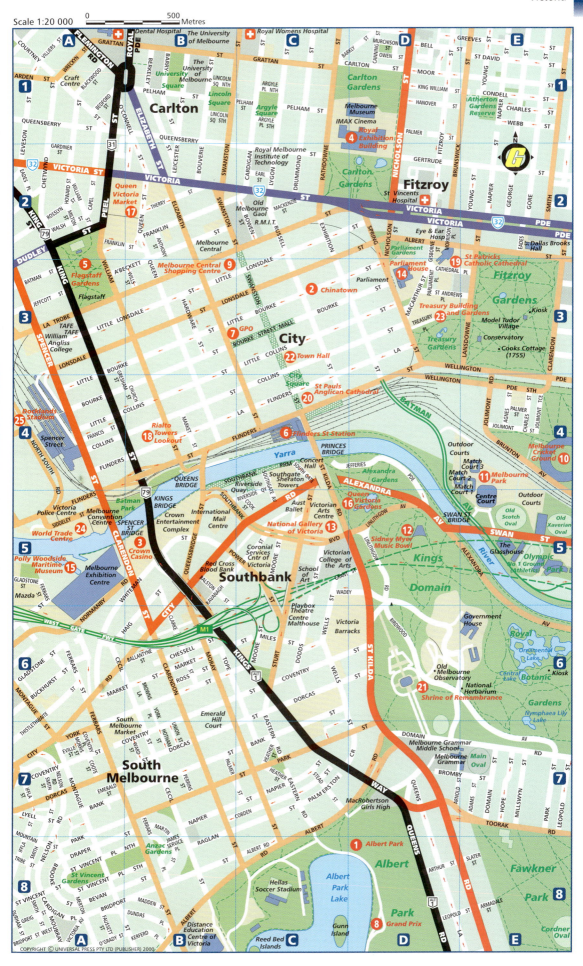

Scale 1:20 000

0   500 Metres

Scale 1:200 00

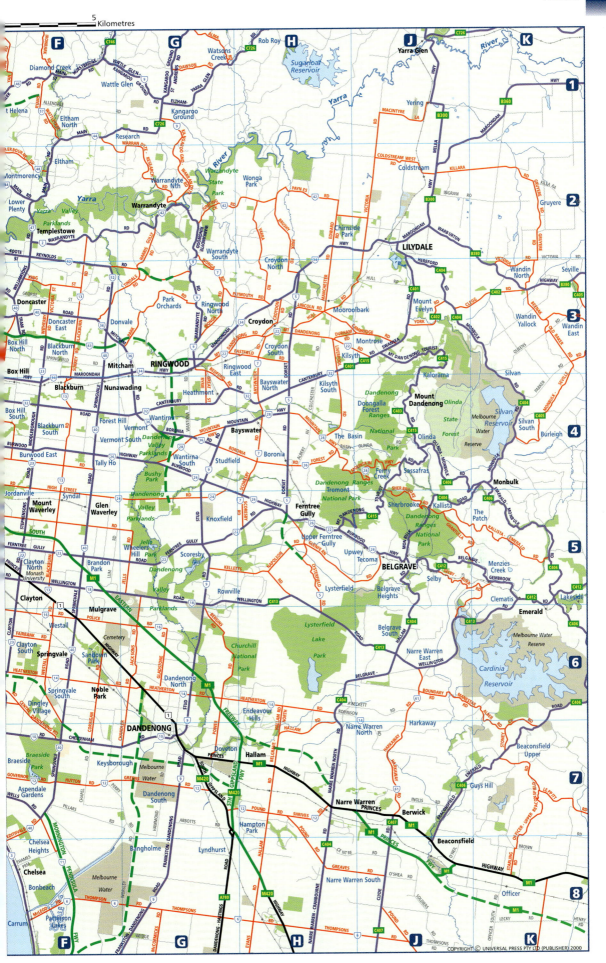

A   **B**   **C**   **D**   **E**

1

Portarlington

Grassy Point

HOOD
TOWER RD ROAD   *Point George*

Indented
Head

2

Indented Head

COATSWORTH

HARVEY RD

OLD ST LEONARDS RD

St Leonards

C125

BLUFF RD

Port

3

*Edwards
Point
State
Faunal
Reserve*

Edwards Point

Swan   *Duck Island*

Bay

Swan Point

4

Swan Island

QUEENSCLIFF

Phillip

Balcombe

Balcombe Point   C783

Mt Martha

Martha Point

*Dromana
Bay*
Safety Beach

C783

*Nepean
Bay*

Ticonderoga Bay

5

PORTSEA   *Point Franklin*

POINT

Point King

NEPEAN

Sorrento

DROMANA

NEPEAN HWY

ROAD

B110   C789   11   C787

Mornington

HOTHAM   RD

MELBOURNE

B110

West Sister
East Sister

McCrae

BOUNDARY   RD

Dromana South

Arthurs Seat
State Park

Blairgowrie

ROSEBUD

Rosebud West

PENINSULA

Red Hill

Arthurs
Seat
State
Park

ARTHURS

SEAT

C789 RD

6

Peninsula

ROAD   **Rye**

B110

EASTBOURNE   RD

11

NEPEAN
POINT

B110 RD

PURVES RD

C789

C787

Tootgarook

Rosebud
South

JETTY

Main
Ridge

SHANDS RD

ROAD

ST

TRUEMANS

C777

BROWNS RD

BROWNS

JETTY RD

MAIN

CREEK

FLINDERS

National

BROWNS

DUNDAS

SANDY

BONEO

LIMESTONE RD

Boneo

Mornington

RD

C787

BALDRYS

MUSK CREEK

TUCKS RD

7

St Andrews
Beach

TRUE MAINS

RD

C777

Peninsula

National

MORNINGTON

RD

C787

FLINDERS

MELKMANS

KEYS

BOYDS

RD

Park

MAIN

BONEO

C787

8

Bass   *Strait*

CAPE   SCHANCK

Cape
Schanck

C777

*Cairns
Bay*

RD

Cape Schanck

*Bushrangers
Bay*   *Picnic Point*

A   **B**   **C**   **D**   **E**

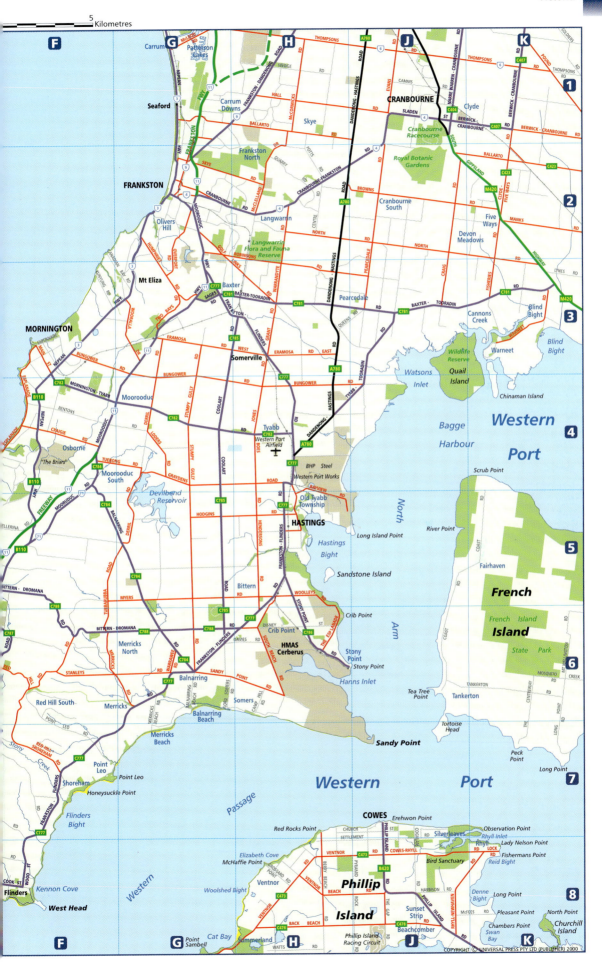

5 Kilometres

F G H J K

Carrum
Patterns Lakes
Seaford
Carrum Downs
Skye
Frankston North
FRANKSTON
Olivers Hill
Langwarrin
Mt Eliza
Langwarrin Flora and Fauna Reserve
Baxter
Baxter-Tooradin
MORNINGTON
Somerville
Eramosa
Bungower
Mornington-Tyabb
Moorooduc
Tyabb
Western Port Airfield
Osborne
"The Briars"
Moorooduc South
Devilbend Reservoir
Hodgins
HASTINGS
Old Tyabb Township
BHP Steel Western Port Works
Bittern
Bittern-Dromana
Merricks North
HMAS Cerberus
Crib Point
Stony Point
Red Hill South
Merricks
Balnarring
Somers
Balnarring Beach
Merricks Beach
Point Leo
Shoreham
Honeysuckle Point
Flinders
Flinders Bight
West Head
Kennon Cove

CRANBOURNE
Clyde
Cranbourne Racecourse
Royal Botanic Gardens
Cranbourne South
Devon Meadows
Five Ways
Pearcedale
Baxter - Tooradin
Cannons Creek
Warneet
Blind Bight
Blind Bight
Watsons Inlet
Quail Island
Chinaman Island

Western Port
Bagge Harbour
Scrub Point
River Point
Long Island Point
Hastings Bight
Sandstone Island
Crib Point
North Arm
Stony Point
Hanns Inlet
Fairhaven
French Island
State Park
Tea Tree Point
Tankerton
Tortoise Head
Peck Point
Long Point

Sandy Point

Western Port
Passage

COWES
Erehwon Point
Red Rocks Point
Silverleaves
Observation Point
Rhyll
Lady Nelson Point
Fishermans Point
Reid Bight
Elizabeth Cove
McHaffie Point
Bird Sanctuary
Ventnor
Phillip
Denne Bight
Long Point
Island
Sunset Strip
Beachcomber
Pleasant Point
Chambers Point
Swan Bay
North Point
Churchill Island
Point Sambell
Cat Bay
Summerland
Phillip Island Racing Circuit

1 2 3 4 5 6 7 8

Scale 1:900 00

A   B   C   D

DANGGALI
CONSERVATION

1

PARK

TARAWI NATURE RESERVE

Springwood
Cooinda

Wild Dog Tank
Nialia Lake

SILVER

Windamingle
Yelta L.
Manilla

Nearie L.
NEARIE LAKE
NATURE RESERVE

Travellers Lake

Aston

Hypurna
Belmore
Belmore Tank

CITY

Bunneringee

Warrawenia Lake

Milkengay L.

Trelega

CHOWILLA
REGIONAL

2

RESERVE

Huntingfield

HWY

Twelve Mile

Burtundy

125

Pine Camp
Lake Victoria

Darling

SILVER

DARLING

Tapio

Fletchers Lake

CHOWILLA
GAME RESERVE
Old Customs House
Chaffey

Cal Lal
Rufus River

Lake Victoria

MURRAY

Warranangra

CITY

Curlwaa
Wentworth

Dareton
Mildura

28

Buronga

3

MURRAY RIVER
NATIONAL PARK
Renmark
Paringa
14

Yamba

STURT

MURRAY

Moorna

Lake Wallawalla

Meringur North

A20

Cullulleraine

30
A79

Merbein
Birdwoodton
Merbein South

Koorlong
Cardross

6
Gol Gol
Monak
20

Red Cliffs

15

78

A20

HWY

44

Taldra

Bugle

Morkalla

Karween

Meringur
Yarrara

254
Bambill

Werrimull

Merrinee
Perlta

Benetook

C254

Yatpool
50
Karado
C253

4

Tunart

Kurnwill

Tarrango

Carwarp

95

Nowingi

Taplan
adda

CALDER

32

tribah

PHEENYS

N
G

MURRAY - SUNSET

TRACK

Rocket Lake

A79

Hattah

5

Paruna
Millewa Bore

NATIONAL PARK

The Rock Holes

Mt Crozier
+ 111m
Mt Cowra
+ 86m

34

Peel
da

Berrook

PEEBINGA
CON. PARK

Karte

KARTE
CON. PARK

74

Goongee

Mulcra

Duddo

Cowangie

Dry Lakes
+ Mt Jess
126m

Kiamal

Galah

29
B12

Walpeup

20

Torrita

F.R.A.

C247

Timberoo South

34

6

Chandos

46

Pinnaroo
Panitya
Carina

B12

Murrayville
Danyo

Tutye

MALLEE

Boinka

Linga

60

Underbool

See page 78

Mt Observatory 111m

A   B   C   D

South Australia see pages 142 to 169

20 Kilometres

E

Eulo

Pooncarie

ethere

F

Panban

G

Garnpung Lake

Gol Gol

H

Manfred

Mandelman

Binda

1

Top Hut

MUNGO

NATIONAL

PARK

Mungo

Boree Plains

Lake Mungo

Marona

Hatfield

2

Arumpo

THE WALLS OF CHINA

Chibnalwood Lakes

Iona

Langleydale

Turlee

Wamberra

New South Wales see pages 22 to 67

3

MALLEE CLIFFS

NATIONAL PARK

Prungle

Tin Tin Lake

Bidura

Box

97

Macomnin Lake

Ganaway Lake

Penarie

Pitarpunga Lake

4

STURT **80**

Nangiloc

Benanee

L. Benanee

RIVER

Colignan

Euston

Robinvale

L. Caringay

MURRUMBIDGEE

Lake Tala

78

HWY

Balranald

YANGA NATURE RESERVE

76

HATTAH-KULKYNE

Kulkyne

MURRAY-

17

20

C251

B400

Bannerton

C252

8

MURRAY VALLEY

Boundary Bend

Yangalake

Yanga Lake

KULKYNE

NATIONAL

PARK

C252

Wemen

55

75

Yungera

Koorkab

Piamble

Kenley

Haysdale

55

5

Cramenton

HWY

43

Annuello

Kooloonong

Natya

Goodnight

Kyalite

Perekerten

Winnambool

Bolton

80

E

Ouyen

55

Kulwin

Kulwyne

Manangatang

42

HWY

B12

Piangil

Tooleybuc

Stony Crossing

Edward

R.

6

Wagant

16

Cocamba

Miralie

Wood Wood

Koraleigh

40

Nyah

Dilpurra

69

Nunga

41

A79

Mittyack

23

Chinkapook

Yarraby

64

Nyah West

Vinifera

Speewa

Tyntynder Central

Bronzewing

Pira

Nowie Nth

38

SUNRAYSIA HWY

Pier Millan

42

Chillingollah

Tyntynder South

Gypsum

E

Nandaly

46

F

See page 79

G

Woorinen

B400

Swan Hill

H

Scale 1:900 00

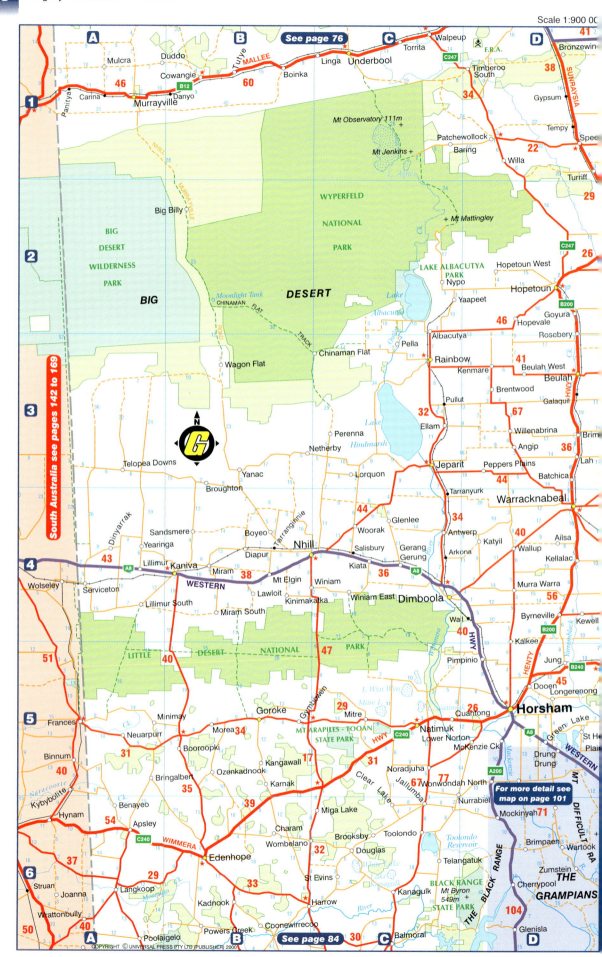

20 Kilometres

New South Wales see pages 22 to 67

See page 77

For more detail see map on page 99

See page 85

See page 80

COPYRIGHT ©UNIVERSAL PRESS PTY LTD (PUBLISHER) 2000

Scale 1:900 00

For more detail see map on page 94

See page 86

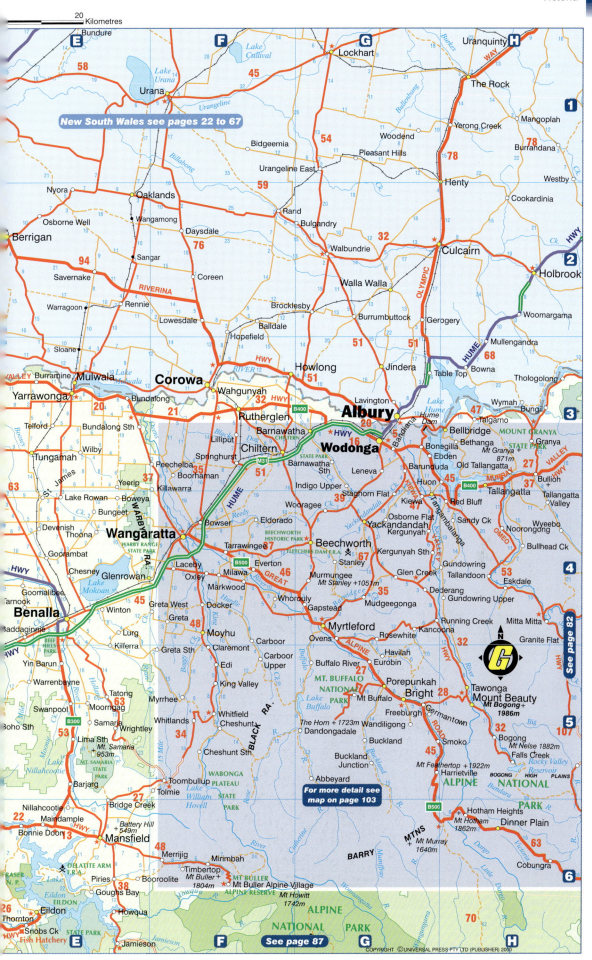

New South Wales see pages 22 to 67

See page 82

For more detail see map on page 103

COPYRIGHT ©UNIVERSAL PRESS PTY LTD (PUBLISHER) 2000

Scale 1:900 00

A **B** **C** **D**

Bowna · Tho Aolong · Talmalmo · Walwa · Cabramurra · Tumut Pond Reservoir

Burrowye · 61 · Tooma · Welaregang

Wymah · Bungil · MOUNT LAWSON · 31 · Burrowa Pine Mtn. · 34 · Tintaldra · 83 · Lake Eucumbene · Adaminaby

47 · Talgarno · 1041m + Mt Lawson · Guys Forest · Cudgewa Nth · Towong · 19 · Eucumbene · Buckenderra

MOUNT GRANYA · STATE PARK · 1300m + Mt Burrowa · Cudgewa Falls · 31 · HWY

Granya · NATIONAL · PARK · Cudgewa · 31 · Corryong · Khancoban · NATIONAL

Mt Granya + 871m · 27 · 37 · Koetong · Shelley · Thowgla · WAY

Old Tallangatta · Bullioh · + Mt Bullioh 684m · Berringama · Colac Colac · Khancoba Pondage · MTNS

B400 · Tallangatta · 31 · Lucyvale · Biggara · Lake Jindabyne

Tallangatta Valley · WABBA · Thowgla Upper · Mt Unicorn + 944m · Geehi · Guthega · Blue Cow Mountain · East Jindabyne

Noorongong · Wyeebo · Mt Cudgewa 1099m · WILDERNESS · Nariel Creek · Perisher Village · Smiggin Holes · Jindabyne

OMEO · Bullhead Ck · Cravensville · PARK · 55 · Gentle Annie + 1121m · Mt Kosciuszko + 2228m · Charlotte Pass · WAY

53 · Tallandoon · Bucheen Ck · Nariel · 111 · ALPINE · Thredbo Village · Moonbah

Eskdale · For more detail see map on page 103 · Mt Sassafras +1587 · Tom Groggin · WAY · Beloka

Mitta Mitta · Dartmouth · Sassafras Gap · SNOWY · Ingebyra

Granite Flat · Lake Dartmouth · ALPINE · Mt Hope 1558 · BARRY · 116 · PARK

See page 81 · HWY · NATIONAL · Buenba · RIVER

Mount Beauty · Mt Cooper +1318m · Mt Pendergast 1462m · Suggan Buggan

Mt Bogong + 1986m · Big · 107 · 79 · PARK · Mackillop Bridge · Delegate River

32 · Bogong · Mt Nelse 1882m · Sunnyside · Deddick · Tubbut · 31

Falls Creek · Rocky Valley Reservoir · Glen Valley · Uplands · Cabanandra · Bonang

ALPINE · BOGONG HIGH PLAINS · NATIONAL · PARK · Benambra · Wulgulmerang · SNOWY · 76

Hotham Heights · Anglers Rest · Lake Omeo · Gelantipy · RIVER · RANGE · Goongerah

Dinner Plain · Hinnomunjie · Butchers Ridge · Malinns

63 · Cobungra · BOWEN MTNS · 90

70 · Omeo · Bindi · NATIONAL · Mt Murrungowar +728m

Mt Livingstone + 1227m · Timbarra · 50 · PARK · Murrungowar

Cassilis · Tongio · Mt Nugong 1482m · Mt Buck + 507m

Tongio West · Swifts Creek · Murrindal · 56 · MURRUNGOWAR F.R.A.

Doctors Flat · Buchan Caves · Buchan · Jarrahmond · Cabbage Tree Creek

Dargo · Morris Peak + 789m · Ensay · 97 · Buchan Sth · Bete Bolong · Orbost · 34

Castleburn · Tabberabbera · Mt Sugarloaf + 890m · Tambo Crossing · FAINTING RA. · Brodribb River · Marlo

Michell River N.P. · ASH · DIVIDING RA. · B500 · GREAT · 49 · Wairewa · 55 · Newmerella · CAPE CONRAN S.P.

Glenaladale · 90 · Bullumwaal · Mt Little Dick 320m · FAIRY DELL F.R.A. · Nowa Nowa · PRINCES · 57 · Lake Corringle

Lindenow · Mt Taylor · Wiseleigh · Bruthen · COLQUHOUN · LAKE TYERS S.P. · Cape Conran

GREAT · Lindenow Sth · Wuk Wuk · Calulu · Sarsfield · Johnsonville · 22 · Tambo Upper · REGIONAL PARK · Lake Tyers · Marlo Inlet

Fernbank · Nicholson · 35 · Swan Reach ·

HWY A1 · Bairnsdale · NYERIMILANG PARK · Lake Tyers · BASS

53 · Eagle Pt · Lake King · Metung · Lakes Entrance · For more detail see map on page 90

Perry Bridge · Paynesville · Goon Nure · Raymond I. · Sperm Whale Head

62 · Bengworden · Meerlieu · THE LAKES NATIONAL PARK

Clydebank · Hollands · Loch Sport

COPYRIGHT © UNIVERSAL PRESS PTY LTD (PUBLISHER) 2000

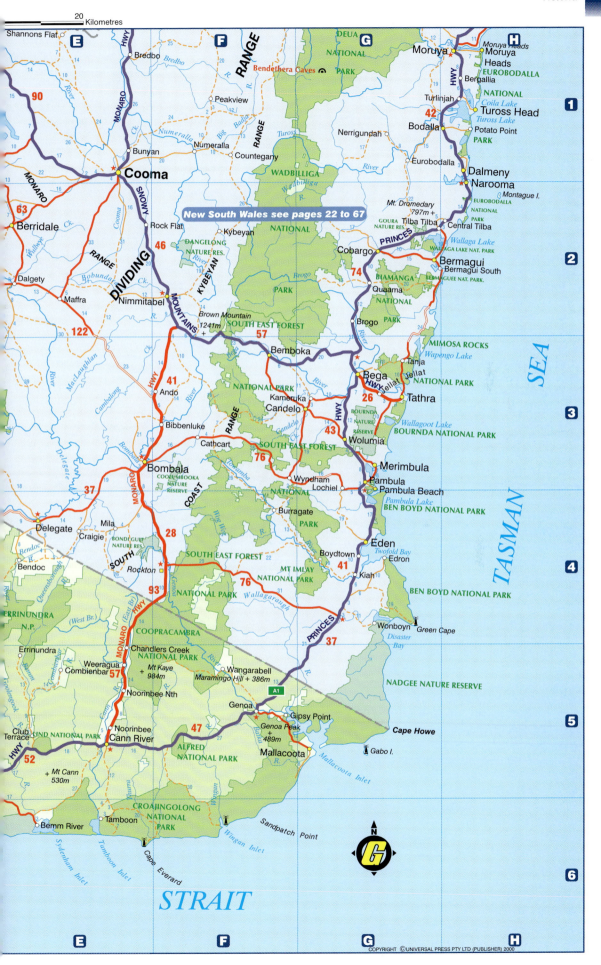

20 Kilometres

Shannons Flat

E   **F**   **RANGE**   DEUA NATIONAL PARK   **G**   Moruya   Moruya Heads   **H**

Bredbo   *Bredbo*   Bendethera Caves   Peakview   Moruya   Bergallia   EUROBODALLA NATIONAL PARK

90   Numeralla   RANGE   Turlinjah   Coila Lake   **1**
Numeralla   Countegany   **42**   Tuross Head   *Tuross Lake*
Bunyan   WADBILLIGA   Nerrigundah   Bodalla   Potato Point   PARK
    River   Eurobodalla
Cooma   New South Wales see pages 22 to 67   Dalmeny   EUROBODALLA   Narooma   Montague I.

63   Rock Flat   Kybeyan   NATIONAL   Mt. Dromedary 797m +   NATIONAL   PARK
Berridale   DANGELONG NATURE RES.   GOURA NATURE RES.   Tilba Tilba   Central Tilba   **2**
46   PRINCES   Wallaga Lake   WALLAGA LAKE NAT. PARK
Dalgety   RANGE   Cobargo   Bermagui   Bermagui South
    DIVIDING   **74**   BIAMANGA   BERMAGUEE NAT. PARK
Maffra   Nimmitabel   KYBEYAN   Quaama   NATIONAL
122   Brown Mountain 1241m +   SOUTH EAST FOREST   Brogo   PARK
    MOUNTAINS   **57**   MIMOSA ROCKS
    Bemboka   Wapengo Lake   NATIONAL PARK   SEA
41   PARK   Tanja   **3**
Ando   NATIONAL PARK   Bega   Jellat   NATIONAL PARK
Bibbenluke   RANGE   Kameruka   **26**   Tathra
    Candelo   HWY   BOURNDA NATURE   Wallagoot Lake
Cathcart   **43**   Wolumia   BOURNDA NATIONAL PARK
Bombala   COOLUMBOOKA NATURE RESERVE   **76**   Merimbula
37   COAST   Wyndham   Lochiel   Pambula   Pambula Beach
    Burragate   Pambula Lake   BEN BOYD NATIONAL PARK   **4**
Delegate   Mila   **28**   NATIONAL   Eden
Craigie   BONDI GULF NATURE RES.   Boydtown   Edron
Bendoc   Rockton   MT IMLAY NATIONAL PARK   **41**   Kiah   Twofold Bay
    SOUTH   **76**   BEN BOYD NATIONAL PARK
ERRINUNDRA N.P.   **93**   NATIONAL PARK   *Wallagaraugh*   PRINCES   Wonboyn   Green Cape
Errinundra   COOPRACAMBRA   **37**   Disaster Bay   **5**
Weeragua   Chandlers Creek   NADGEE NATURE RESERVE
Combienbar   **57**   Mt Kaye 984m   Wangarabell   Maramingo Hill + 386m
    Noorinbee Nth   Genoa   A1   Cape Howe
Club Terrace   Noorinbee   Gipsy Point   Genoa Peak + 489m   Gabo I.
52   **47**   Cann River   Mallacoota   *Mallacoota Inlet*
+ Mt Cann 530m   ALFRED NATIONAL PARK
Bemm River   Tamboon   CROAJINGOLONG NATIONAL PARK   Sandpatch Point   **N**   **G**
    Cape Everard   *Wingan Inlet*

STRAIT

E   **F**   **G**   **H**

Scale 1:900 00

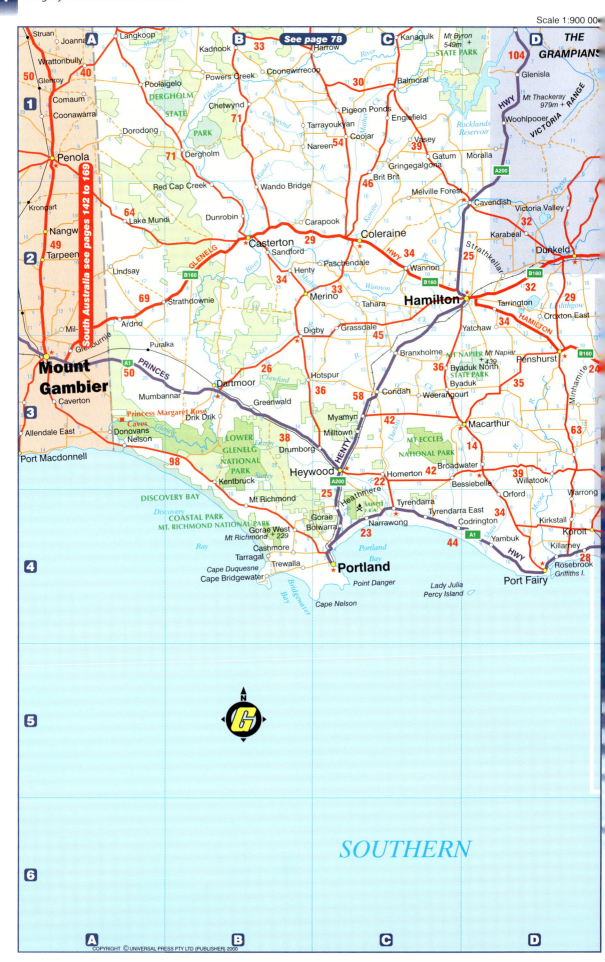

THE GRAMPIANS

SOUTHERN

20 Kilometres

E Bellellen 29 Great Western F Crowlands **See page 79** G 23 Talbot Campbelltown H Sandon
GRAMPIANS Pomonal 47 Armstrong Amphitheatre Caralulup Dunach Glengower Yandoit
(GARIWERD) Jallukar CHINAMAN F.R.A. MT BUANGOR Mt Lonarch 63 Evansford 49 Ullina Hepburn 28 Springs
NATIONAL Mt William STATE PARK 45 Lexton Clunes Smeaton Blampied Newlyn 31
PARK 1167m Moyston Denicull Ck Langi Logan Buangor Chute 23 Waubra 43 Coghills Dean Mollongghip Creswick Wallace 33
66 Barton 19 Maroona Raglan Waterloo B220 Mt Beckworth Learmonth 18 Pootilla MIDLAND
For more detail see map on page 101 Rossbridge Tatyoon Nth 45 Beaufort Miners Rest A300 M8 HWY
37 Willaura B180 Trawalla Burrumbeet Cardigan Village **Ballarat** Mount Helen 31
Mininera 31 Mt Emu Lake Goldsmith Haddon B160 Scotsburn
18 Westmere B160 Streatham Pittong Smythesdale 50 Buninyong Napoleons Lal Lal
26 Wickliffe 47 Carranballac Skipton Linton Scarsdale Enfield Grenville Elaine Meredith 89

OCEAN

Scale 1:900 00

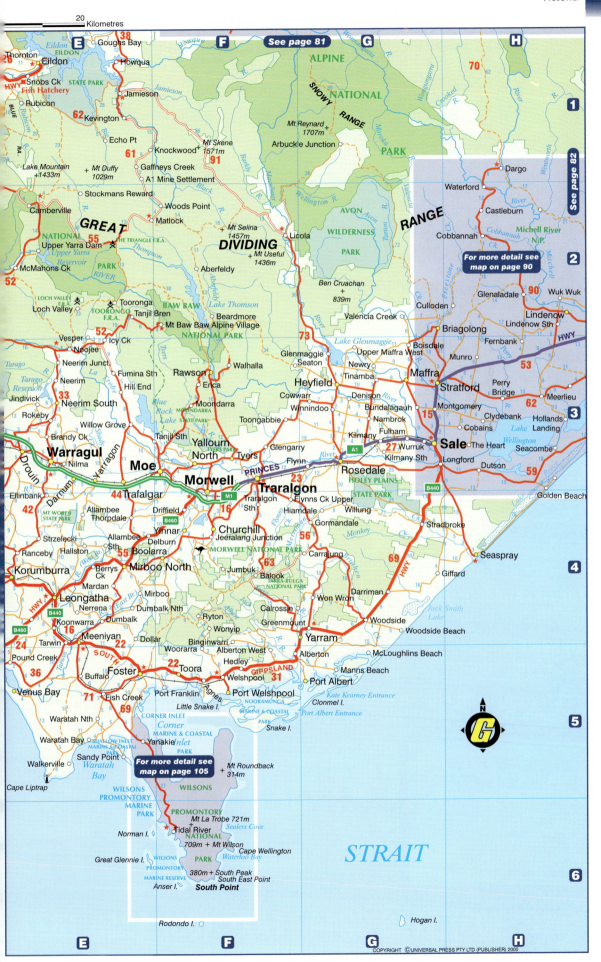

20 Kilometres

See page 81

See page 82

ALPINE

SNOWY RANGE NATIONAL PARK

Thornton
Eildon
EILDON
Goughs Bay
Howqua

Snobs Ck
Fish Hatchery

Rubicon
Jamieson

Kevington

Echo Pt
Knockwood
Mt Skene 1571m

Mt Reynard 1707m
Arbuckle Junction

Dargo
Waterford

Lake Mountain +1433m
Mt Duffy 1029m
Gaffneys Creek
A1 Mine Settlement

Castleburn

For more detail see map on page 90

Camberville
Stockmans Reward
Woods Point
Matlock

Mt Selina 1457m
Licola

RANGE
Cobbannah

GREAT
NATIONAL
Upper Yarra Dam
THE TRIANGLE F.R.A.
Upper Yarra Reservoir

DIVIDING
Mt Useful 1436m
Aberfeldy

AVON WILDERNESS PARK

Michell River N.P.

McMahons Ck

Ben Cruachan + 839m

Culloden
Glenaladale
Wuk Wuk

LOCH VALLEY F.R.A.
Loch Valley
Tooronga
Tanjil Bren
Beardmore
Mt Baw Baw Alpine Village

Valencia Creek

Briagolong
Lindenow
Lindenow Sth

Vesper
Icy Ck
Noojee

BAW BAW NATIONAL PARK
TOORONGO F.R.A.

Lake Glenmaggie
Upper Maffra West
Boisdale
Fernbank

Neerim Junct.
Neerim
Rawson
Erica
Walhalla

Glenmaggie
Seaton
Newry
Tinamba
Maffra
Stratford

Munro
Perry Bridge
Meerlieu

Jindivick
Hill End
Moondarra
Heyfield
Cowwarr
Denison
Bundalaguah

Montgomery
Clydebank
Hollands Landing

Rokeby
Neerim South
Winnindoo
Nambrok
Fulham
Cobains
Seacombe

Willow Grove
Toongabbie
Kilmany
Wurruk
Sale
The Heart

Brandy Ck
Tanjil Sth
Yallourn North
Tyers
Glengarry
Flynn
Kilmany Sth
Longford
Dutson

Warragul
Nilma
Moe
PRINCES
Rosedale
Golden Beach

Drouin
Morwell
Traralgon
HOLEY PLAINS STATE PARK

Ellinbank
Trafalgar
Driffield
Traralgon Sth
Flynns Ck Upper
Hiamdale
Willung
Gormandale
Stradbroke

MT WORTH STATE PARK
Allambee Thorpdale
Yinnar
Churchill
Jeeralang Junction

Strzelecki
Allambee Sth
Delburn
MORWELL NATIONAL PARK
Carrajung

Ranceby
Hallston
Boolarra
TARRA-BULGA NATIONAL PARK
Seaspray

Korumburra
Berrys Ck
Mirboo North
Jumbuk
Balook
Giffard

Mardan
Mirboo
Darriman

Leongatha
Nerrena
Dumbalk Nth
Ryton
Calrossie
Won Wron
Woodside

Koonwarra
Dumbalk
Wonyip
Greenmount
Woodside Beach

Tarwin
Meeniyan
Dollar
Binginwarri
Alberton West
Yarram
McLoughlins Beach

Pound Creek
Woorarra
Hedley
Alberton
Manns Beach

SOUTH GIPPSLAND
Toora
Welshpool
Port Albert

Venus Bay
Buffalo
Foster
Fish Creek
Port Franklin
Port Welshpool
Manns Beach
Kate Kearney Entrance

Waratah Nth
Little Snake I.
Clonmel I.
Port Albert Entrance

Waratah Bay
SHALLOW INLET MARINE & COASTAL PARK
Yanakie
NOORAMUNGA MARINE & COASTAL PARK
Snake I.

Sandy Point
For more detail see map on page 105
Mt Roundback + 314m

Walkerville
Waratah Bay

Cape Liptrap
WILSONS PROMONTORY MARINE PARK
WILSONS

STRAIT

WILSONS PROMONTORY MARINE RESERVE
Norman I.
Great Glennie I.

Mt La Trobe 721m
Tidal River
709m + Mt Wilson
Sealers Cove
Cape Wellington
Waterloo Bay

380m + South Peak
South East Point
Anser I.
South Point

Rodondo I.
Hogan I.

N G

200 kilometres around Melbourne
by A Caddick and K Firth

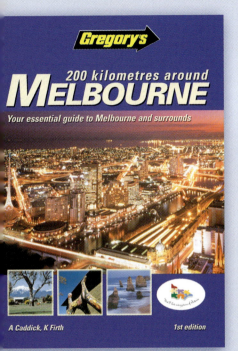

Gregory's
200 kilometres around
MELBOURNE
Your essential guide to Melbourne and surrounds

A Caddick, K Firth   1st edition

YOUR 200 KILOMETRE PLAYGROUND

With *Gregory's 200 kilometres around Melbourne*, you'll never be short of great ideas for that day trip, weekend escape or more leisurely exploration. The guide covers the main attractions and hidden marvels of 12 regions. Written by locals with inside information that only locals know about, the guidebook features:

- Must see, must do attractions for each region
- Information on natural features, history, festivals, localities, towns, national parks recreational activities & much more
- Special feature panels
- Detailed locality, walking and touring maps
- Over 450 colour photographs

This guidebook is perfect for maximizing your precious leisure time and makes an ideal gift.

Available from all good bookshops and department stores.

We've Got Australia Covered

Gippsland Lakes

Lying parallel to Bass Strait and hemmed in by Ninety Mile Beach, the Gippsland Lakes is Australia's largest system of inland waterways, with 400km² of lakes and waters.

Stretching from Yarram in the west to Lakes Entrance in the east and the foothills of Vic's high country to the north, this region is a rich water playground, drawing visitors to explore its many attractions.

Promoted as the Victorian Riviera – temperatures can be up to 6° warmer than in Melbourne – the region is dotted with holiday villages, providing easy access to every imaginable form of watersport. Opportunities for fishing abound, making Gippsland Lakes a drawcard for anglers.

Must Visit

- Bairnsdale
- Lakes NP
- Metung
- Ninety Mile Beach
- Paynesville

ℹ Tourist Information

Central Gippsland Visitor Information Centre
8 Foster St, Sale 3850
Ph: (03) 5144 1108
Freecall: 1800 677 520

Gippsland Lakes

Great Ocean Road

This legendary coastal route, starting at Torquay and extending 285km west to Warrnambool, is a journey along a stretch of spectacular coastline via seaside holiday towns, stark surf beaches, rugged cliffs, expansive ocean, lush rainforest and fragrant woodlands.

Built between 1919 and 1932 as a memorial to soldiers who died in WWI and as employment for returned servicemen, the road was designed to be a tourist route of world repute in this wild, forested terrain. Also known as the 'Shipwreck Coast' due to the more than 100 ships sunk by the treacherous Southern Ocean and rock formations, the stretch to Peterborough is a stark reminder of the perils of this jagged coastline.

Sightseeing is one of the region's most obvious charms, with the stunning surroundings providing

Twelve Apostles

many photo opportunities. The seaside havens provide safe sandy beaches for more sedate activities, while surfing beaches abound. Whale watching, horseriding, bushwalking, mountain bike riding, or sampling fish and chips from one of the many waterfront vendors, are just some of the attractions of this remarkable region.

The 12 Apostles

These majestic rock formations on the Great Ocean Road were once part of the mainland's limestone cliffs, demonstrating the power of the coastlines waves. Rising up 65m from the ocean and stretching along the coastline, they are an impressive sight.

ℹ Tourist Information

Geelong and Great Ocean Rd Visitor Information Centre
Stead Park, Princes Hwy, Geelong 3214
Ph: (03) 5275 5797
Great Ocean Rd Visitor Information Centre
Great Ocean Rd, Apollo Bay 3233
Ph: (03) 5237 6529
www.greatoceanrd.org.au

Main Attractions

★ **Anglesea**
Anglesea is renowned for its large population of grey kangaroos inhabiting Anglesea Golf Course.
★ **Cape Otway Lightstation**
Built in 1848, this is Australia's oldest standing lighthouse.
★ **Fairy Penguins**
To observe a colony of fairy penguins, cross at low tide to Middle Island from Thunder Pt Coastal Reserve, Warrnambool.
★ **Lorne**
Surrounded by densely forested bushland with plunging waterfalls, Lorne is a prime holiday location.
★ **Qdos**
This arts complex is set in a constantly changing sculpture garden within the Otway Forest.
★ **Torquay**
Torquay is the centre of the surf culture on the Great Ocean Rd.
★ **Whale watching**
From June to late September see Southern Right Whales at Logan's Beach, Warrnambool.

Hopkins River Boatshed, Warnambool

Scale 1:588 40

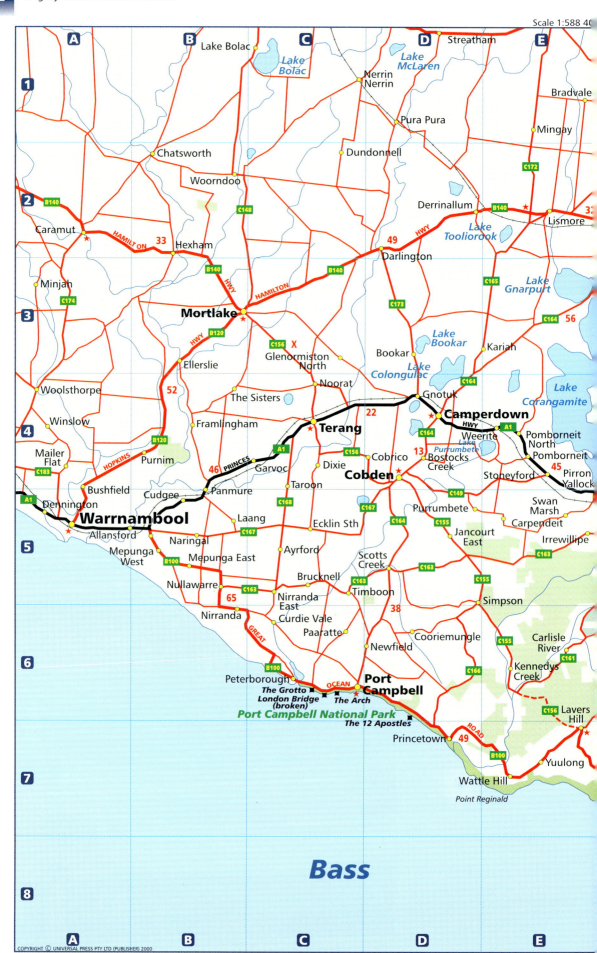

Bass

Macedon Ranges and Sunbury Wineries

Must visit

- Blackwood
- Daylesford Lake
- Hepburn Springs Spa Resort
- Lake House Restaurant

Tourist Information

Daylesford Tourist Information Centre
Vincent St, Daylesford 3460
Ph: (03) 5348 1339
Kyneton Visitor Information Centre
Jean Hayes Reserve
High St, Kyneton 3444
Ph: (03) 5422 6110

Boasting over 100 mineral springs within a concentrated radius, this region is gaining popularity as a holiday destination due to the resurgence of belief in the healing properties of mineral water. Located only a short distance from Melbourne, the Macedon Ranges and Sunbury Wineries are an ideal locale for 'taking the waters'. This European tradition dates back to the 1800s, when the large Swiss-Italian community realised the potential of the waters surrounding them. Mineral water has been bottled here since 1850 and the towns have been spa resorts in the European style since the natural springs were discovered in the 1880s. Alternative and natural therapies, including herbal baths and massages, are now also on offer.

A great place to get away from it all, the district also offers wineries and relics of the old goldfields. The

Lake Daylesford

surrounding rugged bushland is dotted with local reserves, which are ideal for horseriding, fishing and picnicking. Littered with lakes and forests, the district offers a relaxing, tranquil holiday destination, with a diversity of landscapes and local culture to enjoy.

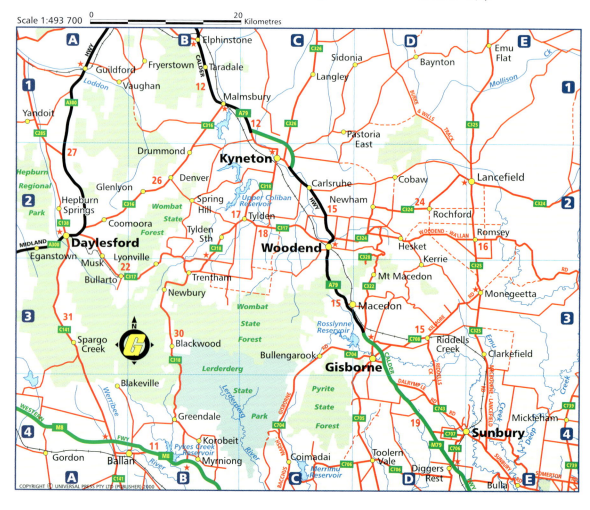

Scale 1:493 700   0 — 20 Kilometres

Phillip Island

Penguin Parade

Located in Bass Strait, near the calm waters of Western Port and only a 1½hr drive from Melbourne, Phillip Island is now joined to the mainland by Narrows Bridge from San Remo.

Once ferries began running from Stony Point in the 1890s, Phillip Island became a popular destination for the summer holidays. It is now Victoria's premier destination for international visitors. Boasting an array of wildlife, including the famed little penguins (the island's drawcard), superior surfing and unspoilt beaches, Phillip Island is an ideal holiday location for nature lovers and watersports fans.

Phillip Island also has some outstanding geological formations, including The Colonnades (ancient columns of basalt), the Forest Caves (large sea-eroded caverns) and Pyramid Rock (columns of basalt in the shape of a pyramid).

Golden cypress trees line the avenue into Cowes, the major town and administrative centre of the island. The majority of the accommodation is here. There are also holiday attractions, and the unspoilt beaches are ideal for swimming and other watersports.

Must Visit

- Cape Woolamai Surf Beach
- George Bass Coastal Walk
- Koala Conservation Centre
- Penguin Parade

ℹ️ Tourist Information

Phillip Island Information Centre
Phillip Island Tourist Rd,
Newhaven 3925
Ph: (03) 5956 7447
Freecall: 1300 366 422
www.phillipisland.net.au

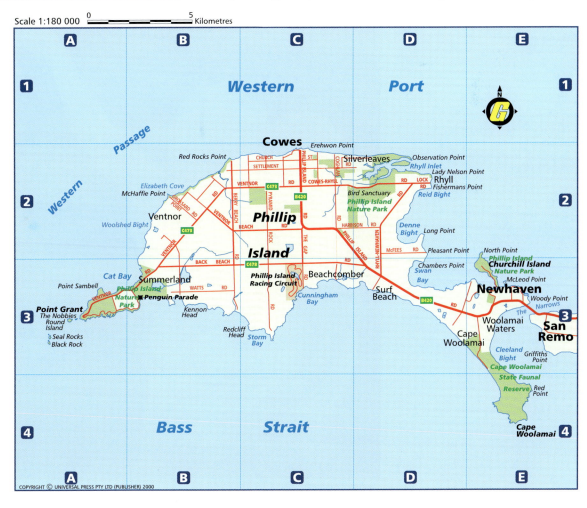

The Dandenongs

Puffing Billy

This vintage steam train has run almost continuously since its debut in 1900. On total fire ban days, diesel locomotives replace it. The short journey between Belgrave and Emerald Lake is beautiful and includes travelling over timber trestle bridges and through forests.

Only an hour's drive from Melbourne, the beautiful Dandenong Ranges form a natural backdrop to Vic's capital city, attracting hordes of city visitors annually to this green haven of hills and forests. Rising to an average elevation of 500-600m, the Dandenong Ranges peak at 633m, at Mt Dandenong, the highest point.

Colourful, inviting and cool, especially in summer, the Dandenongs are popular for day trips, not only for their intrinsic beauty but also for the many beautiful gardens and the great variety of European and native trees. The smattering of art galleries, antique shops and tearooms in the townships

Horseriding in the Dandenongs

littering the Dandenongs provide excellent detours from exploring the region's stunning scenery.

ℹ Tourist Information

Dandenong Ranges & Knox Visitor Information Centre
1211 Burwood Hwy,
Upper Ferntree Gully 3156
Ph: (03) 9758 7522
www.dandenongranges.tourism.asn.au

Main Attractions

★ **Belgrave**
Belgrave is home to the beloved vintage steam train Puffing Billy and the Steam Museum. Puffing Billy runs a 13km route with spectacular valley views.

★ **Dandenong Ranges NP**
See the world's tallest flowering plant in the Dandenongs — the mountain ash tree.

★ **Mt Dandenong Lookout**
This lookout offers a breathtaking vantage point for panoramic views over Melbourne, Port Phillip Bay and Western Port.

★ **Olinda**
An ideal time to visit Olinda is in the spring, when a floral festival is in full bloom.

★ **Sassafras**
Picturesque Sassafras offers charming stores and galleries.

★ **William Ricketts Sanctuary**
This sanctuary is a testimony to the work of Ricketts, who spent much time with the Aboriginal people of Central Australia. The setting of fern gardens and rock waterfalls provide a natural gallery for his kiln-fired sculptures of Aboriginal people.

William Ricketts Sanctuary, Dandenongs

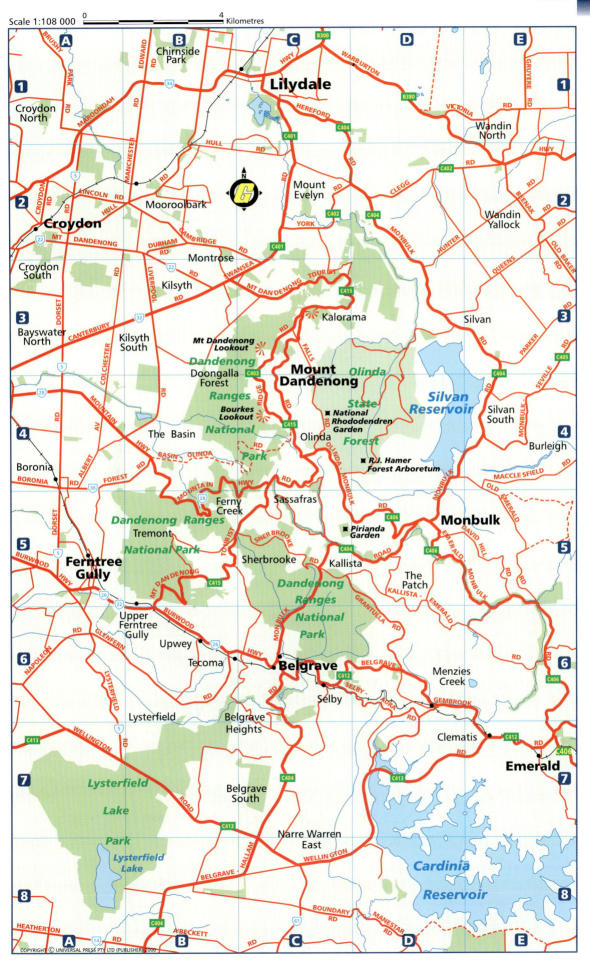

Scale 1:108 000

0   4   Kilometres

The Goldfields

Situated just over 100km west of Melbourne, the Goldfields are a treasure trove for anyone wishing to bring the goldrush era back to life.

In 1851 news of the discovery of gold spread like wildfire around the colonies of Vic and NSW, and reached as far as China, England and the USA. A population explosion occurred — 8000 hopeful prospectors had arrived by October 1851; this swelled to 30 000 a year later; and by 1856 a record number of 100 000 people were trying their luck on the goldfields. Tiny settlements became boomtowns virtually overnight, while Melbourne was deserted — 20 000 of its 25 000 population abandoned the capital for the Mt Alexander diggings in 1851.

As prosperity spread to the growing trades, services and agricultural industries that grew to support the gold miners and developing mining companies, the towns became thriving regional centres, bearing the hallmarks of wealth.

Sovereign Hill, Ballarat

The area's rich history is evident everywhere, providing many opportunities for visitors to learn about the goldrush era, with activities such as prospecting, fossicking, camping and bushwalking. Other attractions include the area's established wineries, art galleries and antiques, gardens and intriguing wildlife.

The Goldrush

The goldrush made Melbourne the largest city in Australia at that time, due to the immense wealth from the diggings. The status of the country was transformed from a colonial settlement with a dubious reputation to a respectable place for migration and investment.

ℹ Tourist Information

Ballarat Visitor Information Centre
39 Sturt St, Ballarat 3350
Ph: (03) 5320 5741
www.ballarat.com

Main Attractions

★ **Ararat**
Ararat was officially founded in 1857, when a group of 700 Chinese discovered alluvial lead there.
★ **Ballarat**
This is the site of the infamous Eureka Stockade uprising.
★ **Ballarat Wildlife Park**
Meet emus, koalas, wallabies, wombats and other Australian animals at Ballarat Wildlife Park.
★ **Bendigo**
Built on its goldrush prosperity, Bendigo's past prominence has yet to fade.
★ **Buda Historic Home and Gardens**
Visit this colonial home and see the best of 19th and 20th century landscaping.
★ **Castlemaine**
Castlemaine is noted as much for its artistic endeavours as for its goldrush past. Castlemaine Art Gallery boasts a fine collection of Australian art.
★ **Clunes**
This was Victoria's first gold town.
★ **Golden Dragon Museum**
This museum is a tribute to the Chinese miners who flocked to the goldfields.

Chinese Joss House, Ballarat

The Goldfields Wineries

Although the Goldfields are known mostly for their goldrush heritage, the region also offers an array of impressive wineries that are well worth visiting. The foothills of the ranges boast a cluster of noted vineyards and wineries. The best known of these is Seppelt Great Western Winery, a household name throughout Australia.

The French game petanque is a common pastime at many of the local wineries. In late November, the region pays tribute to the game by hosting the Pyrenees Vignerons Petanque Festival. Australian Petanque champions teach the finer details of the game in a festive environment of fine regional food and wine.

NAME	ADDRESS	PHONE	OPEN
Blue Pyrenees Estate	Vinoca Rd, Avoca	(03) 5465 3202	*10am–4:30pm, Mon–Fri*
			10am–5pm, Sat–Sun
Dalwhinnie Vineyard	Taltarni Rd, Moonambel	(03) 5467 2388	*10am–5pm daily*
Kara Kara	Sunraysia Hwy, 10km	(03) 5496 3294	*10am–6pm daily*
	south of St Arnaud		
Mt Avoca Vineyard	Moates La, Avoca	(03) 5465 3282	*9am–5pm, Mon–Fri,*
			10am–5pm, weekends
			and public holidays
Redbank Winery	Sunraysia Hwy, Redbank	(03) 5467 7255	*9am–5pm, Mon–Sat,*
			10am–5pm Sun
Seppelt Great Western Winery	Moyston Rd, Great Western	(03) 5361 2222	*10am–5pm daily*
Summerfield	Main Rd, Moonambel	(03) 5467 2264	*9am–6pm, Mon–Sat,*
			10am–6pm Sun
Taltarni	Taltarni Rd, off Avoca-Stawell Rd	(03) 5467 2218	*10am–5pm daily*
Warrenmang Vineyard Resort	Mountain Creek Rd, Moonambel	(03) 5467 2233	*10am–5pm daily*

Scale 1:992 000

The Grampians NP

This bizarre landscape of stark ridges and strangely shaped rocky outcrops rises spectacularly from western Vic's flat wheat plains and grazing fields. Renowned for its priceless Aboriginal rock art and heritage, more than 80% of the state's Aboriginal art sites are located within this impressive region. Archaeologists have dated campfire charcoal to 5000 years ago, although the earliest rock art suggests Aboriginal activity in the area as far back as 22 500 years ago.

The distinctive sandstone forms dominate the landscape, punctuated by 4 main ranges – Mt Difficult to the north, Mt William to the east, Mt Serra to the south and Mt Victoria to the west. Protected by one of Vic's largest national parks, the Grampians covers 167 000ha of stunning scenery, delicate wildflowers, panoramic mountain views and intricate ecosystems.

Rich in natural significance, almost a third of Vic's indigenous flora, 35 species of native mammals, 200 bird species and 27 reptile species reside in this unique habitat.

Boroka Lookout, Grampians

To preserve this natural wonderland visitors are required not to pick any of the plants or bring in pets, and to observe fire restrictions, stay on marked walking tracks and remember that all native birds and animals are protected.

Activities include: rock climbing and abseiling; horseriding through the rugged wilderness; enjoying unusual views from the vantage point of a hot air balloon; bushwalking to see the more secluded and powerful sights of the Grampians; and camping out.

Aboriginal Art Sites

The Grampians NP is an important area for studying the history of Aboriginal rock art. Rock paintings are believed to serve many functions, such as recording days or visits, retelling stories, communicating laws and teaching spiritual principles.

ℹ Tourist Information

Grampians NP Information Centre
Grampians Tourist Rd,
Halls Gap 3381
Ph: (03) 5356 4381
www.parks.vic.gov.au

Main Attractions

★ **Aboriginal Art Tour**
Run by the Brambuk Aboriginal Cultural Centre, these tours incorporate excursions to the region's main art shelters.
★ **Dunkeld**
This town is a convenient departure point for a tour of The Grampians.
★ **Grampians Camel Tours**
This tour company offers memorable camel-back adventures.
★ **Halls Gap Wildlife Park and Zoo**
See a diverse range of animals, including monkeys, red deer and kangaroos. This 8ha park also has BBQ's and playground.
★ **Heatherlie**
This region's astonishing rock formations led to the development of a stonemason industry.
★ **MacKenzie Falls**
This spectacular waterfall is a worthwhile detour from a visit to the Wonderland Range.
★ **The Piccaninny**
An easy 2.4km walk to this intriguing rock formation offers magnificent views of the area.

Ararat Town Hall

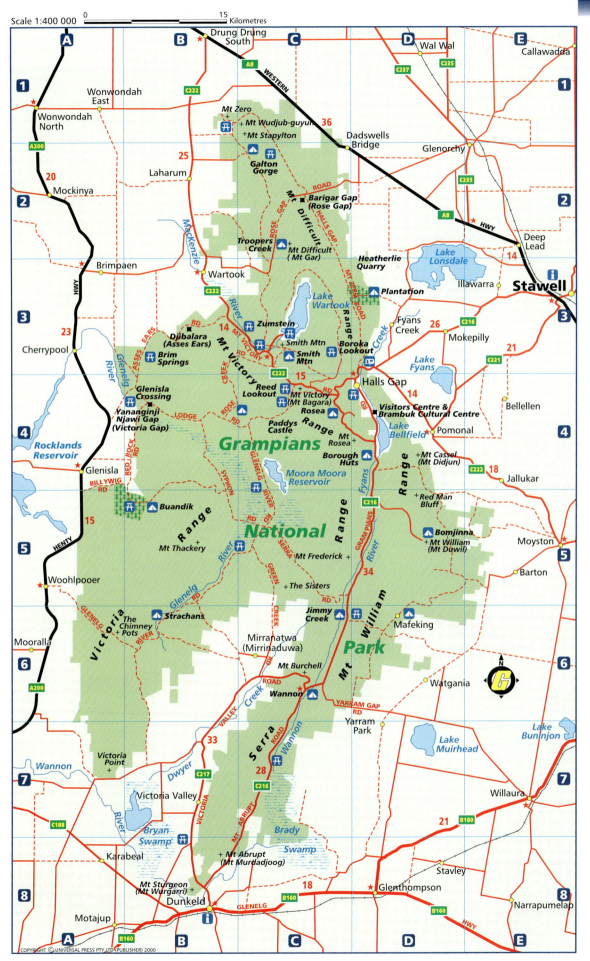

Scale 1:400 000

0   15   Kilometres

Drung Drung South

WESTERN   A8

Wal Wal

Callawadda

Wonwondah East

C222

Mt Zero

Mt Wudjub-guyun   36

Dadswells Bridge

Glenorchy

C237   C235

Wonwondah North

A200

Galton Gorge

Mt Stapylton

25

Laharum

20

Mockinya

Mt Difficult

Barigar Gap (Rose Gap)

Troopers Creek

Mt Difficult (Mt Gar)

Heatherlie Quarry

Lake Lonsdale

C235

A8   HWY

Deep Lead

14

Stawell

Brimpaen

C222

Wartook

Lake Wartook

Plantation

Fyans Creek

26   C216

Mokepilly

Cherrypool

23

Djibalara (Asses Ears)

RD   14

Zumstein

Smith Mtn

Smith Mtn

Boroka Lookout

Lake Fyans

21

C221

Brim Springs

C222

Reed Lookout

15

Mt Victory (Mt Bagara)

Rosea

Halls Gap

14

Bellellen

Glenisla Crossing

Yananginji Njawi Gap (Victoria Gap)

LODGE

Rosea

Paddys Castle

Visitors Centre & Brambuk Cultural Centre

Pomonal

Rocklands Reservoir

Grampians

Mt Rosea

Lake Bellfield

Glenisla

Moora Moora Reservoir

Borough Huts

Mt Cassel (Mt Didjun)

C222   18

Jallukar

BILLYWIG RD

15

Buandik

National

Range

Red Man Bluff

Bomjinna

Mt William (Mt Duwil)

Moyston

Mt Thackery

Range

Mt Frederick

Barton

Woohlpooer

The Sisters

34

Mooralla

A200

Strachans

The Chimney Pots

Mirranatwa (Mirrinaduwa)

Jimmy Creek

Mafeking

Park

Mt Burchell

Wannon

Watgania

YARRAM GAP RD

Victoria Point

33

Dwyer

C217

Yarram Park

Lake Muirhead

Lake Bunjnjon

Willaura

Victoria Valley

28

C216

Bryan Swamp

C188

Brady Swamp

21   B180

Karabeal

Mt Abrupt (Mt Murdadjoog)

Stavley

Mt Sturgeon (Mt Wurgarri)

18

Glenthompson

Narrapumelap

Motajup

Dunkeld

B160   GLENELG

B160   HWY

COPYRIGHT © UNIVERSAL PRESS PTY LTD (PUBLISHER) 2000

Victorian Alps

Where to ski

Resorts cater for different levels of skiers. Mt Hotham and Mt Buffalo have ski runs for immediate skiers. Mt Baw Baw is more suited to beginners. Falls Creek has runs for all levels. Around Lake Mountain there are some excellent cross-country runs.

ℹ Tourist Information

Gateway Visitor Information Centre
Gateway Village, Lincoln Causeway, Wodonga 3690
Ph: (02) 6041 3875
Wangaratta and Region Visitor Information Centre
Cnr Tone Rd & Handley St, Wangaratta 3677
Ph: (03) 5721 5711

Main Attractions

★ **Alpine NP**
This NP encompasses a large part of the Victorian Alps and is home to many of the region's ski resorts.
★ **Beechworth**
This perfectly preserved gold town is rich in history.
★ **Bright**
Bright is a picturesque town that began in the 1850's as a gold town. Today it is the centre of the local timber, walnut, chestnut and tourism industries.
★ **Bogong**
The annual Bogong Moth Festival celebrates the town's namesake.
★ **Falls Creek**
Falls Creek has what are considered to be Victoria's best ski runs. Spectacular views of Fall's Creek can be seen from Roper's Lookout. The walk to Mt Nelse traverses colourful slopes covered with Alpine wildflowers.
★ **Mt Buffalo NP**
This stunning NP covers the huge plateau surrounding Mt Buffalo.

The Victorian Alps are the southern-most part of the Great Dividing Ra. These dramatic yet rounded mountains are far less challenging for skiers than the extremely jagged peaks of their northern hemisphere counterparts, the European Alps.

Located approximately 75km east of Wangaratta, the Victorian Alps cover a vast and rugged terrain that is mostly protected by national parks. The ski resort towns dotting the mountains are within an hour's radius of each other, so there are many opportunities for skiing and ice skating, although the conditions are best for either downhill or cross-country skiing.

The Victorian snow season usually starts in June, lasting at least until September, although some years it has extended as late as November. Bushwalking,

Falls Creek in winter

horseriding, paragliding, hang gliding and trout fishing are some of the many recreational activities that attract visitors during the warmer months.

Bright in autumn

Milawa Gourmet Region

Lying east of Wangaratta, the townships of Milawa and Oxley are renowned for their regional produce, particularly wines and cheeses. The temperate climate is ideal for viniculture and dairying, and many of the local restaurants and cafes showcase the region's produce. Orchards and vineyards dot this charming region, with attractions such as Wabonga Plateau and an impressive amphitheatre at Paradise Falls creating ideal picnic spots for indulging in the local offerings. Many of the region's wineries can be found in the King Valley's northern end, where visitors can enjoy a stunning combination of excellent food and wine.

One of Australia's leading wine exporters, Brown Brothers of Milawa, is a centrepiece for wine tasting visitors to the region.

Other drawcards include Milawa Mustards, conveniently located in the centre of town; Milawa Cheese Co, which offers tastings of its award-winning Milawa Blue cheese on the premises; and King River Café in Oxley, renowned for offering one of the region's finest dining experiences.

King Valley wineries include: Avalon, King River Estate, La Cantina, Chrismont Vineyard, Lana Trento and Dalzotto Wines. Wineries located in Milawa and Oxley include: John Gehrig Wineries, Brown Brothers of Milawa Vineyard, Ciavarella Wines, Reads Winery and Wood Park Estate Wine.

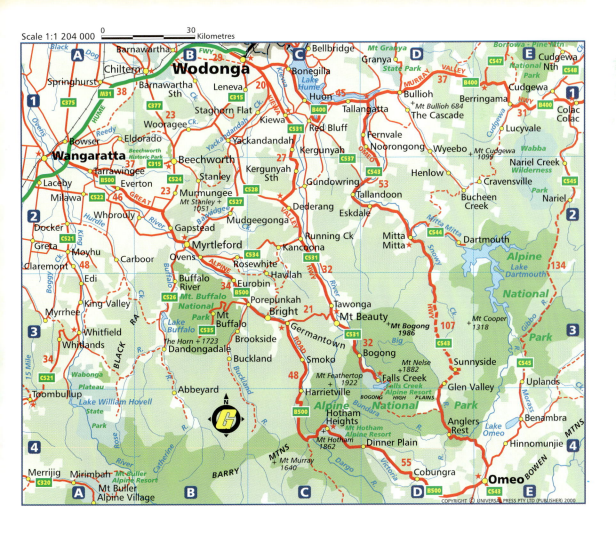

Scale 1:1 204 000

Wilsons Promontory

O nce part of the ancient land bridge to Tas, Wilsons Promontory, the southern-most point of the Australian mainland, is protected by one of Vic's oldest and most spectacular national parks, reserved in 1898. Its pristine beaches and coves, rugged rivers and creeks, and isolated mountain ranges, set among a dramatic backdrop of granite ranges, are preserved by their remoteness; however, the camping grounds at Tidal River are lively during summer and school holidays.

Squeaky Bay, Wilsons Promontory

Visitors have always been intrigued by Wilsons Promontory's majestic coastline and botanical abundance - 'The Prom' features over 700 native plant species growing in diverse habitats. There are tall eucalypts, moist and luxuriant fern gullies, groves of brown and yellow stringy-barks, copses of banksias and tea-trees, and salt marshes.

When to visit 'The Prom'

Visit in the spring and see the abundant wildflowers or visit in the autumn when temperatures are cool and ideal for walking. Conditions can be cold and bleak but sometimes fresh and bracing in winter, while in summer it is extremely crowded.

ℹ Tourist Information

Wilsons Promontory NP
Park Office and Visitors Centre,
Tidal River 3960
Freecall: 1800 350 552
www.parks.vic.gov.au

Main Attractions

★ **Mt Oberon**
Mt Oberon is popular for its panoramic views of the surrounding bays and islands.
★ **Norman Bay**
This sweeping bay is worth visiting for its lovely views, stretching out to the horizon.
★ **Sealer's Cove**
Pack a picnic lunch to enjoy the 9.5km day walk to this spectacular sheltered cove. The shallow waters allow for excellent and secluded swimming.
★ **South East Cape Lighthouse (1859)**
Providing breathtaking vistas of the Promontory, the lighthouse is an 18.5km walk, best done as an overnight journey.
★ **West Coast Beaches**
A string of stunning beaches speckles the Promontory's west coast, overlooking the waters of Bass Strait.
★ **Wilsons Promontory NP**
It is possible to swim or surf at many of the Prom's beaches and the park is ideal for all levels of bushwalkers.

Wilsons Promontory National Park

Scale 1:200 000

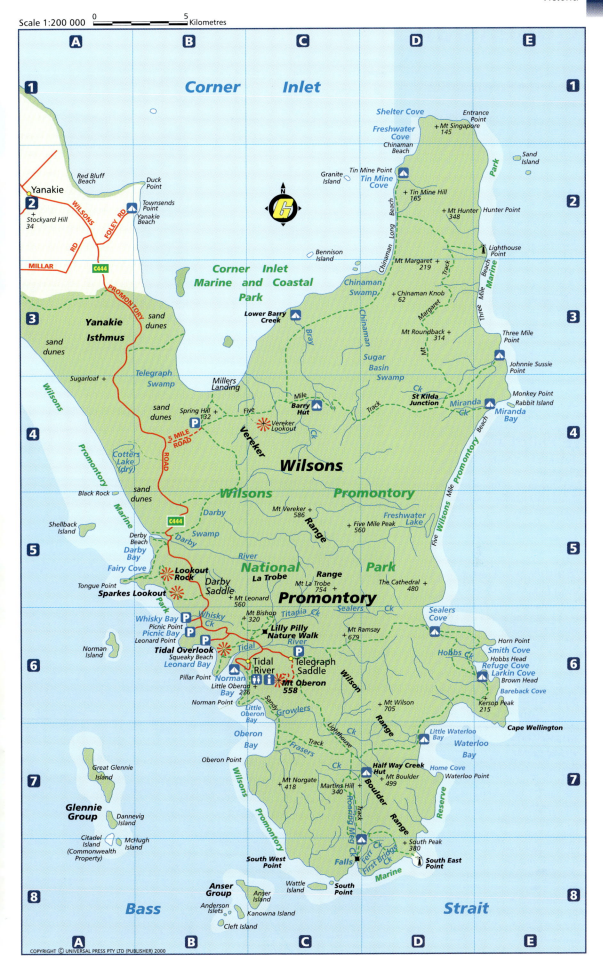

Queensland

QLD: The Sunshine State

- Area = 1 727 530 sq km
- Occupies 22.5% of Australia
- Length of coast = 5207km

Cooktown Orchid   *Koala*

ℹ️ Tourist Information

Queensland Government Travel Centre
243 Edward St, Brisbane 4000
Ph: (07) 3874 2800
www.tq.com.au

Main Attractions

★ **Brisbane**
This city is located on the banks of the Brisbane River, and is an attractive tropical city and close to an array of excellent beaches.

★ **Cairns**
Cairns is the point of departure for the Great Barrier Reef.

★ **Fraser Island**
Except for a few small freehold areas, Fraser Is is a World Heritage listed national park.

★ **Gold Coast**
The Gold Coast is full of theme parks, beaches and backed by high-rise developments and an upmarket shopping centre.

★ **Sunshine Coast**
This is a region of unhurried and unspoilt beaches.

★ **The Scenic Rim**
This is a lush region of national parks.

★ **Whitsundays**
This group of idyllic islands lies in the balmy waters of the Great Barrier Reef.

The State of Qld occupies the NE portion of the Australian continent. It is Australia's second largest state. There are 7 distinct tourist regions; Gold Coast, Darling Downs, Central Coast, Northern Qld, Great Barrier Reef and Western Qld. With beaches and islands among its key attractions, Qld has 5207km of coastline and from north to south its greatest distance is 2092km. Inland, the greatest distance from east to west is 1448km.

This huge expanse of land covers a diversity of terrains, ranging from the lush, tropical rainforests of Cape York, to the temperate sub-tropical climes around the State's capital Brisbane, to the harsh, rugged and dry landscapes of the State's interior.

Although weather conditions vary from one region to another, with the seasons in the northern-most tip being wet and dry, its abundant sunshine and warmth make Qld

Whitsunday Islands

ideal for holidays and touring. Its capital Brisbane, for instance, boasts an average temperature of 25°C and dry winters.

The population of Qld is Australia's most rural — it is the only State with a higher proportion of people living outside its capital than in it.

Mooloolaba, Pt Cartwright

Queensland Key Map and Distance Chart

All distances shown in the chart below have been measured over highways and major roads, not necessarily by the shortest route.

City Map
Brisbane, page 109

Suburban Maps
Brisbane, pages 110 to 113

State Maps
pages 114 to 125

Region Maps

Cairns District, page 127

Fraser Coast, page 129

Gold Coast, page 131

Rockhampton-
 Capricorn Coast, page 133

Sunshine Coast, page 135

The Scenic Rim, page 137

Toowoomba-
 Eastern Downs, page 139

Whitsunday, page 141

Approximate Distance	Bourke NSW	Bowen	Brisbane	Bundaberg	Cairns	Charleville	Charters Towers	Emerald	Gladstone	Longreach	Mackay	Maryborough	Moree NSW	Mt Isa	Rockhampton	Roma	Toowoomba	Townsville	Tweed Heads NSW	Warwick
Bourke NSW		1533	924	1102	1835	454	1353	966	1156	968	1346	1016	445	1610	1139	613	791	1488	1013	766
Bowen	1533		1181	812	542	1079	277	567	627	848	187	922	1292	1033	520	968	1160	195	1281	1244
Brisbane	924	1181		369	1701	754	1360	887	540	1186	980	259	479	1828	647	486	125	1376	100	158
Bundaberg	1102	812	369		1346	832	1025	560	185	973	617	110	714	1615	292	564	409	1007	469	493
Cairns	1835	542	1701	1346		1381	482	955	1169	1053	729	1442	1790	1117	1062	1356	1702	347	1801	1786
Charleville	454	1079	754	832	1381		899	512	811	514	892	762	629	1156	780	268	629	1034	832	713
Charters Towers	1353	277	1360	1025	482	899		473	848	571	464	1121	1308	756	741	874	1235	135	1438	1319
Emerald	966	567	887	560	955	512	473		375	413	380	648	835	1055	268	401	762	608	965	846
Gladstone	1156	627	540	185	1169	811	848	375		788	440	281	789	1430	107	543	544	822	640	628
Longreach	968	848	1186	973	1053	514	571	413	788		793	1061	1143	642	681	700	1061	706	1264	1145
Mackay	1346	187	980	617	729	892	464	380	440	793		713	1105	1220	333	781	973	382	1080	1057
Maryborough	1016	922	259	110	1442	762	1121	648	281	1061	713		628	1703	380	494	323	1117	359	407
Moree NSW	445	1292	479	714	1790	629	1308	835	789	1143	1105	628		1785	772	434	346	1443	568	321
Mt Isa	1610	1033	1828	1615	1117	1156	756	1055	1430	642	1220	1703	1785		1323	1342	1703	891	1906	1787
Rockhampton	1139	520	647	292	1062	780	741	268	107	681	333	380	772	1323		526	640	715	739	724
Roma	613	968	486	564	1356	268	874	401	543	700	781	494	434	1342	526		361	1009	564	445
Toowoomba	791	1160	125	409	1702	629	1235	762	544	1061	973	323	346	1703	640	361		1355	203	84
Townsville	1488	195	1376	1007	347	1034	135	608	822	706	382	1117	1443	891	715	1009	1355		1476	1454
Tweed Heads NSW	1013	1281	100	469	1801	832	1438	965	640	1264	1080	359	568	1906	739	564	203	1476		245
Warwick	766	1244	158	493	1786	713	1319	846	628	1145	1057	407	321	1787	724	445	84	1454	245	

Brisbane

The northern-most of Australia's State capitals, Brisbane is an attractive sub-tropical city lying 14km inland on the banks of the Brisbane River. Although for many years Brisbane was a capital with the atmosphere of a large country town, the Commonwealth Games in 1984 and the World Expo in 1988 helped change that image. Visitors will find a modern and sophisticated city that is full of vitality.

Settled in 1825 by a detachment of 45 convicts and their guards, Brisbane was originally a penal settlement situated at Redcliffe, north of the city's current location. The choice of the capital's location was initially unpopular with northern developers, who believed that the Government was too far away to effectively deal with their needs.

The move to Brisbane's present and more pleasant site beside the river was due to a lack of fresh water supplies, the failure of introduced

Southbank street theatre

crops and unrest among the Aboriginals. The riverside position has since played a pivotal role in the life of this vibrant, steamy city. Paddlesteamers, yachts, floating restaurants, ferries, cruise boats and bridges can be seen from many vantage points on Brisbane River's picturesque banks, which form a focal point for the outdoors lifestyle of Brisbane's 1.6 million residents.

ℹ Tourist Information

Brisbane Tourism Information Centres
Queen St Mall, Brisbane 4000
Ph: (07) 3229 5918
City Hall, King George Sq,
Brisbane 4000
Ph: (07) 3221 8411
www.brisbanetourism.com.au

Main Attractions

★ **Brisbane Botanical Gardens**
Formal gardens, bicycle tracks and duck ponds are some of this gardens attractions.

★ **Fortitude Valley, Chinatown**
This cosmopolitan area boasts a wide range of cafes and restaurants, as well as clubs and a shopping mall.

★ **Mt Coot-tha Lookout**
This is Brisbane's other official botanical gardens. Features include a scented garden and the Sir Thomas Brisbane Planetarium.

★ **Queen St Mall**
With its blend of traditional and modern architecture, Queen St Mall brings life to the city's shopping centre.

★ **Queensland Cultural Centre**
Located on Brisbane River's south bank, this cultural centre consists of Qld Museum, Qld Art Gallery, State Library and the huge Performing Arts Complex.

★ **South Bank Parklands**
This is a recreation area providing entertainment for all with gardens, waterways, riverside walkways, cafes, restaurants, BBQ facilities and an IMAX cinema.

Brisbane city sunset

Places of Interest

1. Anzac Sq   **C4**
2. Brisbane Convention & Exhibition Centre   **B6**
3. Casino   **B5**
4. Eagle St Pier & Riverside Markets   **D4**
5. Festival Hall   **C5**
6. Kangaroo Pt   **E4**
7. Old Government House   **C6**
8. Old Windmill Observatory   **B4**
9. Queensland Art Gallery and Museum   **B5**
10. Queensland Maritime Museum   **C7**
11. Queensland Sciencentre   **C5**
12. Riverside Centre   **D4**
13. St Johns Anglican Cathedral   **D4**
14. Story Bridge   **E4**
15. Victoria Barracks   **A4**
16. Victoria Park   **B1**

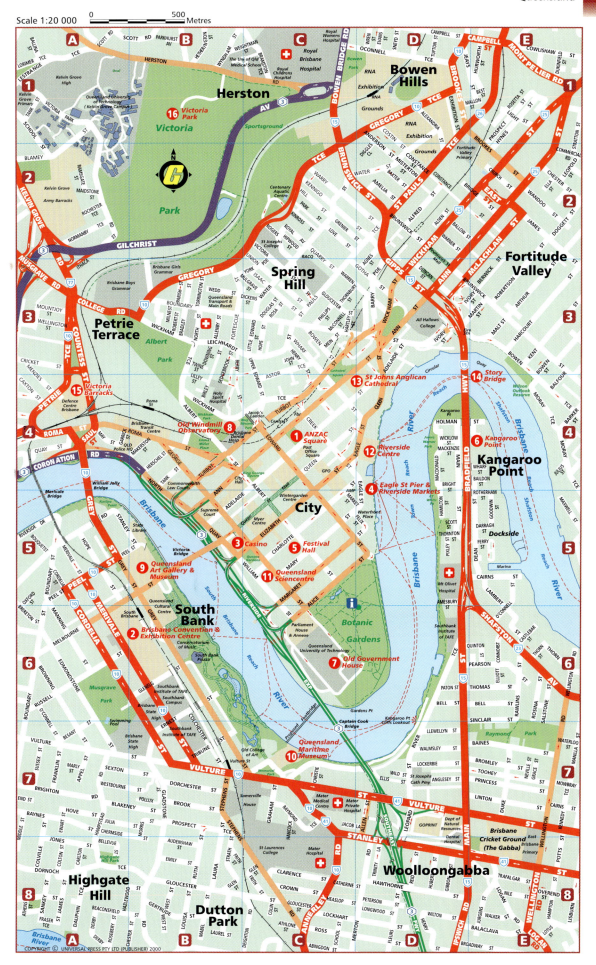

Scale 1:20 000

0   500 Metres

Scale 1:180 000

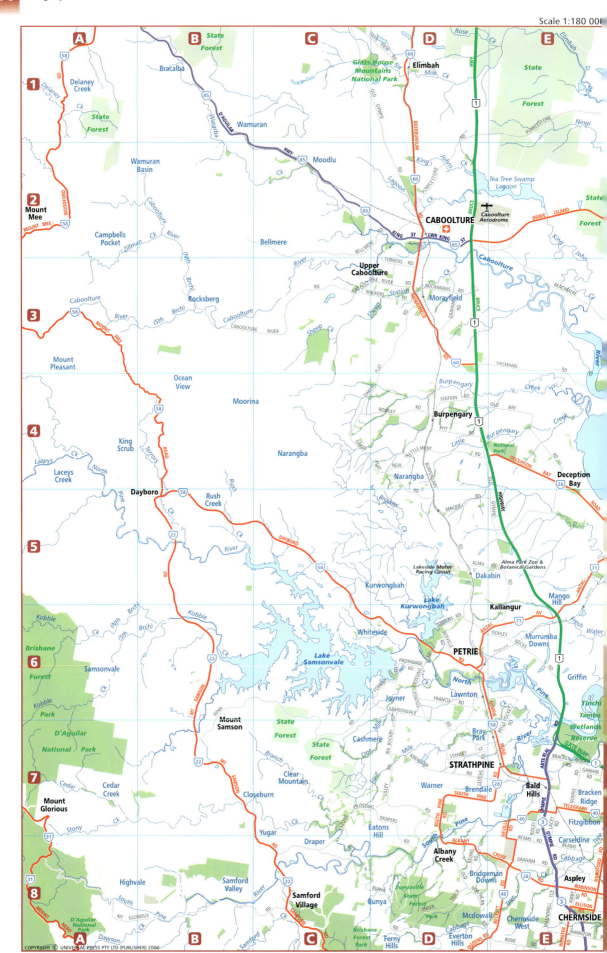

5
Kilometres

F G H J K

Coral

Sea

Donnybrook

Bribie
Island
National
Park

Bribie

Island

Meldale
Creek RD

White
Patch

Toorbul

Banksia
Beach

*Bribie
Island
National
Park*

1

Bellara

Woorim

Ningi

Sandstone
Point

Bongaree

2

Godwin
Beach

*Woody
Bay*

To Moreton Island

Beachmere

3

Deception

Sea

Bay

4

Scarborough
Boat Harbour

Castlereagh Point

Scarborough

Moreton

5

Redcliffe
Aerodrome

Rothwell

ANZAC

Osbourne Point

Kippa-
Ring

REDCLIFFE

Redcliffe Point

To Moreton Island

Margate

Inlet

Clontarf

Woody
Point

Bay

6

Creek

Woody Point

River

Bramble

Bay

Brighton

7

SANDGATE

Cabbage Tree Head

Deagon

Shorncliffe

*Mud
Island*

North Boondall

Nudgee
Beach

Taigum

Boondall

Zillmere

Nudgee

Juno
Point

Virginia

Port of
Brisbane

BISHOP

8

Banyo

**Brisbane
Airport**

Pinkenba

**Container
Terminals**

Fisherman
Islands

St Helena Island
**St Helena Island
National Park**

Waven
Heights

F

Domestic
Terminal

G

H

J

K

Scale 1:180 00

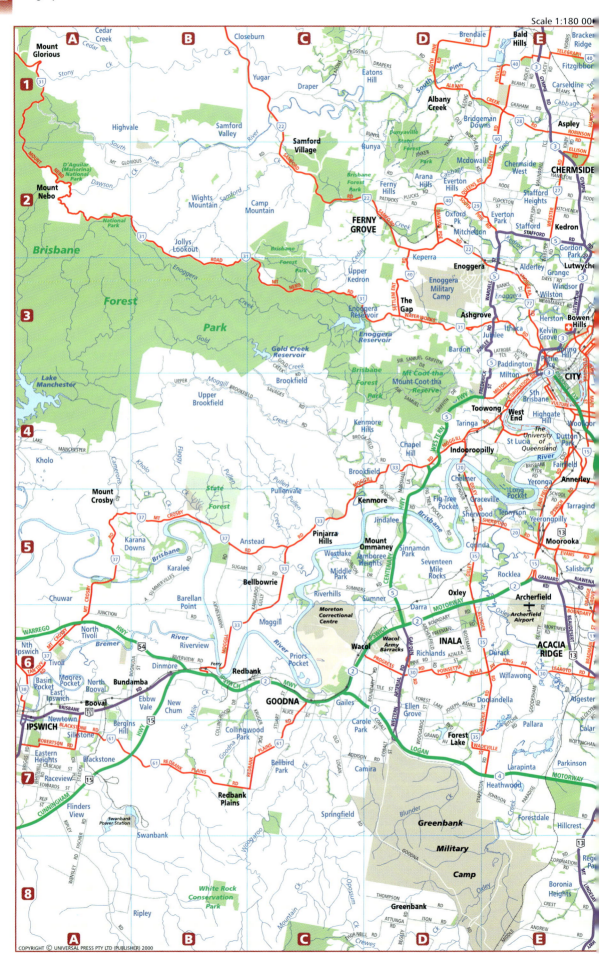

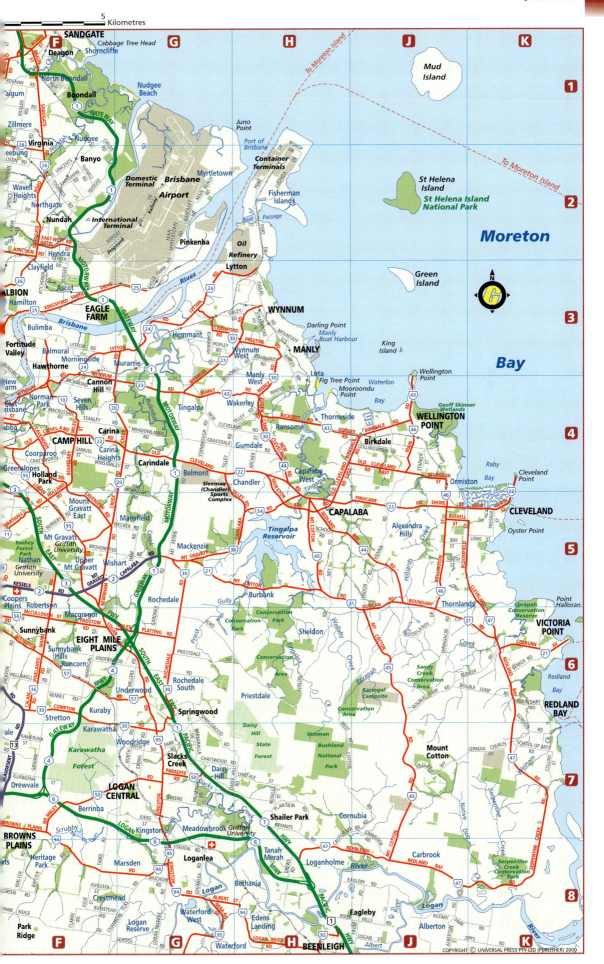

Scale 1:2 600 00

GULF OF CARPENTARIA

Rocky I.

Thabugan Point

Halls Point

Mornington

Lingnoonganee I.

Cape Van Dieman

Gee Wee Point

Island

Gunana

WELLESLEY ISLANDS

Sydney I.

Bountiful I.

Denham I.

Pains I.

Forsyth I.

FORSYTH ISLANDS

Bayley I.

Horseshoe I.

Oaktree Point

Allen I.

Bentinck I.

Point Burrowes

Point Austin

Sweers I.

SOUTH WELLESLEY ISLANDS

Fitzmaurice Point

Tarrant Point

Westmoreland

Hells Gate Roadhouse

295

Corinda (ruin)

Bowthorn

Punjaub

Kangaroo Point

Gore Point

Escott Resort

Burketown

Tirranna
Roadhouse

Doomadgee

Armraynald

71

117

Almora

Floraville

84

Wernadinga

McAllister

Karumba

Alligator Point

KARUMBA
DEV. RD

Normanton

Magowra

Burke &
Wills Cairn

Glenore

Mutton
Hole

Inverleigh

153

Milgarra

Maggieville

Lawn Hill

Planet Downs

Gregory Downs

69

Augustus Downs

Neumayer Valley

195

Warren Vale

Highland Plains

LAWN HILL
NATIONAL
PARK

Adels Grove

Mended Hill

Silver Star

76

Talawanta

68

84

Nardoo

Bang Bang

Wondoola

Vena Park

83

Donors Hills

Cowan Downs

Iffley

Gallipoli

126

Mellish Park

Lorraine

Myally

77

DEVELOPMENTAL

DEVELOPMENTAL

Burke & Wills
Roadhouse

Myola

Taldora

Riversleigh

Norfolk

Mt Gordon

Mt Oxide

Chidna

Kamileroi

Canobie

Morstone Downs

Undilla

Thorntonia

Lady
Annie

Gunpowder
Resort

Gleeson

Boomarra

84

Monstraven

234

Alcala

91

Rocklands

Split Rock

Mammoth

180

Coolullah

BURKE

Brinard

Spoonbill

Camooweal

66

CAMOOWEAL
CAVES N.P.

Don

188

Kajabbi

Granada

Sedan Dip

Clonagh

BARKLY

HWY

Avon Downs

Yelvertoft

See page 118

Calton Hills

Gypsy
Downs

Dalgonally

COPYRIGHT © UNIVERSAL PRESS PTY LTD (PUBLISHER) 2000

Northern Territory see pages 200 to 229

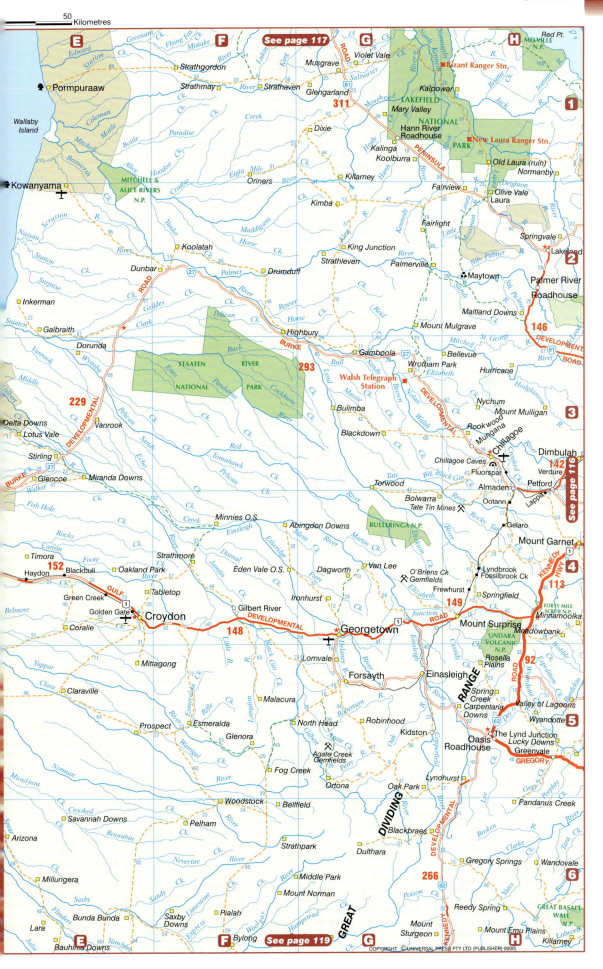

50 Kilometres

See page 117
See page 116
See page 119

E   F   G   H

1
2
3
4
5
6

Pormpuraaw
Wallaby Island
Kowanyama
Inkerman
Galbraith
Delta Downs
Lotus Vale
Stirling
Glencoe
Fish Hole
Timora
Haydon
Blackbull
Green Creek
Golden Gate
Croydon
Coralie
Claraville
Mittagong
Prospect
Esmeralda
Glenora
Arizona
Millungera
Lara
Bauhinia Downs
Bunda Bunda
Saxby Downs
Pialah
Bylong
Middle Park
Mount Norman
Woodstock
Bellfield
Pelham
Strathpark
Dulthara
Savannah Downs

Strathgordon
Strathmay
Strathaven
Glengarland
Musgrave
Violet Vale
Bizant Ranger Stn.
Kalpowar
Mary Valley
Hann River Roadhouse
New Laura Ranger Stn.
Dixie
Kalinga
Koolburra
Old Laura (ruin)
Normanby
Killarney
Oriners
Fairview
Olive Vale
Laura
Kimba
Fairlight
Springvale
Lakeland
Koolatah
King Junction
Strathleven
Palmerville
Palmer River Roadhouse
Dunbar
Drumduff
Maytown
146
Highbury
Maitland Downs
Mount Mulgrave
293
Gamboola
Bellevue
Hurricane
Wrotham Park
Walsh Telegraph Station
Bulimba
Nychum
Mount Mulligan
Blackdown
Rookwood
Mungana
Chillagoe
Dimbulah
142
Chillagoe Caves
Fluorspar
Verdure
Petford
Terwood
Almaden
Tate
Bolwarra
Tate Tin Mines
Ootann
Lappa
Minnies O.S.
Abingdon Downs
Bulleringa N.P.
Gelaro
Mount Garnet
Strathmore
Van Lee
O'Briens Ck Gemfields
Lyndbrook
Fossilbrook Ck
113
Eden Vale O.S.
Dagworth
Frewhurst
Springfield
Ironhurst
149
Mount Surprise
Minnamoolka
Gilbert River
Forty Mile Scrub N.P.
Meadowbank
148
Georgetown
Lornvale
Undara Volcanic N.P.
92
Forsayth
Einasleigh
Rosella Plains
Malacura
Spring Creek
Carpentaria Downs
Valley of Lagoons
North Head
Robinhood
Wyandotte
Agate Creek Gemfields
Kidston
The Lynd Junction
Lucky Downs
Oasis Roadhouse
Greenvale
Fog Creek
Ortona
Gregory
Oak Park
Lyndhurst
Blackbraes
Gregory Springs
Wandovale
266
Reedy Spring
Great Basalt Wall N.P.
Mount Sturgeon
Mount Emu Plains
Killarney

311
229
152
Pormpuraaw

MITCHELL & ALICE RIVERS N.P.
STAATEN RIVER NATIONAL PARK

LAKEFIELD NATIONAL PARK

Scale 1:2 600 000

GREAT BARRIER REEF

MARINE PARK

(CAIRNS SECTION)

For more detail see
map on page 127

GREAT BARRIER REEF MARINE PARK

(CENTRAL SECTION)

See page 115

See page 120

See page 127

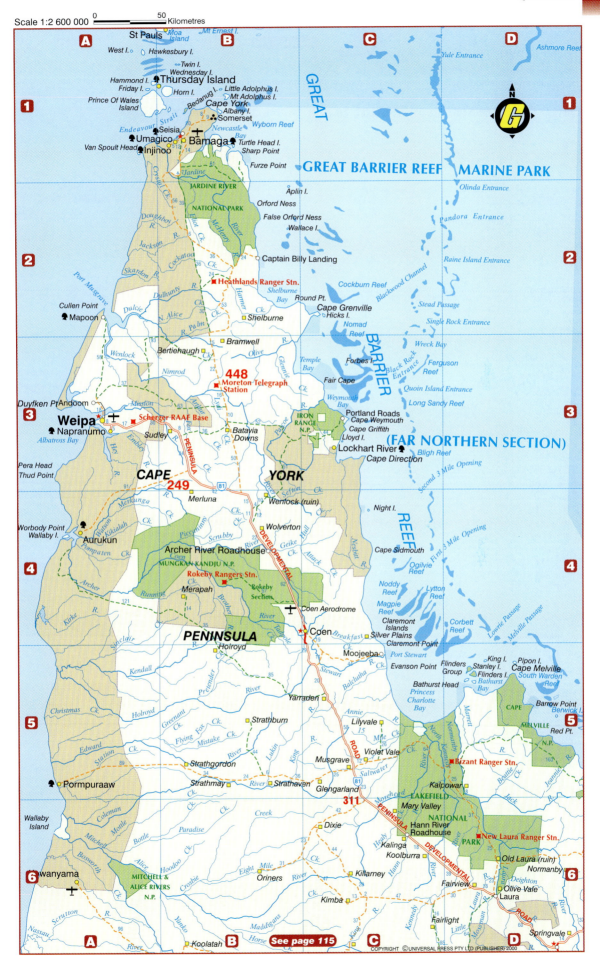

Scale 1:2 600 000

GREAT BARRIER REEF MARINE PARK

(FAR NORTHERN SECTION)

CAPE 249 YORK

PENINSULA

See page 115

Scale 1:2 600 000

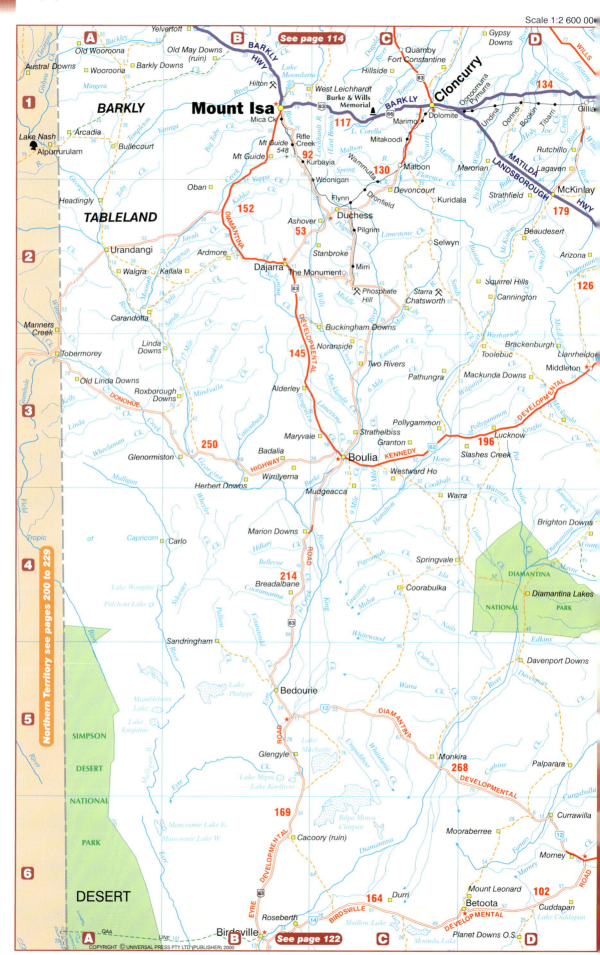

See page 114

See page 122

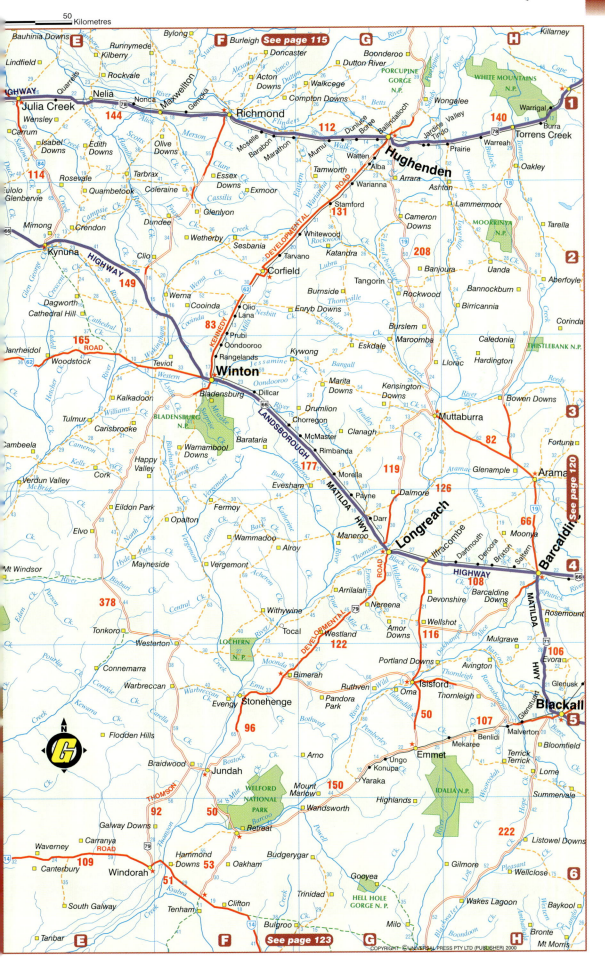

See page 115
See page 120
See page 123

50 Kilometres

Scale 1:2 600 000

Barrington • Southern Cross
Balfes Ck
107 A
Thalanga
Mungunburra
Homestead
Kimburra
Cape River
Pentland 1
Milray
Corea Plains
204
Longton
Mirtna
2
Yarromere
Bowie
Kyong
Doongmabulla
Fleetwood
3
Lake Dunn • Eastmere
Fortuna
Dunrobin
Albro
Springvale
Boongoondoo
Forrester
181
Rangers Valley
GREAT
See page 119
Stirling
Garfield
Hobartville
4
Lochnagar • Busthinia
Alice
Springvale
138
Jericho
Beta
Armagh
Lancevale
CAPRICORN
Clover Hills
Tumbar
163
Alpha
Yalleroi
Glen Avon
Glenusk
Skye
Thrungli
DIVIDING
5
LANDSBOROUGH
101
Kelpum
Summervale
DAWSON
Gartmore
Tambo
Malta
Minnie Downs
Lansdowne
Caldervale
116
Lumeah
Chatham
Coolabri
MATILDA
6
Baykool • Noella
Barfion
Wansey Downs
Augathella A

Brittania
Mount Cooper
Harvest Home
Scartwater
Lake Dalrymple
Bungobine
Mt Coolon
Belyando Crossing
Pasha
Disney
Avon Downs
Moray Downs
167
Frankfield
Laglan
Beresford
EPPING FOREST N.P.
Blair Athol Mine
Peak Vale
Islay Plains
Mt Tabletop 823+
Drummond
Hannams Gap
Bogantungan
Mt Portwine +748
Durabrook
Mantuan Downs
Castlevale
246
DEVELOPMENTAL
Tandera
Cungelella
Carwell
CARNARVON NATIONAL PARK
Mt King 806+
Babbiloora
Mt Tabor
Lorne
Crystalbrook
Hillside
Oak Vale
Moorak
Waverley
RANGE
See page 124

B
Ravenswood
Carse O Gowrie
Dalberg
See page 116
Burdekin Falls Dam
Heidelberg
Strathmore
Conway
Newlands Mine
Glenden
180
Elphinstone
Villafranca
Moranbah
Mt McLaren
ROAD
PEAK
DOWNS
Clermont
Langlop
Kahn
Nanya
Retro
Chimside
Jurema
Amah
Kabelbarra
Anakie Gemfields
Rubyvale
Sapphire
66
Willows Gemfields
Anakie
Taraborah
171
HIGHWAY
Willows
Borilla
63
Zamia
Vandyke
Joe Joe
Echo Hills
Riverside
Kareela

C
Pring
Armuna
Mookarra
Aberdeen
Longford Ck
Binbee
83
Eriaba
Almoola
Collinsville
McNaughton
Birralee
Havillah
For more detail see map on page 141
Eungella
Hatton
Glenden
Finch Hatton
Riverside Mine
Goonyella Mine
Wotonga
Mindi
Bolingbroke
Waitara
Braeside
29
Coppabella
Ingsdon
Red Mountain
Iffley
67
Saraji Mine
Dysart
Norwich Park Mine
PEAK RANGE N.P.
German Creek Mine
Oakey Ck Mine
Capella
Tieri
Gregory Mine
Yan Yan
Fairhill
Yamboyna
106
Curragh
Crew
Emerald
Blackwater
Yamala
Lochmead
Comet
Burngrove
75
Gindie
Kammel
Kinrola Mine
Koorilgah Mine
Fernlees
South Blackwater Mine
Springsure
Somerby
70
DAWSON HWY
Rolleston
Goomally
Springwood
Consuelo
Basalt Creek
77
Carnarvon
Wyseby
Carnarvon Lodge
178
Warrong
Westgrove
Ridgelands
C

D
George Pt
Hayman I.
Hook Island
Earlando
Border I.
Airlie Beach
Shutehaven
Hamilton I.
Proserpine
Thoopara
Conway
Shaw
Cape Conway
Blacksmith
Goldsmith I.
Bloomsbury
Yaboroo
Carlisle
Brampton I.
Rabbit I.
124
Seaforth
Mount Ossa
Kuttabul
Marion
80
Gargett
Mirani
Eton
36
Sarina
Yukan
Keumala
53
Hatfield
106
Balook
Croydon
Cosmos
242
May Downs
181
Middlemount
Junee
Royles
Yarrabee
DEVELOPMENTAL
Blackwater
Bluff
Walton
Umolo
CAPRICORN
46
Dingo
Goonwarra
Tryphi
BLACKDOWN TABLELAND N.P.
122
Woorabinda
Planet Downs
Bauhinia Downs
CARNARVON
DEVELOPMENTAL
PALMGROVE N.P.
Bedourie
Reedy Creek
EXPEDITION N.P.
Gwambegwine
Glenhaughton
Baroondah
D

COPYRIGHT © UNIVERSAL PRESS PTY LTD (PUBLISHER) 2000

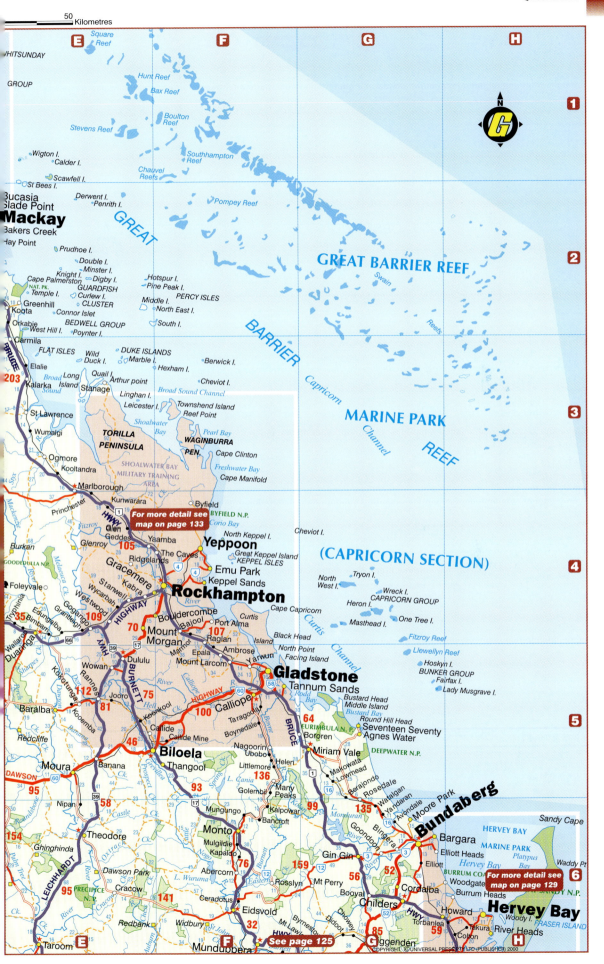

50 Kilometres

WHITSUNDAY
GROUP

Square Reef
Hunt Reef
Bax Reef
Boulton Reef
Stevens Reef

Wigton I.
Calder I.
Scawfell I.
St Bees I.

Bucasia
Slade Point
Mackay
Bakers Creek
Hay Point

Derwent I.
Penrith I.

Southhampton Reef

Chauvel Reefs

Pompey Reef

GREAT BARRIER REEF

Prudhoe I.
Double I.
Minster I.
Knight I.
Digby I.
Cape Palmerston
GUARDFISH
Temple I.
Curlew I.
Greenhill
CLUSTER
Koota
Connor Islet
Orkabie
West Hill I.
BEDWELL GROUP
Poynter I.

Hotspur I.
Pine Peak I.
PERCY ISLES
Middle I.
North East I.
South I.

GREAT

Swain
Reefs

Reefs

203

Jarmila
FLAT ISLES
Elalie
Kalarka
Broad
Long
Sound
Island

Wild
Duck I.
DUKE ISLANDS
Marble I.
Quail I.
Stanage
Arthur point
Linghan I.
Leicester I.

Hexham I.
Berwick I.

Cheviot I.

BARRIER

Capricorn

MARINE PARK

St Lawrence
Wumalgi
Ogmore
Kooltandra

**TORILLA
PENINSULA**
SHOALWATER
Bay
SHOALWATER BAY
MILITARY TRAINING
AREA

Townshend Island
Reef Point

**WAGINBURRA
PEN.**
Pearl Bay
Cape Clinton
Freshwater Bay
Cape Manifold

Channel

REEF

3

Marlborough
Kunwarara
Princhester

Byfield
BYFIELD N.P.

Cheviot I.

For more detail see map on page 133

Corio Bay

1
HWY
Burkan
Glen
Geddes
105
Glenroy
GOODEDULLA N.P.
Gracemere
Ridgelands
Yaamba
The Caves

North Keppel I.
Great Keppel Island
KEPPEL ISLES

(CAPRICORN SECTION)

4

Foleyvale
Kabra
Stanwell
Westwood
109
Wycarbah
Granteleigh

Yeppoon

Emu Park
Keppel Sands

North
West I.

Tryon I.

Wreck I.
CAPRICORN GROUP
Heron I.
One Tree I.
Masthead I.

Tnyphnia
35
Edungalba
Bimbam
Gogango
70
Rockhampton
Bouldercombe
Bajool
107
Port Alma
Curtis

Cape Capricorn

Fitzroy Reef

**Mount
Morgan**
Marmor
Raglan
Epala
Wowan
Dululu
Mount Larcom

Black Head
North Point
Facing Island

Llewellyn Reef
Hoskyn I.
BUNKER GROUP
Fairfax I.
Lady Musgrave I.

Waltpa
Duaringa
112
Rannes
Jooro
75
Koonkool
100
Calliope
Taragoola
Boynedale

Ambrose
Yarwun
Gladstone
Tannum Sands

Rodd
Bay
Bustard Head
Middle Island
Bustard Bay

5

Baralba
81
Kooemba
Callide
Redcliffe
46
Callide Mine
Biloela
Thangool
Nagoorin
Uboba
64
Bororen
EURIMBULA N.P.
Miriam Vale
Round Hill Head
Seventeen Seventy
Agnes Water

Moura
Banana
93
Golembil
Littlemore
Heleri
Many
Peaks
136
Kalpowar
99
Makowata
Lowmead
Berajondo
Rosedale
DEEPWATER N.P.

95
Nipan
58
Mungungo
Bancroft
135
Yandaran
Avondale
Moore Park

HERVEY BAY

Sandy Cape

154
Ghinghinda
Theodore
Monto
Mulgildie
Kapaldo
76
159
Gin Gin
Goondoon
Bingera
52
Elliott Heads
Bargara
MARINE PARK

Bundaberg

Platypus
Bay
Waddy Pt

95
PRECIPICE
N.P.
Cracow
141
Abercorn
Rosslyn
Mt Perry
56
Booyal
Cordalba
Elliott
BURRUM COAST
Woodgate
Burrum Heads
For more detail see map on page 129

Dawson Park
L. Wuruma

Redbank
Widbury
Ceradotus
Eidsvold
32
Mt Lawn
Didcot
Chowey
85
Howard
Torbanlea
Takura
Colton
River Heads
59

Hervey Bay
Woody I.
FRASER ISLAND

See page 125

Taroom
Mundubbera
Eidsvold
Ggenden

COPYRIGHT © UNIVERSAL PRESS PTY LTD (PUBLISHER) 2000

Scale 1:2 600 000

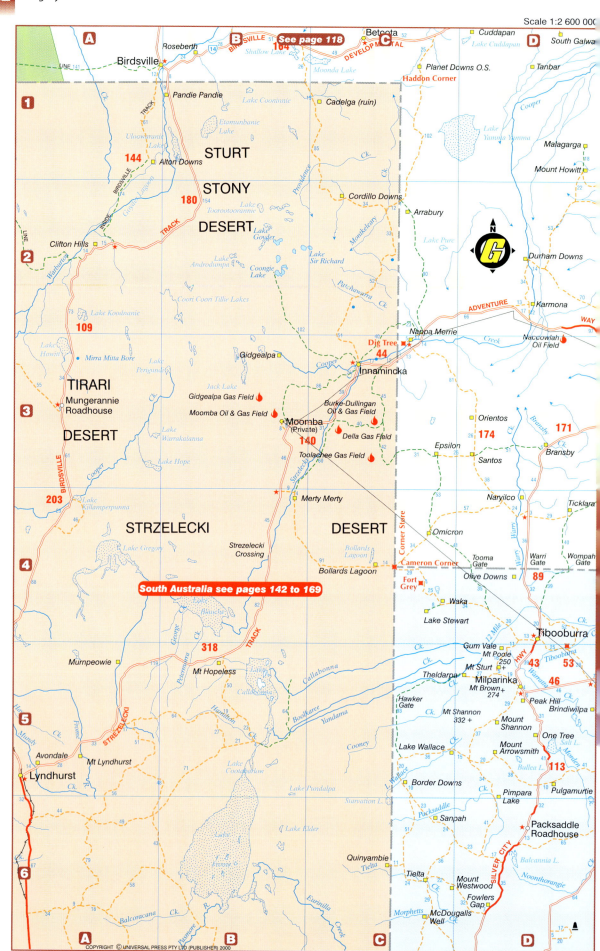

See page 118

STURT

STONY

DESERT

TIRARI

DESERT

STRZELECKI

DESERT

South Australia see pages 142 to 169

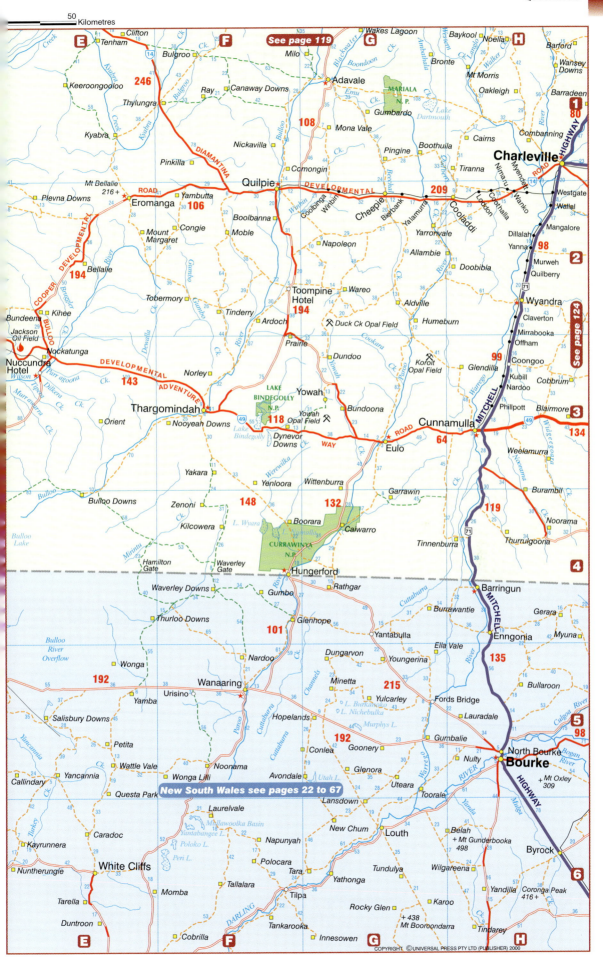

50 Kilometres

See page 119

See page 124

New South Wales see pages 22 to 67

COPYRIGHT ©UNIVERSAL PRESS PTY LTD (PUBLISHER) 2000

Scale 1:2 600 000

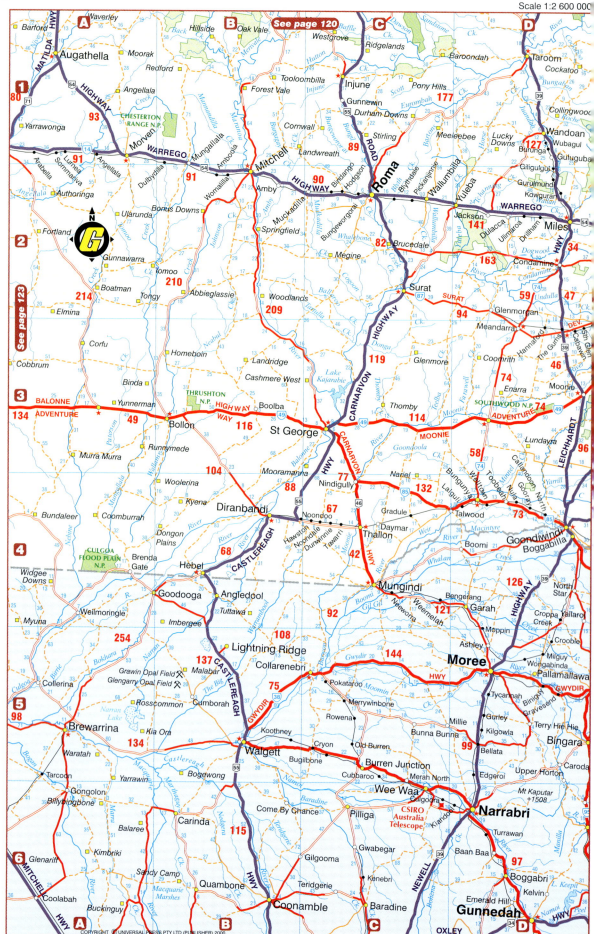

50 Kilometres

See page 121

Hervey Bay
Woody I.
FRASER ISLAND

For more detail see map on page 129

For more detail see map on page 135

Maryborough

Gympie

GREAT SANDY N.P.

Noosa Heads
Nambour
Maroochydore
Caloundra

Bribie Island
Cape Moreton

Caboolture
MORETON ISLAND N.P.
Moreton Island

Redcliffe
Moreton Bay
Mud I.

Amity Pt
Pt Lookout

For more detail see map on pages 110 - 113

Kingaroy

Nanango

Dalby

BRISBANE
North Stradbroke Island

Toowoomba

Gatton
Ipswich
Beenleigh
Stradbroke Island

For more detail see map on page 139

For more detail see map on page 131

Nerang
Surfers Paradise
Tweed Heads
Kingscliff

For more detail see map on page 137

Warwick
Beaudesert

Murwillumbah
Pottsville Beach
Ocean Shores
Brunswick Heads
Nimbin
Bangalow
Cape Byron
Byron Bay
Lennox Head
Ballina

Lismore

Casino
Alstonville
Coraki

Tenterfield

Iluka
Yamba
Maclean
Brooms Head

New South Wales see pages 22 to 67

Inverell
Glen Innes

Grafton
Minnie Water
Wooli
Red Rock
Arrawarra
Woolgoolga
Emerald Beach

Coffs Harbour
Sawtell

Armidale
Nambucca Heads
Scotts Head

COPYRIGHT ©UNIVERSAL PRESS PTY LTD (PUBLISHER) 2000

Cairns

The Eden-like environment of Cairns and its surrounding districts is a succulent green belt bordered by the Coral Sea's temperate waters and the brilliant green plains that sweep down from the northern-most section of the Great Dividing Ra. Inland from the balmy, humid coast, the Atherton Tableland is elevated 600–900m above sea level. Known as the 'cool tropics', here it is usually warm and sunny during the day, while the night provides calm relief.

The region offers an abundance of waterfalls, rolling hills, lush rainforests, idyllic tropical beaches, extinct volcanoes and crater lakes to explore. Home to Qld's most northerly city, the region attracts millions of tourist dollars each year, taking pride of place as an international holiday destination. The townships feature an eclectic combination of colonial tropical architecture, modern resorts and wild vegetation. Visitors can choose

Millaa Millaa Falls, Atherton

from an array of warm-climate outdoor activities to keep themselves entertained.

Crater Lakes

Lake Barrine and Lake Eacham have formed in the craters of extinct volcanoes, which have existed for millions of years. Lake Eacham was an early settler's camp. Aborigines believed it to be haunted and steered clear of the vicinity calling it, 'No Man's Land of Devil Devils'.

ℹ️ Tourist Information

Tourism Tropical North Queensland Visitor Information Centre
51 The Esplanade, Cairns 4870
Ph: (07) 4031 7676
www.information@tnq.org.au

Main Attractions

★ **Daintree NP**
This NP features lush rainforest where activities include crocodile tours, forest walks and birdwatching.
★ **Kuranda**
This resort town's attractions include markets, Tjapukai Aboriginal Dance Theatre, Butterfly Sanctuary, Scenic Railway and the Wildlife Noctarium.
★ **Mossman Gorge**
This river gorge is surrounded by rainforest. The Kuku Yalangi Aboriginal community give guided tours.
★ **Port Douglas**
This is now an upmarket tourist resort.
★ **Skyrail Rainforest Cableway**
The cable cars make their 7.5km journey hovering above the tree tops.
★ **Tjapukai Aboriginal Cultural Park**
This park showcases the internationally acclaimed Tjapukai Aboriginal Dance Theatre. There is also a campsite, restaurant and history theatre.
★ **Wooroonooran NP**
Within this park are Josephine Falls, The Boulders, Walshs Pyramid and Qld's highest mountain, Bartle Frere.

Scuba Dive, Great Barrier Reef

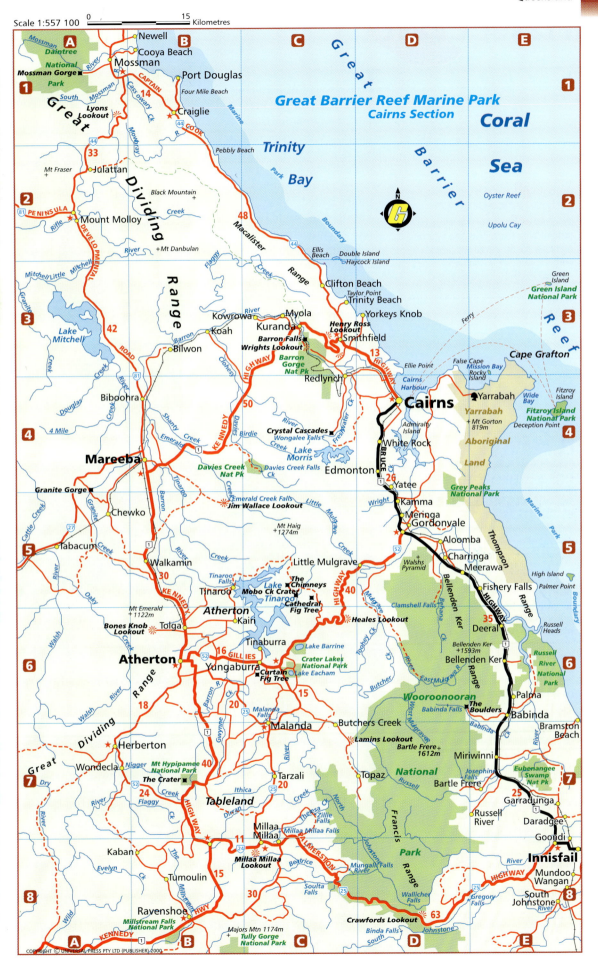

Scale 1:557 100

0   15
Kilometres

Great Barrier Reef Marine Park
Cairns Section

Coral

Sea

Great

Barrier

Reef

Trinity

Bay

Great

Dividing

Range

Oyster Reef

Upolu Cay

Green
Island

Green Island
National Park

Cape Grafton

Fitzroy
Island

Fitzroy Island
National Park
Deception Point

Yarrabah
Aboriginal
Land

Newell
Cooya Beach
Mossman
Mossman Gorge
National
Park
Port Douglas
Four Mile Beach
Lyons
Lookout
Craiglie
Pebbly Beach

Mt Fraser
Julatten
33

Black Mountain
Mount Molloy
48
Creek
Macalister

Range
+Mt Danbulan

Ellis
Beach
Double Island
Haycock Island

Clifton Beach
Taylor Point
Trinity Beach
Yorkeys Knob

Lake
Mitchell
42

Bilwon

Kowrowa
Koah
Kuranda
Barron Falls
Wrights Lookout
Barron
Gorge
Nat Pk

Myola
Henry Ross
Lookout
Smithfield
13

Ellie Point
Cairns
Harbour

False Cape
Mission Bay
Rocky
Island

Cairns

4 Mile

Biboohra

50

Mareeba

Granite Gorge
Chewko

Crystal Cascades
Wongalee Falls

Davies Creek
Nat Pk
Davies Creek Falls
Ck

Lake
Morris

Redlynch

White Rock

Edmonton
26
Yatee

Admiralty
Island

Yarrabah
+Mt Gorton
819m

Wide
Bay

Grey Peaks
National Park

Tabacum
Walkamin
30

Emerald Creek Falls
Jim Wallace Lookout

Mt Haig
+1274m

Kamma
Meringa
Gordonvale
Aloomba
Charringa
Meerawa
Fishery Falls

High Island
Palmer Point

Russell
Heads

Tinaroo
Mobo Ck Crater

Little Mulgrave
The
Chimneys
Cathedral
Fig Tree

Walshs
Pyramid

Bellenden Ker
Range

Mt Emerald
+1122m
Tolga
Bones Knob
Lookout
Atherton
Kairi

Lake
Tinaroo

Heales Lookout
40

Clamshell Falls

Bellenden Ker
+1593m

Deeral
35

Russell
River
National
Park

Atherton
16 GILLIES
Yungaburra
Curtain
Fig Tree
18
20
Malanda
Falls
15

Tinaburra
Lake Barrine
Crater Lakes
National Park
Lake Eacham

Malanda

Butchers Creek

Lamins Lookout
Bartle Frere
+1612m

Wooroonooran
Babinda Falls
The
Boulders
Babinda

Bellenden Ker
Palma
Bramston
Beach

Herberton
Wondecla
Mt Hypipamee
National Park
The Crater
40

Tarzali
20

Topaz

National

Bartle Frere

Josephine
Falls
Miriwinni

Eubenangee
Swamp
Nat Pk
25

Garradunga

Kaban
24
Tableland
Millaa
Millaa
11
Millaa Millaa Falls
Millaa Millaa
Lookout

Park

Russell
River
Daradgee

Goondi

Tumoulin
15
30
Crawfords Lookout
63
Binda Falls

Innisfail
Mundoo
Wangan
South
Johnstone

Ravenshoe
Millstream Falls
National Park
Majors Mtn 1174m
Tully Gorge
National Park

Fraser Coast

The magnificent natural playground of the Fraser Coast hosts diverse and unique landscapes, from intriguing coloured sands, silent rainforests, giant sand dunes and towering cliffs to tranquil lakes, spectacular scenery, pristine beaches and lush national parks.

Boasting the world's largest sand island and magnificent waterways, the Fraser Coast offers the full gambit of watersports including swimming, fishing, scuba diving and boating. The seaside townships dotting the mainland coast, such as Tuan, Tinnanbar and Poona, provide many sightseeing adventure opportunities and more sedate and relaxed activities.

A major attraction for visitors are the majestic humpback whales, which pass through the region en route to Antarctica.

Rainforest, Fraser Island

Shipwreck Survivor

After the wreck of the *Stirling Castle* in 1836, Eliza Fraser was cast ashore on Fraser Island where she lived with the Aboriginies. She was rescued by 'Wandi', the escaped convict, David Bracefell.

i Tourist Information

Fraser Coast & South Burnett Regional Tourism Development Board Ltd
388 Kent St, Maryborough 4650
Ph: (07) 4122 3444
www.info@frasercoast.org.AU

Main Attractions

★ **'The Cathedrals'**
These strikingly coloured sand cliffs at Cathedral Beach on Fraser Island change colour depending on the light available and the time of day.

★ **Eli Creek**
The crystalline Eli Creek is the largest creek on the east coast of Fraser Island, and is ideal for swimming.

★ **Fraser Island**
This island is famous for its coloured sands, vast sand dunes and rainforests.

★ **Great Sandy NP**
Bushwalking tracks offer opportunities to explore the 165 000ha wilderness more closely, with 43 short walks ranging in levels of difficulty.

★ **Hervey Bay Natureworld**
At Natureworld visitors can hand feed native animals and birds, touch koalas and handle a snake.

★ **Maryborough**
Picturesque Maryborough has many historic buildings.

★ **Whale Watching**
A good time to see whales is between August and October, when they return to the Antarctic.

Catamarans, Hervey Bay

Scale 1:720 000

0   20   Kilometres

A   B   C   D   E

1
Sandy Cape Lighthouse
Sandy Cape
Rooney Point
Manann
Beach

2
Bargara
Kellys Beach
Innes Park
Elliott Heads
Riverview
Coonarr
Ngkala Rocks
Marloo Bay
Orchid Beach
Waddy Pt
Middle Rocks
Indian Head
Hervey Bay
Marine Park
Platypus
Wathumba Creek
Bay

Hervey   Bay

3
Burrum Coast National Park
Woodgate
Burrum Coast National Park
Burrum Point
Walkers Point
Buxton
Burrum Heads
Isis Junction
Burrum Coast National Park
The Cathedrals
Lake Bowarraly
Dundubara
Cathedral Beach Resort
The Pinnacles
Great Sandy National Park
Fraser

4
BRUCE
Howard
Toogoom
Craignish
Point Vernon
Hervey Bay
Moon Point
Sandy Point
Big Woody Island
Urangan
"Maheno" Wreck
Yidney Scrub
Island
HWY
Dundowran
Takura
Nikenbah
Walligan
33
Torbanlea
Mangrove Point
River Heads
Kingfisher Bay
Lake Garawongera
Happy Valley
Yidney Rocks
Lake McKenzie
Lake Wabby
Poyungan Rocks
Coral

5
Lake Lenthall
Colton
34
25
Maryborough West
Yengarie
Maryborough
Tinana
86
Sandy Straits
Turkey Island
Great Sandy
Central Station
Ungowa
Eurong
Wanggoolba Ck
Lake Boomanjin
Sea

6
Mungar
Yerra
1
HWY
Poona National Park
Maaroom
Boonooroo
Tuan
Garrys Anchorage
Dilli Village
Conservation
Park
Five
Seventy
Tiaro
39
Tinana
Poona
Tawan
Tinnanbar
60
Hook Point
Inskip Point

7
Netherby
Mt Bauple National Park
Bauple
1
Gundiah
Paterson
Theebine
Glenwood
Miva
36
Wide Bay Military Training Area
Carlo Point
Tin Can Bay
Toolara
13
Cooloola Village
Rainbow Beach
Wide
Bay
Great Poona Sandy Lake
National Park
Double Island Point
Lake Freshwater

8
Gundalda
Neerdie
Kia Ora
Toolara Forest
41
Great Sandy
(Cooloola Section)
National Park
Cooloola Beach
33
Curra
Goomboorian
Rossmount
Wonga Lower
Chatsworth
Wolvi
Coondoo
Neusa Vale
49
BRUCE
River
12
Upper Widgee
Gympie
Glastonbury

Gold Coast

Surfers Paradise

Located only 1hr south of Brisbane and stretching along 70km of coastline lies Australia's biggest, busiest and brassiest tourist resort — the Gold Coast. The narrow coastal strip features high-rise accommodation, eateries, tourist shops, international standard resorts, neon signs and nightclubs parallel to one of Australia's most famous stretches of beach, the aptly named Surfers Paradise.

With its idyllic climate — the annual average temperature is 23°C, with an overwhelming 300 sunny days per year — and the stunning backdrop of the cooler, sub-tropical mountain ranges in the hinterland, it is obvious why the Gold Coast has become so popular with both tourists and retirees. Lying behind the commercial strip, expensive canal developments are testimony to the region's popularity with people who have been attracted by the Gold Coast's sunshine and relaxed, breezy lifestyle.

Boasting 35 beaches and 5 key waterways, the Gold Coast offers every imaginable watersport.

Surfing, windsurfing, boogie boarding, swimming, sailing, scuba diving, jet skiing, fishing and canoeing make this a prime holiday destination for sun and surf fans. A myriad of theme parks jostle for attention with the world-class shops, restaurants and outdoor activities on offer to the 3.9 million plus visitors flocking to the Gold Coast each year. This vibrant resort town does not sleep — a casino, nightclubs and bustling bars provide a hectic nightlife.

ℹ Tourist Information

Gold Coast Tourism Bureau Ltd
Level 2, 64 Ferny Ave, Surfers
Paradise 4217
Ph: (07) 5592 2699

Main Attractions

★ **Burleigh Heads NP**
Several tracks wander through the rainforest, open forest and grassy tussocks of this park.

★ **Coolangatta**
Greenmount Beach at Coolangatta is a delightfully calm beach, with shallow waters making it ideal for families.

★ **Currumbin Sanctuary**
Visitors to this wildlife sanctuary can feed colourful lorikeets, see koalas, visit the snake pit and the animal nursery and ride a mini train.

★ **Dreamworld**
This fantasy adventure park offers rides, a wildlife park, 12 theme 'worlds' and a huge cinema screen.

★ **Sea World**
Sea World features a dolphin show, fun rides and waterski displays.

★ **Surfers Paradise**
With popular beaches and a waterfront promenade, this tourist hotspot is the heart of the Gold Coast.

★ **Warner Bros Movie World**
Billed as 'Hollywood on the Gold Coast', this is a film and TV-based theme park.

Currumbin Sanctuary

Scale 1:258 600

0   10   Kilometres

Beenleigh
Beenleigh Rum Distillery
Stapylton
Windaroo
Yatala
Darlington Park International Raceway
Ormeau
Kingsholme
Woongoolba
Norwell
Pimpama
Willow Vale
Tamborine National Park
Wongawallan
Upper Coomera
Eagle Heights
Heritage Centre
North Tamborine
Guanaba
Mt Tamborine
Clagiraba
Mt Nathan
Nerang
Land
Warfare
Centre
Advancetown
Gilston
Hinze Dam
Tallai
Mudgeeraba
Advancetown Lake
War Museum
Bonsai World
Neranwood
Beechmont
Numinbah Valley
Bonogin
Lamington National Park
Binna Burra Lodge
Springbrook National Park

Long Island
Lagoon Island
Steiglitz
Rocky Point Sugar Mill
Russell Island
North Stradbroke Island
Cobby Cobby Island
Tabby Tabby Island
Eden Island
Crusoe Island
Jumpinpin
Jacobs Well
Kangaroo Island
Southern Moreton Bay Islands National Park
Woogoompah Island
South Stradbroke Island
Conservation Park
Coomera
Sanctuary Cove
Dreamworld
Hope Island
Paradise Point
Hollywell
Coombabah
Movie World
Wet'nWild Water World
Helensvale
Cable Ski World
Runaway Bay
Biggera Waters
Gaven
Arundel
Labrador
The Spit
Ernest
Southport
Main Beach
Sea World
Nerang
Carrara
Bundall
Surfers Paradise
Broadbeach
Jupiters Casino
Mermaid Beach
Merrimac
Mermaid Waters
Robina
Miami
Bond University
Burleigh Heads
Burleigh Waters
David Fleay Wildlife Park
Palm Beach
Elanora
Currumbin
Tallebudgera
Currumbin Bird Sanctuary
Tugun
Currumbin Waters
Bilinga
Tallebudgera Valley
Coolangatta
Coolangatta Airport
Tweed Heads
Olsons Bird Gardens
Queensland
N.S.W.
Piggabeen
Currumbin Rock Pool
Currumbin Valley
Tweed Heads West
Bilambil Heights
Terranora Broadwater
Fingal Head

Coral Sea

Pacific Highway

Rockhampton and Capricorn Coast

Dreamtime Cultural Centre

This centre is located on an important ancient site where Aboriginal people once gathered for tribal meetings. The museum aims to promote understanding of 40 000 years of Aboriginal history.

ℹ Tourist Information

Capricorn Tourism & Development Organisation
Capricorn Information Centre, 'The Spire', Gladstone Rd, Rockhampton 4700
Ph: (07) 4927 2055
Gladstone Area Promotion & Development Ltd
Gladstone Marina Ferry Terminal, Bryan Jordan Dr, Gladstone 4680
Ph: (07) 4972 4000
www.gladstoneregion.org.au

Main Attractions

★ **Curtis Island**
This is a serene island of remote beaches, rugged headlands and a sweeping coastline.
★ **Great Keppel Island**
This lively, sun-drenched island is accessible via ferry from Rosslyn Bay harbour in Yeppoon.
★ **Heritage Village**
An active township museum where visitor's can experience Rockhampton's colourful history.
★ **Koorana Crocoldile Farm**
This farm is famed for breeding estuarine crocodiles.
★ **Lake Awoonga**
This vast and magnificent lake is a haven for waterbirds and a recreation area where watersports can be enjoyed.
★ **Mt Morgan**
Mt Morgan is an old gold mine, which ceased in 1981. It now houses a local history and geology museum.
★ **Olsen's Capricorn Caverns**
A spectacular system of 16 limestone caves. A popular cavern is the Cathedral, which has fantastic natural acoustics and old church pews to sit on.

Straddling the Tropic of Capricorn, the Capricorn Coast is an inviting combination of glorious beaches, raging rivers, intricate reef islands and rugged, sun-bathed outback towns. A contrast of dramatic volcanic outcrops, hazy beaches, vast grazier's estates, estuarine mudflats, scenic headlands and wooded hills, the region is dotted with historic townships whose elegant buildings hint at the wealth of former times.

Also rich in history, the area was once the site of a goldrush and flourished due to its abundant natural resources – from gold and copper mines to vast cattle country properties. Relics provide evidence of this prosperous past.

The region's interesting Aboriginal history is another drawcard for visitors: there are bora rings, museums and artefacts of the Darumbal people, whose territory once stretched from inland Mt Morgan to the Keppel Bay coastline. The region's diverse landscapes offer

Dreamtime Cultural Centre

the delights of surf, land and sea. This is a place where visitors can enjoy some of the world's best fishing and scuba diving, bushwalking, caving, camping and sightseeing.

Auckland Hill Waterfall, Gladstone

Scale 1:1 000 000
0   30 Kilometres

Coral

Sea

Great Barrier Reef
Marine Park

Arthur Point
Stanage

Cape Townshend
Collins Island
Leicester Island
Townshend Island
Broome Head
Reef Point

"Couti Uti"
Torilla
"Waratah"
Shoalwater
Sabine Point
Bay
Pearl Bay
Waginburra
Peninsula
North East Point

"Torilla Plains"
Peninsula
Port Clinton
Cape Clinton

"Rasberry Vale"

"Banksia"
Shoalwater   Bay
Cliff Point
"Manifold"
Cape Manifold

"Rasberry Creek"
Ck
Military   Training
Area
"Brampton Vale"

"Tilpal"
Tilpal Ck
State Forest
Stockyard Point
Boundary

Herbert
Byfield
Byfield National Park
Water Park Point
Corio Bay

Kunwarara
State Forest
"Maryvale"
Keppel Islands National Park
North Keppel Island

BRUCE
Canal Creek"
Cooberrie
Bangalee
Marine

49
Glen Geddes
Rossmoya
Park
Great Keppel Island
Barren Island

Fitzroy
Yeppoon
Boondoola
Yaamba
Mt Etna Caves Nat Park

Garmant
The Caves
41
18
Mulambin
Kinka
Great Keppel Island

HWY
23
Cawarral
Tanby
19
Emu Park

Ridgelands
Pandoin
Mt Arthur Nat Park
Coowonga
Keppel Sands

Dalma
Kawana
Coolcorra
Nankin

Rockhampton
Yeppen
27
Keppel

State Forest
Gracemere
Bay
Cape Keppel

Stanwell
Kabra
Gavial
River
Cattle Point

Warren
56
Midgee
Casuarina Island
Cape Capricorn

Wycarbah
66
Bouldercombe
39
34
Archer
Balaclava Island
Port Alma
Curtis Island National Park

Westwood
17
Bajool
25
Marmor
Curtis
Black Head

CAPRICORN
Mt Morgan
41
Raglan
State Forest
Island

66
Gogango
26
31
Epala
Butlerville
Southend

39
State Forest
Ambrose
Facing

BURNETT
Mt Larcom
Aldoga
32
Gladstone
Island

Dululu
"Prior Vale"
Yarwun
19
58
17

Wowan
34
State Forest
60
State Forest
Tannum Sands

Don
Dee River
BURNETT
Calliope River
60
12
Benaraby

34
45
17
Stirrat
HWY
Calliope
BRUCE

Rannes
Jooro
60
Fry
67
Awonga Dam
Taragoola

8
39
Jambin
Bell Ck
DAWSON
60
Castle Tower National Park
Boynedale

Koonkool
State Forest
State Forest

Sunshine Coast

Northof Brisbane, the 48km coastal stretch bound by Caloundra to the south and Noosa Heads to the north is called the Sunshine Coast. The name conjurs vivid images of the region's glistening surf beaches, expanding to the horizon; its picturesque lakes; unspoilt rainforests; and cliffs of rainbow coloured sand.

The Sunshine Coast offers a quieter, more relaxed alternative to the Gold Coast's excesses. With an average temperature that does not drop below 20°C year-round and a wide choice of accommodation to suit every taste and budget, the Sunshine Coast invites visitors to experience its balmy, laid-back way of life. These once sleepy coastal villages and modest holiday destinations have become glamorous retreats for the glitterati; others retain the charm of quieter times.

Sunshine Plantation

Legend of the Coloured Sands

According to the Kabi Kabi Aboriginies, the coloured sands at Rainbow Beach were formed when the Rainbow Spirit was shattered by a boomerang in a fight over a woman. The pieces fell onto the sand cliffs, colouring them forever.

ℹ Tourist Information

Cooloola Regional Development Bureau
224 Mary St, Gympie 4570
Ph: (07) 5482 5444
www.cooloola.org.au

Main Attractions

★ **The Big Pineapple**
This park is based on a working pineapple and macadamia plantation. The Big Pineapple itself, is a tower with a lookout at the top.
★ **Dolphin Viewing**
Tin Can Bay is a great place for viewing humpback dolphins.
★ **Eumundi Markets**
These popular markets sell all manner of wares.
★ **Maroochydore**
This is a modern beachside town, which features the indoor children's playground called Maze Mania 4 Kids.
★ **Mooloolaba**
This is a thriving beachside town. One of its attractions is Underwater World, which features a seal show.
★ **Noosa**
Noosa offers great beaches, world-class shopping and sophisticated restaurants, surrounded by Noosa NP.
★ **Tewantin**
Tewantin is home to the House of Bottles, constructed from over 35 000 bottles, plus a giant beer bottle built from 17 000 stubbies.

Alexandra Bay

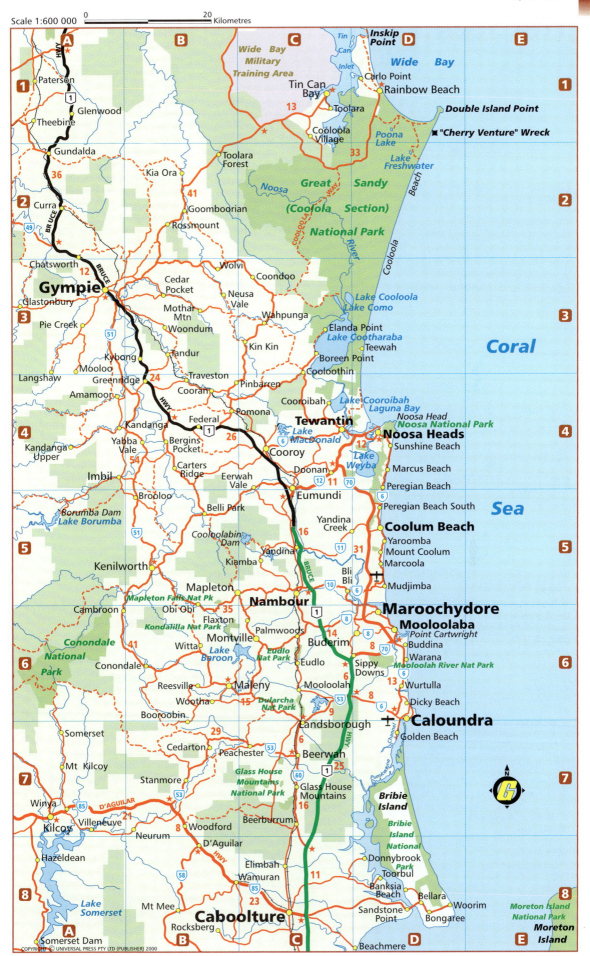

Scale 1:600 000

0   20   Kilometres

Coral

Sea

Wide Bay Military Training Area

Inskip Point

Tin Can Inlet

Wide **Bay**

Carlo Point

Rainbow Beach

Tin Can Bay

13

Toolara

Double Island Point

Coolola Village

Poona Lake

Lake Freshwater

■ "Cherry Venture" Wreck

33

Paterson

Glenwood

Theebine

Gundalda

36

Kia Ora

41

Toolara Forest

Great   Sandy

(Coolola   Section)

National Park

Curra

49

Goomboorian

Rossmount

Chatsworth

12

Gympie

Glastonbury

Cedar Pocket

Wolvi

Coondoo

Neusa Vale

Wahpunga

Lake Cooloola Lake Como

Pie Creek

51

Mothar Mtn

Woondum

Kin Kin

Elanda Point

Lake Cootharaba

Teewah

Kybong

Tandur

Boreen Point

Cooloothin

Mooloo

Greenridge

24

Traveston

Cooran

Pinbarren

Cooroibah

Lake Cooroibah Laguna Bay

Langshaw

Amamoor

Pomona

Cooroibah

Noosa Head

Noosa National Park

Kandanga

Federal

1

Tewantin

Lake MacDonald

Noosa Heads

Kandanga Upper

Yabba Vale

54

Bergins Pocket

26

Cooroy

Doonan

Lake Weyba

Sunshine Beach

Marcus Beach

Imbil

Carters Ridge

Eerwah Vale

12

11

70

Peregian Beach

Brooloo

Belli Park

Eumundi

Peregian Beach South

Sea

Borumba Dam Lake Borumba

51

Cooloolabin Dam

Yandina

16

Yandina Creek

11

31

Coolum Beach

Yaroomba

Mount Coolum

Marcoola

Kenilworth

Kiamba

Bli Bli

10

6

Mudjimba

Mapleton

Mapleton Falls Nat Pk

Obi Obi

35

Nambour

1

8

Maroochydore

Mooloolaba

Point Cartwright

Buddina

Cambroon

Flaxton

Palmwoods

14

Buderim

Kondalilla Nat Park

Montville

Witta

Lake Baroon

Eudlo Nat Park

Eudlo

8

70

Warana

Mooloolah River Nat Park

Conondale

National

Park

41

Conondale

Sippy Downs

6

Reesville

Wootha

Maleny

15

Dularcha Nat Park

Mooloolah

13

Wurtulla

8

Dicky Beach

Booroobin

9

Somerset

29

Cedarton

Peachester

53

Landsborough

6

Caloundra

Golden Beach

Mt Kilcoy

Stanmore

Beerwah

Glass House Mountains National Park

60

25

Winya

85

D'AGUILAR

53

Glass House Mountains

16

Bribie

Island

N

Kilcoy

Villeneuve

21

Neurum

8

Woodford

Beerburrum

Bribie Island National Park

Hazeldean

D'Aguilar

58

Elimbah

Wamuran

11

Donnybrook

Toorbul

Banksia Beach

Bellara

Woorim

Mt Mee

23

Caboolture

Rocksberg

Sandstone Point

Bongaree

Moreton Island National Park

Moreton

Island

Lake Somerset

Somerset Dam

Beachmere

The Scenic Rim

Slow Progress

The cliffs, waterfalls and dense rainforest in the Springbrook area made the going so difficult that in 1863 it took a surveyor 6 months to survey a distance of just 5km from Springbrook to the Numinbah Valley.

Located south of Brisbane, the Scenic Rim's mountain rainforests form a temperate wall between the Darling Downs and the coastal flats of the Gold Coast. A testament to nature's diversity, this lush expanse of sub-tropical rainforest hides wild national parks, breathtaking Lamington Plateau, majestic waterfalls, remote river valleys and fertile farmlands, all with the backdrop of stunning mountain ranges.

A veritable bushwalker's oasis, the Scenic Rim offers much to explore for day trippers, bushwalkers, campers and those with more time. The region combines well trodden paths with more isolated tracks, so visitors have the choice of either joining, or escaping, the crowds. Three mountain groups dominate the landscape, providing the source of the numerous rivers and streams that keep this verdant region well watered.

Tamborine National Park

ℹ️ Tourist Information

Ipswich Visitors and Tourist Information
Cnr Brisbane St and d'Arcy Doyle Pl,
Ipswich 4305
Ph: (07) 3281 0555

Main Attractions

★ **Binna Burra**
Binna Burra is the NE portion of Lamington NP. Binna Burra Lodge is a privately run resort.
★ **Green Mts**
This section of Lamington NP offers panoramic views.
★ **Helidon**
Helidon is renowned for its natural and sandstone spas.
★ **Ipswich**
This is Qld's oldest provincial city.
★ **Lake Apex Fauna Sanctuary**
This sanctuary features over 150 species of animals.
★ **Lamington NP**
This NP protects Australia's largest remaining sub-tropical rainforest.
★ **O'Reilly's Rainforest Guesthouse**
A feature of visiting this guesthouse is the Treetop Walk.
★ **Springbrook NP**
This park showcases the Springbrook Plateau, Mt Cougal and Natural Bridge.
★ **Tamborine Mt**
Mt Tambourine features sweeping views and galleries, cafes and gardens.

Numinbah Valley, Lamington NP

Laidley Creek Valley

This secluded valley encapsulates the Scenic Rim's charms. It boasts a combination of stunning views, rural farmlands and homesteads, and natural attractions. With panoramic vistas of Mt Beau Brummel and Mt Castle, which flank the valley, Schultz's Lookout provides the best vantage point for viewing the valley from above.

Attractions include Grandchester Railway Station, Qld's oldest train station, and Bigge's Camp, marking the original settlement of Grandchester. Bigge's Camp Park has picnic facilities, shelter sheds and monuments to local Aboriginal history, which are dotted among the spotted-gum forest.

In Laidley itself is the Pioneer Village, containing a century old school, blacksmith's shop, police cells, pioneer cottage and stores. Das Neumann Haus is an unusual timber building constructed in 1893 and now houses a museum, arts and crafts shop and a German cafe. Laidley market is held on the last Saturday of each month. Laidley Bakery is housed in a 2-storey brick building that dates back to 1904. Narda Lagoon, set picturesquely opposite the Pioneer Village, provides a welcome habitat for the region's wildlife. Denbigh Farm and Teahouse is an ode to the valley's pioneering past. For a change of pace, the tiny township of Forest Hill features many historic pubs.

Old Bakery, Laidley

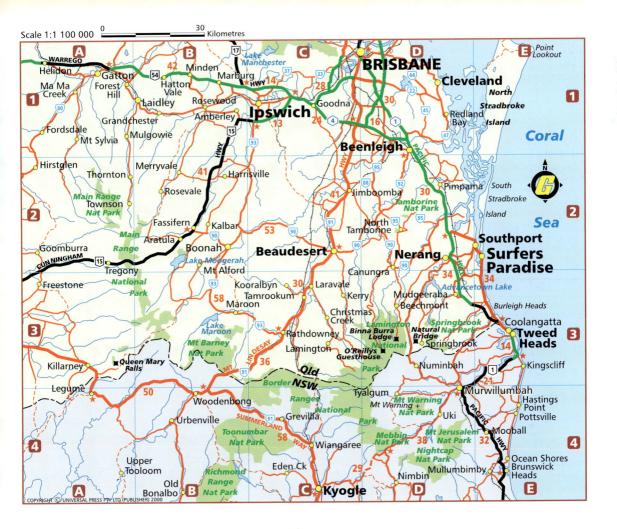

Scale 1:1 100 000

Toowoomba and Eastern Downs

Located 100km inland from Brisbane, the verdant plains of the Darling Downs are dotted with farmhouses, pastures, crops and grazing lands. The rich black soil is a by-product of ancient volcanic activity, as are the mountain peaks of the Great Dividing Ra which form the eastern boundary of this region.

Sprawling from Crows Nest in the north to Dalby in the west, the Eastern Downs offers visitors many diversions. Among the farmlands and cotton country there are also wineries, national parks, quaint villages, bustling townships, grand colonial architecture and remnants of the legends left by Steele Rudd in his stories about the realities of life on the land in his time. The Darling Downs are often associated with the grand old pastoralists of SE Qld. The region is ideal for combining

Jondaryn Woolshed

outdoor activities — bushwalking, camping, cycling, horseriding and golf — with more refined and sedate pursuits such as shopping for antiques, bed and breakfast stays, historical tours, Devonshire teas and exploring rural villages.

Road Rage

The famous transport company Cobb & Co had rules for passengers displayed on notices in its carriages. These included no discussion of bushrangers, accidents, politics or religion, and no snoring or removal of shoes.

ℹ Tourist Information

Toowoomba and Golden West Regional Tourist Association
Downs Business Centre
4 Little St, Toowoomba 4350
Freecall: 1800 688 949

Main Attractions

★ **Bell**
This pretty township is well worth visiting.
★ **Cobb and Co Museum, Toowoomba**
This museum houses many types of horse-drawn carriages.
★ **Crows Nest**
This picturesque town provides an intriguing insight into pioneer life.
★ **Crows Nest NP**
Not far inside the park's entrance lies the renowned Valley of Diamonds, named for the shimmering effect of sunlight streaming onto the rockface of the gorge.
★ **Empire Theatre, Toowoomba**
This heritage listed theatre is the largest regional theatre in Australia.
★ **Jondaryan Woolshed**
This sheep station now features sheepdog and blacksmithing demonstrations.
★ **Rimfire Vineyards and Winery**
This winery is located in Maclagan, 35km north of Jondaryan.
★ **Rudd's Pub, Nobby**
This is a museum and pub at the birthplace of Arthur Hoey Davis, otherwise known as Steele Rudd and the creator of the fabled 'Dad 'n' Dave' tales.

Sunflower field, Toowoomba

Scale 1:857 150

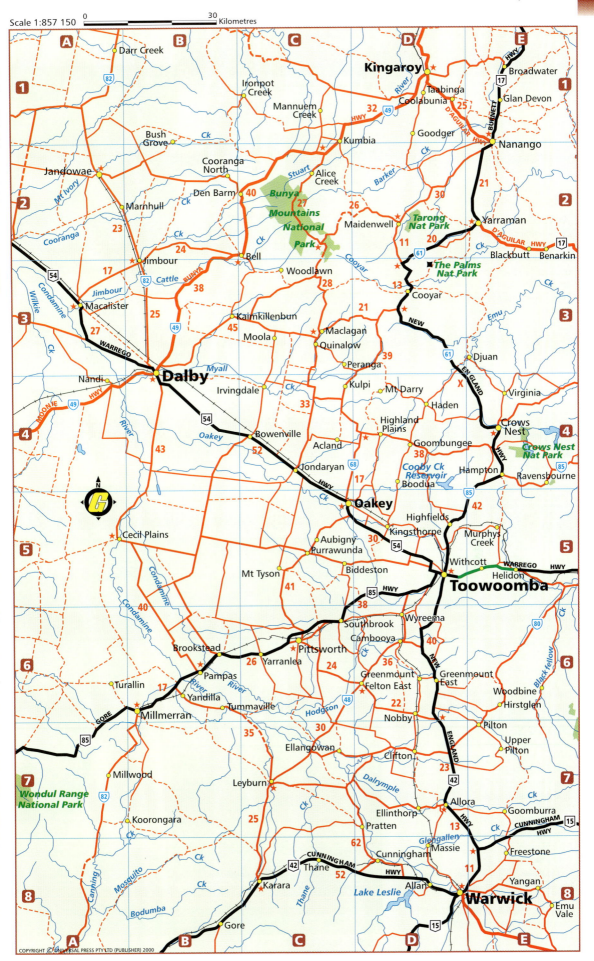

Whitsunday Islands

Airlie Beach

With the exotic perimeters of the Great Barrier Reef and Conway Ranges NP, Airlie Beach is a prime holiday destination. Offers a range of pursuits related to land, sea and air and all styles of accommodation. The perfect base for exploring the region's many diversions.

ℹ️ Tourist Information

Whitsunday Information Centre
Bruce Highway,
Proserpine 4800
Freecall: 1800 801 252
www.whitsundayinformation.com.au

When Captain James Cook entered what is now known as the Whitsunday Passage on Whit Sunday, 3 June 1770, he spent much time surveying the beautiful islands he encountered. Home to 74 tropical islands, only 8 of which are inhabited, the Whitsunday Group lies parallel to the stretch of mainland coast between Mackay and Bowen.

With an estimated 8.25hr sunshine per day and an average yearly temperature of 23°C, the sun-bathed Whitsunday coast is an idyllic retreat. With all you would expect from a tropical island oasis, this region boasts unspoilt coral-fringed islands, pristine beaches, luminescent waters, balmy weather and alluring seaside resorts. Offering consistently perfect conditions for swimming, snorkelling, scuba diving, fishing, sailing and cruising in the warm turquoise waters, the Whitsunday coast is a beach-lovers' dream destination.

Charter and tour companies based on the mainland offer a wide variety of tour and recreation

Airlie Beach

options. Explore the area by boat or seaplane, sightsee from a scenic flight, or try parasailing, bungy jumping and tandem skydiving with the region's spectacular scenery as a backdrop. Excellent fishing opportunities can be found at Funnel Bay, Dingo Beach and Hydeaway Bay. The Whitsundays offer a full range of accommodation to suit all tastes and budgets, from a camping haven on a deserted island to a suite in a luxurious five-star resort.

Main Attractions

★ **Barefoot Bushman's Wildlife Park**
This park houses an assortment of over 700 native animals.
★ **Brampton Island**
This is a resort island.
★ **Conway Range NP**
Behind the Whitsunday's stretch of coastal townships, this national park has lush rainforest and is worth visiting.
★ **Daydream Island**
This is a resort island.
★ **Hamilton Island**
The resort is the key landmark.
★ **Hayman Island**
This is a resort island.
★ **Lindeman Island**
This island is home to Australia's first Club Med resort.
★ **South Long Island**
Renowned as the Great Barrier Reef's most natural and adventurous island, this is a secluded retreat.
★ **South Molle Island**
With unspoilt NP fringed by scenic beaches, this island is great for family groups.

Sailing, Shute Island

Scale 1:550 000

0   20   Kilometres

Coral

George Point

Armit Island

Grassy Island

Earlando

Dryander

National

Grimston Point

Park

Pioneer Bay

Airlie Beach

Cannonvale

Nth Molle Island

Pioneer Point

Resort Sth Molle Island

Cid Island

11

Shutehaven

Strathdickie

Sugarloaf

24

Proserpine

Mt Conway +333

Conway

National

Mt Proserpine +444

Wilson

Conway

Long Island

Resort

Dent Island

Hayman Island

Resort

Pinnacle Point

Hook Peak +459

Hook Island

Underwater Observatory

Border Island

Whitsunday Islands

WHITSUNDAY GROUP

Mt Robinson +390

Captain Cook Memorial

National Park

Harold Island

Edward Island

Whitsunday Island

Haselwood Island

Lupton Island

Pioneer Bay

Whitsunday Craig +354

Craig Point

Resort Hamilton Island

Sea

Great Barrier Reef Marine Park

Central Section

Park

Long Island Sound

Round Head

Genesta Bay

Pentecost Island

Maher Island

Lindeman Island

LINDEMAN GROUP

Resort

Mansell Island

Cape Conway

Kennedy Sound

Shaw Island

Lindeman Islands National Park

Thomas Island

Channel

Repulse Bay

Lethebrook

38

Thoopara

Repulse Islands National Park

Repulse Islands

Cumberland

Silversmith Island

Laguna Quays

Midge Point

Midge Point

Blacksmith Island

Hammer Island

SIR JAMES SMITH GROUP

Smith Islands National Park

Goldsmith Island

Linne Island

Tinsmith Island

Bloomsbury

Tonga Mtn +233

Hillsborough

Brampton Island National Park

Carlisle Island

Resort Brampton Island

BRUCE

31

Yalboroo

Mt Beatrice National Park

1

Wagoora

Pindi Pindi

Calen

Wootaroo (St Helens)

Newry Islands National Park

Newry Island

Resort

Port Newry

Halliday Bay

Ball Bay

Cape Hillsborough

Great Barrier Reef Marine Park

Mackay-Capricorn Section

Channel

Mt Consuelo +717

Eungella

National

Mt William +1259

Park

9

18

Mt Ossa

Seaforth

Cape Hillsborough National Park

Andrews Point

Sand Bay

22

Mt Jukes East

Shoal Point

Mt Charlton

18

Kuttabul

Beallah

Blackwood National Park

Habana

Bucasia

Eimeo

Finch Hatton

Mt Martin

Aminunga

7 HWY

1

9

Farliegh

14

12

Slade Point

Andergrove

Mackay Harbour

21

Glenella

North Mackay

Pinnacle

Gargett

27

10

Marian

25

Pioneer

Playstowe

DOWNS

HWY

River

Mackay

Walkerston

Mirani

Creek

Teemburra Dam

Kinchant Dam

PEAK

70

1

South Australia

SA: The Festival State

- Area = 984 381sq km
- Occupies 12.5% of Australia
- Length of coast = 3540km

Sturt's Desert Pea

Wombat

ℹ️ Tourist Information

South Australian Travel Centre
18 King William St, Adelaide 5000
Freecall: 1300 655 276
www.visit-southaustralia.com.au

Located in Australia's southern central section, SA is in the unique position of bordering all the country's mainland states. Its predominantly flat, low-lying terrain consists of large tracts of desert, broken by the Flinders and Musgrave Ra, and gigantic saline lakes.

South Australia can be divided into 12 distinct regions, including the Barossa Valley, the South-East, Kangaroo Island, Peninsula Country, the Flinders Ranges, the Riverland and Outback regions.

Although SA is the continent's driest state, the SE corner is well watered by the Murray River. This area offers renowned regional produce including, cheeses, fruit and world class wines.

Much of the State's population live in its capital city, Adelaide. The majority of the population live within the SE corner due to the climate and conditions being moderate in comparison to the rest of the State.

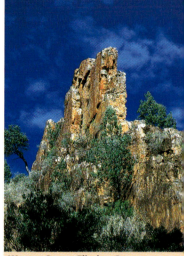
Warren Gorge, Flinders Ranges

Despite its considerable size, some of its varied attractions are within a 3 hour radius of Adelaide.

While the outback is quite a distance from Adelaide, it still has much to offer. Far from the centres of civilization are the opal fields of Coober Pedy and Andamooka, as well as Lake Eyre, Australia's largest lake.

Main Attractions

★ **Adelaide**
Adelaide has become known for its thriving cultural scene, excellent restaurants and fine wines.

★ **Barossa Valley**
The Barossa Valley has long been reputed as one of Australia's premier wine-producing regions.

★ **Fleurieu Peninsula**
This striking peninsula features a string of fine beaches dotting Gulf St Vincent's pretty coastline.

★ **Flinders Ranges**
The distinctive landforms of the Flinders Ranges consist of colourful cliffs, granite peaks and deep gorges.

★ **Kangaroo Island**
This sparsely populated island offers secluded camping spots, bushwalking tracks, scenic coastal areas and reef diving sites.

★ **Mt Gambier**
This coastal region offers 35 national and conservation parks.

★ **Riverland**
This region is dominated by the Murray River.

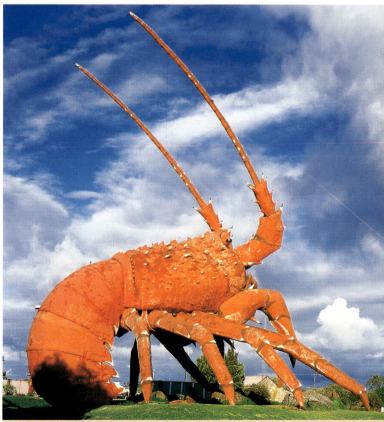
The Big Lobster, Kingston

South Australia Key Map and Distance Chart

All distances shown in the chart below have been measured over highways and major roads, not necessarily by the shortest route.

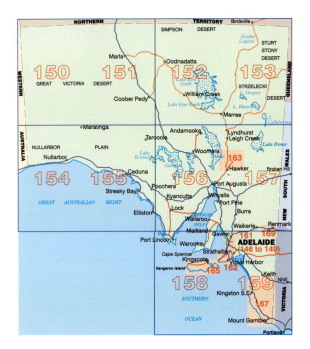

City Map
Adelaide, page 145

Suburban Maps
Adelaide, pages 146 to 149

State Maps
pages 150 to 159

Region Maps

Barossa Valley, page 161

Fleurieu Peninsula, page 162

Flinders Ranges, page 163

Kangaroo Island, page 165

Mt Gambier District, page 167

Riverland, page 169

Approximate Distance	Adelaide	Bordertown	Broken Hill NSW	Ceduna	Coober Pedy	Eucla WA	Innamincka	Kulgera NT	Leigh Creek	Mount Gambier	Murray Bridge	Peterborough	Pinnaroo	Port Augusta	Port Lincoln	Port Pirie	Renmark	Streaky Bay	Whyalla	Woomera
Adelaide		267	514	769	837	1256	1033	1251	548	435	74	261	236	305	642	223	247	695	378	484
Bordertown	267		781	1036	1104	1523	1300	1518	815	183	193	528	132	572	909	490	279	962	645	751
Broken Hill NSW	514	781		878	946	1365	1064	1360	579	870	588	281	674	414	751	387	424	804	487	593
Ceduna	769	1036	878		996	487	1213	1410	728	1204	843	597	972	464	404	546	861	107	449	643
Coober Pedy	837	1104	946	996		1483	896	414	487	1272	911	665	1040	532	869	614	923	922	605	369
Eucla WA	1256	1523	1365	487	1483		1700	1897	1215	1691	1330	1084	1459	951	891	1033	1392	594	936	1130
Innamincka	1033	1300	1064	1213	896	1700		1310	485	1468	1107	783	1204	749	1086	817	1087	1139	822	789
Kulgera NT	1251	1518	1360	1410	414	1897	1310		901	1686	1325	1079	1454	946	1283	1028	1337	1336	1019	783
Leigh Creek	548	815	579	728	487	1215	485	901		983	622	298	719	264	601	332	602	654	437	380
Mount Gambier	435	183	870	1204	1272	1691	1468	1686	983		361	696	315	740	1077	658	462	1130	813	919
Murray Bridge	74	193	588	843	911	1330	1107	1325	622	361		335	162	379	716	297	207	769	452	558
Peterborough	261	528	281	597	665	1084	783	1079	298	696	335		421	133	470	106	300	523	206	312
Pinnaroo	236	132	674	972	1040	1459	1204	1454	719	315	162	421		508	845	437	147	898	581	687
Port Augusta	305	572	414	464	532	951	749	946	264	740	379	133	508		337	82	391	390	73	179
Port Lincoln	642	909	751	404	869	891	1086	1283	601	1077	716	470	845	337		419	724	294	264	420
Port Pirie	223	490	387	546	614	1033	817	1028	332	658	297	106	437	82	419		316	472	155	261
Renmark	247	279	424	861	923	1392	1087	1337	602	462	207	300	147	391	724	316		777	460	566
Streaky Bay	695	962	804	107	922	594	1139	1336	654	1130	769	523	898	390	294	472	777		375	569
Whyalla	378	645	487	449	605	936	822	1019	437	813	452	206	581	73	264	155	460	375		252
Woomera	484	751	593	643	369	1130	789	783	380	919	558	312	687	179	420	261	566	569	252	

Adelaide

Adelaide
Convention & Tourism Authority
A U S T R A L I A

As Australia's first planned city for free settlers, Adelaide has no convict history — settlement began due to overcrowding and unemployment in NSW. In 1831, the State initially began as a settlement driven by private enterprise and managed by the South Australia Company before it was officially declared a State in 1836.

Named after Queen Adelaide, the wife of King William IV, Adelaide's affluent past is evident in its glorious architecture. Today it retains the grandeur of its gracious 18th century buildings, interspersed with those built in the Italian Renaissance style with goldrush wealth. The tree-lined North Terrace is an excellent example – it is the site of many of the city's finest civic and civilian buildings.

Housing a population of almost one million residents, this planned city is easy to navigate due to its gridiron design. Its prime position on the banks of the picturesque Torrens River, among superb gardens with the blue haze of the Adelaide Hills as a backdrop, lends the city a relaxed ambience. Adelaide experiences 4 distinctly different

HMS 'Buffalo', Glenelg

seasons, making it a charming place to visit at any time of the year.

Its long history of immigration – initially Europeans predominantly from Great Britain, Germany, Eastern and Southern Europe, and more recently from places as diverse as Asia and Africa – has influenced the city's development. The cafe culture has long been part of Adelaide life, while the ethnic diversity is reflected in the city's markets and restaurant scene. Now Adelaide is known more for its restaurants, wines and festivals than it is for its churches.

Tourist Information
South Australian Travel Centre
18 King William St, Adelaide 5000
Freecall: 1300 655 276
www.visit-southaustralia.com.au

Main Attractions
★ **Adelaide Botanic Gardens**
These gardens are very popular and house the oldest glasshouse in an Australian botanic garden.
★ **Adelaide Festival Centre**
This centre offers free concerts on Sundays during summer.
★ **Art Gallery of South Australia**
This is one of Australia's oldest galleries.
★ **Central Market**
The markets are a culinary adventure and reflect Adelaide's diverse ethnic population.
★ **Glenelg**
Glenelg Beach is the most popular of Adelaide's long, sandy beaches.
★ **Gouger St**
Gouger St is one of Adelaide's premier eat streets, featuring food from around the world.
★ **Rundle Mall**
The retail hub of Adelaide is situated in Rundle Mall.
★ **South Australian Museum**
This museum features a fascinating collection of Aboriginal artifacts.

Adelaide Festival Centre

Places of Interest

① Adelaide Casino **C4**
② Adelaide Town Hall **C5**
③ Adelaide Zoo **D3**
④ Ayers House **D4**
⑤ Edmund Wright House **C5**
⑥ Elder Hall **C4**
⑦ Government House **C4**
⑧ Montefiore Hill **B3**

⑨ Mortlock Library of South Australiana **C4**
⑩ Museum of Exploration, Surveying and Land Heritage **C5**
⑪ Old Adelaide Gaol **A4**
⑫ Parliament House & Old Parliament House **C4**
⑬ Scots Church **C4**

Scale 1:30 000

Scale 1:160 000

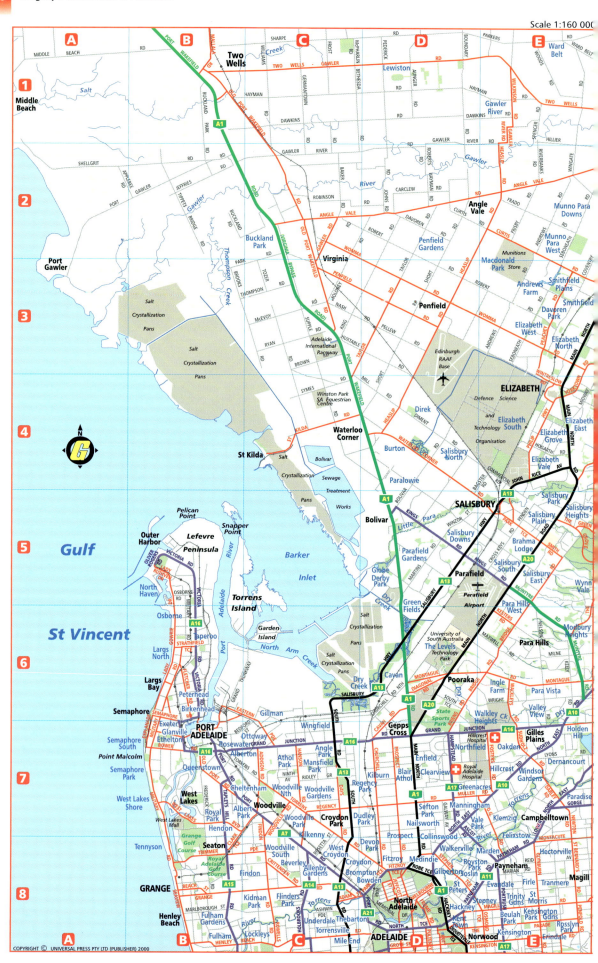

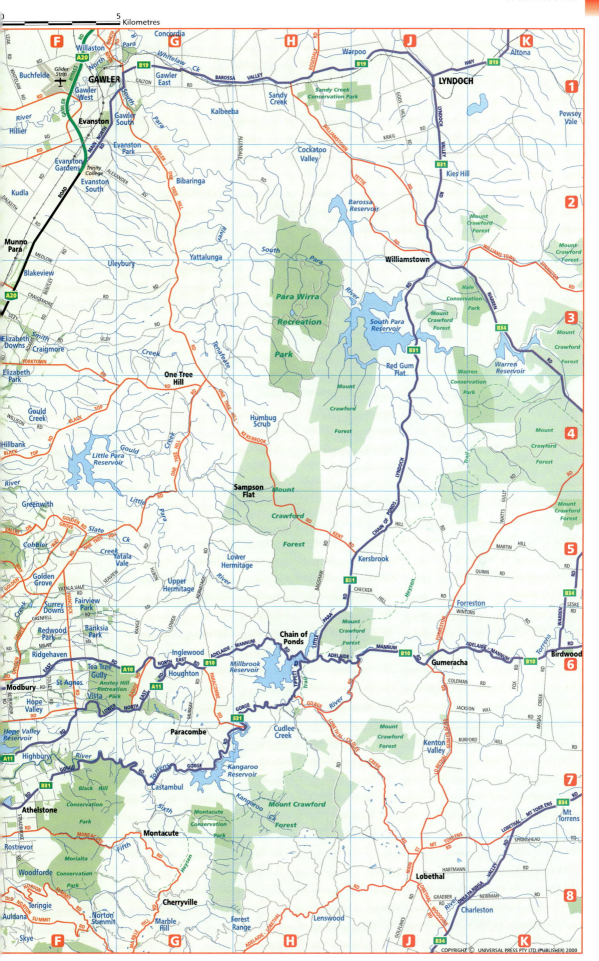

Scale 1:160 00

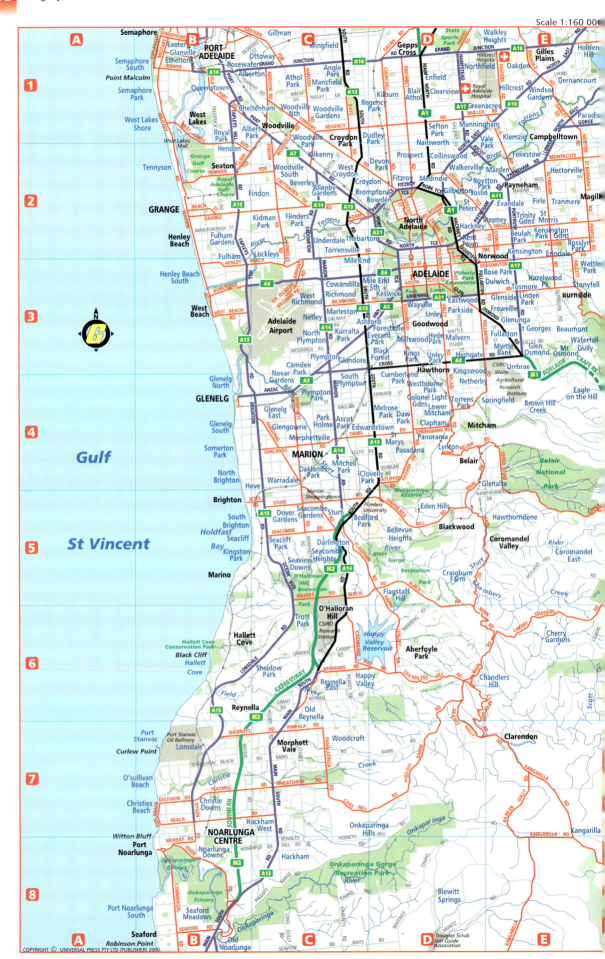

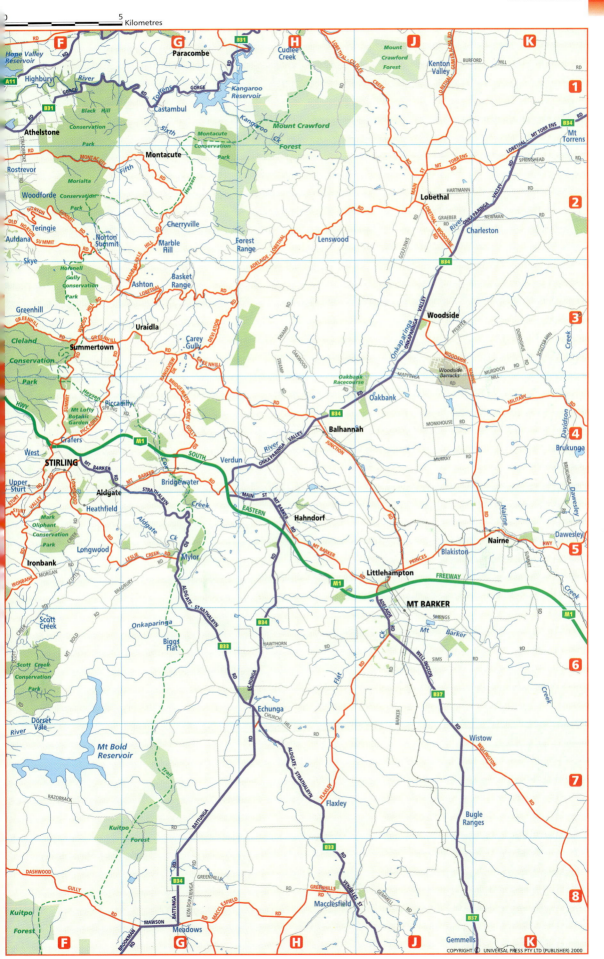

Scale 1:1 995 000

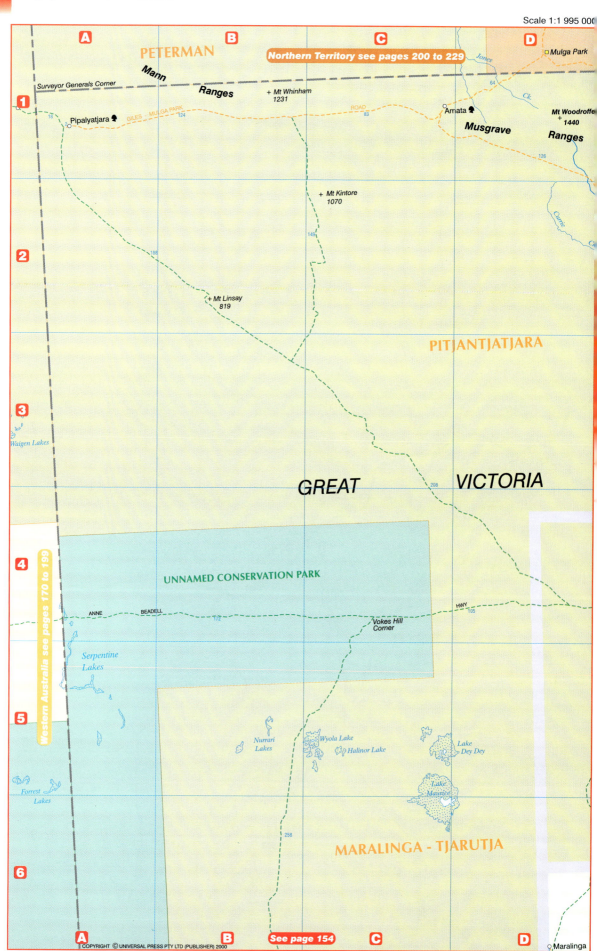

A · B · C · D

PETERMAN

Mann · Ranges

Northern Territory see pages 200 to 229

Surveyor Generals Corner

+ Mt Whinham 1231

Mulga Park

GILES - MULGA PARK

ROAD

Pipalyatjara

Amata

Mt Woodroffe + 1440

Musgrave · Ranges

+ Mt Kintore 1070

+ Mt Linsay 819

PITJANTJATJARA

Waigen Lakes

GREAT · VICTORIA

Western Australia see pages 170 to 199

UNNAMED CONSERVATION PARK

ANNE · BEADELL

HWY

Vokes Hill Corner

Serpentine Lakes

Nurrari Lakes

Wyola Lake

Halinor Lake

Lake Dey Dey

Forrest Lakes

Lake Maurice

MARALINGA - TJARUTJA

A · B · **See page 154** · C · D

Maralinga

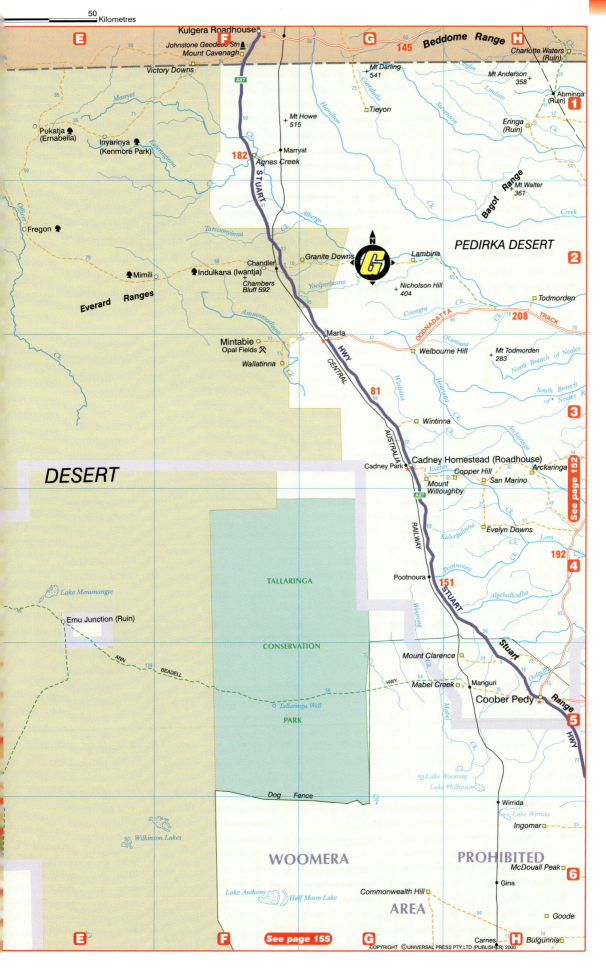

50 Kilometres

COPYRIGHT ©UNIVERSAL PRESS PTY LTD (PUBLISHER) 2000

Scale 1:1 995 000

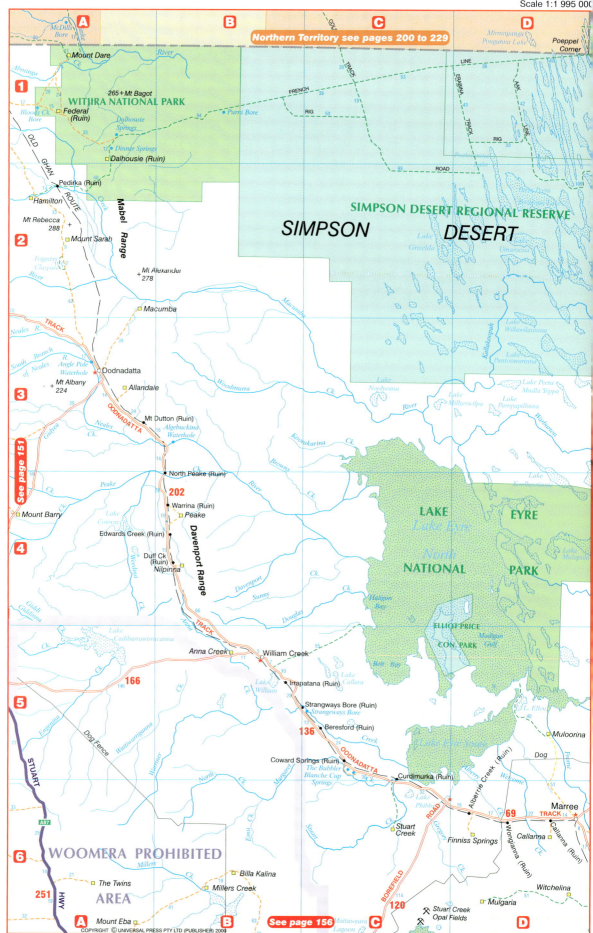

Northern Territory see pages 200 to 229

SIMPSON DESERT REGIONAL RESERVE

SIMPSON DESERT

WITJIRA NATIONAL PARK

Mount Dare
265 + Mt Bagot
Federal (Ruin)
Dalhousie Springs
Dinner Springs
Dalhousie (Ruin)
Pedirka (Ruin)
Hamilton
Mt Rebecca 288
Mount Sarah
Mt Alexander 278
Macumba

Oodnadatta
Allandale
Mt Dutton (Ruin)
Algebuckina Waterhole

North Peake (Ruin)
202
Warrina (Ruin)
Peake
Mount Barry
Edwards Creek (Ruin)
Duff Ck (Ruin)
Nilpinna

LAKE EYRE
Lake Eyre

EYRE

NATIONAL

PARK

North

ELLIOT PRICE CON. PARK

Halligan Bay

Belt Bay

Anna Creek
William Creek
Irrapatana (Ruin)
Lake William
Lake Callara

166

Strangways Bore (Ruin)
Strangeways Bore
136
Beresford (Ruin)

Muloorina

Coward Springs (Ruin)
The Bubbler Blanche Cup Springs
Curdimurka (Ruin)
Lake Phibbs
Alberrie Creek (Ruin)
Wonganna (Ruin)
Callanna
69
Marree
Callanna (Ruin)
Finniss Springs

STUART HWY

Dog Fence

WOOMERA PROHIBITED

AREA

Stuart Creek

BOREFIELD ROAD

The Twins
Billa Kalina
251
Millers Creek

Stuart Creek Opal Fields
120

Witchelina
Mulgaria

See page 151

See page 156

Mount Eba

Poeppel Corner

Mount Dare
McDills Bore

A   B   C   D

1   2   3   4   5   6

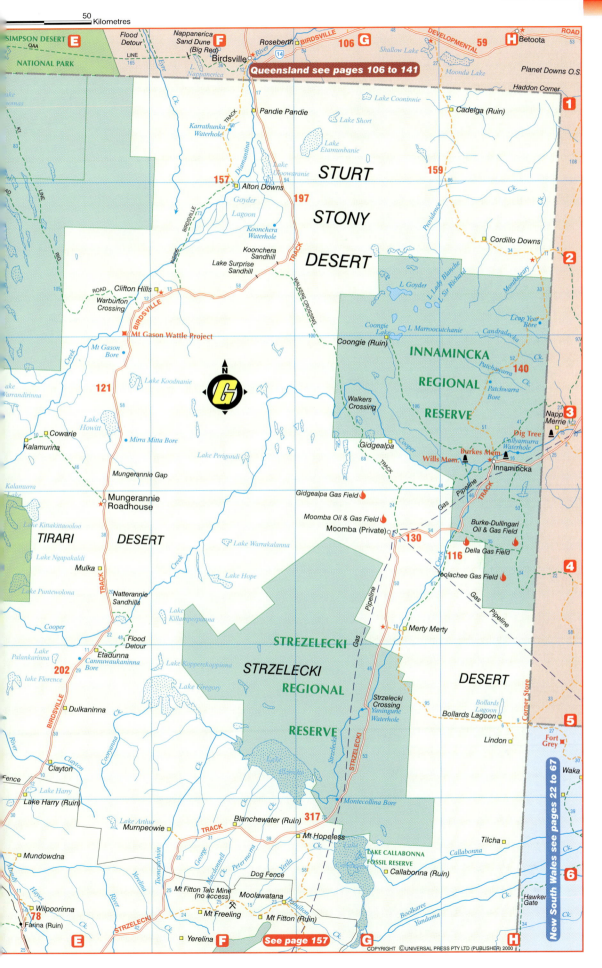

50 Kilometres

SIMPSON DESERT **E**
QAA
NATIONAL PARK

Flood Detour

Nappanerica Sand Dune (Big Red) **F**
Roseberth **BIRDSVILLE G** 106

DEVELOPMENTAL 59 **H** Betoota ROAD

Birdsville
L. Nappanerica

Queensland see pages 106 to 141

Shallow Lake
Moonda Lake
Planet Downs O.S
Haddon Corner

Pandie Pandie
Lake Cooninnie
Cadelga (Ruin) **1**

Karrathunka Waterhole
Lake Short

Lake Etamunbanie

STURT

157
Alton Downs
159

197
Goyder Lagoon
Koonchera Waterhole

STONY

Cordillo Downs **2**

Koonchera Sandhill
Lake Surprise Sandhill

DESERT

L Goyder
L Lady Blanche
L Sir Richard
Monkeleary

Clifton Hills
Warburton Crossing

Coongie Lake
L. Marroocutchanie
Leap Year Bore
Candradecka

Mt Gason Wattle Project

Coongie (Ruin)

INNAMINCKA

Patchawarra
140
Patchwarra Bore

Mt Gason Bore

Walkers Crossing

REGIONAL

Napp Merrie **3**

121
Lake Koodnanie
Lake Howitt
58

Walkers Crossing

RESERVE

Dig Tree
Cullyamurra Waterhole

Cowarie
Kalamurina
Mirra Mitta Bore

Gidgealpa

Cooper

Wills Mem.
Burkes Mem
Innamincka

Lake Perigundi

Gidgealpa Gas Field

Gas Pipeline
46

Mungerannie Gap

Moomba Oil & Gas Field
Moomba (Private)

130

Burke-Dullingari Oil & Gas Field
Della Gas Field

Kalamurra

Mungerannie Roadhouse

TIRARI **DESERT**
Lake Kittakittaooloo
Lake Ngapakaldi

Lake Warrakalanna

116
Toolachee Gas Field **4**

Mulka

Lake Hope

Gas Pipeline

Natterannie Sandhills

Lake Killamperpunna

Merty Merty

Cooper
Lake Puntewolona

Flood Detour

Lake Palankarinna
lake Florence
202
Etadunna
Cannuwaukaninna Bore

Lake Kopperekoppunna

Lake Gregory

STRZELECKI

Corner Store

DESERT

Pipeline

45

Bollards Lagoon
Bollards Lagoon **5**

Dulkaninna

STRZELECKI

Strzelecki Crossing
Yaningurie Waterhole
95

Lindon

Fort Grey

REGIONAL

Clayton
Lake Harry

RESERVE

Waka

Fence
Lake Harry (Ruin)

Lake Arthur

Montecollina Bore

Murnpeowie
Blanchewater (Ruin)
317
Mt Hopeless

Tilcha

Mundowdna

Dog Fence
LAKE CALLABONNA FOSSIL RESERVE
Callabonna (Ruin)

Lake Callabonna

Wilpoorinna
Mt Fitton Talc Mine (no access)
Moolawatana

Hawker Gate **6**

78
Farina (Ruin)
Mt Freeling
Mt Fitton (Ruin)

STRZELECKI

E
Yerelina
F
See page 157
G
H

COPYRIGHT © UNIVERSAL PRESS PTY LTD (PUBLISHER) 2000

New South Wales see pages 22 to 67

Scale 1:1 995 0

Western Australia see pages 170 to 199

See page 150

Maraling

AUSTRALIAN

TRANS   Cook

NULLARBOR REGIONAL RESERVE

PLAIN

NULLARBOR

Ivy Tank Motel

EYRE

143   A1

NULLARBOR NATIONAL PARK

Nullarbor
Roadhouse

Koonalda

Head
of Bight

193

HWY   A1

Eucla   Border Village

EYRE   *Eucla Telegraph Station (ruin)*

GREAT AUSTRALIAN BIGHT MARINE PARK

GREAT
AUSTRALIAN
BIGH

GREAT   *AUSTRALIAN*

SOUTHERN

50 Kilometres

See page 151

E   F   G   H

Goode

WOOMERA   PROHIBITED   AREA

Carnes   Bulgunnia

Dog Fence

Mulgathing

1

Malbooma   Tarcoola

Idea   RAILWAY

Ferguson

Mt Finke
349 +

Lake Evrard

YELLABINNA REGIONAL RESERVE

2

Yalata
Yalata Roadhouse

YUMBARRA
C.R.

YUMBARRA CONSERVATION PARK

Dog   Fence

HWY

Nundroo

81   Bookabie

WAHGUNYAH
C.R.

Glen Boree

Coorabie   FOWLERS BAY

Penong   EYRE

Kalanbi

O.T.C. Earth Station

PUREBA
CONSERVATION

Kondoolka

3

ARINE
PARK

Fowlers Bay

Fowlers
Bay

CHADINGA
C.R.

A1

70

Koonibba

Wandana

PARK

NUNNYAH
C.R.

Cape Adieu

Point
Fowler

Point Sinclair

Lake
Macdonnell

Maltee

KOOLGERA
C.R.

Cape Nuyts

Denial Bay

Ceduna

Mudamuckla
Puntabie

Nunjikompita

POINT BELL C.P.
Point Bell

Point Peter
St Peter I.

Laura Bay

FLINDERS

90

HWY

Pimbaacia

Wirrulla

Denial
Bay

Carawa

Petina

Yantanabie

NUYTS ARCHIPELAGO
C.P.

Goat I.

Eyre I.

Smoky Bay

107

45

A1

Evans I.

Smoky
Bay

Haslam

Poochera

Nuyts Archipelago

Franklin Is.

Point Brown

ACKAMAN CREEK
C.P.

Chilpanunda

Cungena

4

Isles of
St Francis

St Francis I.
Masillion I.

Streaky
Bay

B100

61

Chandada
Inkster

Karcultab

ISLES OF
SAINT FRANCIS
C.P.

Cape Bauer

Gibson Pen.

Streaky Bay

Corvisart
Bay

BIGHT

Point Westhall

Yanerbie Beach

CALPATANNA
WATERHOLE
C.P.

62

HWY

Colley

KULLIPARU
C.P.

Sceale Bay
Cape Blanche

Calca

Port Kenny

KULLIPARU
C.P.

Calca Pen.

Cape Radstock

Baird Bay

VENUS BAY C.P.

Venus Bay
Point
Weyland

Talia

5

Anxious
Bay

66

LAKE NEWLAND C.P.

Colton

Waldegrave Is
Cape Finniss

Elliston

Flinders I.

Investigator Group

INVESTIGATOR GROUP C.P.

Pearson Isles

OCEAN

6

E   F   G   H

See page 156

Scale 1:1 995 0

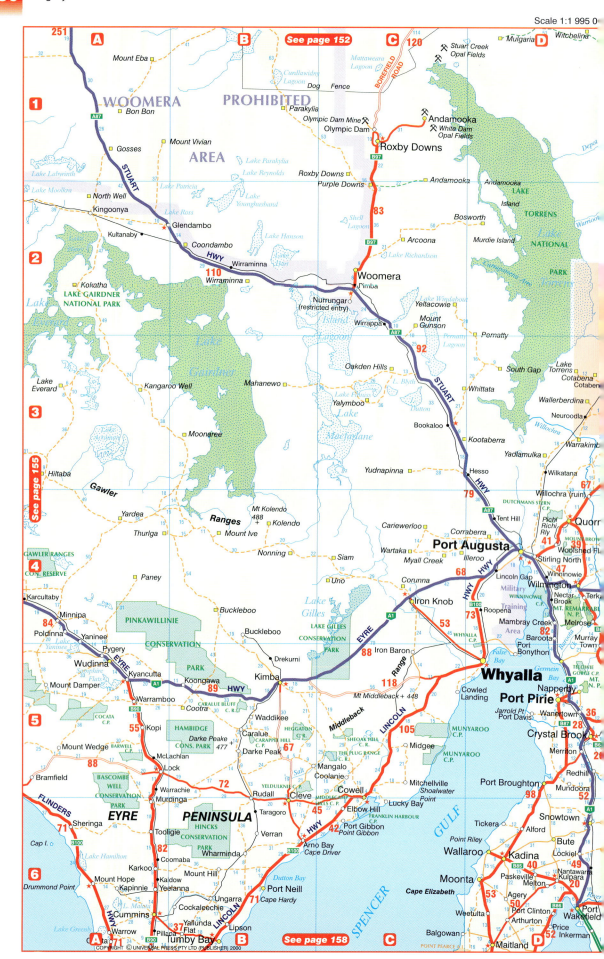

See page 152

See page 155

See page 158

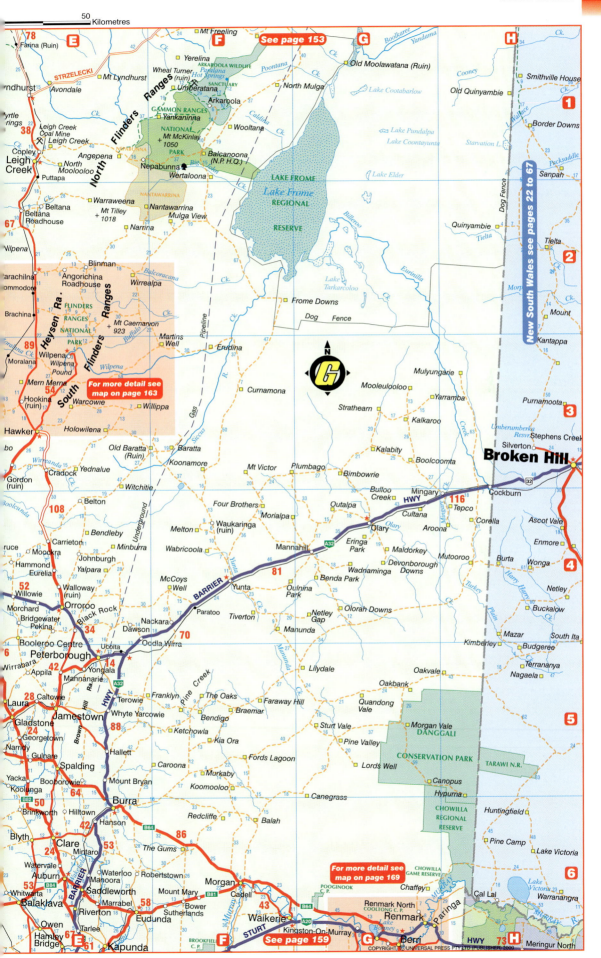

Scale 1:1995 0

See page 156

For more detail see map on pages 146 - 14

For more detail see map on page 165

A Cummins
Yallunda
Flat
Pillana
B Lipson
Tumby Bay
Warrow
Coulta **71**
Edillilie **42**
Koppio
White Flat
Wanilla
Pearlah
46
Louth Bay
Poonindie
North Shields
Coffin Bay
Pen.
Coffin Bay
Point Sir Isaac
Wangary
Coffin Bay
Coomunga
Point Avoid
22
Port Lincoln
Boston I.
Cape Donington
Jussieu
LINCOLN
N.P.
Taylor I.
Cape Carnot
Sleaford Bay
Pen.
Linguanea I.
West Point
Williams I.
Thistle I.
Waterhouse Point
Gambier Is.
GAMBIER ISLANDS C.P.
Neptune Is.
NEPTUNE ISLANDS C.P.
Reevesby I.
SIR JOSEPH BANKS
Sir Joseph Banks Group
C.P.
Spilsby I.

SPENCER

C

West Cape
INNES N.P.
Inneston
Marion Bay
Stenhouse Bay
Cape Spencer
WARRENBEN C.P.
53

D
Weetulta
Arthurton
Port Clinton
Port
Wakefield
Price
52
Balgowan
Maitland
POINT PEARCE
South Kilkerran
Ardrossan
Port Victoria
Wardang I.
Urania
Sandilands
YORKE
PENINSULA
47 48
Pine Point
Black Pt
Port Rickaby
Hardwick Bay
Cutramulka
Port Julia
Bluff Beach
Minlaton
78
Port Vincent
Brentwood
31
Hardwicke Bay
Stansbury
Corny Point
Corny Point
Warooka
43
Coobowie
Yorketown
36
Edithburgh
Sturt Bay
Troubridge Point
GULF ST VINCENT

INVESTIGATOR   *STRAIT*

Normanville
North Cape
Rapid Bay
77
Stokes Bay
Kingscote
Cape Jervis
54
WESTERN RIVER W.A.
Cygnet River
Nepean Bay
Penneshaw
Cape Borda
CAPE TORRENS W.A.
Pamdana
American River
DUDLEY
C.P.
Cape
Willoughby
RAVINE DES CASOARS
FLINDERS
CHASE
N.P.
KANGAROO ISLAND
B23
Cape
Hart
WILDERNESS AREA
SEAL BAY
C.P.
CAPE GANTHEAUME
C.P.
D'Estree Bay
Rocky River
FLINDERS
CHASE
W.A.
Vivonne Bay
Cape Du Couedic
FLINDERS
CHASE
N.P.
CAPE BOUGER
W.A.
VIVONNE BAY
C.P.
CAPE GANTHEAUME
W.A.
Cape Gantheaume

SOUTHERN

50 Kilometres

For more detail see map on page 161

See page 157

For more detail see map on page 169

For more detail see map on page 162

For more detail see map on page 167

MURRAY - SUNSET NATIONAL PARK

OCEAN

Barossa Valley

Barossa Festivals

German influence remains with some of the Barossa festivals. The biennial Vintage Festival, held from Easter Monday during years of odd numbers, attracts more than 100 000 people. Other festivals include Essenfest (March), Melodienacht (May) and the Barossa Classic Gourmet Weekend (August).

ℹ Tourist Information

Barossa Wine & Visitor Centre
66–68 Murray St, Tanunda 5352
Ph: (08) 8563 0600
Freecall: 1800 812 662
www.barossa-region.org

Main Attractions

★ **Angaston**
This picturesque town is home to some of the Barossa's oldest winemakers.
★ **Bethany Wines**
This hillside winery, located in an old quarry, produces wine and port.
★ **Chateau Yaldara Estate**
Specialising in sweet and sparkling European–style wines, this winery is housed in a 19th century flourmill.
★ **Lyndoch**
One of SA's oldest towns, Lyndoch was settled in 1839. Although wine has always been produced here, wheat was the primary crop until 1896.
★ **Penfolds Wines**
Established in 1844, Penfolds is the Barossa's largest winery, showcasing some of Australia's best known wines.
★ **Seppeltsfield**
Founded in 1851, this winery is the Barossa's most spectacular. An avenue of date palms leads to the Seppelt family mausoleum.
★ **Wolf Blass Wines Map:**
This winery produces prize–winning wines of consistent quality.

Although small, the Barossa Valley is Australia's best known wine-growing area and a major tourist attraction. Thousands of visitors make the pilgrimage every year, with the main aim of touring the vineyards, tasting the wines and making cellar door purchases.

As the German immigrants who initially settled the region discovered in colonial times, the Barossa's Mediterranean-like climate and differing soil types make it an ideal place for growing diverse varieties of grapes, producing consistently high quality wines.

In 1847 the valley's first vines were planted at the Orlando vineyards. This compact region is in a prime position for producing an array of wines, ranging from shiraz and chardonnay to excellent riesling and pinot noir.

While the Barossa Valley boasts over 50 wineries, from household names such as Penfolds to boutique wineries like Charles Melton and Grant Burge Wines, the region also offers lots of other attractions, including its history and scenic beauty. The valley is dotted with small Lutheran

Chateau Yaldara, Lyndoch

churches, another legacy of the German settlers escaping religious persecution, as well as quaint townships featuring rural trappings such as antique stores, bakeries and old-fashioned pubs.

The Barossa's close proximity to Adelaide makes it an ideal day trip destination, especially as its attractions are also within a relatively limited area. With a range of great accommodation options available, it is also an excellent place to explore at leisure.

Seppelt Winery

Scale 1:120 000

0   5   Kilometres

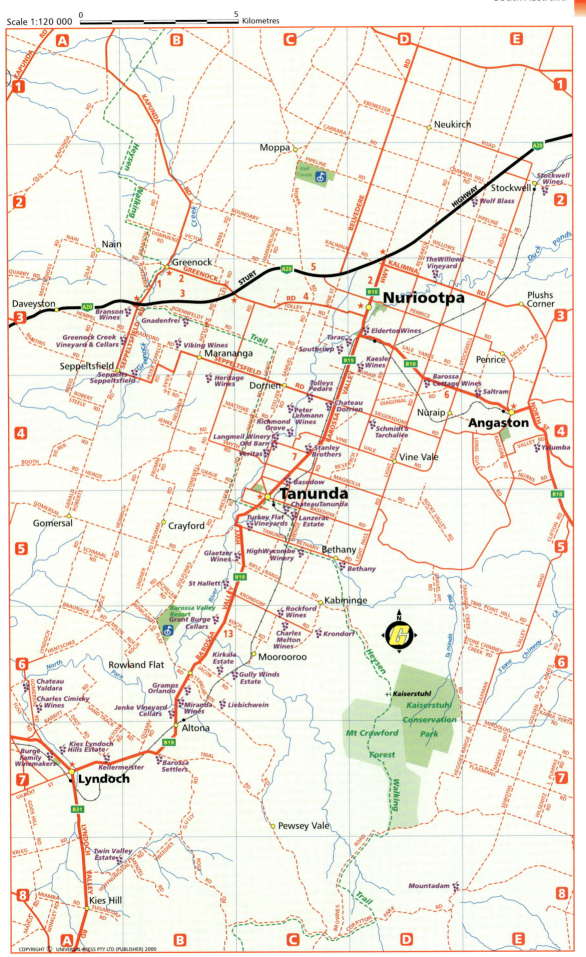

Fleurieu Peninsula

Its close proximity to Adelaide and outstanding combination of seaside resorts surrounded by idyllic rural townships, set among rolling hills and vineyards, make the Fleurieu Peninsula an ideal holiday destination.

Boasting great surfing and swimming beaches, islands which are home to penguins and waters frequently visited by southern right whales, both sides of the Peninsula's coast offer a full range of waterfront attractions.

In contrast, the lush green interior hosts 20-plus conservation parks, 1500km of nature trails, sleepy villages and world–class wineries. The region's noted natural beauty has made it a haven for artists and craftspeople, whose works are showcased in galleries and at weekend craft markets.

The region's attractions can be enjoyed in any season, due to its Mediterranean climate.

Must Visit
- Cape Jervis
- Coorong NP
- Deep Creek Conservation Park

ℹ Tourist Information

McLaren Vale and Fleurieu Visitor Centre
Main Rd, McLaren Vale 5171
Ph: (08) 8323 9944
www.visitorcentre.com.au

Granite Island, Victor Harbour

Scale 1:450 000

Flinders Ranges

This isolated area is a land of legends, telling tales of adventure, hardship, success and failure. Located only 192km north of Adelaide, the ancient landscape of the Flinders Ranges bears the evidence of thousands of years of activity in its quiet planes, incredible rock formations, daunting arid peaks and endless sunburnt plains.

Granite rocks found here date back 1600 million years, while some areas are estimated to be as much as 1800 million years old. Seashell remains have been found in the midst of rocky inland deserts and there are fossilised palm tree remnants near Coober Pedy.

For over 40 000 years, Aboriginal people lived in this area — the silent sites of their ceremonial grounds, cave paintings and carvings are a testimony to this time.

There are many options for exploring this furrowed region of

Sunset at Cazneaux Tree

vast salt lakes, historic mining areas, distinctive rock formations, outstanding gorges and picturesque waterholes — a haven for rare wildlife and plants. With much to discover, it is ideal for 4WD tours, driving or even camel trekking, while the Ghan and Pichi Richi railways are a must for train buffs. However, it is important to be adequately prepared and check weather conditions, as they are renowned for being changeable.

Must Visit

- Arkaroola Wilderness Sanctuary
- Beltana
- Flinders Ranges NP
- Gammon Ranges NP

ℹ Tourist Information

Wadlata Outback Centre
41 Flinders Tce, Port Augusta 5700
Ph: (08) 8641 0793
wadlata@wadarid.mtx.net

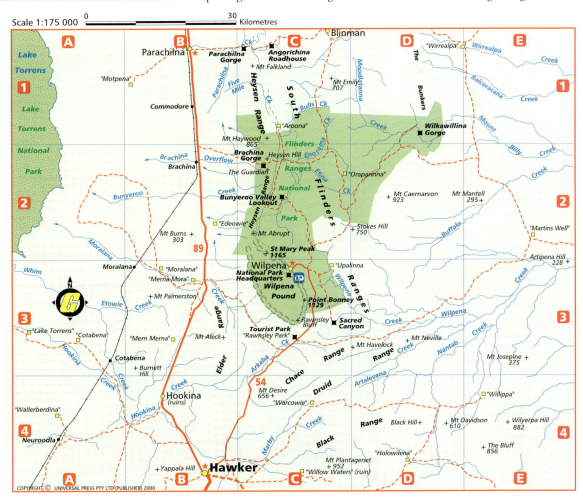

Kangaroo Island

The third largest island off the Australian coastline, Kangaroo Island is an astonishing 155km long and 55km at its widest point — many visitors are surprised by its size, not realising it is so large. Its reputation as a haven for native wildlife and flora is well deserved, with 30% of its total area covered by national parks where pets are not permitted.

Even in peak season, the island's size protects it from feeling crowded, although its tiny townships swell to incredible proportions. It offers a relaxed lifestyle and endless opportunities for water-based activities such as fishing, swimming, sailing, surfing, scuba diving and boating, plus the rare opportunity to see fascinating creatures such as little penguins, Australian sea lions and its very own Kangaroo Island kangaroo in their natural habitat.

The spectacular coastline offers outstanding coastal views, historic lighthouses and remnants of shipwrecks off the perilous coast.

Remarkable Rocks, Flinders Chase

Its easy pace and superb natural environment make Kangaroo Island a perfect, secluded retreat where visitors can truly unwind.

History

Kangaroo Island was discovered in 1802 by Mathew Flinders, who named it after the dark-furred kangaroos. For some years the island was inhabited by escaped convicts, ship deserters and renegade whalers. Life was violent and barbaric during this time.

Tourist Information

Gateway Information Centre
Howard Dr, Penneshaw 5222
Ph: (08) 8553 1185
www.tourkangarooisland.com.au

Main Attractions

★ **Cape Willoughby Lighthouse**
Completed in 1852, the Cape Willoughby lighthouse was the first in South Australia.

★ **Emu Bay**
With shallow, clear water, Emu Bay is one of the island's most popular swimming spots.

★ **Kingscote**
As SA's first settlement site at nearby Reeves Pt, Kingscote is rich in history.

★ **Penneshaw**
Penneshaw is a sheltered beach ideal for swimming. See little penguins at dusk as they come ashore to nest in the sandhills.

★ **Seal Bay**
This sandy beach and dune area is the resting place of Australian sea lions and where they come to nurse their young.

★ **Stokes Bay**
A rock pool in this bay offers protected swimming, while small caves provide shelter from the sun.

National Trust Museum, Kingscote

Island Produce

Due to its relative seclusion and limited industry, Kangaroo Island is in the enviable position of remaining a clean and green environment. Enterprising Islanders have seized this opportunity to develop Kangaroo Island into one of Australia's premier alternative primary production areas. The island now offers an increasing and diverse range of regional produce, with a growing export market. The fox–free island produces high quality, corn fed, free–range chickens, while its seafaring location makes it ideal for fresh seafood — King George whiting is a regional specialty, featured on many local restaurant menus. To taste the island's tempting treats visit:

★ **Clifford's Honey Farm:** Regarded as the only place in the world with a pure strain of Ligurian bee, the Farm offers free tastings and sells home–made honey icecream.

★ **Dudley Partners, Kangaroo Island:** Offering locally grown and produced red and white wines, Hog Bay River Vineyards is developing a reputation for its fine Cabernet Merlot.

★ **Gum Creek Marron Farm:** Try and buy marron, a freshwater crustacean resembling lobster, in this picturesque farm setting.

★ **Island Pure Sheep Dairy:** Producing world–class sheep cheeses and yoghurts based on Greek, Cypriot, Italian and Spanish recipes, the Dairy offers opportunities to observe milking, plus tastings and sales.

Crayfish in bucket

Scale 1:550 000

Mt Gambier District

Known as the 'South East', SA's southern-most corner is rich in natural attractions, with an arc of pristine beaches stretching along the coastline to the Victorian border.

Volcanic activity sculpted the landscape, with the Crater Lakes among its most stunning natural attractions.

Regarded as the Limestone Coast due to its incomparable concentration of limestone craters, caves and cliffs, the Mt Gambier District offers visitors a range of activities and attractions in a spectacular natural setting. The fascinating geography reflects the fact that millions of years ago this region was under water. The countryside around the Mt Gambier district contains conservation reserves that are world standard.

The Bvandik or Bunganditj tribe occupied this region at least 30 000 years ago, if not earlier. The land was plentiful for its inhabitants. On land there was an array of wildlife and plants to hunt, while in the sea, lakes and swamps, shell-fish and fish were abundant. After discovery by the Europeans in 1800, this district was taken away from its original inhabitants.

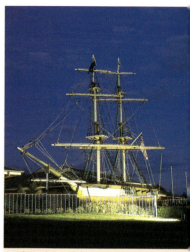

Lady Nelson Visitor Centre, Mt Gambier

Visit Beachport

This historic whaling port features excellent angling opportunities from SA's second longest jetty. Visit the Butcher's Gallery in SA's first butcher shop, the National Trust Museum and Beachport Conservation Park.

ℹ Tourist Information

'The Lady Nelson' Visitor and Discovery Centre
Jubilee Hwy East, Mt Gambier 5290
Ph: (08) 8724 9750
Freecall: 1800 087 187
www.mountgambiertourism.com.au

Main Attractions

★ **Blue Lake**
Blue Lake, the district's most famous tourist destination, was originally a volcanic crater.

★ **Camp Coorong**
Learn about traditional Aboriginal life by visiting the Ngarrindjeri people in the area where they have lived for thousands of years.

★ **Coonawarra**
Coonawarra is one of Australia's greatest wine districts.

★ **Coorong NP**
This NP has many species of birds that migrate from northern Asia.

★ **Naracoorte Caves**
The region's largest limestone caves are in this World Heritage listed park.

★ **Pool of Siloam**
This salt lake is 7 times saltier than the sea and is said to relieve symptoms of arthritis and rheumatism.

★ **Robe**
A holiday destination for over 150 years, Robe is an historic fishing village.

Naracoorte Caves

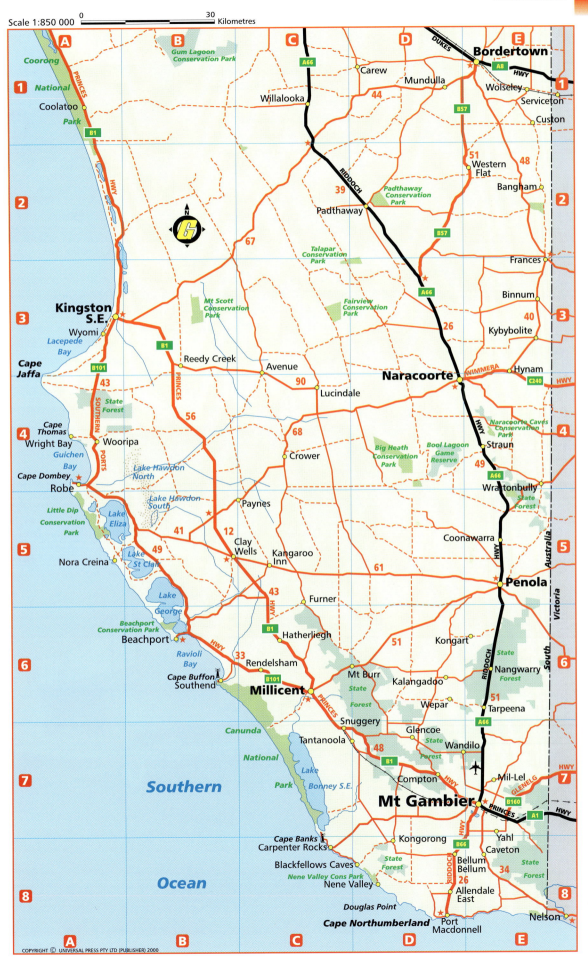

Scale 1:850 000

0   30
Kilometres

COPYRIGHT © UNIVERSAL PRESS PTY LTD (PUBLISHER) 2000

Riverland

This region features the Murray River, one of the world's great waterways, carving its way through the terrain past a changing landscape. Not only does the river dominate the region's landscape, it also influences its economy — providing the lifeblood to its orchards, dairy pastures and vineyards.

The Riverland actually produces more than half of SA's wine grapes and is becoming increasingly known as a wine area in its own right. The Riverland is the heart of the fruit bowl of SA, where more than 90% of the state's citrus, stone fruit and nuts are produced; local produce can be sampled from stalls along the roadside.

There is no better way to explore the might of the Murray River than

Pelican Bredl's Wildflife Park

by travelling on it — houseboats fully equipped with home comforts are an ideal holiday option. The water–rich environment is ideal for anglers, where catches of the day include Murray cod, redfin and fresh yabbies. Dotted with tiny towns, rich in the history of pioneering days, this regions offers much to explore.

The Overland Corner Hotel

Constructed in 1858, this hotel was the first stone building in the Riverland. Weary bullock teamsters used it as a stop on the original stock route to Adelaide. The hotel remains at Overland Corner, although today it is a museum.

Tourist Information

Berri Tourist & Travel Centre
24 Vaughan Tce, Berri 5343
Ph: (08) 8582 1655

Main Attractions

★ **Barmera**
As SA's country music capital, Barmera has hosted the State's annual country music festival for over 20 years.

★ **Berri**
Renowned across Australia for its citrus and stone fruits, Berri is an ideal base for exploring the region.

★ **Kingston Estate**
This popular winery offers cellar door sales and tastings.

★ **Loxton Historical Village**
This historical village was voted the 'Best Tourist Attraction' in the 1994 Riverland Tourism awards.

★ **Renmark**
This township on the Murray River offers an insight into early river history. Worth visiting is Ruston's Rose Garden, containing 50 000 rose bushes.

★ **The Big Orange**
Located on the Sturt Hwy in Berri, The Big Orange is a tribute to the region's all–important citrus industry, featuring sales of local produce, a lookout, and children's playground.

PS Industry Paddlesteamer

Cruising the Mighty Murray

Since the first paddlesteamer, the *Mary Ann*, was launched in 1853 near Mannum, river transport has been a popular way to see the Murray River. Offering many cruising opportunities, the river can be travelled by houseboats, paddleships and historic paddlesteamers past quaint townships, vast vineyards, fruitful orchards, ancient terrain and scenic wilderness. Options can also include eco cruises, where exploring nature is the aim. For a Murray adventure contact:

Big River Holidays: Enjoy personalised service in these fully equipped, owner–operated and easy to operate houseboats for 2–12 people.

Breeze Houseboats: Explore the tranquil setting in the privacy of a houseboat.

Green and Gold Houseboats: Available for day hire or longer periods, these luxury houseboats for 2–12 people have facilities for people with a disability.

Proud Australia Holidays: Board the elegant *Proud Mary* for nature cruises.

PS Industry: This historic paddlesteamer operates from Renmark, and is a leisurely way to enjoy the river's attractions.

PS Murray Princess: Offering luxury cruising on SA's largest inland water paddlewheeler, trips depart from Mannum and include speed boat rides, visits to an Aboriginal site and waterskiing.

River Murray Houseboats: Reasonably priced, these fully equipped houseboats are 2–10 berth, with economical twin 4–stroke motors.

Riverscape Adventure Centre: Operating daily river cruises and eco tours from Murray Bridge, this is a relaxed and friendly way to see the river.

Murray Princess

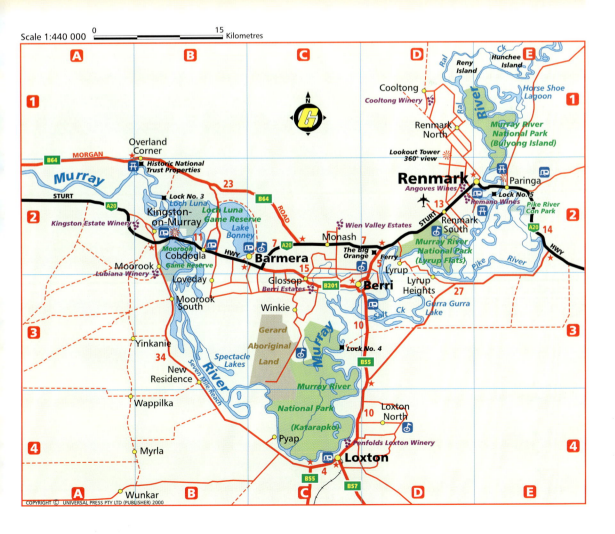

Western Australia

WA: Wildflower State

- Area = 2 527 633 sq km
- Occupies 32.9% of Australia
- Length of coastline = 7000km

Kangaroo Paw

Numbat

ℹ Tourist Information

Western Australia Tourist Centre
Forrest Pl, cnr Wellington St,
Perth 6000
Freecall: 1300 361 351
www.tourism.wa.gov.au

Main Attractions

★ **Bunbury**
This is a charming and peaceful town and WA's second largest population centre.

★ **Caves District**
This area is characterised by caves, wineries, fine restaurants and secluded hideaways.

★ **Fremantle**
This city has developed an alternative, arty atmosphere in recent years.

★ **Mandurah-Pinjarra**
This region is renowned for its idyllic beaches, waterways and the karri forest of the Darling Ranges.

★ **Perth**
This state capital enjoys the enviable position of experiencing more sunshine hours than any other Australian capital.

★ **Rottnest Island**
This island is a popular holiday resort with secluded beaches and beautiful coves.

★ **Stirling Range NP to Albany**
This region has the majestic granite headlands of the Porongurups, Stirling Range, and Albany, which is a popular place to visit.

Bound by desert to the east and coastline to the west, WA covers approximately one-third of the Australian continent and embraces a number of climatic and time zones.

Despite this vast land mass, WA has a relatively small population, less than 0.5% of the nation's population. Most residents live in the capital, Perth, which is closer to Jakarta and Singapore than to Sydney or Melbourne.

Rich in natural resources — including iron ore, gold, gas, petroleum products, wheat, wool and minerals — it is essentially a primary industry state, although the fastest growing industry is now tourism. The state has many national parks with spectacular natural attractions, ranging from magnificent desert landscapes and wildflower carpeted forests to beautiful coastal waters, drawing visitors in increasing numbers.

The state's climate is seasonally based, with a combination of tropical, temperate and arid climes. The southern section experiences

Burswood Casino

cool winters and hot, dry summers. The monsoonal north maintains high, humid temperatures in its wet and dry seasons. In contrast, the interior crackles, with temperatures rising to over 40°C in the middle of its summer days.

Eagle Bay, Leeuwin – Naturaliste National Park

Western Australia Key Map and Distance Chart

All distances shown in the chart below have been measured over highways and major roads, not necessarily by the shortest route.

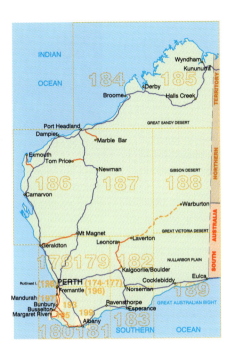

City Map
Perth, page 173

Suburban Maps
Perth, pages 174 to 177

State Maps
pages 178 to 189

Region Maps
Bunbury District, page 193
Caves District, page 195
Fremantle, page 196
Mandurah-Pinjarra, page 197
Rottnest Island, page 198
Stirling Ranges NP to
 Albany, page 199

Approximate Distance	Albany	Broome	Bunbury	Busselton	Carnarvon	Derby	Esperance	Eucla	Geraldton	Halls Creek	Kalgoorlie/Boulder	Kununurra	Mandurah	Meekatharra	Merredin	Narrogin	Norseman	Northam	Perth	Port Hedland
Albany		2582	361	372	1292	2736	474	1386	819	3196	799	3554	468	1116	463	269	676	439	406	1988
Broome	2582		2538	2592	1461	222	912	3082	1934	682	2185	1040	2441	1466	2304	2313	2372	2143	2372	614
Bunbury	361	2538		54	1069	2554	687	1599	596	3004	764	3362	1027	924	422	170	889	261	182	1796
Busselton	372	2592	54		1123	2608	698	1610	650	3058	818	3416	161	978	482	224	900	315	236	1850
Carnarvon	1292	1461	1069	1123		1615	1600	2300	473	2075	1161	2433	972	620	1125	1078	1590	964	903	867
Derby	2736	222	2554	2608	1615		2728	3236	2088	544	2267	902	2447	1620	2458	2467	2526	2297	2378	768
Esperance	474	912	687	698	1600	2728		912	1319	3188	389	3486	710	1108	562	535	202	828	714	1980
Eucla	1386	3082	1599	1610	2300	3236	912		1827	3696	897	4054	1502	1616	1175	1433	710	1336	1433	2488
Geraldton	819	1934	596	650	473	2088	1319	1827		2548	988	2906	499	540	652	605	1117	491	430	1340
Halls Creek	3196	682	3004	3058	2075	544	3188	3696	2548		2799	358	2907	2080	2918	2927	2986	2757	2838	1228
Kalgoorlie/Boulder	799	2185	764	818	1161	2267	389	897	988	2799		3157	663	719	336	594	187	497	594	1591
Kununurra	3554	1040	3362	3416	2433	902	3486	4054	2906	358	3157		3265	2438	3276	3285	3344	3115	3196	1586
Mandurah	468	2441	1027	161	972	2447	710	1502	499	2907	663	3265		827	327	175	792	166	75	1698
Meekatharra	1116	1466	924	978	620	1620	1108	1616	540	2080	719	2438	827		838	847	906	677	758	872
Merredin	463	2304	422	482	1125	2458	562	1175	652	2918	336	3276	327	838		258	465	161	258	1710
Narrogin	269	2313	170	224	1078	2467	535	1433	605	2927	594	3285	175	847	258		723	170	192	1719
Norseman	676	2372	889	900	1590	2526	202	710	1117	2986	187	3344	792	906	465	723		626	723	1778
Northam	439	2143	261	315	964	2297	828	1336	491	2757	497	3115	166	677	161	170	626		97	1549
Perth	406	2372	182	236	903	2378	714	1433	430	2838	594	3196	75	758	258	192	723	97		1630
Port Hedland	1988	614	1796	1850	867	768	1980	2488	1340	1228	1591	1586	1698	872	1710	1719	1778	1549	1630	

Perth

F ounded in 1829 and built on the banks of the Swan River, Perth is a scenic and sophisticated city, renowned for its abundant sunshine, relaxed lifestyle and easy-going manner.

Perth's modern skyline blends with magnificent colonial architecture, housing excellent retail outlets, particularly around Hay and Murray Sts and the malls running between them. King St, the historic and lovingly restored commercial precinct, is now renowned for its fashion houses, cafes, art galleries and specialist book stores.

Within minutes of the CBD is the world's oldest operating mint as well as a number of art galleries and museums, historic buildings and numerous parklands.

Perth's prime position, flanking both the broad reaches of the Swan River and the open waters of the Indian Ocean, makes it an ideal

Hay Street mall

place for enjoying alfresco dining. The riverside and beach front both boast an array of cafes and restaurants, while nearby there are more than 80km of white sandy beaches. Further afield, many of WA's key attractions are located within close proximity to Perth, which makes it an ideal base for exploring the surrounding attractions.

Tourist Information

Western Australian Tourist Centre
Forrest Pl, cnr Wellington St,
Perth 6000
Ph: (08) 9483 1111
Freecall: 1300 361 351
www.westernaustralia.net

Main Attractions

★ **Government House**
Completed in 1864 and home to the State Governor, Government House is set in romantic English-style gardens and includes an elegant ballroom.

★ **Kings Park**
Affording excellent views from Mt Eliza, the glorious Kings Park has 400ha of parkland and boasts natural bushland and showcases WA's famed wildflowers.

★ **London Court**
This Tudor-style shopping arcade is Perth's most photographed attraction.

★ **Perth Mint**
Visit the past in the Mint's Old Melting House, see hourly gold bar pouring demonstrations or watch the workings from the viewing gallery.

★ **Old Perth Boys' School**
This ecclesiastical-style sandstone building, constructed between 1852 and 1854, now houses Reveleys Cafe and wine bar and the Perth Institute of Contemporary Arts.

Perth at night

Places of Interest

❶ Barracks Archway   A4
❷ His Majesty's Theatre   B4
❸ Parliament House   A4
❹ Perth Cultural Centre   E5
❺ Perth Town Hall   B4
❻ Perth Zoo   B7
❼ Queens Gardens   D5

❽ St George's Anglican Cathedral   C4
❾ St Mary's Catholic Cathedral   C4
❿ Stirling Gardens   B4
⓫ Supreme Court Gardens   B5
⓬ The Old Mill   A6
⓭ Western Australian Museum   C3

Scale 1:25 000

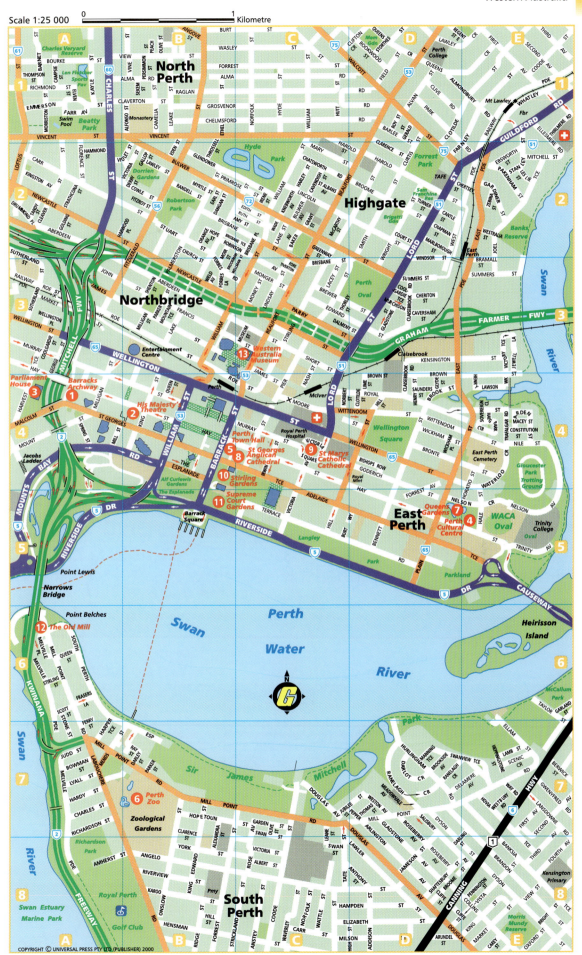

Scale 1:160 000

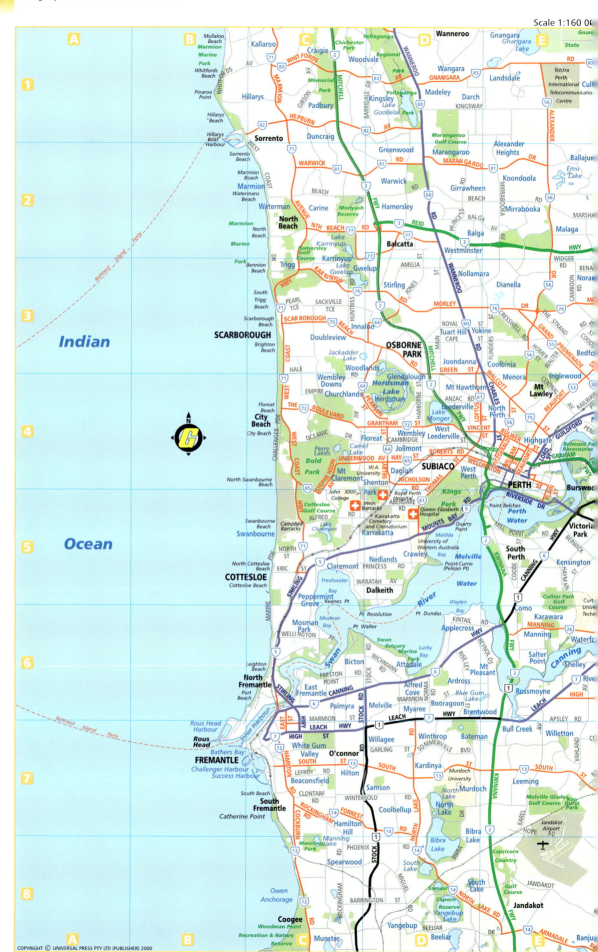

Indian

Ocean

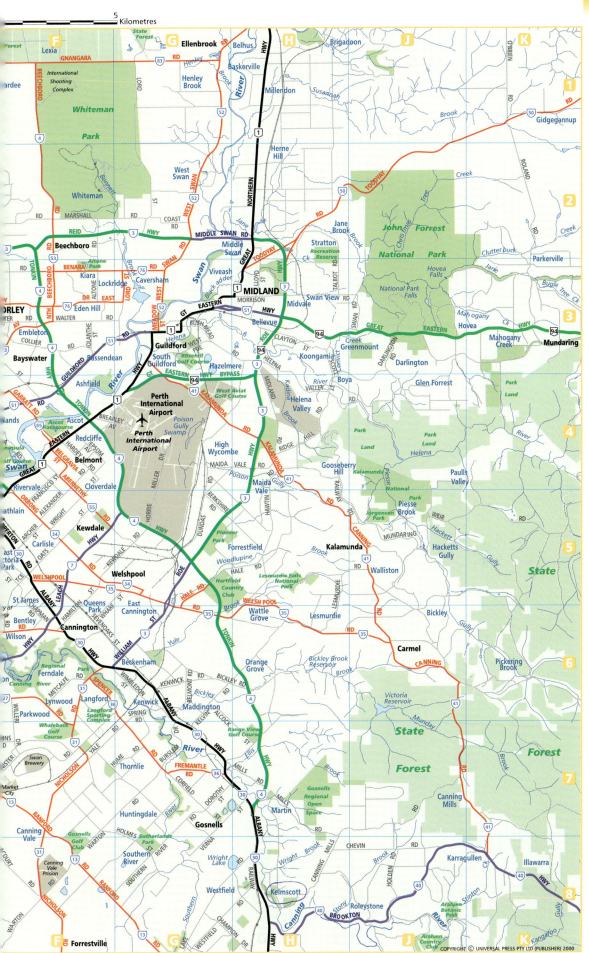

Scale 1:160 000

5 Kilometres

Scale 1:1 870 00

INDIAN

OCEAN

PERTH

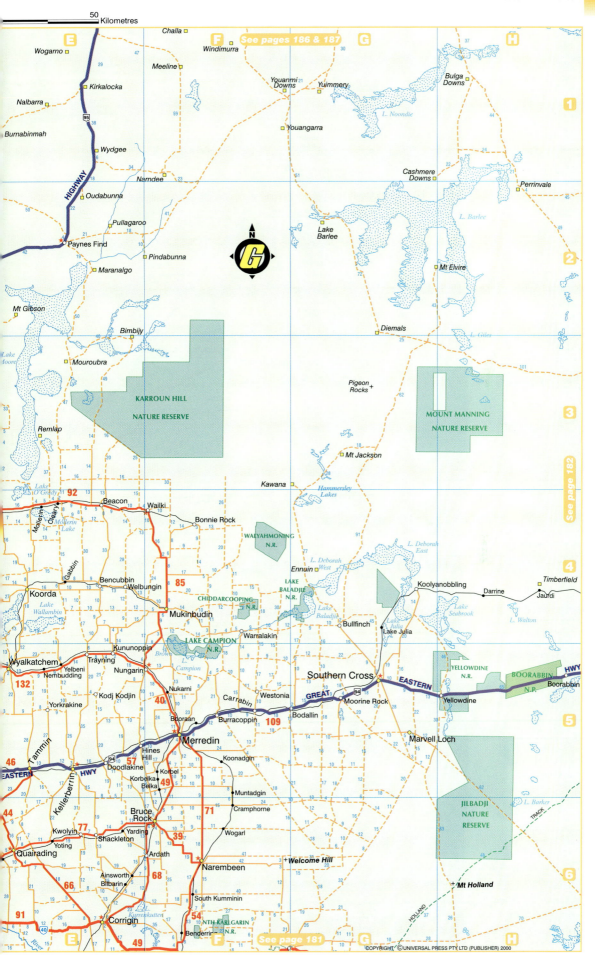

50 Kilometres

Wogarno
Challa
Windimurra
See pages 186 & 187
Meeline
Youanmi Downs
Yuimmery
Bulga Downs
Kirkalocka
Nalbarra
L. Noondie
Burnabinmah
Youangarra
Wydgee
Cashmere Downs
Perrinvale
Narndee
L. Barlee
HIGHWAY
Oudabunna
Lake Barlee
Pullagaroo
Paynes Find
Pindabunna
Mt Elvire
Maranalgo
Mt Gibson
Bimbijy
Diemals
L. Giles
Lake Moore
Mouroubra
Pigeon Rocks
MOUNT MANNING
NATURE RESERVE
KARROUN HILL
NATURE RESERVE
Remlap
Mt Jackson
Kawana
Hammersley Lakes
Lake O'Grady
92
Beacon
Wailki
Mollerin
Clean
Mollerin Lake
Bonnie Rock
L. Deborah East
WALYAHMONING N.R.
L. Deborah West
Ennuin
Koolyanobbling
Darrine
Jaurdi
Timberfield
Gabbin
Bencubbin
Welbungin
85
Koorda
CHIDDARCOOPING N.R.
LAKE BALADJIE N.R.
Lake Baladjie
Lake Seabrook
L. Walton
Lake Wallambin
Mukinbudin
Bullfinch
Lake Julia
L. Julia
Wyalkatchem
Kununoppin
LAKE CAMPION N.R.
Brown
Warralakin
Trayning
Yelbeni
L. Campion
Southern Cross
YELLOWDINE N.R.
BOORABBIN
HWY
Nembudding
Nungarin
132
Nukarni
40
Carrabin
Westonia
EASTERN
GREAT
Yellowdine
Boorabbin
N.P.
Boorabbin
Yorkrakine
Kodj Kodjin
Booraan
Burracoppin
109
Bodallin
Moorine Rock
Bodallin
Merredin
Marvell Loch
46
Hines Hill
Koonadgin
EASTERN
HWY
Doodlakine
Korbel
Kellerberrin
57
Korbelka
Belka
49
Muntadgin
Tammin
44
Bruce Rock
71
Cramphorne
Kwolyin
77
Yarding
Wogarl
Shackleton
39
Yoting
Ardath
Welcome Hill
JILBADJI
NATURE
RESERVE
L. Barker
TRACK
Quairading
Narembeen
68
Ainsworth
Bilbarin
66
South Kumminin
Mt Holland
HOLLAND
91
Corrigin
54
NTH KARLGARIN N.R.
Benderrin
49
See page 181

Scale 1:1 870 00

INDIAN

OCEAN

See page 178

Seabird
Guilderton
Bindoon
Bolgart
Goomalling

Gingin
YEAT
N.R.
Muchea
MOONDYNE
N.R.

Two Rocks
Yanchep
YANCHEP
N.P.
L. Pinjar
Bullsbrook
130
Jennacubbine
46
Jennapullin
Southern
Brook

Quinns Rock
85
Clackline
Spring
Hill
Grass
Valley
27
Northam
58

Burns
Wanneroo
54
Wundowie
Wooroloo
Bakers
Hill
97
York
Greenhills
69

PERTH
Midland
95
The Lakes
66
Beverley

Rottnest I.
For more detail see
map on page 198
For more detail see
map on pages 174 - 177
Mt Dale
Mount
Kokeby
YENYENINC
LAKES
N.R.

Fremantle
75
Armidale
Byford
BROOKTON
137
Westdale
Brookton
Aldersyde

Kwinana
Rockingham
Garden I.
Cape Peron
Mundijong
86
Jarradale
Serpentine
Mt Randall
LUPTON
N.P.
BOYAGIN
N.R.
Pingelly

Becher Pt
Golden Bay
Singleton
Madora
Keysbrook
North Dandalup
160
For more detail see
map on page 196

Mandurah
Ravenswood
North Bannister
69

Dawes
Cape Bouvara
jarra
Dwellingup
Bannister
Wandering
Popanyinning
For more detail see
map on page 197

L. Clifton
Coolup
LUPTON
K.P.
Cuballing
Congelin

YALGORUP
N.P.
Waroona
127
Marradong
Boddington
Narrogin
32

Preston Beach
Yarloop
LANE
POOLE
RES
Quindanning
Williams
Highbury

L. Preston
112
Harvey
97
LANE
POOLE
C.P.
85
Piesseville
39
29

Myalup Beach
Binningup Beach
Worsley
Refinery
Brunswick
Darkin
90

Australind
Pt. Casuarina
Brunswick
Junction
Allanson
Collie
Arthur
River
107

Bunbury
Burekup
For more detail see
map on page 193
Bowelling
Muja Coal Mine
Darkin

54
Stratham
Boyanup
Mumballup
125
Moodiarrup
55

Cape Naturaliste
Eagle Bay
Busselton
Capel
Donnybrook
Dinninup
Kojonup

LEEUWIN NATURALIST N.P.
Dunsborough
Geographe
Bay
Kirup
Boyup
Brook
Muradup

Yallingup
Cape Clairault
Vasse
Carbunup
River
59
93
Balingup
Greenbushes

124
Gracetown
Cowaramup
45
Nannup
Bridgetown
114
65

Margaret River
Cape Menteile
Prevelly
For more detail see
map on page 195
Witchcliffe
45
37
Palgarup
Yornup

Cape Freycinet
LEEUWIN-NATURALISTE N.P.
BROCKMAN
73
Manjimup
Nyamup
Frankland

Karridale
Hamelin Bay
Kudardup
Cape Hamelin
44
SCOTT
N.P.
79
BEEDELUP
N.P.
Quinninup
MUIRS
N.R.
Rocky Gully
161

Augusta
Cape Leeuwin
Flinders
Bay
GINGILUP
SWAMPS
N.R.
Pemberton
50
SHANNON
N.P.

Black Pt
58
MT FRANKLAND
N.P.
68

D'ENTRECASTEAUX N.P.
Northcliffe
113
SOUTH

Cape D'Entrecasteaux
D'ENTRECASTEAUX N.P.
Broke Inlet
Bow
Bridge

WALPOLE - NORNALUP N.P.
Chatham I.
Pt Nuyts
Walpole
Nornalup
Peaceful
Bay
Parry
Beach
Hillier

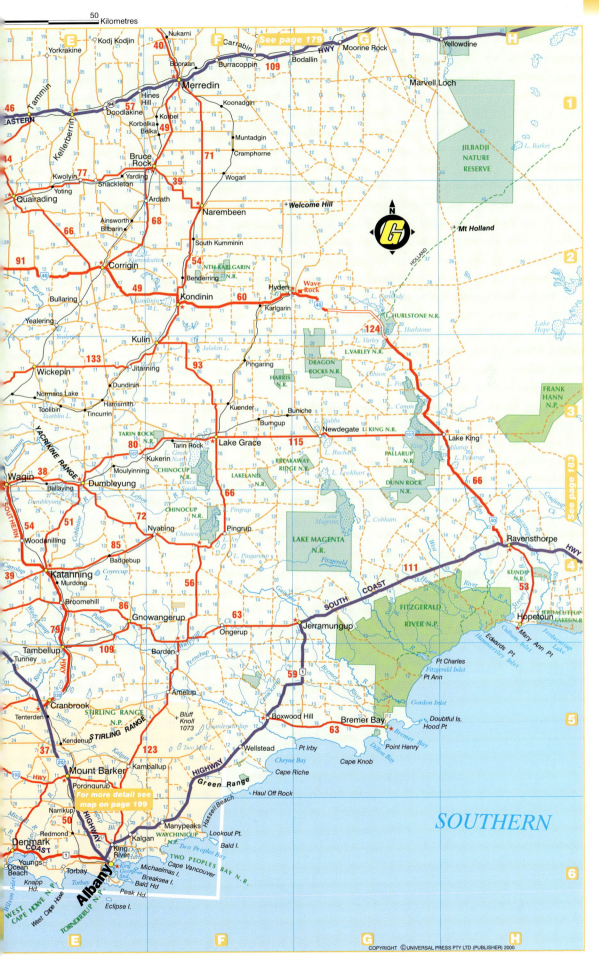

50 Kilometres

SOUTHERN

COPYRIGHT ©UNIVERSAL PRESS PTY LTD (PUBLISHER) 2000

Scale 1:1 870 000

0   50 Kilometres

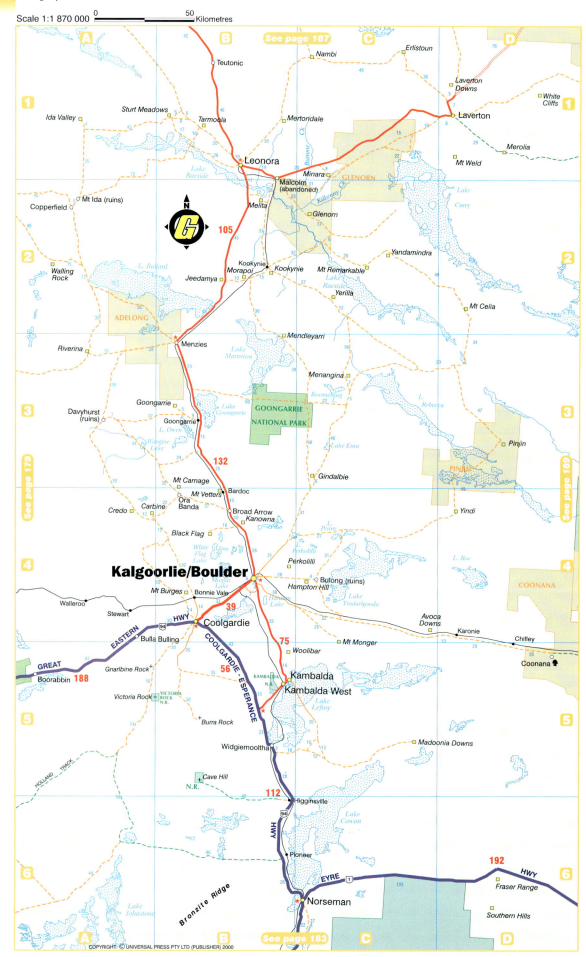

Scale 1:1 870 000

0   50 Kilometres

Scale 1:3 900 000

INDIAN OCEAN

Seringapatam Reef

Scott Reef
SCOTT REEF NATURE RES.

Browse I.

Adele I.

Buccaneer Archipelago

Resort
Koolan

Hidden I.
Koolan I.
Cockatoo I.
Koolan I.

Cape Leveque
Kooljaman Resort
One Arm Pt (Bardi)
Lombardina (Djarindjin)
PENDER BAY
Pender Bay
Pender

Beagle Bay
Beagle Bay
BEAGLE BAY

King Sound

Mermaid Reef

Country Downs
Fraser R.
Derby

COULOMB POINT N.R.
Mowanjum
Willare Br. Roadhouse
42
Yeeda

Rowley Shoals
ROWLEY SHOALS MARINE PARK
Clerke Reef

Kilto **146**
Bedunburru
Tjarramba

Imperieuse Reef

Waterbank
34
Roebuck Roadhouse
Yakka Munga

Broome
Ganthaeume Pt.
Roebuck Plains
Roebuck Bay
Broome Bird Observatory
Thangoo

Dampier Downs

HIGHWAY

Cape Latouche Treville
Mowla Bluff
Mowla Bluff **203**

Port Smith Caravan & Bird Pk
Lagrange Bay
Cape Bassut
287
Bidyadanga (Lagrange)
Admiral Bay
Frazier Downs
FRAZIER DOWNS

Nita Downs

Anna Plains

DRAGON TREE N.R

Eighty Mile Beach

Mandora
Wallal Downs
Sandfire Roadhouse

KIDSON

North Turtle I.
Poissonnier Pt
141
GREAT NORTHERN

GREAT

Cape Keraudren

(WAPET RD)

Pardoo
Port Hedland
De Grey
Pardoo Roadhouse

De Grey R.

Cape Thouin
Boodarie
32
South Hedland
Strelley
142
Nimingarra
Coongan
Muccan
Callawa
Warrawagine

TRACK

Mundabullangana
Indee
Wallareenya
Tabba Tabba
Carlindie
Eginbah
Bamboo Creek Mine
143

See page 187

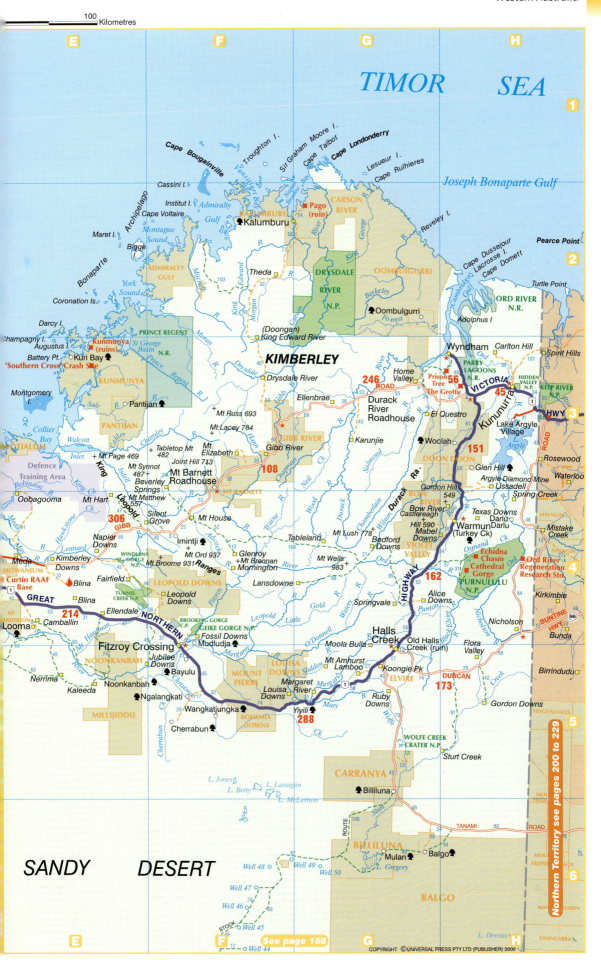

100 Kilometres

Scale 1:3 900 000

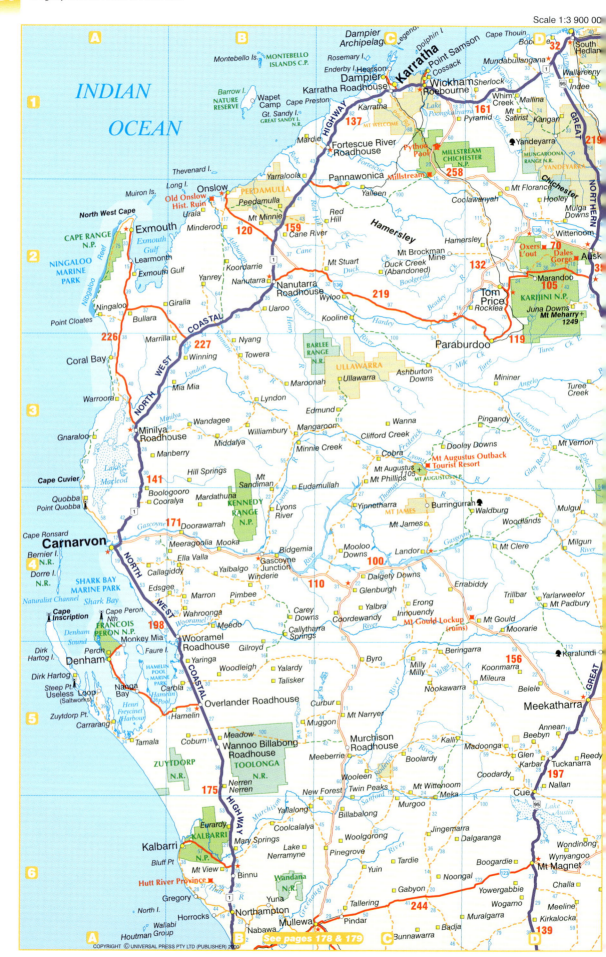

INDIAN

OCEAN

See pages 178 & 179

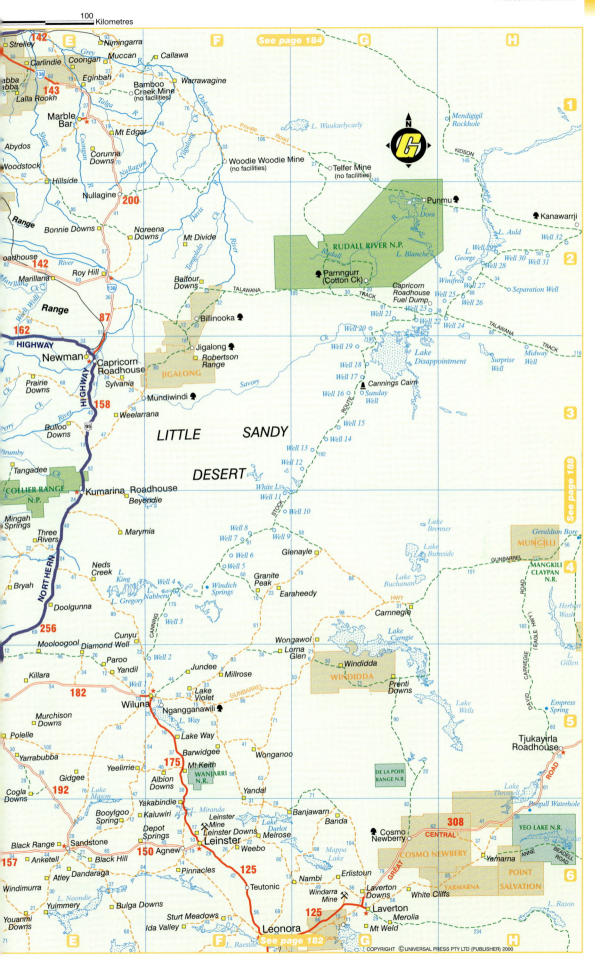

See page 184
See page 188
See page 182

100 Kilometres

Strelley
Nimingarra
Muccan
Coongan
Callawa
Carlindie
abba bba
Eginbah
Warrawagine
Lalla Rookh
Bamboo Creek Mine (no facilities)
Marble Bar
Mt Edgar
Abydos
Corunna Downs
Woodstock
Woodie Woodie Mine (no facilities)
Telfer Mine (no facilities)
Mendigigil Rockhole
Hillside
Nullagine
Range
Bonnie Downs
Noreena Downs
Mt Divide
Rudall River N.P.
Punmu
Kanawarrji
oadhouse
Marillana
Roy Hill
Balfour Downs
Parnngurr (Cotton Ck)
Capricorn Roadhouse Fuel Dump
Range
Billinooka
Jigalong
Robertson Range
Cannings Cairn
Newman
Capricorn Roadhouse
Sylvania
JIGALONG
Prairie Downs
Mundiwindi
Bulloo Downs
Weelarrana
LITTLE SANDY DESERT
COLLIER RANGE N.P.
Kumarina Roadhouse
Beyondie
Mingah Springs
Three Rivers
Marymia
Glenayle
MUNGILLI
Geraldton Bore
Neds Creek
Windich Springs
Granite Peak
Earaheedy
Carnegie
MANGKILI CLAYPAN N.R.
Bryah
Herbert Wash
Doolgunna
Cunyu
Wongawol
Lorna Glen
Mooloogool
Diamond Well
Paroo
Yandil
Jundee
Millrose
Windidda
WINDIDDA
Prenti Downs
Killara
Wiluna
Ngangganawili
Lake Violet
Lake Way
Empress Spring
Murchison Downs
Tjukayirla Roadhouse
Polelle
Barwidgee
Wonganoo
Yarrabubba
Mt Keith
WANJARRI N.R.
Yeelirrie
Albion Downs
Yandal
DE LA POER RANGE N.R.
Gidgee
Peegull Waterhole
Cogla Downs
Yakabindie
Kaluwiri
Banjawarn
Banda
YEO LAKE N.R.
Booylgoo Spring
Depot Springs
Miranda
Leinster Downs
Melrose
Cosmo Newberry
CENTRAL
Black Range
Sandstone
Leinster
Weebo
Mappa Lake
COSMO NEWBERRY
Yamarna
Anketell
Black Hill
Agnew
Pinnacles
Nambi
Erlistoun
POINT SALVATION
Windimurra
Atley
Dandaraga
Teutonic
Windarra Mine
Laverton Downs
White Cliffs
YARMARNA
Youanmi Downs
Yuimmery
Bulga Downs
Sturt Meadows
Ida Valley
Leonora
Mt Weld
Laverton
Merolia

COPYRIGHT ©UNIVERSAL PRESS PTY LTD (PUBLISHER) 2000

Scale 1:3 900 000   0 ——— 100 Kilometres

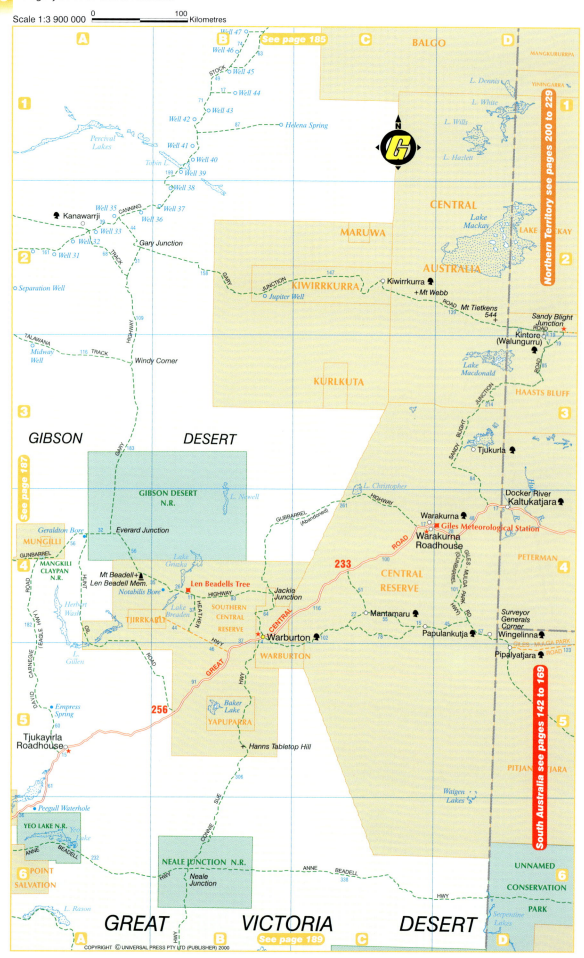

Scale 1:3 900 000

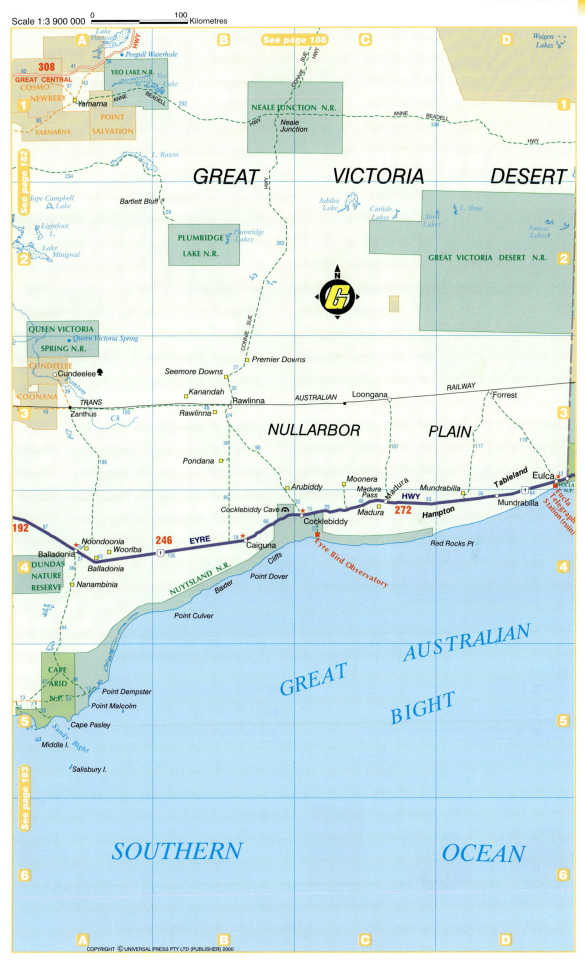

FINE WOODCRAFT GALLERY PEMBERTON

AUSTRALIA'S FINEST COUNTRY GALLERY

The Wood work

The Furniture

The Gardens

The Gallery

The Gift Shop

The Garden Cafe

The Total Gallery Experience

- Professional customer service
- Highest quality
- World-wide freight service
- Specialty make-to-order facilities
- Exceptional range and variety
- Handcrafted in Western Australia

There's much to discover at Fine Woodcraft Gallery

Open daily. 9am - 5pm, Dickinson Street, Pemberton, Western Australia 6260
Tel: (08) 9776 1399 or 9776 1090, Fax: (08) 9777 1355
E-mail: finewood@karriweb.com.au

Bunbury District

Manjimup

This region is best known for its karri forests and is also home to the 'Four Aces' - 4 giant karri trees over 400 years old. The other karri trees here are hundreds of years old and grow up to 75m tall.

Tourist Information

Bunbury Visitor Information Centre
Old Railway Station, Carmody Pl, Bunbury 6230
Ph: (08) 9721 7922

The capital of the region known as the South West and WA's second largest population centre, Bunbury's waters mark the point where the warm Indian Ocean waters collide with those of the cooler Southern Ocean. This area is renowned for its abundant wildlife, boasting game birds such as ducks and swans, as well as fish-filled rivers.

The city was named over 150 years ago after Lt Henry William St Pierre Bunbury, who was sent to further explore the region in 1836. It now provides visitors with an excellent base for their own regional explorations, although the city itself offers many attractions — a stretch of golden beaches, caves and inlets, beach and sea fishing opportunities, tranquil lagoons, superior yachting facilities and picturesque picnic spots and dolphin cruises.

The surrounding hinterland features superb karri forests, spectacular coastline, pretty orchards, verdant grassland and farmstay opportunities.

Dolphins at Koombana Bay

For instance, Donnybrook is known for its apple orchards, wineries, arts and crafts, while at Harvey visitors will find some of WA's prime beef and best oranges.

Main Attractions

★ **Australind**
This historic town is popular for boating, sailing, fishing, prawning, crabbing and windsurfing.

★ **Bunbury**
Offering a cosmopolitan seaside atmosphere of beaches, cafes, shopping and many nature based attractions, such as the Mangrove Boardwalk.

★ **Dolphin Discovery Centre**
Experience the sight and sounds of these amazing creatures through an audiovisual show.

★ **Koombana Bay dolphins**
The bay is famed for its dolphins, who frolic in its protected waters.

Mangrove Boardwalk
These mangroves are about 25 000 years old.

★ **Old Goldfields Orchard and Cider Factory**
Here the workings of Donnybrook's historic goldrush era are recreated, with gold panning just one of the activities available. There is a boutique cider factory where adults can taste different brews.

Mangrove Boardwalk

Caves District

The Magical Cave System

Millions of years have provided perfect conditions for the formation of caves in the long, limestone range between Cape Leeuwin and Cape Naturaliste. Of the 120–200 known caves, 4 of the most spectacular are open to the public and worth a visit.

ℹ Tourist Information

Margaret River Tourist Bureau
Bussell Hwy, Margaret River 6285
Ph: (08) 9757 2911

The Caves District boasts one of the world's most extensive limestone cave systems. It is also known as the 'Cape to Cape' area due to its swathe of capes, from Cape Naturaliste in the north to Cape Leeuwin in the south and 5 other capes in between.

The district is an ideal holiday destination, with a winning combination of caves and rolling pastures in the hinterland, bordered by a spectacular coastline of reefs and bays, with wineries and gourmet dining opportunities dotted in between. The infamous Roaring Forties winds create challenging surf conditions, making the coastline a beacon for surfers and windsurfers from other parts of Australia and beyond. The tranquil waters of Geographe Bay attract anglers, waterskiers, snorkellers, windsurfers and beach lovers, while the network

Leeuwin-Naturaliste National Park

of some 300 caves draws abseilers, cavers and bushwalkers from around the globe.

Wine enthusiasts will appreciate the close proximity to the vineyards and wineries of one of Australia's up-and-coming wine-producing regions and gourmands will also find much to enjoy in the Caves District.

Main Attractions

★ **Augusta**
This is a beautiful fishing town.

★ **Busselton**
With 30km of white sandy beaches, this premier seaside resort town has twice been voted 'WA's Top Tourism Town'.

★ **Dunsborough**
Home of the SWAN dive wreck and artificial reef, its sheltered waters, peaceful coves and scenic bushland make it an ideal family holiday retreat.

★ **Jewel Cave**
Regarded as the region's best cave, it features fragile formations such as helictites.

★ **Lake Cave**
The Cave is guarded by an ancient karri tree and inside a unique table is suspended over a subterranean lake.

★ **Margaret River**
The success of the vineyards here, only established in early 1970s, is legendary and has spread world-wide.

Lake Cave, near Margaret River

Scale 1:400 000

0   15 Kilometres

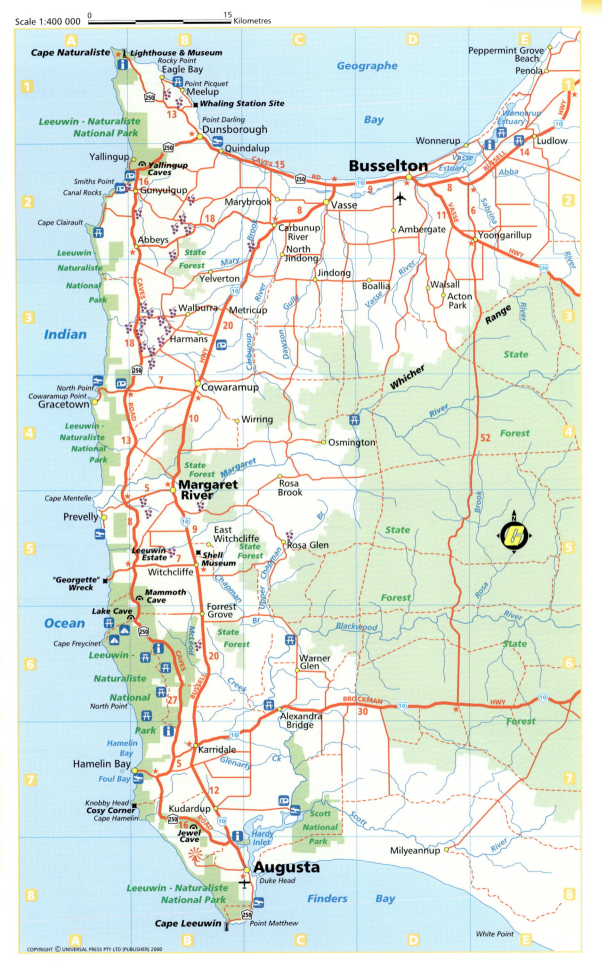

A **B** **C** **D** **E**

Cape Naturaliste
Lighthouse & Museum
Rocky Point
Eagle Bay
Point Picquet
Meelup
Whaling Station Site

Geographe

Peppermint Grove
Beach
Penola

1

Leeuwin - Naturaliste
National Park

13

Point Darling
Dunsborough

Quindalup

CAVES 15

Bay

Wonnerup
Estuary

Wonnerup
Ludlow
14

Vasse
Estuary

1

Yallingup

Yallingup
Caves

250

Busselton

Abba

Smiths Point
Canal Rocks
Gunyulgup
16

Marybrook

8

Vasse

Ambergate

11 6

Sabrina

Yoongarillup

2

Cape Clairault

18

Abbeys

State
Forest

Carbunup
River
North
Jindong

Jindong

Boallia

Walsall
Acton
Park

HWY

104

2

Leeuwin -
Naturaliste
National
Park

Yelverton

Walburra

Mary
River

Metricup

20

Harmans

Gully

Dawson

Vasse
River

Whicher

Range

State

Forest

3

Indian

18

7

North Point
Cowaramup Point
Gracetown

250

ROAD

13

Cowaramup

10

Wirring

Carbunup River

River

52

Forest

4

Leeuwin -
Naturaliste
National
Park

Osmington

4

Cape Mentelle

State
Forest

5

Margaret
River

Margaret
River

Rosa
Brook

Br

River

State

5

Prevelly

8

Leeuwin
Estate

9

7

East
Witchcliffe
State
Forest
Shell
Museum

Rosa Glen

Upper Chapman

Forest

Brook

Rosa

State

5

"Georgette"
Wreck

Witchcliffe

Chapman

Mammoth
Cave

Lake Cave

250

Forrest
Grove

Br

Blackwood

River

6

Ocean

Cape Freycinet

Leeuwin -

Naturaliste

National

North Point

27

CAVES

BUSSELL

20

Warner
Glen

30

BROCKMAN HWY

10

10

Forest

6

Park

Hamelin
Bay

Hamelin Bay
Foul Bay

5

Karridale

Glenarty

Ck

Alexandra
Bridge

7

Knobby Head
Cosy Corner
Cape Hamelin

12

Kudardup

250 ROAD

16
Jewel
Cave

10

Hardy
Inlet

Scott
National

Park

Scott

River

Milyeannup

7

Augusta

Duke Head

8

Leeuwin - Naturaliste
National Park

250

Cape Leeuwin
Point Matthew

Finders

Bay

White Point

8

A **B** **C** **D** **E**

Fremantle

'Freo' — as it is affectionately known by locals — is Perth's port and a maritime playground, with lively street theatre and a thriving cafe culture and alternative arts scene amid the workings of a fully functioning port.

Since hosting the 1987 America's Cup, this once sleepy port village has become a cosmopolitan tourism and recreation centre. Its renowned markets — such as the National Trust classified Fremantle Markets and the E Shed Markets — sidewalk cafes and seaside ambience attract weekenders and holiday-makers.

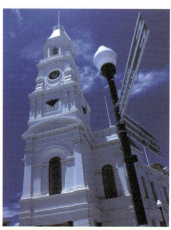

Fremantle Town Hall

Must Visit

- Fremantle Fishing Boat Harbour
- Fremantle History Museum
- Old Fremantle Prison
- Fremantle Town Hall
- The Round House

Tourist Information

Fremantle Tourist Bureau
Town Hall, Kings Square, High St
Fremantle 6160
Ph: (08) 9431 7878

Places of Interest

❶ Army Museum of WA	E1	
❷ E Shed Markets	C2	
❸ Esplanade Hotel	D2	
❹ Fremantle Markets	D2	
❺ Fremantle Museum and Arts Centre	E1	
❻ Historic Boats Museum	C2
❼ Old Fire Station	C2
❽ Samson's House Museum	E2
❾ Success Yacht Harbour	D4
❿ Wildflower Factory	D1
⓫ World of Energy	D1

Scale 1:20 000

Mandurah-Pinjarra

In the heart of WA's Peel region, Mandurah-Pinjarra encompasses 5700km² of diverse landscapes, ranging from rolling farm pastures and striking jarrah forests in the east to coastal plains bordered by the shimmering waters of the Indian Ocean in the west.

With a combination of popular attractions and its close proximity to Perth, this is one of the State's premier tourist destinations.

Calm and protected inlet waters dominate the landscape, providing an aquatic playground that offers excellent boating, swimming and fishing venues. The foreshores feature an array of idyllic picnic spots with BBQs, tables, shelters and change rooms. The open ocean provides abundant opportunities for crabbing, prawning, windsurfing, scuba diving and yachting. Locals rejoice when the 'crab run' begins, as boat owners armed with drop

Fishing at Mandurah Beach

nets arrive to lure away the bountiful blue swimmer crabs. Golf is also a popular pastime: the region boasts 3 world-renowned golf courses — designed by Ian Baker-Finch, Graham Marsh and Robert Trent Jones Jnr, respectively.

Must Visit

- Hotham Valley Tourist Railway
- Pinjarra Heritage Trail
- Harvey Estuary
- Peel Inlet

Tourist Information

Mandurah Tourist Bureau
75 Mandurah Tce, Mandurah 6210
Ph: (08) 9550 3999

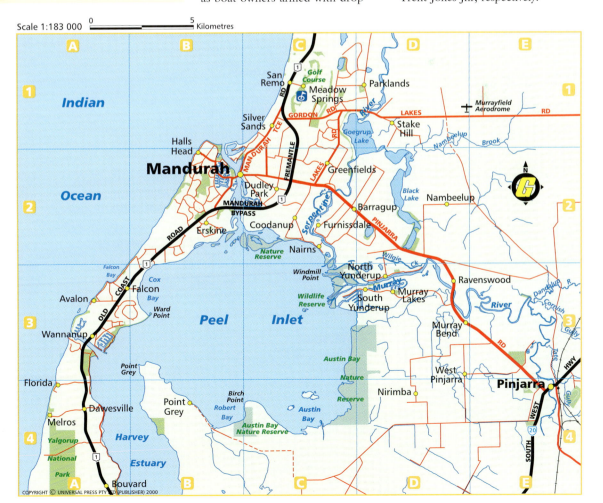

Scale 1:183 000   0   5 Kilometres

Rottnest Island

Must Visit

- Rottnest's Colonial Architecture
- Rottnest Museum
- Historic Oliver Hill Light Railway
- Thompson Bay

ℹ **Tourist Information**

Rottnest Island Visitor and Information Centre
Thompson Bay, Rottnest Island 6161
Ph: (08) 9372 9752
www.rottnest.wa.gov.au

This sandy island is home to quokkas, small indigenous beaver-like marsupials that were mistakenly identified as rats in 1696 by a Dutch explorer, who subsequently named the island 'Rats Nest'. Today, holiday-makers are drawn to Rottnest Island in their thousands each year. Bicycles, available everywhere for hire, are the main mode of transport on the island — so there is almost no motorised traffic.

'Rotto', 18km west of Fremantle, is only 11km long and less than half that wide. Its pristine beaches are a major drawcard, as they boast crystal clear water and some of the world's southern-most coral reefs. These sparkling waters are extremely popular for water-based activities, with the sheltered emerald bays providing idyllic conditions for snorkelling, surfing, scuba diving, swimming or just soaking up the

Secluded Bay, Rottnest Island

sun. The reefs surrounding the island offer excellent abalone, rock lobster, squid and many species of fish. Due to its close proximity to Perth and Fremantle, by ferry or aeroplane, Rottnest is an ideal daytrip destination, but has much to offer visitors who choose to settle into its easygoing pace.

Scale 1:75 000

0   3 Kilometres

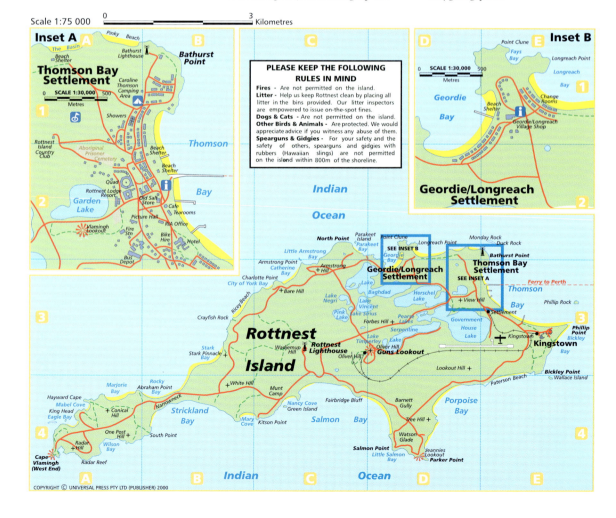

PLEASE KEEP THE FOLLOWING RULES IN MIND

Fires - Are not permitted on the island.
Litter - Help us keep Rottnest clean by placing all litter in the bins provided. Our litter inspectors are empowered to issue on-the-spot fines.
Dogs & Cats - Are not permitted on the island.
Other Birds & Animals - Are protected. We would appreciate advice if you witness any abuse of them.
Spearguns & Gidgies - For your safety and the safety of others, spearguns and gidgies with rubbers (Hawaiian slings) are not permitted on the island within 800m of the shoreline.

Stirling Range NP to Albany

Blessed with immense natural beauty, the Great Southern region is a treasure trove for holiday-makers. Its diverse landscape incorporates sweeping rural vistas, rugged cliff-covered coastline, gentle coves and bays, raging rivers and rugged mountain ranges. Unspoilt national parks of majestic karri and tingle forest are dotted with ancient rock formations, while the tranquil bays invite calving southern right and humpback whales to give birth to their young each year. Some of WA's most beautiful wildflowers grace the granite ranges, which date back 1000 million years. Today, these ranges offer excellent hiking and bushwalking opportunities.

This region was settled before Perth — its defacto capital, Albany was WA's first European settlement, and the site of its original farm is still there. Now, Great Southern is being increasingly feted for its rural

Sheep grazing, Stirling Range

charm and regional produce — it is fast becoming one of Australia's largest wine regions, with over 30 wineries to visit.

Must Visit

- Albany Whaleworld
- King River
- Middleton Beach
- Mt Barker wine-producing region

ℹ️ Tourist Information

Albany Tourist Bureau
Old Railway Station, Proudlove Pde,
Albany 6330
Ph: (08) 9841 1088
Freecall: 1800 644 088
www.albanytourist.com.au

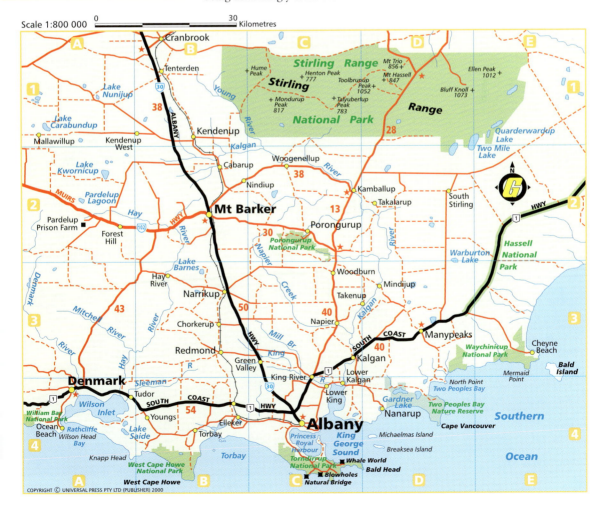

Scale 1:800 000

Northern Territory

NT: Outback Australia

- Area = 1 346 200 sq km
- Occupies 17.5% of the continent
- Length of coastline = 6200km

Sturt's Desert Rose   *Red Kangaroo*

ℹ️ Tourist Information

Northern Territory Visitors Centre
Tourism Northern Territory
1st Floor, 22 Cavenagh St,
Darwin 0800
Ph: (08) 8941 1394
www.northernterritory.com

Main Attractions

★ **Alice Springs**
Surrounded by red desert, Alice Springs is the NT's second largest centre. There is much to explore around the town.

★ **Darwin**
Darwin is a cosmopolitan, modern town with a relaxed, tropical atmosphere.

★ **Kakadu NP**
One of Australia's icons, this NP is on the World Heritage List for both its natural and cultural significance.

★ **Nitmiluk (Katherine Gorge) NP**
This NP is home to the magnificent 12m Katherine Gorge, carved over centuries by the Katherine River.

★ **Uluru-Kata Tjuta NP — Ayres Rock (Uluru)**
Ayres Rock is the Australian outback's most famous icon. This 3.6km long site is also a sacred site for the local Anangu Aboriginals.

★ **Litchfield NP**
This NP encompasses the Tabletop Range and has spectacular waterfalls and crocodile-free swimming spots.

Covering approximately one-sixth of Australia, the NT is the country's most barren region. The Territory's rich Aboriginal past dates back as far as 50 000yrs, and the sunburnt terrain is dotted with evidence of this heritage. Their ceremonies, rock art and intimate knowledge of the land and its seasons attest to their special link with the Territory. About 45% of the Territory is classified as Aboriginal land, where only visitors with special permits are allowed to enter.

Uluru (Ayres Rock)

The stunning ochre colours and vibrant red sands of the Centre are epitomised by the MacDonnell Ranges and the Simpson Desert; in contrast are the verdant greens of the rainforests and savanna woodlands that merge into the monsoonal Timor and Arafura seas.

The remoteness and diversity of the NT make it an ideal location for visitors wanting to go beyond the beaten track. It is excellent for 4WD touring, and camel treks can be organised from Alice Springs, with 2 week journeys to Rainbow Valley just one of the options. Bushwalkers will find much to discover on a range of walking tracks ranging in degrees of difficulty. Scenic flights are a more leisurely sightseeing option, while the Centre's dry heat creates ideal conditions for gliding.

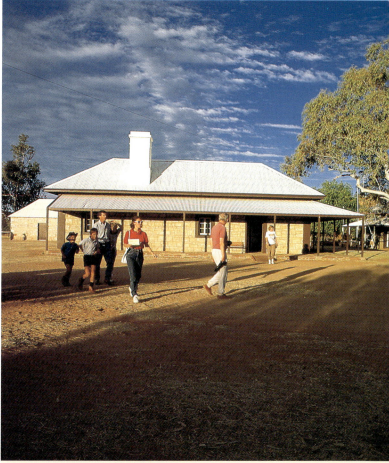

Old Telegraph Station, Alice Springs

Northern Territory Key Map and Distance Chart

All distances shown in the chart below have been measured over highways and major roads, not necessarily by the shortest route.

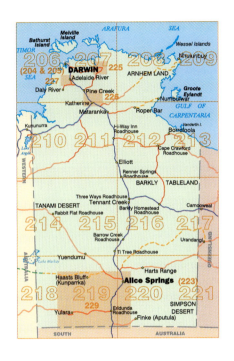

City Map
Darwin, page 203

Suburban Maps
Darwin, pages 204 and 205

Territory Maps
pages 206 to 221

Region Maps
Alice Springs, page 223
Kakadu National Park, page 225
Katherine Gorge, page 226
Litchfield National Park, page 227
Uluru/Kata Tjuta-
Alice Springs, page 229

Approximate Distance	Adelaide River	Alice Springs	Ayers Rock/Yulara	Borroloola	Camooweal QLD	Darwin	Erldunda	Hi-Way Inn	Jabiru	Katherine	Kulgera	Kununurra WA	Mataranka	Nicholson WA	Pine River SA	Tennant Creek	Ti-Tree	Top Springs	Tobermorey	Wauchope
Adelaide River		1385	1827	585	1293	107	1584	477	288	202	1660	714	308	902	111	871	1180	492	1799	985
Alice Springs	1385		442	1214	988	1492	199	908	1468	1183	275	1695	1077	1464	1274	514	205	1054	570	400
Ayers Rock/Yulara	1827	442		1656	1430	1934	243	1350	1910	1625	319	2137	1519	1906	1716	956	647	1496	1012	842
Borroloola	585	1214	1656		746	967	1413	383	943	658	1489	1151	552	1011	749	700	1009	601	1628	814
Camooweal QLD	1293	988	1430	746		1400	1187	816	1376	1091	1263	1603	985	1372	1182	474	783	962	1402	588
Darwin	107	1492	1934	967	1400		1691	584	243	309	1767	821	415	1009	218	978	1287	599	1906	1092
Erldunda	1584	199	243	1413	1187	1691		1107	1667	1382	76	1894	1276	1663	1473	713	404	1253	769	599
Hi-Way Inn	477	908	1350	383	816	584	1107		560	275	1183	768	169	628	366	394	703	218	1322	508
Jabiru	288	1468	1910	943	1376	243	1667	560		285	1743	797	391	985	194	954	1263	575	1882	1068
Katherine	202	1183	1625	658	1091	309	1382	275	285		1458	512	106	700	91	669	978	290	1597	783
Kulgera	1660	275	319	1489	1263	1767	76	1183	1743	1458		1970	1352	1739	1549	789	480	1329	845	675
Kununurra WA	714	1695	2137	1151	1603	821	1894	768	797	512	1970		618	327	603	1181	1490	550	2109	1295
Mataranka	308	1077	1519	552	985	415	1276	169	391	106	1352	618		797	197	563	872	396	1491	677
Nicholson WA	902	1464	1906	1011	1372	1009	1663	628	985	700	1739	327	797		791	950	1259	410	1878	1064
Pine River SA	111	1274	1716	749	1182	218	1473	366	194	91	1549	603	197	791		760	1069	381	1688	874
Tennant Creek	871	514	956	700	474	978	713	394	954	669	789	1181	563	950	760		309	540	928	114
Ti-Tree	1180	205	647	1009	783	1287	404	703	1263	978	480	1490	872	1259	1069	309		849	619	195
Top Springs	492	1054	1496	601	962	599	1253	218	575	290	1329	550	396	410	381	540	849		1468	654
Tobermorey	1799	570	1012	1628	1402	1906	769	1322	1882	1597	845	2109	1491	1878	1688	928	619	1468		814
Wauchope	985	400	842	814	588	1092	599	508	1068	783	675	1295	677	1064	874	114	195	654	814	

Darwin

ℹ️ Tourist Information

Darwin Region Tourism Association
Beagle House, cnr Knuckey & Mitchell Sts, Darwin 0800
Ph: (08) 8981 4300
www.ntholidays.com.au

The Territory's capital, perched on a picturesque harbour, is closer to Jakarta and Singapore than it is to Sydney and Melbourne. Home to the Larrakeyah Aboriginal people for thousands of years, it was first settled by Europeans in 1869, when SA Surveyor-General Goyder arrived to establish a city in the Top End. Darwin was the terminus for the Overland Telegraph link to England, which began operating in 1872. This telegraph line indirectly provided Darwin's first economic and migrant boom. Darwin now serves primarily as an administration centre for government and the mining industry.

Its isolation and steamy tropical climate give Darwin a relaxed, easygoing atmosphere and way of life. Few historic buildings remain, due to repeated air raids during WWII and to the devastation of Cyclone Tracy on Christmas Day in 1974, making it one of Australia's most modern cities.

Shopping Mall, Darwin

Darwin is an outdoors city. The renowned Mindil Beach Sunset Markets are extremely popular. The palm-fringed night markets, held on one of Darwin's favourite beaches, feature food stalls reflecting the city's eclectic multicultural mix. The historic Wharf Precinct was once the domain of anglers and skateboarders; now the old wharves are becoming a tourist attraction, with restaurants, museums and tours.

Main Attractions

⭐ **Aquascene**
At high tide daily, witness the spectacular sight of hundreds of milkfish, mullet, catfish and other fish competing for hand-fed white bread.

⭐ **Australian Pearling Exhibition**
This world class exhibit provides an insight into the romance of the local pearling industry.

⭐ **Darwin Botanic Gardens**
Explore the 42ha gardens and discover mangroves, orchids, rainforest, open woodlands and other tropical habitats.

⭐ **East Pt Reserve**
A dusk visit will reveal Fannie Bay's spectacular sunset, as wallabies come out in their hordes. The 200ha Reserve features natural mangroves and forest, parklands and safe saltwater swimming.

⭐ **Indo-Pacific Marine**
Boasting living coral reef ecosystems, the night program offers a torchlight tour and a seafood buffet dinner.

Sunset at Fannie Bay

Places of Interest

1. Cenotaph **C7**
2. Chinese Temple **D7**
3. Darwin Entertainment Centre **C6**
4. Darwin Wharf Precinct **E8**
5. Fannie Bay Gaol Museum **C1**
6. Government House **D7**
7. Mindil Beach Lookout **A4**
8. Old Court House **D7**
9. Parliament House **D7**
10. Smith St Mall **D7**
11. Vestey's Beach **C2**
12. Victoria Hotel **D7**

Scale 1:25 000

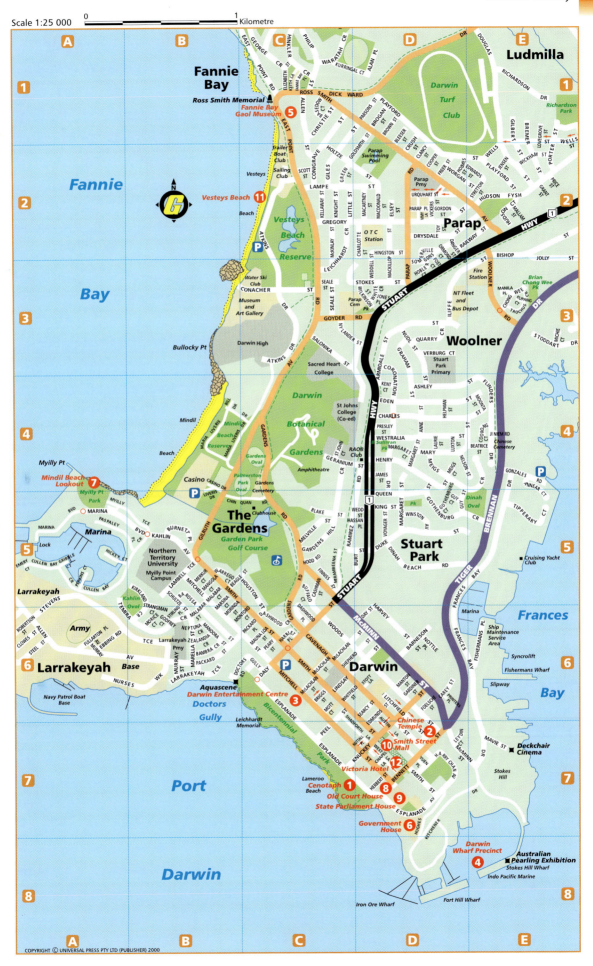

0   1 Kilometre

Fannie Bay

Ross Smith Memorial
Fannie Bay Gaol Museum

Ludmilla

Darwin Turf Club

Richardson Park

Parap

Woolner

Vesteys Beach

Fannie

Bay

Vesteys Beach Reserve

Water Ski Club CONACHER

Museum and Art Gallery

Bullocky Pt

Darwin High

Brian Chong Wee Pk

Chinese Cemetery

Parap Swimming Pool

OTC Station

Parap Cem

NT Fleet and Bus Depot

Fire Station

Stuart Park Primary

Mindil

Darwin Botanical Gardens

Sacred Heart College

St Johns College (Co-ed)

RAOB Club

Gardens Oval

Amphitheatre

Myilly Pt

Mindil Beach Lookout

Myilly Pt Park

Casino

Palmerston Park Oval

Gardens Cemetery

Dinah Oval

Cruising Yacht Club

Marina

Lock

Larrakeyah

Army

Northern Territory University Myilly Point Campus

Kahlin Oval

The Gardens

Garden Park Golf Course

Stuart Park

Frances Bay

Ship Maintenance Service Area

Syncrolift

Larrakeyah Base

Navy Patrol Boat Base

Aquascene
Darwin Entertainment Centre

Leichhardt Memorial

Bicentennial Park

Darwin

Doctors Gully

Fishermans Wharf

Slipway

Frances Bay

Deckchair Cinema

Chinese Temple

Smith Street Mall

Victoria Hotel

Stokes Hill

Port

Lameroo Beach

Cenotaph

Old Court House
State Parliament House

Government House

Darwin Wharf Precinct

Australian Pearling Exhibition
Stokes Hill Wharf
Indo Pacific Marine

Darwin

Iron Ore Wharf

Fort Hill Wharf

Scale 1:80 00

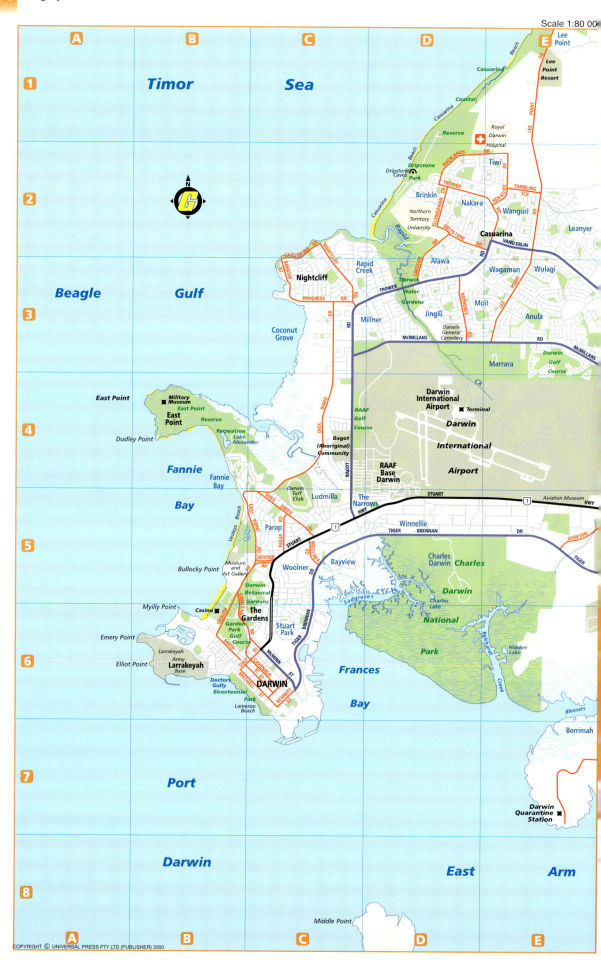

Timor   Sea

Lee Point

Lee Point Resort

Casuarina

Coastal

Casuarina Reserve

Royal Darwin Hospital

Dripstone Caves

Dripstone Park

Rocklands

Tiwi

Brinkin

Nakara

Wanguri

Leanyer

Northern Territory University

Casuarina

Tambling Tce

Beagle   Gulf

Nightcliff

Rapid Creek

Darwin Water Gardens

Alawa

Wagaman

Wulagi

Trower

Millner

Jingili

Moil

Anula

Coconut Grove

Darwin General Cemetery

McMillans

Marrara

Darwin Golf Course

McMillans

Darwin International Airport

Terminal

East Point

Military Museum

East Point

East Point Reserve

Darwin

Dudley Point

Recreation Lake Alexander

RAAF Golf Course

International

Bagot (Aboriginal) Community

Airport

Fannie

Fannie Bay

Darwin Turf Club

Ludmilla

RAAF Base Darwin

Stuart

Aviation Museum

Bay

The Narrows

Winnellie

Hwy

Vesteys Beach

Parap

Tiger Brennan

Johnson

Bullocky Point

Museum and Art Gallery

Woolner

Bayview

Charles Darwin

Charles

Tiger

Myilly Point

Casino

The Gardens

Darwin Botanical Gardens

Darwin

Charles Lake

National

Emery Point

Garden Park Golf Course

Stuart Park

Hidden Lake

Elliot Point

Larrakeyah

Army Base

Larrakeyah

Park

Frances

Bleesers

Doctors Gully Bicentennial Park

DARWIN

Berrimah

Lameroo Beach

Bay

Port

Darwin Quarantine Station

Darwin

East   Arm

Middle Point

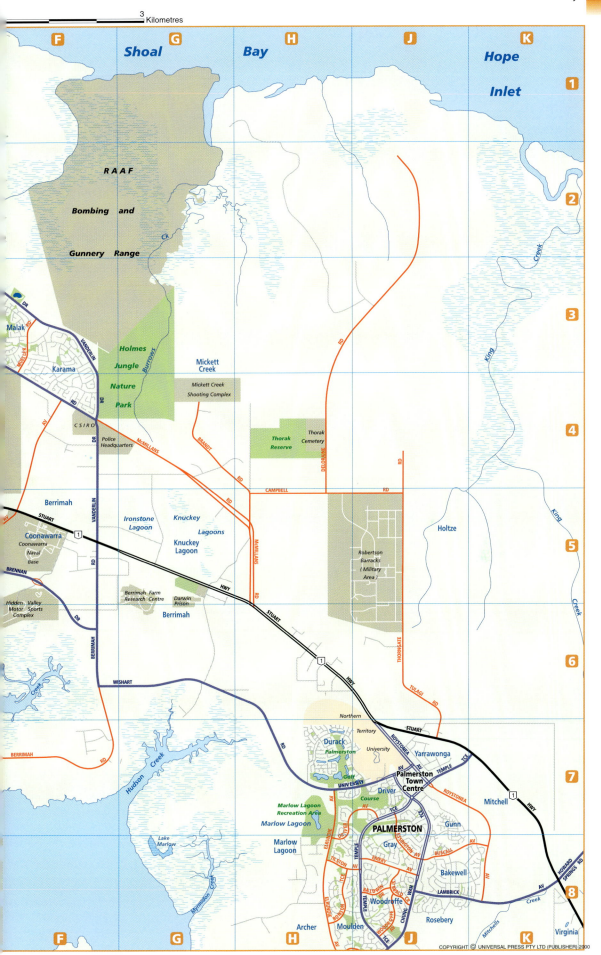

3 Kilometres

F G H J K

Shoal   Bay

Hope

Inlet

1

R A A F

Bombing   and

2

Gunnery   Range

Ck

Malak

3

Holmes

Karama

Jungle

Burrows

Nature

Mickett
Creek

Park

Mickett Creek
Shooting Complex

CSIRO

Thorak
Cemetery

4

Police
Headquarters

McMillans

BRANDT

Thorak
Reserve

DELORAINE

RD

CAMPBELL   RD

RD

Berrimah

King

Knuckey

5

STUART

Ironstone
Lagoon

Lagoons

Holtze

Coonawarra

Knuckey
Lagoon

1

Coonawarra
Naval
Base

McMILLANS

Robertson
Barracks
(Military
Area)

BRENNAN

Creek

King

Hidden Valley
Motor Sports
Complex

Berrimah Farm
Research Centre

Darwin
Prison

DR

Berrimah

HWY

STUART

Creek

THORNGATE

6

1

HWY

WISHART

TULAGI   RD

BERRIMAH

Hudson

Northern

STUART

BERRIMAH   RD

RD

Creek

Territory
University

Durack

ROYSTONEA

Yarrawonga

TCE

7

Palmerston

Goff

Palmerston
Town
Centre

TEMPLE

HOWARD

Driver

ROYSTONEA

Mitchell

1

SPRINGS

HWY

UNIVERSITY

Course

Marlow Lagoon
Recreation Area

Marlow Lagoon

TCE

Gunn

RD

Lake
Marlow

Marlow
Lagoon

PALMERSTON

Gray

BUSCH

Bakewell

Creek

8

Woodroffe

LAMBRICK

CHUNG

Myrmidon

Archer

Moulden

Rosebery

Mitchells

Virginia

F G H J K

Scale 1:2 000 00

	A	B	C	D
1				
2				
3				
4				
5				
6				

Tiwi Islands

Cape Van Dieman

St Asaph Bay

Shark Bay

Cape Lavery

Radford Pt.

Snake Bay

Lethbridge Bay

Deception Pt.

Pularumpi

Milikapiti

Bathurst Island

Rocky Pt.

Gordon Bay

Wurankuwu

Melville Island

46

26

Tiwi Wilderness Lodge
Cape Helveticus

12

21

Pickertaramoo

Nguiu
(Police Stn.)

54

Cape Fourcroy

Cape Gambier

Clarence Strait

Vernon Islands

BEAGLE GULF

Gunn Pt.

10

Shoal Bay

For more detail see map on pages 204 & 205

Lee Pt.

DARWIN

Charles Point

Mandorah

20

TIMOR

13

31

Quail I.

Belyuen

Berry Springs

Grosse I.

34

Dundee Beach

Manton Dam

25

32

Darwin R. Dam

11

Finniss River

Fog Bay

16

Finniss

51

Rum Jungle

Point Blaze

DELISSAVILLE/WAGAIT/LARRAKIA

R

Florence Falls

31

11

For more detail see map on page 227

Batchelor

13

14

Camp Creek

Peron I. Nth

Wangi

SEA

Welltree

Tolmer Falls

The lost City

Peron I. Sth

Reynolds

LITCHFIELD

25

Adelaide

Anson Bay

Litchfield

N.P.

Robin Falls

Cape Ford

Daly

18

24

Cape Scott

Elizabeth Downs

28

32

27

Cape Dombey

19

(Police Stn)*Tipperary*

Hyland Bay

18

Daly River

Cape Hay

Moyle

82

River Bamboo

JOSEPH BONAPARTE

Peppimenarti

River

Wadeye
(Port Keats)
(Police Stn)

GULF

44

28

Palumpa

42

DALY RIVER/PORT KEATS

Pearce Point

UPPER DALY

50 Kilometres

ARAFURA SEA

Croker Point
Lawson I.
McCluer I.
Vashon Head
Smith Pt.
Danger Pt.
Croker Island
Minjilang
Grant I.
Point Jahleel
Trepang Bay
Black Point (Ranger Stn.)
Darch I.
Templer I.
Cape Cockburn
Seven Spirit Lodge
Cobourg Peninsula
Cape De Courcy Head
Cape Don
GURIG NATIONAL PARK
Victoria Settlement
Valencia I.
Mountnorris Bay
Brogden Pt.
Nth Goulburn I.
Soldier Pt.
Napier Bay
Burford I.
COBOURG MARINE PARK
Morse I.
Murgenella (Ranger Stn.)
Goulburn Islands
Sth Goulburn I.
Cape Keith
Greenhill I.
Sir George Hope Islands
Endyalgout I.
Auran Bay
Warruwi
Cobham Bay
Turner Pt.
Arrlg Bay
Cuthbert Pt.
Conder Pt.

TIWI LAND CENTRAL LAND COUNCIL COUNCIL

VAN DIEMEN GULF

Cape Hotham
Pt. Stuart
West Alligator Hd.
Point Farewell
Field I.
Murgenella R.
102
Adam Bay
DJUKBINJ N.P.
Chambers Bay
Finke Bay
King R.
Cooper Creek
172
Woolner
Swim Creek
West Alligator R.
South Alligator R.
22
15
Nabarlek
See page 208
Howard Springs
Shady Camp
Melaleuca
Carmor Plains
Ubirr Rock
Border Store (Manbiyarri)
11
12
Oenpelli (Police Stn.)
Goomadeer R.
Nungbalgarri Ck.
38
Humpty Doo
Middle Point
5
21
Opium Ck
Pt. Stuart Lodge
KAKADU
Jabiluka M.L.
Tin Camp Ck.
Fog Dam
13
Wildman River Lodge
Cashew Nut Farm
7
For more detail see map on page 225
Ranger M.L.
DJUKBINJ N.P.
94
7
5
Ranger Stn.
17
Wildman R.
35
Nourlangie
Jabiru
Bowali Visitor Centre (Park H.Q.)
Liverpool R.
ARNHEM
Corroboree Pk Inn
Rockhole
Park Entrance Stn.
87
HWY
Frontier Kakadu Village
17
Goyder R.
76
125
Bark Hut Inn
West R.
36
45
29
16
HWY
10
Nourlangie Rock
Koongarra Mineral Lease
Gas
Mary R.
Annaburroo Billabong
Cooinda Lodge
27
6
Jim Jim Billabong
Mt Ringwood
90
Ck.
NATIONAL
River
29
McKinlay R.
79
132
Jim Jim Ck.
ARNHEM LAND
Mt Bundy
Margaret R.
Woolwonga
21
Coongong R.
Barramundie Ck.
PARK
Mann R.
Adelaide River
11
Mary River
Gunlom Falls
Gimbat R.
Ban Ban Springs
49
21
Jarrangbarnmi (Koolpin Gorge)
17
STUART
Hayes Creek Roadhouse
Burrundie
Frances Ck
Park Entrance Stn.
13
Gimbat
Mainoru R.
23
2
28
Spring Hill
KAKADU
10
14
Mary River Roadhouse
Douglas
25
12
20
62
Gimbet R.
111
Emerald Springs Roadhouse
18
15
BUTTERFLY GORGE N.R.
26
Pine Creek
Wardie Ck.
Mountain Valley
Douglas Experimental Farm
Douglas Hot Springs
22
1
Bonrook
MANYALLALUK
18
Ooloo
21
Jindare
Umbrawarra Gorge
NITMILUK
For more detail see map on page 226
MANYALLALUK
Fox R.
247
Lukies Farm
Daly R.
92
91
19
Edith Falls (KATHERINE GORGE)
Katherine R.
24
ARNHEM ROAD
Mann R.
Granite
N.P.
Manyallaluk
29
Florina
Ferguson R.
Gundagai
27
Katherine Gorge (Nitmiluk)
30
King River
Barunga
CENTRAL
62
Dorisvale
Katherine
TAWOYN
Tindal RAAF Base
52
Maranboy (Police Stn.)
Beswick
BESWICK
Carbeen Park
VICTORIA HWY
Cutta Cutta Caves
Roper R.
Chambs Ck.
45
30
16
See page 211

See page 208
For more detail see map on page 225
For more detail see map on page 226
See page 211

Scale 1:2 000 0[...]

ARAFURA   SEA

A   **B**   **C**   **D**

1

2

Nth Goulburn I.

Goulburn Islands

Sth Goulburn I.

Aurari Bay

North Crocodile Reef

Warruwi

Turner Pt.   Cuthbert Pt.

Arla Bay   Braithwaite Pt.

N.W. Crocodile I.

Drysdale I.

Graham I.

King R.

River

Junction Bay

Goomandeer Pt.

Hawkesbury Pt.

Cape Stewart

Crocodile Islands

Mooroongga I.

Elcho Island

Cooper

172

Entrance I.

Skirmish Pt.

Boucaut Bay

Rabuma I.

Galiwinku

Napier Pen.

Brown R.

3

Creek

15

Nabarlek

Goomadeer

Nungbalgan R.

29

Maningrida
(Police Stn.)

Milingimbi

Milingimbi I.

Castlereagh Bay

Howard I.

26

Banyan I.

Ramingining

Woden R.

Buckingham Bay

Flinders Peninsula

Gapuwiyak

25

4

River

Liverpool River

Cadell River

Immbar Ck.

Blyth

Glyde

74

Goyder River

105

CENTRAL

155

Mitchell Range

Koolatong

Maidjunga R.

Harbgood

Mann

ARNHEM LAND

Blyth

Goyder Ck.

River

Parsons Ra.

Walker

Bath Ra.

Blue Bay

5

ARNHEM   LAND

Wilton

90

Annie River

Harris Ck.

Bulman

Mainoru

Flying Fox River

70   ROAD

Lindsay Ck.

Mountain Valley

18

Mainoru

Waldoo River

Manouk R.

ARNHEM

Phelp River

Rose River

Wukayinyanya

Numbulwar

6

29

24

247

62

CENTRAL   72

River

Turkey Creek

156

Lagoon

Nyanpinti Pt.

Edward I.

Beswick

Chambers R.

Creek

River

River Ck.

A   **B**   **See page 212**   **C**   **D**

Warrakunta Pt.

See page 207

See page 213

Scale 1:2 000 00

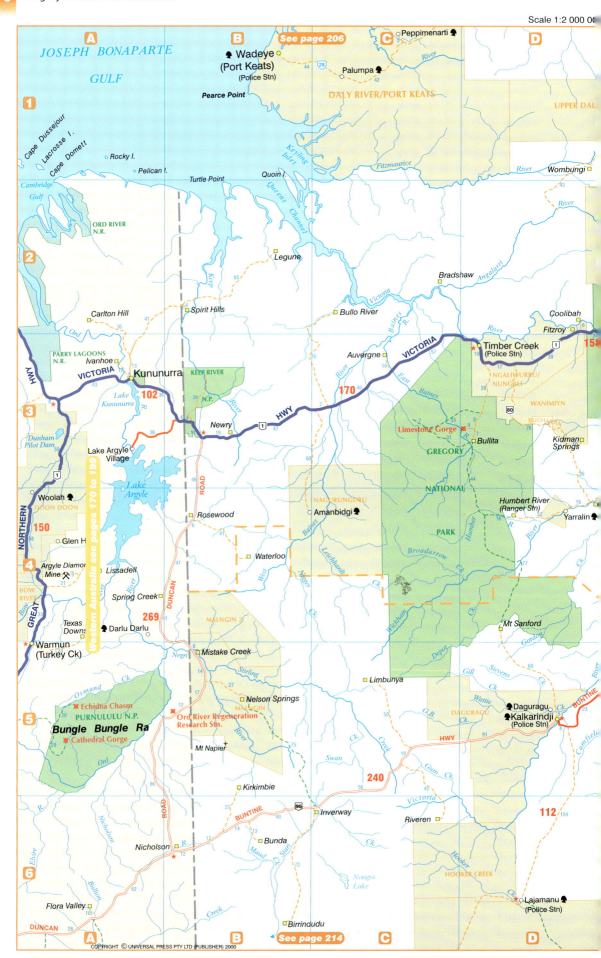

See page 206

See page 214

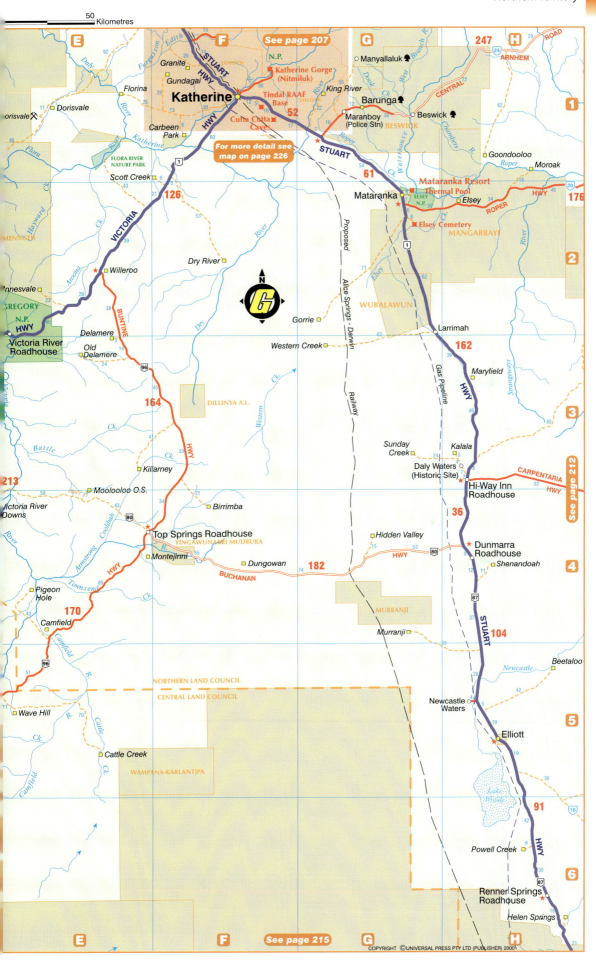

50 Kilometres

See page 207

N.P.

Manyallaluk

ARNHEM ROAD

247

E

F

G

H

Granite
Gundagai
Florina
Dorisvale
Dorisvale

Katherine
Katherine Gorge (Nitmiluk)
King River

Barunga
Beswick

BESWICK

CENTRAL

Tindal RAAF Base
52
Maranboy (Police Stn)

STUART HWY

Carbeen Park
Cutta Cutta Caves

For more detail see map on page 226

STUART

Goondooloo
Moroak

Roper

Flora River Nature Park
Scott Creek
126

Mataranka Resort Thermal Pool
Elsey
HWY
176
20

61
Mataranka
Elsey N.P.
Elsey Cemetery
MANGARRAYI

1

VICTORIA

Dry River

Willeroo
Gorrie

WUBALAWUN

Elsey

BUNTINE

GREGORY N.P.
HWY
Victoria River Roadhouse

Delamere
Old Delamere

Larrimah
162

Western Creek

Maryfield

164

HWY
Killarney

DILLINYA A.L.

Railway

Gas Pipeline

Sunday Creek
Kalala
Daly Waters (Historic Site)

Hi-Way Inn Roadhouse

CARPENTARIA HWY

See page 212

213
Victoria River Downs

Mooloola O.S.
Birrimba
80

Top Springs Roadhouse
YINGAWUNARRI MUDBURA
Montejinni

Hidden Valley
HWY
80

Dunmarra Roadhouse
Shenandoah

36

Dungowan
182
BUCHANAN

MURRANJI

Murranji

87

STUART
104

Pigeon Hole
170
Camfield
96

Beetaloo

NORTHERN LAND COUNCIL

CENTRAL LAND COUNCIL

Newcastle Waters

Wave Hill

5

Cattle Creek

WAMPANA-KARLANTJPA

Elliott

Lake Woods

91
HWY

Powell Creek

87

Renner Springs Roadhouse

Helen Springs

6

E

F

See page 215

G

H

Scale 1:2 000 00

See page 208

A ARNHEM ROAD CENTRAL
247
1 Beswick ♣
Goondooloo
Moroak
Roper
Mataranka Resort Thermal Pool
ELSEY N.P.
Elsey
34
ROPER
176
Roper Valley
Elsey Cemetery
MANGARRAYI

B
Roper Bar
66
HWY
20
46

C
Urapunga
(Police Stn)
Ngukurr ♣
YUTPUNDJI-DJINDIWIRRITJ
Roper
87
Port Roper

D
Numbulwar
Nyanpinti Pt.
Edward I.
Warrakunta Pt.
Port Roper
Limmen Bight
MARRA
Maria I.

2
62
Larrimah
162
Maryfield
HWY
3
Kalala
24
Hi-Way Inn Roadhouse
82
CARPENTARIA
36
80
4 Dunmarra Roadhouse
Shenandoah
12
87
STUART
104
39
Ck.
Newcastle
Beetaloo
42
5 Newcastle Waters
19
Elliott
19
30

See page 211

Miniyeri ♣
ALAWA 1
Hodgson River
ALAWA
Nutwood Downs
18

The Four Archers
341
Nathan River
Rosie
Lorella Springs
Pine

JANDANKU
Bauhinia Downs
24
Tawallah
58
Broadmere
Billengarrah

270
HWY
Tanumbirini
57
October
22
O.T. Downs
44
CARPENTARIA
Cape Crawford Roadhouse
McArthur River
Balbirini
11
Mailapunyah
30

Amungee Mungee

Entry to Aboriginal Lands is Prohibited without a permit from: The Permits Officer, Northern Land Council P.O. Box 42921 Casuarina, NT, 0871 Telephone (08) 8920 5178 Facsimile (08) 8945 2633 ▶

WAMPAYA

HWY
153
67

6
Powell Creek
91
HWY
Gas Pipeline
87
Renner Springs Roadhouse
Helen Springs
18

Ucharonidge
30
Mungabroom
48
250
BARKLY
STOCK
ROUTE
39
Eva Downs
78
31

Walhallow
Anthony Lagoon
7
Cresswell Downs (Abandoned)
11
CALVERT
16
TABLELANDS HWY

A

B See page 216

C

D TABLELANDS HWY

50 Kilometres

See page 209

E   F   G   H

Eylandt
Ungwariba Pt.

South Pt.   ARNHEM LAND

Cape Beatrice

ANINDILYAKWA LAND COUNCIL

1

GULF OF CARPENTARIA

2

SIR EDWARD PELLEW GROUP

WURRALIBI A.L.   North I.

West I.   WURRALIBI A.L.
Bing Bong   McArthur River Mine
Loading Facility
South   Centre I.   Vanderlin I.
West I.

Batten Pt

36   Creek   River

21   3

14   River   Manangoora

Borroloola   River

12   28

18   HWY   23
8   River

19   NARWINBI   18   Greenbank

33   **113**   16   Seven Emu

62   River

River   **200**   26

26

McArthur River   **GARAWA**   River

148

Spring Creek   55   River

34   Pungalina

Robinson   Running   Ck
River   Ck

48   Gold

1   Ck

Wollogorang Gulf
30   34   Wilderness
Kiana   Redbank   Lodge

58   24

Calvert Hills   36   Westmoreland

ROAD   16   18   Hells Gate
Bluey   95   Roadhouse

Puzzle   Ck   **295**   Cliffdale

276   32

132   Nicholson   River   Corinda (ruin)   Doomadgee

Benmara   Bowthorn

Creek   WAANYI/GARAWA

Elizabeth

Creek   Fish Hole   Ck   Ck   Creek

See page 217

Queensland see pages 106 to 141

3

4

5

6

Scale 1:2 000 00

A **B** See page 210 **C** **D**

HOOKER CREEK

Nongra
Lake

Flora Valley

1 DUNCAN 28

Lajamanu
(Police Stn)

Creek

Birrindudu

Gordon Downs
(ruins)

YINGUALYALYA

121

Winnecke

229

Cairn

Wilson

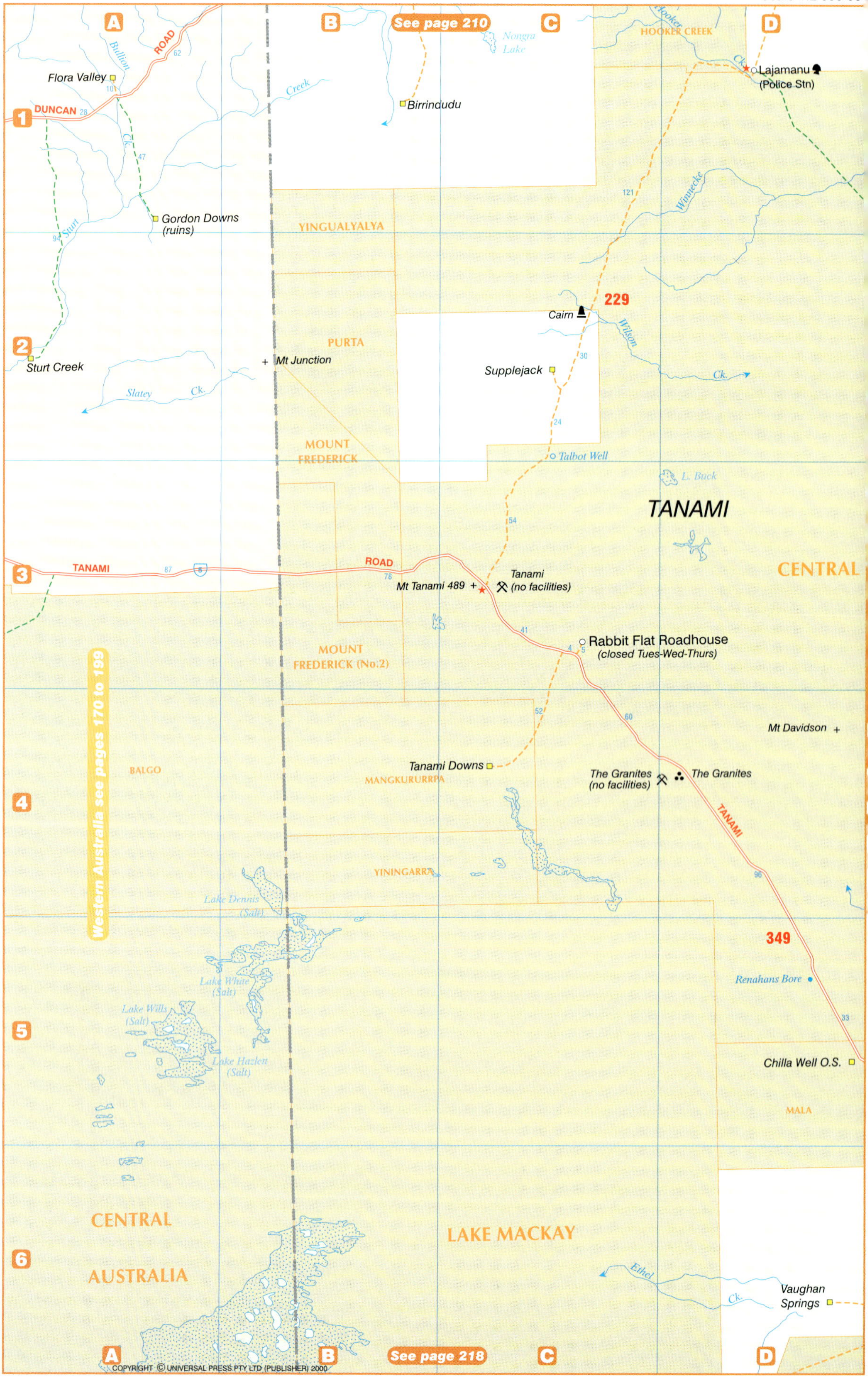

2 Sturt Creek

+ Mt Junction

PURTA

Supplejack

30

Ck.

Slatey Ck.

24

MOUNT
FREDERICK

Talbot Well

L. Buck

TANAMI

54

CENTRAL

3 TANAMI 87 6

ROAD

78

Mt Tanami 489 +

Tanami
(no facilities)

41

Rabbit Flat Roadhouse
(closed Tues-Wed-Thurs)

4
5

MOUNT
FREDERICK (No.2)

52

60

Mt Davidson +

Tanami Downs

BALGO

MANGKURURRPA

The Granites
(no facilities)

The Granites

TANAMI

4 Western Australia see pages 170 to 199

YININGARRA

96

Lake Dennis
(Salt)

349

Lake White
(Salt)

Renahans Bore

Lake Wells
(Salt)

33

5 Lake Hazlett
(Salt)

Chilla Well O.S.

MALA

CENTRAL

6 **AUSTRALIA**

LAKE MACKAY

Ethel

Ck.

Vaughan
Springs

A **B** See page 218 **C** **D**

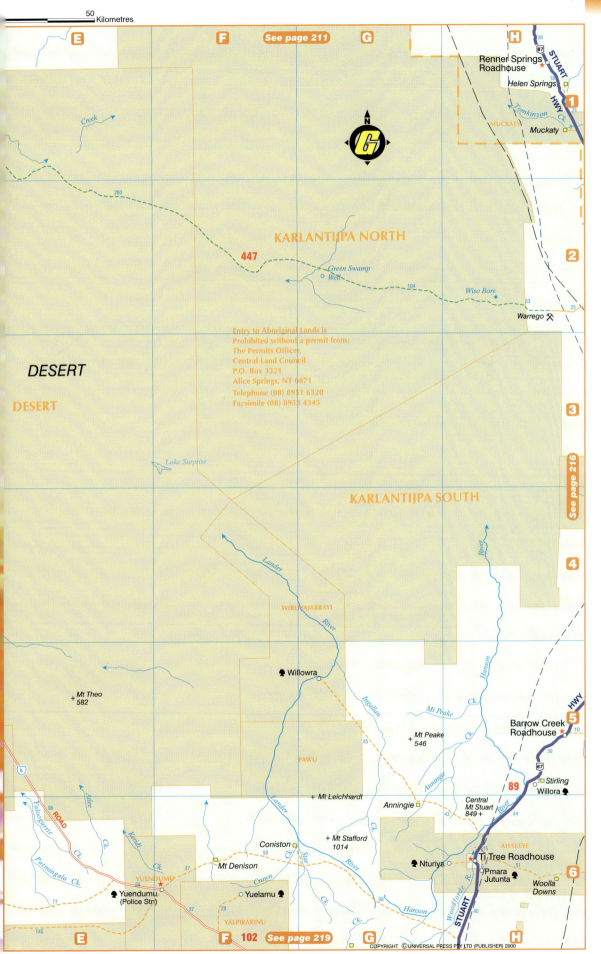

50 Kilometres

See page 211

E   F   G   H

Renner Springs
Roadhouse

Helen Springs

87   STUART

MUCKATY

Muckaty

HWY

30

15

21

1

Creek

260

KARLANTIJPA NORTH

447

Green Swamp
Well

104

Wiso Bore

33

Warrego

25

2

Entry to Aboriginal Lands is
Prohibited without a permit from:
The Permits Officer,
Central Land Council
P.O. Box 3321
Alice Springs, NT 0871

Telephone (08) 8951 6320
Facsimile (08) 8953 4345

DESERT

DESERT

Lake Surprise

See page 216

3

KARLANTIJPA SOUTH

River

Lander

4

WIRLIWAJARRAYI

River

Willowra

+ Mt Theo
582

Ingallan

Mt Peake

Ck.

HWY

Barrow Creek
Roadhouse

5

10

+ Mt Peake
546

85

30

87

89

Stirling
Willora

PAWU

Lander

Anningie

Ck.

Central
Mt Stuart
849 +

River

44

43

AHAKEYE

+ Mt Leichhardt

Anningie

Ck.

98   ROAD

Alice

Ck.

Kendi   Ck.

Ck.

Yaloogarrie

Patmingala Ck.

Ck.

37

Coniston

Mt Denison

+ Mt Stafford
1014

Stuart

River

Nturiya

15

Ti Tree Roadhouse

51

YUENDUMU

Yuendumu
(Police Stn)

77

Yuelamu

Crown

Ck.

Pmara
Jutunta

Woolla
Downs

6

40

STUART

Hanson

Woodforde R.

145

28

37

50

YALPIRAKINU

E   F   102

See page 219

G   H

98

Scale 1:2 000 00

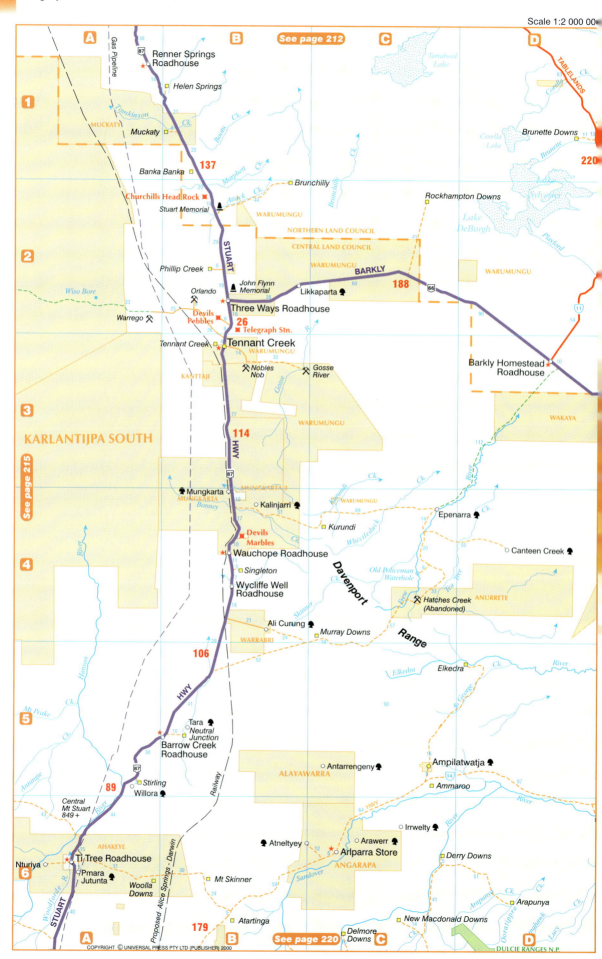

See page 212

TABLELANDS

A   B   C   D

Gas Pipeline

Renner Springs
Roadhouse
Helen Springs

Tarrabool
Lake

Brunette Downs

220

1

MUCKATY
Muckaty

Tomkinson

Banka Banka

137

Morphett Ck.

Brunchilly

Corella
Lake

Rockhampton Downs

Corella Ck.

Brunette

Sylvester

Lake
DeBurgh

Playford

WARUMUNGU

Churchills Head Rock
Stuart Memorial

NORTHERN LAND COUNCIL

CENTRAL LAND COUNCIL

WARUMUNGU

BARKLY

2

Phillip Creek

STUART

Wiso Bore

Orlando
Devils
Pebbles
Warrego

John Flynn
Memorial
Three Ways Roadhouse

Telegraph Stn.

Likkaparta

188   66

WARUMUNGU

11

Tennant Creek   Tennant Creek

26

Nobles
Nob

Gosse
River

Barkly Homestead
Roadhouse

WARUMUNGU

3

KARLANTIJPA SOUTH

KANTTAJI

WARUMUNGU

114

WAKAYA

HWY

See page 215

77

Kurundi Ck.

112

Mungkarta
MUNGKARTA

Bonney

MUNGKARTA 2

Kalinjarri

WARUMUNGU

Epenarra

Kurundi

Canteen Creek

Devils
Marbles
Wauchope Roadhouse

Whistleduck Ck.

Old Policeman
Waterhole

4

Singleton

Wycliffe Well
Roadhouse

Davenport

Skinner Ck.

Hatches Creek
(Abandoned)

ANURRETE

Ali Curung
WARRABRI

Murray Downs

Range

Elkedra

Elkedra

George River

106

HWY

Hanson River

52

Tara
Neutral
Junction
Barrow Creek
Roadhouse

Ampilatwatja

ALAYAWARRA

Antarrengeny

Ammaroo

14

5

Mt Peake Ck.

Stirling
Willora

Annunge River

89

Central
Mt Stuart
849+

Railway

Irrwelty

River

AHAKEYE

Atneltyey

Arawerr

Derry Downs

6

Nturiya

Ti Tree Roadhouse
Pmara
Jutunta
Woolla
Downs

Proposed Alice Springs - Darwin

Mt Skinner

Arlparra Store

ANGARAPA

Sandover River

Arapunya Ck.

Arapunya

STUART

Woodforde R.

New Macdonald Downs

179

Atartinga

Delmore
Downs

DULCIE RANGES N.P.

See page 220

A   B   C   D

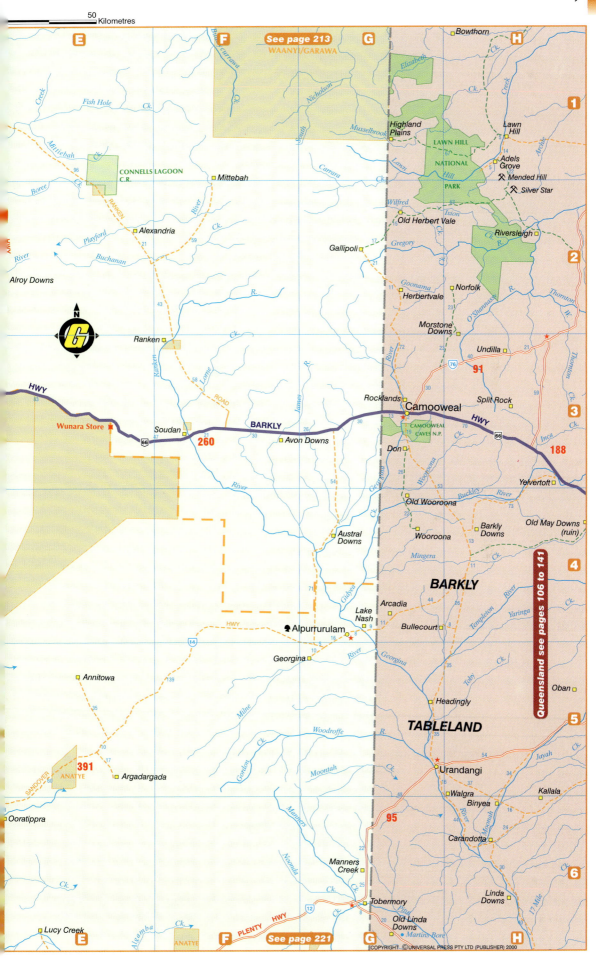

50 Kilometres

See page 213
WAANYI/GARAWA

E   F   G   H

1

2

3

4

5

6

Bowthorn

Highland Plains

Lawn Hill

LAWN HILL

NATIONAL

Adels Grove

Mended Hill

Silver Star

PARK

Riversleigh

Old Herbert Vale

Gallipoli

Norfolk

Herbertvale

Goonama

Morstone Downs

O'Shannassy

Undilla

91

Rocklands

Camooweal

Split Rock

CAMOOWEAL CAVES N.P.

HWY

188

Don

Old Wooroona

Yelvertoft

Old May Downs (ruin)

Wooroona

Barkly Downs

Mingera

Arcadia

BARKLY

Bullecourt

Templeton

Yaringa

Oban

Headingly

Toby

TABLELAND

Urandangi

Juyah

Kallala

Walgra

Binyea

95

Carandotta

Linda Downs

17 Mile

Manners Creek

Tobermory

Old Linda Downs

Martins Bore

Fish Hole Ck.

CONNELLS LAGOON C.R.

Mittebah

Mittebah

Alexandria

Boree

Playford

Buchanan

Alroy Downs

Ranken

N

G

96

21

43

Ranken

58

HWY

83

Wunara Store

Soudan

66

260

BARKLY

Avon Downs

260

21

87

ROAD

James

River

54

30

Austral Downs

71

Gidyea

Lake Nash

Alpurrurulam

HWY

14

Georgina

Georgina River

Annitowa

39

35

Milne

Woodroffe

391

ANATYE

Argadargada

SANDOVER

60

17

10

Gordon

Moontah

Ooratippra

Manners

Noonda

Lucy Creek

ANATYE

Alcamba Ck.

See page 221

PLENTY HWY

12

Queensland see pages 106 to 141

Scale 1:2 000 00

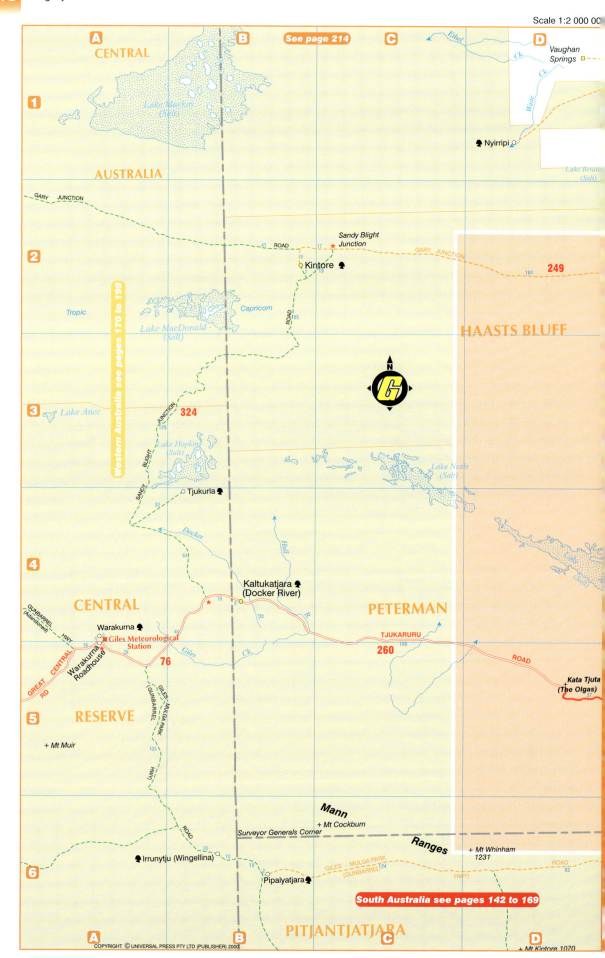

CENTRAL

See page 214

Vaughan Springs

AUSTRALIA

Lake Mackay (Salt)

Nyirripi

GARY JUNCTION

ROAD

Sandy Blight Junction

GARY JUNCTION

HAASTS BLUFF

Kintore

249

184

Tropic of Capricorn

Lake MacDonald (Salt)

JUNCTION

324

Lake Anec

Lake Hopkins (Salt)

Lake Neale (Salt)

SANDY BLIGHT

Tjukurla

Docker

Hull

Kaltukatjara (Docker River)

PETERMAN

CENTRAL

Warakurna

Giles Meteorological Station

TJUKARURU

Warakurna Roadhouse

Giles Ck

76

260

180

ROAD

GUNBARREL (Adandoneji)

GREAT CENTRAL RD

GILES – MULGA PARK (GUNBARREL) HWY

Kata Tjuta (The Olgas)

RESERVE

+ Mt Muir

105

Mann

+ Mt Cockburn

Surveyor Generals Corner

Ranges

+ Mt Whinham 1231

Irrunytju (Wingellina)

ROAD

GILES – MULGA PARK (GUNBARREL) HWY

124

ROAD

83

Pipalyatjara

South Australia see pages 142 to 169

PITJANTJATJARA

+ Mt Kintore 1070

Western Australia see pages 170 to 199

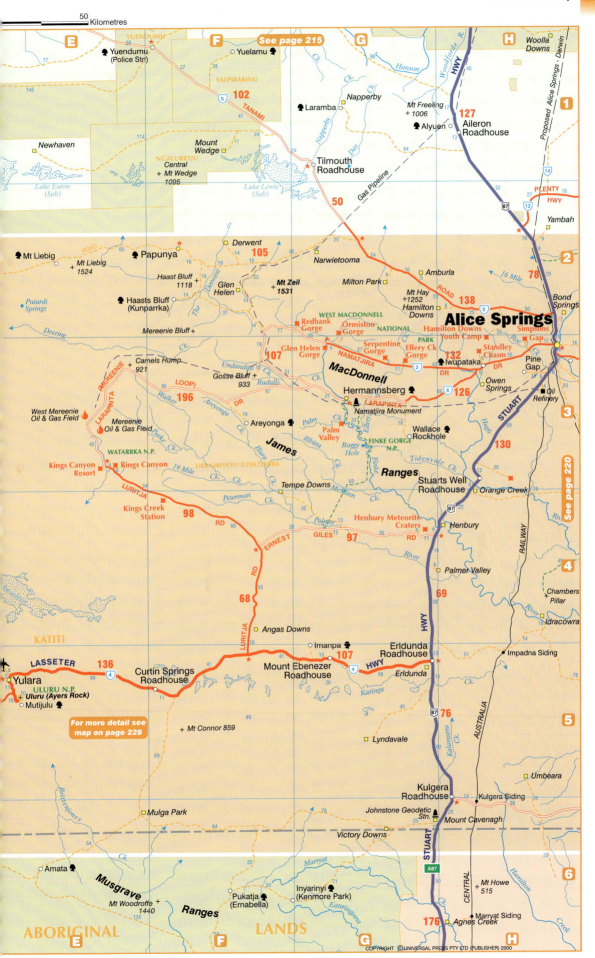

See page 215

50 Kilometres

YUENDUMU
Yuendumu
(Police Stn)
Yuelamu
Woola
Downs

YALPIRAKINU

102
TANAMI

Napperby
Laramba
Mt Freeling
+ 1006
127
Alyuen
Aileron
Roadhouse

Newhaven
Mount
Wedge
NGALURRTJU
Central
+ Mt Wedge
1095
Tilmouth
Roadhouse
Lake Eaton
(Salt)
Lake Lewis
(Salt)
Gas Pipeline
50
Gas Pipeline
PLENTY
HWY
Yambah

Mt Liebig
Papunya
Derwent
105
Narwietooma
Amburla
16 Mile
78

Mt Liebig
+ 1524
Haast Bluff
1118
Glen
Helen
Mt Zeil
+ 1531
Milton Park
Mt Hay
+1252
ROAD
138
Bond
Springs

Haasts Bluff
(Kunparrka)
WEST MACDONNELL
Hamilton
Downs
Alice Springs

Putardi
Springs
Mereenie Bluff +
Redbank
Gorge
Ormiston
Gorge
NATIONAL
Hamilton Downs
Youth Camp
Simpsons
Gap

Deering
107
Glen Helen
Gorge
Serpentine
Gorge
PARK
Ellery Ck
Gorge
NAMATJIRA
132
Iwupataka
Standley
Chasm
DR
Pine
Gap

Carnels Hump
+ 921
LOOP
196
Gosse Bluff +
933
Rudalls
MacDonnell
Hermannsberg
126
Owen
Springs
Oil
Refinery

West Mereenie
Oil & Gas Field
LARAPINTA
MEREENIE
DR
Areyonga
Undandita
Namatjira Monument
LARAPINTA
STUART
130

Mereenie
Oil & Gas Field
Areyonga
Palm
Ilbitta
Palm
Valley
FINKE GORGE
N.P.
Wallace
Rockhole
High

WATARRKA N.P.
James
Boggy
Hole
Finke
Tidenvale Ck

Kings Canyon
Resort
Kings Canyon
19 Mile
UREAMPINYU ILTJILTJARRA
Ranges
Stuarts Well
Roadhouse
Orange Creek
RAILWAY
See page 220

Kings Creek
Station
LURITJA
98
Tempe Downs
Petermann
McMinn
Henbury Meteorite
Craters
Henbury

RD
ERNEST
Palmer
GILES
97
RD
River
River
69

68
River
Palmer Valley
Chambers
Pillar
Idracowra

KATITI
LURITJA
Angas Downs
Imanpa
Erldunda
Roadhouse
Impadna Siding

LASSETER
136
Curtin Springs
Roadhouse
Mount Ebenezer
Roadhouse
107
HWY
Erldunda
AUSTRALIA

Yulara
Uluru N.P.
Uluru (Ayers Rock)
Mutijulu
Karinga
76

For more detail see
map on page 229
+ Mt Connor 859
Lyndavale
Umbeara

Kulgera
Roadhouse
Kulgera Siding

Mulga Park
Johnstone Geodetic
Stn.
Mount Cavenagh
STUART
Victory Downs

Amata
Musgrave
Marryat
Ranges
Inyarinyi
(Kenmore Park)
A87
CENTRAL
+ Mt Howe
515

ABORIGINAL
Mt Woodroffe +
1440
Pukatja
(Ernabella)
LANDS
176
Agnes Creek
Marryat Siding

Scale 1:2 000 00

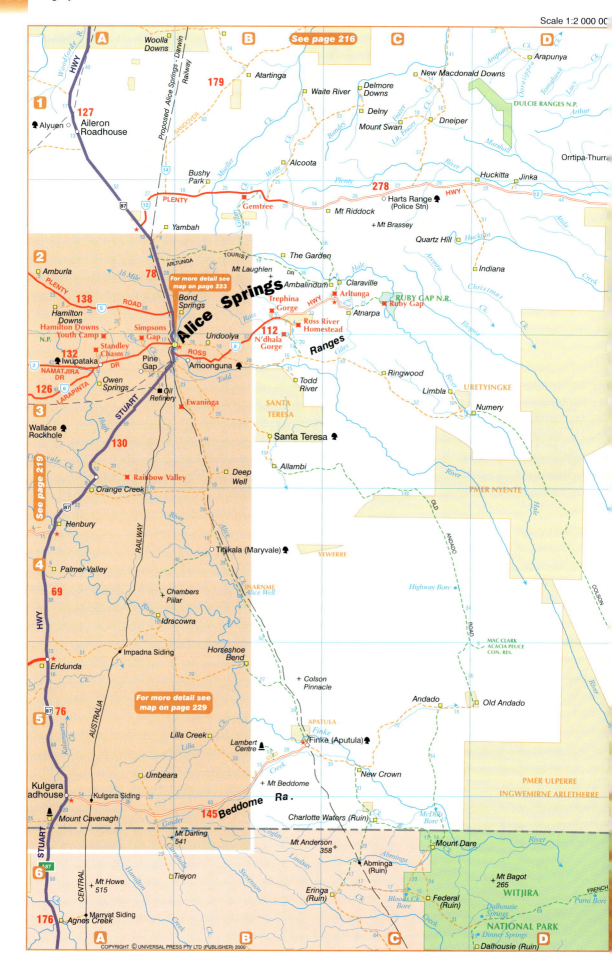

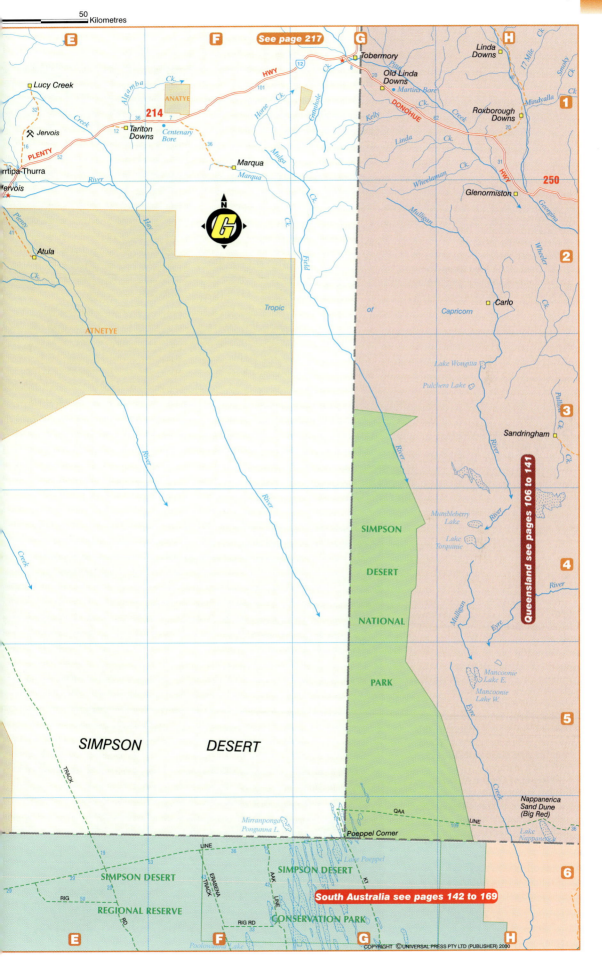

50
Kilometres

See page 217

E
F
G
H

Lucy Creek

ANATYE

214

Tariton
Downs

Centenary
Bore

Jervois

HWY

101

Horse Ck

Greenhole

Tobermory

12

Linda
Downs

17 Mile Ck

Smoky Ck

Old Linda
Downs

Martins Bore

Mindyalla Ck

1

20

DONOHUE

82

Roxborough
Downs

20

31

HWY

250

rtipa-Thurra

PLENTY

52

16

Jervois

River

Marqua

Marqua

Mulga

Ck

Kelly

Linda

Wheelaman

Ck

Ck

Glenormiston

Georgina

N
G

Plenty

41

Atula

Ck

Hay

ATNETYE

Tropic

Field

Ck

River

of

Capricorn

Carlo

Mulligan

Wheeler Ck

2

Lake Wongtta

Pulchera Lake

Palltan Ck

3

Sandringham

River

Queensland see pages 106 to 141

Creek

River

SIMPSON

DESERT

NATIONAL

PARK

Mumbleberry
Lake

Lake
Torquinie

River

Mulligan

River

4

Eyre

Mancoonie
Lake E.

Mancoonie
Lake W.

5

SIMPSON

DESERT

TRACK

Eyre

Creek

Nappanerica
Sand Dune
(Big Red)

Mirranponga
Pongunna L.

QAA

LINE

Lake
Nappanerica

36

6

LINE

Poeppel Corner

Lake Poeppel

19

36

53

SIMPSON DESERT

ERABENA TRACK

LINE

AAK

KI

39

20

RIG

50

REGIONAL RESERVE

RIG RD

SIMPSON DESERT

CONSERVATION PARK

South Australia see pages 142 to 169

E
F
G
H

Poolowanna Lake

Alice Springs

Events in Alice Springs

Most famous is the Henley-on-Todd Regatta in September. This is the only day of the year when bottomless boats are raced along the dry bed of the Todd River! The annual Camel Cup races held in May are another uniquely outback event.

ℹ Tourist Information

Central Australian Tourism Industry Association
60 Gregory Tce, Alice Springs 0870
Ph: (08) 8952 5800
Freecall: 1800 645 199

Main Attractions

★ **Aboriginal Art & Cultural Centre**
At the centre, visitors can learn how to play the didgeridoo and try spear throwing.
★ **Anzac Hill**
Anzac Hill is the most visited landmark in Alice Springs, offering panoramic views beyond the MacDonnell Ranges.
★ **Ghan Preservation Society**
Train enthusiasts will appreciate this museum, which includes a working steam engine, old loco shed, train rides and a tearoom.
★ **Museum of Central Australia**
This fascinating museum contains displays about the regions science, culture and natural history.
★ **Old Stuart Gaol**
Alice Springs oldest surviving building was constructed in 1907–1908, remaining in service until 1938.
★ **Araluen Centre for Arts and Entertainment**
This centre showcases the works of famous Aboriginal artist Albert Namatjira.

The largest settlement in the Australian interior, 'The Alice' is surrounded by the immense natural beauty of the MacDonnell Ranges, making it an excellent base for exploring the surrounding waterholes, gorges, creeks, intricate geological forms, national parks and endemic flora and fauna.

Initially founded in 1870 as an Overland Telegraph line staging post, most of its growth has occurred over the past 30yr, particularly after the 1980s tourist boom. The Alice Springs Telegraph Station Historical Reserve is a memorial to the town's heritage. It is the site of the town's first settlement, and the 2000ha reserve contains the Telegraph Station buildings and Alice's original waterhole.

Alice Springs has remained relatively isolated throughout most of its development — the southern road to Adelaide was only properly sealed in 1987. The Royal Flying Doctor Service still operates from the town. Alice Springs Cultural

Hot air ballooning, Alice Springs

Precinct offers an array of historical and cultural attractions such as the Memorial Cemetery, Aviation Museum of Central Australia and Frank McEllister Park, all located within close proximity of each other.

Frontier Camel Farm

Scale 1:25 000

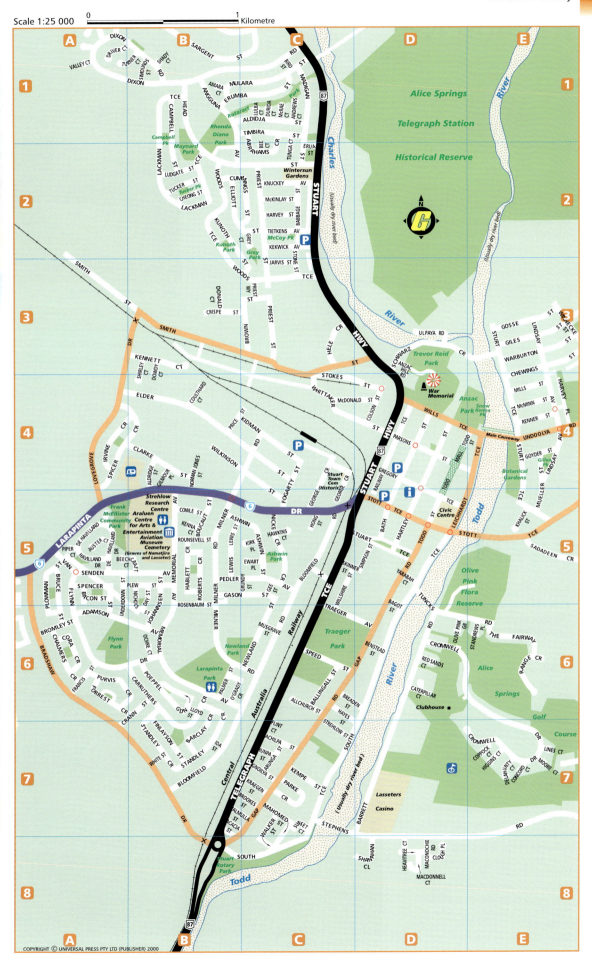

Kakadu NP

The Seasons of Kakadu

The weather is extreme and varied in Kakadu. Its Aboriginal inhabitants believe there are 6 distinct seasons in this region as opposed to just the Wet and Dry. These seasons are Gunumeleng, Gudjewy, Banggereng, Yegge, Wurrgeng and Gurrung.

ℹ Tourist Information

Bowali Visitor Centre
Kakadu Hwy, Kakadu 0886
Ph: (08) 8938 1100

A beacon for visitors to the NT, this World Heritage listed NP is a pristine world of ecosystems in itself. Jointly managed by the Australian Nature Conservation Agency and traditional Aboriginal owners, the park protects a cultural and ecological treasure trove of international importance.

Kakadu's 20 000km² is home to an estimated 10 000 species of insects, 16 000 plant species, 275 bird species, 75 reptile species and 25 species of frogs.

The diverse landscape is characterised by the wet and dry seasons. While the tropical rains entice waterfowl flocks year-round, the entire Park awakens during the rains from November to March, when the floodplains become a vast sea of birdlife, and waterfalls reach their peak.

Aboriginal people have lived continuously in the area for at least 50 000yrs, and the park is scattered

Yellow Water Billabong

with relics including grindstones, shelters, stone tools and ceremonial painting ochre. Dreamtime legends are presented at various significant sites throughout the park, with rock art galleries showcasing images of hunters carrying barbed spears, sprayed hand stencils, and an array of creation beings such as Nglyod the Rainbow Serpent and Namarrgon the Lightning Man.

Main Attractions

★ **Gunlom**
This area offers a striking combination of a waterfall and tranquil plunge pool, making this an idyllic picnic spot.

★ **Jabiru**
This town is set against the spectacular backdrop of the Arnhemland Escarpment.

★ **Koolpin Gorge**
Access to this magical gorge is restricted, but well worth the effort of organising an entry permit and key from the Southern Entry Station.

★ **Nourlangie Rock**
This 1.5km circular walk includes a visit to an ancient Aboriginal shelter where visitors will see impressive art sites.

★ **Yellow Water Billabong**
From the boardwalk visitors can view this pristine waterway, which supports a diverse ecosystem of animals, birds and plants. Sunset is the ideal time to visit.

★ **Maguk**
Enjoy this 2km walk in the forest.

Anbangbang Gallery, Kakadu National Park

Kakadu's Crocs

The park incorporates the South Alligator River's entire drainage basin, providing an ideal habitat for this densely populated park. The river was mistakenly named by an early British explorer after alligators rather than the large community of crocodiles. The park's croc population was hunted almost to the point of extinction at the beginning of this century; now the crocodile is a protected species.

The park provides a haven for 2 crocodile types: the saltwater and the freshwater. 'Freshies' live in freshwater rivers and billabongs, grow up to 3m long and eat small mammals, seafood and birds, and can be found in some of the park's

swimming holes. In contrast, their neighbours the 'Salties' inhabit both salt and fresh water, grow up to 6m in length and have been known to take large mammals such as buffaloes and even people – fully grown, 'salties' are the largest reptiles on earth. An absence of warning signs does not necessarily mean that waterholes are safe for swimming, as the signs are popular souvenirs. A crocodile can remain underwater for up to an hour, as its heart rate can fall to as low as 2 or 3 beats per minute to conserve energy.

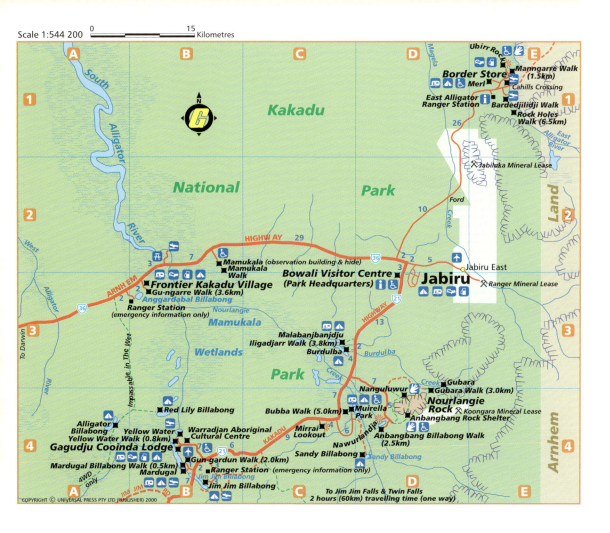

Scale 1:544 200

Katherine Gorge (Nitmiluk) NP

Must Visit

- Cutta Cutta Caves Nature Park
- Edith Falls
- Katherine Gorge
- Katherine River

ℹ️ Tourist Information

Visitor Information Centre
Gorge Rd, Nitmiluk NP, Katherine 0851
Ph: (08) 8972 1886

Nitmiluk NP is renowned for its key drawcard — the magnificent Katherine Gorge — but it also offers over 100km of walks which range from 1hr to 5 days, canoe hire or cruises, birdseye views from plane or helicopter joy flights, swimming opportunities and abundant wildlife within its 3000km².

The Park is the gateway to the NT's Top End, and so shares that region's monsoonal climate, with a humid hot wet season between October and April and a dry season running from May to September.

The Katherine River is the region's lifeblood, as it has been for the local Jawoyn and Dagoman Aboriginal people for thousands of years. Not only does the river function as a reliable water source, it is also a recreational attraction, providing opportunities for swimming, canoeing, fishing and picnicking along its picturesque

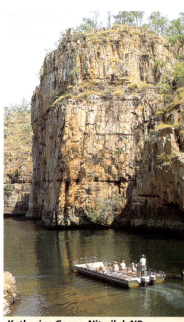

Katherine Gorge, Nitmiluk NP

shores. Other Park activities include croc spotting tours, horse trail rides, 4WDing expeditions, and station stays.

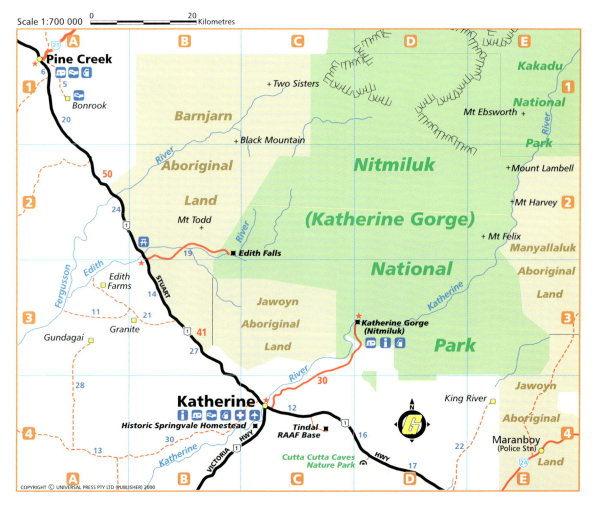

Litchfield NP

Relatively unknown until it was declared a NP in 1986, Litchfield NP is one of NT's underrated attractions. Its 143km² encompass magnetic termite moulds, historic ruins such as Blyth Homestead, monsoonal rainforest, weather-beaten sandstone and shimmering spring-fed streams, making it a beacon for 250 000 visitors annually.

The Park's major attractions are all easily accessible as sealed roads link them, while 4WD vehicles can reach even the most remote locations. However, during the wet season some areas may be difficult to reach and some waterholes may be closed, due to water turbulence.

The spring-fringed plateau of the Tabletop Ra feeds the Park's permanent waterfalls and the Park's waterholes are excellent for swimming and are generally crocodile free. A number of camping

Magnetic Termite mounds

spots requiring permits are dotted throughout the Park, with hotel accommodation offered at nearby Adelaide River. Bushwalking is a popular pastime, while the lush wetlands provide ample fishing opportunities for anglers.

Must Visit

- Adelaide River
- Batchelor Butterfly Farm
- Buley Rockhole
- Florence Falls
- Tjaynera Falls

ℹ Tourist Information

Darwin Regional Tourism Association
38 Mitchell St, Darwin 0800
Ph: (08) 8981 4300

Scale 1:509 300

Uluru-Kata Tjuta NP to Alice Springs

The Olgas

This group of 36 enormous and weathered domes, rising 546m , were described by explorer Ernest Giles as 'monstrous pink haystacks'. He named them after Queen Olga of Wurttemberg. Their descriptive Aboriginal name means 'many heads'.

ℹ Tourist Information

Uluru-Kata Tjuta Cultural Centre
Uluru-Kata Tjuta NP
Yulara 0872
Ph: (08) 8956 2299

The vast terrain west of Alice Springs to Uluru-Kata Tjuta NP is the heart of the red centre, spanning the western section of the MacDonnell Ranges. This stunning but rugged landscape encompasses an ancient and unique terrain dotted with gorges, waterholes, unusual geological formations, tranquil creeks and strange landforms, carved out over hundreds of millions of years.

The arid and seemingly inhospitable landscape is home to an array of endemic flora and fauna — springtime sees the blossoming of colourful wildflowers, while rock wallabies are often seen around the steep ridges and rocky gaps of Simpsons Gap NP.

The NP covers 126 132ha and contains 2 of the world's greatest natural wonders, Uluru (Ayers Rock) and Kata Tjuta (Mt Olga) — both major tourist drawcards. This NP is the most visited site in Australia. The Park also offers much

Kata Tjuta (The Olgas)

more, including spectacular views, guided walks, Anangu Aboriginal heritage, 500 plant species, 24 endemic mammals and 72 species of reptiles. It received international recognition in 1977, when it was declared an International Biosphere Reserve by UNESCO.

Main Attractions

★ **Ayres Rock Resort**
This tourist resort and village is within close proximity to the district's major attractions.
★ **Finke Gorge NP**
This NP's main attraction is Palm Valley. Prehistoric cycads and red cabbage palms have survived the barren terrain for more than 10 000yr.
★ **Kata Tjuta**
These extraordinary rock formations and 36 domes rise from the ground and, like Uluru, their colours change with the light throughout the day. None of the domes are safe to climb.
★ **Standley Chasm**
Sunlight bathes the 80m high walls of this narrow chasm around noon. The chasm was formed by erosion of the softer rock from the red, quartzite walls.
★ **Uluru**
At 384m high, Uluru is the world's largest monolith. The Mala and Kuniya guided walks provide an excellent grounding in the cultural significance of Uluru to the Anangu people.

Glen Helen Gorge, West MacDonnell Ranges

Aboriginal Sites and Land

As the NT encompasses terrain that is Aboriginal land, it is important that visitors who plan to travel through Aboriginal land away from designated highways obtain a permit. Permits can be obtained from relevant the Land Councils, although visitors travelling on organised tours will have their permits prepared for them. The Northern Territory also contains a number of sites that hold special significance to local Aboriginal people; some of these sites are protected by law. Although visitors are permitted to climb Uluru, the Aboriginal owners prefer that they not do so, because the climb is the traditional route ancestral Mala men took upon arriving at the rock.

The Land Councils for the NT are:

Central Land Council
33 Stuart Hwy,
Alice Springs 0871
Ph: (08) 8951 6320

Northern Land Council
9 Rowlings St,
Casuarina 0811
Ph: (08) 8920 5100

Tiwi Land Council
U5/3 Bishop St, Stuart Park,
Winnellie 0821
Ph: (08) 8981 4898

Hand imprint rock painting

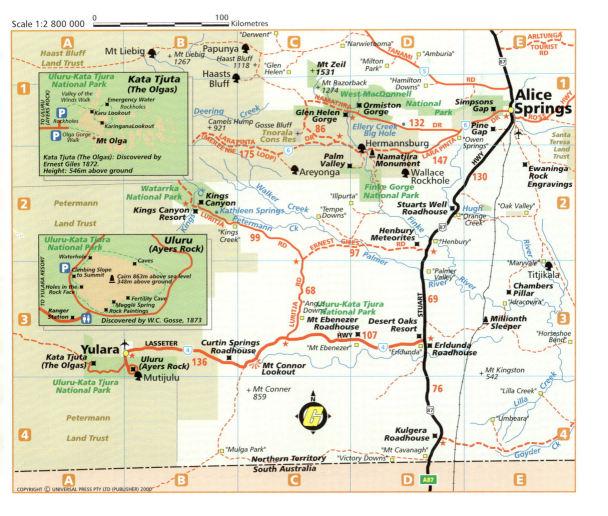

Tasmania

TAS: The Holiday Isle

- Area = 68 500 sq km
- 230km away from mainland Australia
- Length of coastline = more than 3200km

Blue Gum

Tasmanian Devil

ℹ Tourist Information

Tasmanian Travel
& Information Centre
20 Davey St, Hobart 7000
Ph: (03) 6230 8233
Freecall: 1800 806 846

Main Attractions

★ **Cradle Mt-Lake St Clair NP**
This World Heritage listed NP is one of Tasmania's best known and most visited attractions. There are deep, trout-filled lakes and bushwalks that attract walkers from around the world.

★ **Flinders Island and King Island**
Flanking Bass Strait's eastern and western sides, these islands are secluded and idyllic holiday destinations. Both islands are rich in colonial history.

★ **Hobart**
Situated on the picturesque harbour, at the mouth of the Derwent River and backed by glorious mountains, Hobart is a charming blend of colonial heritage and waterfront lifestyle. It is also Australia's second oldest capital city.

★ **Tasman Peninsula**
The east coast is where Tasmanians go for their holidays. A mild climate, surfing beaches, excellent fishing and spectacular scenic attractions make this region an ideal holiday destination.

The turbulent waters of Bass Strait separate Tas from the Australian mainland. Tas is Australia's southernmost State as well as its smallest. This compact space makes it an ideal touring destination, as only relatively short distances separate its many attractions and population centres. Beaches circle its coastline, while national parks and reserves protect its spectacular landmass, which features more than 1000km of world-class walking tracks. Tasmania also boasts the stunning and often remote World Heritage Area; it has the highest percentage of national parks of any Australian State.

As Australia's only island State, Tasmania's isolation has shaped its cultural and historical development. Much of its colonial heritage has survived from the time when it was known as Van Diemen's Land, providing a wealth of historic sites to interest visitors. Well preserved historic towns include Richmond, New Norfolk and Ross.

Its physical diversity ranges from long white beaches, sand dunes and dense rainforest to rugged mountains

Historic Richmond Bridge

and alpine moors covered in snow during the winter months, with many lakes, lush green pastures, convict ruins and fine examples of colonial freestone architecture dotted in between.

Unlike most of Australia, Tas enjoys 4 distinctly different seasons, making it an ideal place to experience the changing of the seasons. Tasmania produces apples, berry fruits, cheeses and world class ales and wines.

Fishing boats, Hobart

Tasmania Key Map and Distance Chart

All distances shown in the chart below have been measured over highways and major roads, not necessarily by the shortest route.

City Map
Hobart, page 233

Suburban Maps
Hobart, pages 234 and 235

State Maps
pages 236 to 241

Region Maps
Cradle Mountain, page 245
Flinders Island-
 King Island, page 247
Tasman Peninsula, page 249

Approximate Distance	Burnie	Campbell Town	Deloraine	Devonport	Geeveston	George Town	Hobart	Launceston	New Norfolk	Oatlands	Port Arthur	Queenstown	Rosebery	St Helens	St Marys	Scottsdale	Smithton	Sorell	Swansea	Triabunna
Burnie		198	100	50	381	152	328	137	290	246	386	148	109	293	259	197	88	316	264	314
Campbell Town	198		98	148	184	120	131	70	127	48	188	253	308	120	85	130	286	118	66	116
Deloraine	100	98		50	281	87	228	51	190	146	286	204	209	207	159	111	188	216	164	214
Devonport	50	148	50		331	102	278	87	240	196	336	198	159	243	209	147	138	266	214	264
Geeveston	381	184	281	331		304	53	254	91	136	148	312	367	304	269	314	469	78	189	139
George Town	152	120	87	102	304		251	50	259	168	308	300	261	170	205	74	240	238	186	236
Hobart	328	131	228	278	53	251		201	38	83	95	259	314	251	216	261	416	25	136	86
Launceston	137	70	51	87	254	50	201		197	118	258	251	246	156	131	60	225	188	136	186
New Norfolk	290	127	190	240	91	259	38	197		79	133	221	276	247	212	257	378	63	174	124
Oatlands	246	48	146	196	136	168	83	118	79		140	261	316	168	133	178	334	70	114	131
Port Arthur	386	188	286	336	148	308	95	258	133	140		354	409	299	268	318	474	70	181	131
Queenstown	148	253	204	198	312	300	259	251	221	261	354		55	407	338	311	236	284	395	345
Rosebery	109	308	209	159	367	261	314	246	276	316	409	55		401	368	306	197	339	450	400
St Helens	293	120	207	243	304	170	251	156	247	168	299	407	401		35	96	381	229	118	168
St Marys	259	85	159	209	269	205	216	131	212	133	268	338	368	35		131	347	198	87	137
Scottsdale	197	130	111	147	314	74	261	60	257	178	318	311	306	96	131		285	248	214	264
Smithton	88	286	188	138	469	240	416	225	378	334	474	236	197	381	347	285		404	352	402
Sorell	316	118	216	266	78	238	25	188	63	70	70	284	339	229	198	248	404		111	61
Swansea	264	66	164	214	189	186	136	136	174	114	181	395	450	118	87	214	352	111		50
Triabunna	314	116	214	264	139	236	86	186	124	131	131	345	400	168	137	264	402	61	50	

Hobart

Tasmania's South
Regional Tourism Association

HOBART
The Gateway To Your Natural State

F ounded in 1804 and declared a city in 1842, Hobart is rich in reminders of its colonial past. Its status as Australia's second oldest city after Sydney is evidenced by its record as the first of the nation's capitals to introduce a tram service in 1893, while electric lighting replaced gas lamps in 1898.

Boasting beautiful Georgian architecture, over 90 of the city's buildings are classified by the National Trust, with most of them — including Australia's oldest theatre, the Theatre Royal — located in historic Macquarie and Davey Sts.

Hobart is nestled at the foot of Mt Wellington, whose peak is often snow-capped in the winter months. Panoramic vistas of the city are available from the mountain's superb lookouts.

Like most Australian capitals, Hobart's lifestyle is defined by water: it is a riverside city with a bustling harbour, surrounded by picturesque

Victoria Dock, Hobart

harbourside warehouses. The waterfront area is the focal point for both locals and visitors alike, as it is the site for many of its tourist attractions and city events. Today, Hobart's residents enjoy a relaxed pace of life, with the many benefits of a big city and a thriving arts and crafts scene. Contemporary and classical performances can be enjoyed alongside a lively streetscape of buskers, string quartets and market stalls.

ℹ️ Tourist Information

Tasmanian Travel & Information Centre
Cnr Davey and Elizabeth Sts, Hobart 7000
Ph: (03) 6230 8233
Freecall: 1800 806 846

Main Attractions

★ **Battery Point**
Hobart's oldest district was once home to sailors, fishermen, prostitutes and shipwrights. It is now a fashionable inner city neighbourhood.

★ **Cadbury Chocolates**
Home to this well known brand of chocolates, the Cadbury factory is a must for chocoholics.

★ **Cascade Brewery**
Australia's oldest brewery produces some of the finest beer in the country. Tours of both the Brewery and museum are available daily.

★ **Royal Tasmanian Botanical Gardens**
Established in 1818, these gardens house an extensive collection of native and exotic plants. Features include a cactus house, herb garden and Japanese Gardens.

★ **Runnymede**
Set in exquisite and tranquil gardens, this National Trust homestead was built in 1837. Open to the public, many items in the home are authentic and the rooms have been lovingly restored.

Salamanca Markets, Hobart

Places of Interest

1. Anglesea Barracks **C6**
2. Derwent River cruise **D5**
3. Elizabeth Mall **D4**
4. Government House **D2**
5. Maritime Museum **E6**
6. Narryna Folk Museum **D5**
7. Parliament House **D5**
8. Princes Park **E5**
9. St David's Park **D5**
10. Town Hall **D4**

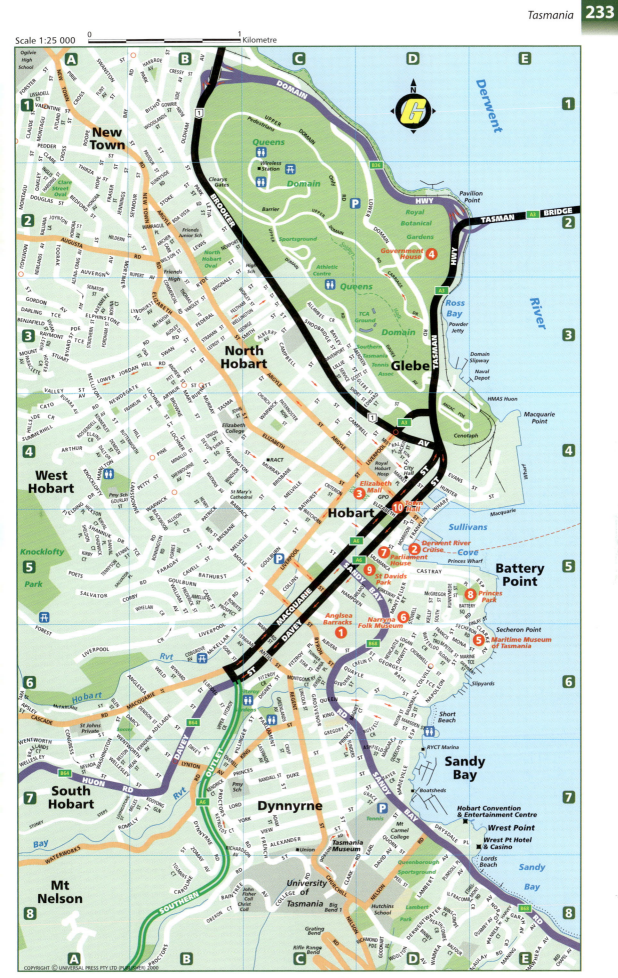

Scale 1:25 000

0   1 Kilometre

New Town

North Hobart

West Hobart

Knocklofty Park

Hobart

Glebe

Derwent

Ross Bay

River

Macquarie Point

Battery Point

Sullivans Cove

Sandy Bay

South Hobart

Dynnyrne

Mt Nelson

University of Tasmania

Queens Domain

Royal Botanical Gardens

Government House

Wrest Point

Hobart Convention & Entertainment Centre

Wrest Point Hotel & Casino

Elizabeth Mall

Parliament House

St Davids Park

Narryna Folk Museum

Anglesea Barracks

Princes Park

Maritime Museum of Tasmania

Derwent River Cruise

Town Hall

Tasmania Museum

Scale 1:80 00

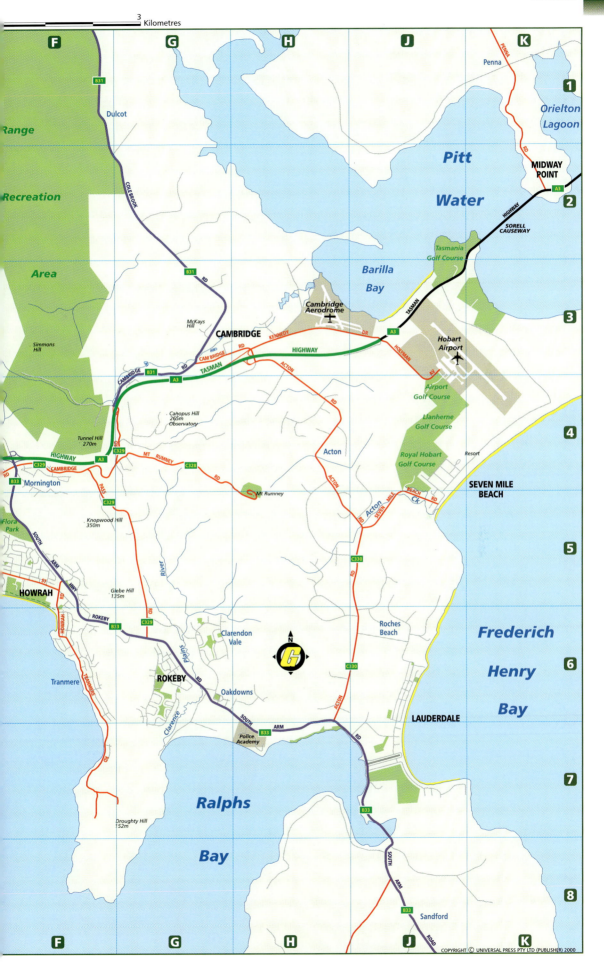

3 Kilometres

F G H J K

Penna

Orielton
Lagoon

Range

Dulcot

MIDWAY
POINT

Pitt

Recreation

Water

Area

SORELL
CAUSEWAY

Tasmania
Golf Course

Barilla
Bay

McKays
Hill

Cambridge
Aerodrome

Simmons
Hill

CAMBRIDGE

Hobart
Airport

HIGHWAY

KENNEDY

CAM BRIDGE

Airport
Golf Course

TASMAN

Canopus Hill
265m
Observatory

ACTON

Llanherne
Golf Course

Acton

Royal Hobart
Golf Course

Tunnel Hill
270m

Resort

HIGHWAY

MT RUMNEY

CAMBRIDGE

SEVEN MILE
BEACH

Mornington

Mt Rumney

Acton

BEACH

Flora
Park

Knopwood Hill
350m

River

Glebe Hill
135m

HOWRAH

Roches
Beach

ROKEBY

Frederich

Clarendon
Vale

Henry

Tranmere

ROKEBY

Oakdowns

LAUDERDALE

Bay

SOUTH

ARM

Police
Academy

Ralphs

Droughty Hill
152m

Bay

Sandford

Scale 1:800 000

See page 239

20 Kilometres

Bass *Strait*

E F G H

1

2

able Cape

Somerset
Burnie
Seabrook
Camdale
Cooee
Wivenhoe
Mooreville
Elliott
Ridgley
West Ridgley
Highclere
ewkesbury
53
Hampshire
Heybridge
Stowport
Cuprona
Natone
Camena
Riana
Upper Natone
South Riana
Preston
Heka
Warringa
South Preston
Nietta
Loongana
South Nietta
Black Bluff
1339
Moina
Wilmot

Penguin
Sulphur Creek
Howth
Ulverstone
Turners Beach
Leith
14
Gawler
North Motton
Sprent
Forth
Spreyton
Kindred
Latrobe
Paloona
Lower Barrington
Barrington
Devils Gate
14
Ambleside
Devonport
Wesley Vale
Northdown
Moriarty
Thirlstane
Harford
Sassafras
Railton
51
Merseylea
Sheffield
Roland
West Kentish
Kimberley
Paradise
Claude Road
Gowrie Park
Weegena
Dunorlan
Moltema
Elizabeth Town
Cethana
Chudleigh
Liena
Mayberry
Marakoopa
Caveside
Mole Creek
Montana
Western Creek
Meander
Lorinna
King Solomon
37
Deloraine
Needles
Lemonthyme
Fisher
Rowallan
Jackeys Marsh
Ironstone Mtn
1443
Blackwood Creek
Liffey
Drys Bluff
1297

Pt Sorell
Hawley Beach
Port Sorell
Yorktown
Beaconsfield
East Sassafras
West Frankford
Frankford
Glengarry
Birralee
Parkham
Rosevale
Westbury
Exton
15
Hagley
Quamby Brook
Golden Valley
Bishopsbourne
Bracknell

Five Mile Bluff
Bellbuoy Beach
West Hd.
Greens Beach
Badger Hd.
Kelso
Clarence Point
Low Hd.
Low Head
George Town
24
Bell Bay
Beauty Point
Rowella
Sidmouth
39
Deviot
Holwell
13
Rosevears
Bridgenorth
Rosevale
Launceston
Westwood
Hadspen
Carrick
Glenore
Whitemore
19
Westbury

Beechford
Stony Hd.
Lulworth
Weymouth
Pipers Brook
Pipers River
Lefroy
Lower Turners Marsh
Mt Direction
Turners Marsh
49
Gravelly Beach
Lanena
Exeter
Dilston
Legana
23
Rocherlea
15
Pateena
Western Junction
32
Longford
23
Perth
Cressy
17

Noland Bay

Visitor Centre
Pencil Pine
Mt Remus
1110
Cradle Valley
Cradle Mtn 1545
Fisher
Rowallan
Breona
57
CENTRAL PLATEAU
PROTECTED AREA
Rats Castle
1392
Reynolds Neck
55
Poatina
Poatina
Cramps

SOUTHW
CONSERVATION
AREA
CRADLE MOUNTAIN
LAKE ST. CLAIR
Mt Ossa
1617
NATIONAL PARK
WORLD
HERITAGE
AREA
WALLS OF JERUSALEM
NATIONAL PARK
Liawenee
Great Lake
Miena
17
Tods Corner
Brazendale I.
Flintstone
Neil I.
Wilburville
Steppes
L. Sorell
Millers Bluff
1210m
LAKE-SORELL
WILDLIFE SANCTUARY
Woods

30
See page 240

For more detail see map on page 245

See page 238

Barren Tier
1186

LYELL HWY
Visitor Centre

3

4

5

6

E F G H

COPYRIGHT © UNIVERSAL PRESS PTY LTD (PUBLISHER) 2000

Scale 1:800 000

0   20 Kilometres

For more detail see
map on page 247

See page 237

See page 241

Scale 1:800 000

0   20
Kilometres

See page 236

See page 240

SOUTHERN

OCEAN

Strahan

Lynchford
John Butters
Crotty Dam
Darwin Dam

Bellinger, 1894
Cape Sorell
Cat I.
Sophia Pt.
Macquarie
Liberty Pt.
Mt Sorell 1144
West Coast Ra.

Gem, 1856
Sloop Rocks
Sloop Pt.
Harbour

Gorge Pt.
Gould Pt.
Convict Ruins
Sarah I.
Gordon
Albina Ck.
River
Birthday Bay

Varna Bay
Modder
Varna, 1857
Pennerowne Pt.
Timbertops
D'Aguilar Ra.

Hibbs Bay
Hibbs Pyramid
Point Hibbs
Hibbs R.
McCarthy R.
Conder Pt.
Spero Bay
Spero R.
Sorell
Endeavour Bay
Wanderer
SOUTHWEST
Hales
Wanderer, 1858
High Rocky Pt.
CONSERVATION
Mainwaring R.
AREA

Acacia, 1904

Lewis
Matilda, 1881
Black Warrior, 1863
Low Rocky Pt.
Elliott Bay
Nye Bay
Elliott Pt.

Scale 1:800 0

For more detail see map on page 245

See page 237

Raglan Ra. 74
LYELL HWY
Derwent Bridge
Waddamana
Big Jim
Bronte Park
25
24
Crotty Dam
Darwin Dam
Lake Echo
Dee Lag.
Lake Echo
C527
C178
46
West Coast Ra.
Engineer Ra.
FRANKLIN-GORDON
Frenchmans Cap 1445
Butlers Gorge
Mt King William I 1359
Mt King William II 1359
Mt Hobhouse 1219
Dee
Lake King William
Tungatinah
Tarraleah
Victoria Valley
Osterley
C603
WILD RIVERS
Mt King William III
King William Range
Deception Ra.
Adelaide R.
Liapootah
Wayatinah
Wayatinah
L. Catagunya
Strickland
LYELL
Bothwell
50
28
NATIONAL
Prince of Wales Range
Princess Range
The Spires
Denison Range
Catagunyah
Wylds Craig 1339
L. Repulse
Repulse
Cluny
Ouse
Lawrenny
Hollow Tree
Pelham
B110
PARK
Mt Humboldt
Nicholls Range
The Pleiades
Clear Hill 1198
Mt Field West 1434
MOUNT FIELD NATIONAL PARK
Hamilton
Meadowbank
Lake Meadowbank
Ellendale
Fentonbury
17
D'Aguilar Ra.
Charles Ra.
Gordon Dam
Gordon
Serpentine Dam
Mt Sprent 1097m
Strathgordon
Teds Beach
Lake Gordon
Adamsfield
ROAD
66
GORDON RIVER RD
Skiing
National Park
Westerway
Junee
Tyenna
Fitzgerald
Maydena
Glenora
Bushy Park
Platform P 979
Rosegarlan
13
Plenty
18
Uxbridge
Moogara
Creepy Crawly Walk
Frodshams Pass
Mt Wedge 1147
McPartlan Pass
Snowy North 1140
New Norfolk
Mt Lloyd
Lachlan
See page 239
Orb Lake
Double Peak 1060
Frankland Range
Lake Pedder
Mt Solitary
Scotts Pk
Scotts Peak Dam
Edgar Dam
Mt Anne 1425
L. Judd
Lake Judd
L. Skinner
Mt Weld 1344
SOUTHWEST
Snowy Ra.
Lonnanvale
Judbury
Crabtree
Lucaston
Apple Museu
Ranelagh
Glen Huon
Piners Peak 696
Pine Ck.
Nye Bay
Elliott Pt.
Brier Holme Hd.
Brier Holme, 1904
Mt Hean 747
De Witt Range
DAVEY
CROSSING TRACK
Mt Hesperus 1098
Arthur Range
PORT
Spring R.
ARTHUR
Mt Picton 1327
Picton Ra.
Weld R.
CONSERVATION
AREA
Hartz Mtns.
HARTZ MTNS NATIONAL PARK
Hartz Pk. 1254m
Franklin
20
South Franklin
Castle Forbes Bay
Port Huon
Geeveston
Waterloo
Surges Bay
Glendevie
WORLD
HERITAGE
Svenor Pt
Hobbs I.
Alfhild, 1907
Wreck Bay
Bathurst Harbour
Mt Norold 792
Federation Pk 1224
Mt Bobs
L. Geeves
Roberts Ra.
Hartz
Police Point
37
Dover
Strathblane
West Pyramid
North Head
Point St Vincent
Geordy, 1816
Eveline, 1891
Hilliard Head
Breaksea I.
Port Davey
SOUTHWEST NATIONAL PARK
AREA
Ray Range
Old Spero R.
Mt La Perouse 1158
Adamsons Pk 1226
Hastings
Hastings
Lune River
Ida Bay
Enchantress, 1835
Southport
Stephens Bay
Wendar
Mutton Bird I.
Flying Cloud Pt.
Melaleuca Bird Observatory
Melaleuca Lagoon
Mt Counsel 800
Mt Melaleuca 595
Louisa Ck.
Louisa R.
Thermal Springs
Historic Railway
Southport Lagoon
Actaeon
Eliza Pt.
Window Pane Bay
Karamu Bay
Wilson Bay
Telopea, 1848
Aleona, 1848
Cox Bight
Cox Bluff
Red Pt.
Louisa Bay
Louisa I.
New River Lagoon
Prion Bay
Havelock Bluff
Point Vivian
Catamaran
Cockle Ck.
Recherche Bay
Fishers Pt.
South West Cape
Ripple, 1877
De Witt I.
SOUTHWEST
Flat Witch I.
NATIONAL PARK
Maatsuyker I.
Maatsuyker Group
Ile du Golfe
Shoemaker Pt.
South Cape
Soldier Bluff
South Cape Bay
Whale Hd
South East Cape
TRACK
COAST

COPYRIGHT © UNIVERSAL PRESS PTY LTD (PUBLISHER) 2000

20 Kilometres

TASMANIA

Australia's Natural State.
Where the scenery is spectacular
and the hospitality is warm and inviting.

Strahan

The award winning Franklin Manor, is a boutique hotel with a relaxed ambience offering fourteen rooms of premium accommodation. With fine food, wine, log fires and friendly service the Manor is perfectly situated for visitors to enjoy the beauty and solitude of the Tasmanian wilderness.
Phone: (03) 6471 7311

Strahan

World Heritage Cruises, pioneered by five generations of the Grining Family, offer you a day to remember aboard either of their state-of-the-art vessels. Visit Hell's Gates and enjoy a guided tour of the infamous Sarah Island before entering the spectacular Gordon River and viewing its ancient rainforests.
Phone: (03) 64 717 174

Cradle Mountain

Lemonthyme Lodge is the perfect place to experience the Tasmanian Wilderness while relaxing in the lap of luxury. Either in the sunny days of Summer or the chilly mountain Winter. You can sit and enjoy the warmth of an open fire or wander through the rainforest then enjoy a sumptuous meal in our award winning restaurant.
Phone: (03) 6492 1112

Freycinet

Freycinet Lodge is Tasmania's premier environmental resort. The property has sixty beautifully appointed cabins. The main lodge overlooks Great Oyster Bay with two restaurants, bar, lounge and conference areas. Freycinet Lodge provides a daily activity program including bush walking, star-gazing, bird watching and 4WD touring.
Phone: (03) 6257 0101

Launceston

Indulge yourself in the romance and intimacy of York Mansions. Centrally located to local restaurants, wineries and the Cataract Gorge chairlift. Catch a trout at the Launceston Lakes, or pamper yourself at the Aquarius Roman Baths.
Phone: (03) 6334 2933

Hobart

Salamanca Inn, Hobart's original contemporary styled all suite hotel has recently completed a million-dollar refurbishment. From accommodation to restaurant and function facilities emphases is placed on Tasmanian products.
Phone: (03) 6223 3300

Solve the puzzle of where to go with Gregory's maps

Go anywhere with Gregory's maps of capital cities, tourist regions, states and territories, Australia and overseas. Gregory's is Australia's largest cartographic company with an extensive range of maps. It is also Australia's oldest cartographic company, continuing a fine tradition of mapping excellence.
Proudly Australian-owned and made, Gregory's is a brand you can trust.
Gregory's are Australia's most popular maps – your passport to a more enjoyable trip.
Available from good service stations, newsagents, bookshops and department stores.

 We've Got Australia Covered

Cradle Mt–Lake St Clair NP

Lake St Clair

This lake was formed by a glacier and is Australia's deepest natural freshwater lake, 17 km long and 200m deep. It is the source of the Derwent River on which Hobart is situated.

i Tourist Information

Cradle Mt Visitor Centre
Park entrance, Cradle Mt Rd,
Cradle Mt-Lake St Clair NP
Ph: (03) 6492 1110
www.dpiwe.tas.gov.au

Main Attractions

★ **Ballroom Forest**
Nestled amongst Cradle Mountains slopes, this temperate, majestic rainforest is a highlight of the Dove Lake Loop Track Walk.

★ **Dove Lake**
The shores of this picturesque lake are ideal for observing the movement of wallabies and wombats in the late afternoon.

★ **Overland Track**
The Overland Track is reputed as one of Australia's premier wilderness walking tracks. This 5 day expedition covers 80km. Highlights include a side-trip to the ascent of Tasmania's highest peak, Mt Ossa. Walkers should always notify the park rangers of their planned movements.

★ **Waldheim Chalet**
The name of this chalet means 'forest home'. Waldheim is located at the northern end of the Overland Track. Waldheim Cabins offer an authentic experience in the wilderness.

Located approximately 85km south of Devonport, Cradle Mt itself, as well as the NP, are drawcards for Australian and international visitors alike — they are one of Tasmania's most popular attractions. Renowned for its excellent bushwalks, including the Overland Track and shorter circuits suitable for a few hours or days, this NP offers walking opportunities to suit a range of fitness levels and time frames. Cradle Mt-Lake St Clair NP is a natural wonderland, boasting shy wildlife, ancient beech forests and trout-filled lakes.

The Park's founding father, Austrian immigrant Gustav Weindorfer, was overwhelmed by the other-worldliness of this area, proclaiming that it 'must be a national park for the people of all time'. His wish was realised, as it is now part of the acclaimed Tasmanian Wilderness World Heritage Area, protecting a diversity of environments waiting to be explored. Its 161 000ha boasts stunning scenery, wild landscapes, buttongrass plains, primordial rainforests and alpine heathlands. The rugged terrain is interspersed with glacial lakes, while icy rivers and streams cascade from the craggy mountains. Its romantically named attractions include the Enchanted

Fergusson Falls, Cradle Mt–Lake St Clair NP

Walk, Forgotten Lake, Ballroom Forest, Shadow Lake and the Acropolis; while the aptly named Pencil Pine Falls, a short stroll from the visitors centre, provides dramatic photo opportunities. The Overland Track is a 5 to 8 day walk.

Facilities include picnic shelters fitted with electric BBQs and a public telephone near the visitors centre, picnic tables, toilets in a few locations, some accommodation, Cradle Mt Lodge Store and Cradle View Restaurant.

Cradle Mountain in winter

Scale 1:300 000

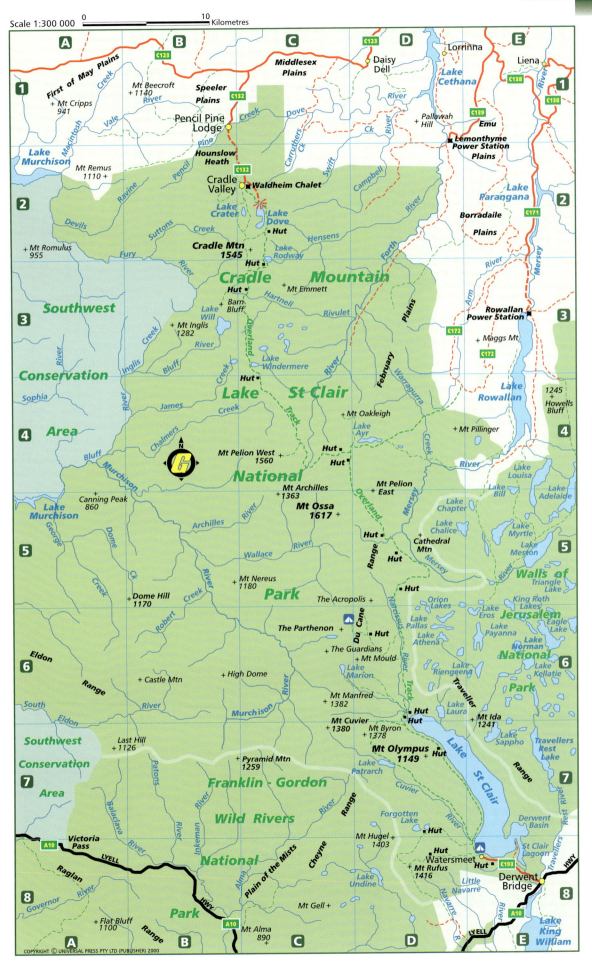

COPYRIGHT © UNIVERSAL PRESS PTY LTD (PUBLISHER) 2000

Flinders Island and King Island

Perched above the east and west of Tasmania's top end, Flinders and King Islands were once centres of the long-banned sealing industry, but now support celebrated agricultural industries of their own.

Flinders Island is the largest in the Furneaux Group, named after pioneer Matthew Flinders, one of the first people to use the term 'Australia'.

Since its colonial settlement, the island has witnessed many changes: in the 1950s a Soldier/Farmer scheme was initiated, leading to 33 559ha being cleared and sown. The island is now an ideal place to escape the stresses of city life, offering many natural attractions and a few artificial ones.

In contrast, King Island lies on the western edge of Bass Strait, covering 126 000ha. The mining of gold and tin were once the island's primary industries; this has shifted to dairy products of international

King Island Lobster

repute, livestock farming, crayfishing, abalone harvesting and even kelp drying.

With more than 145km of picturesque coastline and abundant natural attractions, King Island is an idyllic holiday haven for those truly wishing to get away from it all — but be warned, the island has no ATM or Eftpos facilities.

History of King Island

The first European thought to have discovered this island was Captain James Black. He named it after Philip King, the Governor of NSW in 1801. Nowadays the seal and sea elephant colonies are extinct after extensive sealing and hunting in the past.

ℹ Tourist Information

Tasmanian Travel & Information Centre
20 Davey St, Hobart 7000
Ph: (03) 6230 8233
Freecall: 1800 806 846

Main Attractions

FLINDERS ISLAND
★ **Emita Museum**
This museum displays the history of various groups of pioneer settlers.
★ **Logan Lagoon Wildlife Sanctuary**
This sanctuary has been included on the list of Wetlands of International Importance.
★ **Strzelecki NP**
This 4215ha park offers opportunities to relax with bushwalking, beachcombing, boating and swimming among its attractions. The 756m climb to Mt Strzelecki's summit is a 5hr return walk.
KING ISLAND
★ **Cape Wickham Lighthouse**
Australia's tallest lighthouse was built in 1861 to guide travellers safely into Bass Strait.
★ **King Island Dairies**
The dairy was established in 1902 because dairy products were easier to transport than livestock.
★ **Grassy**
This area is well known for its penguin rookery.

Trousers Pt, Flinders Island

Scale 1:800 000

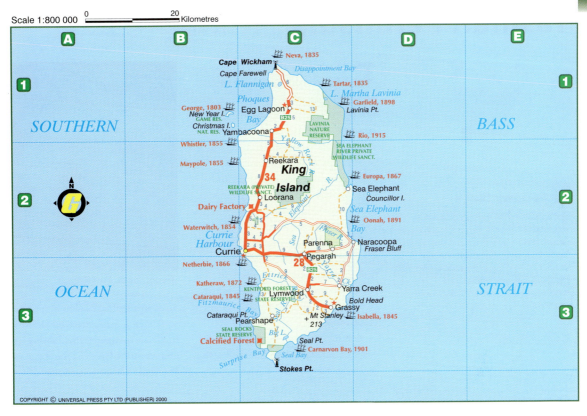

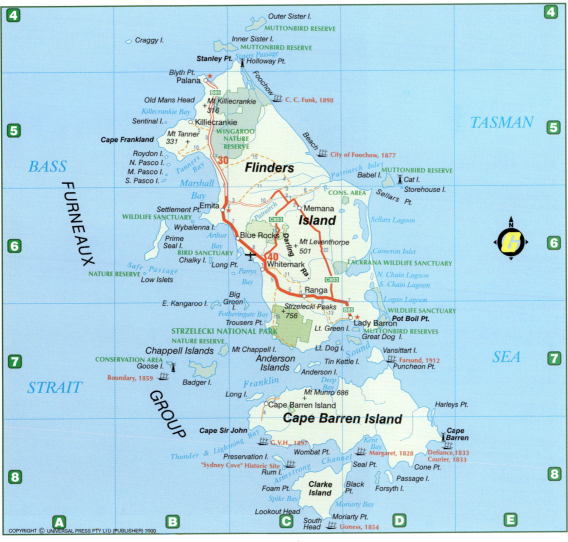

Tasman Peninsula

Eaglehawk Neck

Once guarded by vicious dogs in an attempt to turn the Peninsula into a virtual prison, infamous Eaglehawk Neck is a must to visit. It is the site of many natural wonders including the extraordinary Tessellated Pavement wave platform, Blowhole and Pirates Bay Lookout.

The Tasman Peninsula's landscape is rugged – like much of its history. Its coastline features geological curiosities, fascinating seascapes and spectacular seaside walks, while its inland and islands preserve protected habitats, endangered species and flora and fauna, which are native to Tasmania.

The coastline offers opportunities for adventure, such as abseiling, rock climbing, scuba diving and kayaking. While the vast array of walking trails, horseriding and mountain bike riding tracks allow visitors to view the stunning surroundings at close range.

Bearing evidence of thousands of years of Aboriginal communities, the region is also scattered with

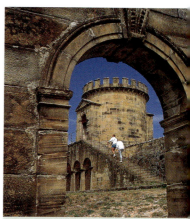

Guard Tower, Port Arthur

Tasmania's oldest colonial and penal settlements. Each layer has left its mark on the landscape, leaving abundant evidence of the Tasman Peninsula's historic heritage.

ℹ️ Tourist Information

Port Arthur Visitor Centre
Port Arthur Historic Site,
Port Arthur 7182
Freecall: 1800 659 101
www.portarthur.org.au

Main Attractions

★ **Isle of the Dead**
Cruises are available across the bay from Port Arthur to the penal settlement's cemetery.
★ **Maria Island NP**
Originally a convict station, this NP's isolation has led to a proliferation of wildlife, with a number of endangered species introduced to boost their numbers.
★ **Port Arthur Historic Site**
Encircled by the waters of a sheltered bay, this is the site of Australia's longest established penal colony, operating between 1830 and 1877. The area is now filled with ruins. Evening lantern lit ghost tours are available.
★ **Tasman NP**
This Park boasts some of Australia's best coastal walks. Australian fur seals breed and rest along the rugged coastline.
★ **Tasmanian Devil Park and Tiger Snake Centre**
This centre offers an opportunity to get close to Tasmanian devils, koalas, kangaroos and wallabies.

Cape Pillar, Tasman Peninsula

Scale 1:350 000

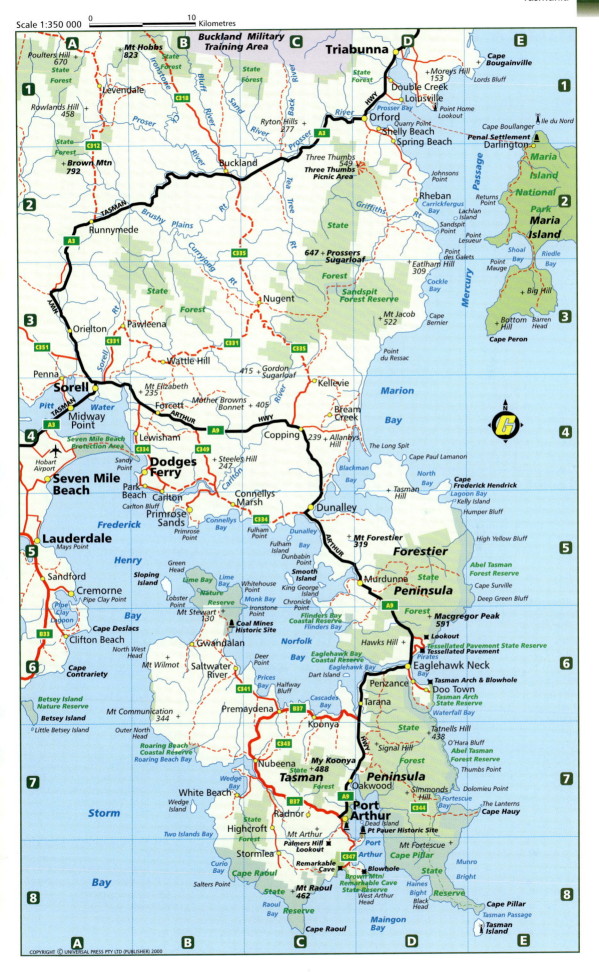

Index and Gazetteer

(Italics = Homesteads)

A1 Mine Settlement, VIC 87 E1
Abbeyard, VIC 81 G5
Abbieglassie, QLD 124 B2
Abercorn, QLD..................121 F6
Aberdeen, NSW..................40 C3
Aberdeen, QLD..................120 C1
Aberfeldy, VIC..................87 F2
Aberfoyle, NSW 35 E5
Aberfoyle, QLD 119 H2
Abergowrie, QLD 116 A5
Abingdon Downs, QLD 115 F4
Abminga (Ruin), SA 151 H1
Abydos, WA 187 E1
Acheron, VIC......................86 D1
Acton Downs, QLD 119 F1
Adaminaby, NSW 44 D3
Adamsfield, TAS 240 C3
Adavale, QLD 123 G1
Adelaide, SA 159 E2
Adelong, NSW 44 C2
Adels Grove, QLD..............114 B5
Adventure Bay, TAS 241 E5
Agery, SA 156 D6
Agnes, VIC........................87 F5
Agnes Creek, SA 151 F1
Agnes Water, QLD 121 G5
Agnew, WA 187 F6
Aileron Roadhouse, NT 219 H1
Ailsa, VIC..........................78 D4
Ainsworth, WA..................181 E2
Aireys Inlet, VIC 86 A4
Airlie Beach, QLD 120 D1
Alawoona, SA..................159 G1
Alba, QLD 119 G1
Albacutya, VIC..................78 C2
Albany, WA 181 E6
Alberrie Creek
  (Ruin), SA........................152 D6
Albert, NSW 39 E3
Alberton, VIC 87 F5
Alberton West, VIC 87 F5
Albion Downs, WA 187 F5
Albro, QLD 120 B3
Albury, NSW......................44 B3
Alcala, QLD 114 D6
Alcomie, TAS....................236 C2
Alcoota, NT 220 B1
Alderley, QLD 118 B3
Aldinga Beach, SA 159 E2
Aldville, QLD 123 G2
Alectown, NSW 39 G4
Alexandra, VIC..................86 D1
Alexandria, NT 217 E2
Alford, SA........................156 D6
Alfred Town, NSW............44 C2
Ali Curung, NT 216 B4
Alice, QLD 120 A4
Alice Downs, WA 185 G4
Alice Springs, NT..............220 B3
Aligator Creek, QLD........116 B6
Allambee, VIC..................87 E4
Allambee South, VIC 87 E4
Allambi, NT 220 B3
Allambie, NSW 37 F2
Allambie, QLD 123 H2
Allandale, SA 152 A3
Allansford, VIC..................85 E4

Allanson, WA 180 C4
Alleena, NSW 39 E6
Allendale, VIC..................85 H1
Allendale East, SA............159 G6
Allies Creek, QLD 125 E1
Allora, QLD......................125 F3
Alma, NSW......................38 A5
Alma, VIC 79 G6
Almaden, QLD..................115 H3
Almoola, QLD 120 C1
Almora, QLD 114 B4
Alonnah, TAS 241 E5
Aloomba, QLD..................116 A3
Alpha, QLD 120 B4
Alpha, QLD 120 B5
Alpurrurulam, NT 217 G4
Alroy, QLD 119 F4
Alroy Downs, NT 217 E2
Alstonville, NSW 35 G3
Alton Downs, SA 153 F2
Alyangula
  (Police Stn), NT 209 A5
Alyuen, NT 219 H1
Amah, QLD 120 C4
Amanbidgi, NT 210 C4
Amata, SA........................150 C1
Ambalindum, NT............220 C2
Ambleside, TAS................237 F3
Amboola, QLD..................124 B2
Ambrose, QLD..................121 F5
Amburla, NT 219 G2
Amby, QLD 124 B2
Amelup, WA 181 F5
American River, SA..........158 D3
Amity Point, QLD 125 G3
Ammaroo, NT 216 C5
Amoonguna, NT 220 B3
Amor Downs, QLD 119 G4
Amosfield, NSW................35 E3
Amphitheatre, VIC............79 G6
Ampilatwatja, NT..............216 C5
Amungee Mungee, NT 212 B4
Anakie, QLD 120 C4
Anakie, VIC 86 A3
Anakie East, VIC 86 A3
Andado, NT 220 C5
Andamooka, SA 156 C1
Andamooka, SA 156 C1
Anderson, VIC 86 D4
Ando, NSW 45 E5
Andoom, QLD 117 A3
Andover, TAS 241 F1
Angas Downs, NT............219 F4
Angaston, SA 159 E1
Angellala, QLD 124 A1
Angellala, QLD 124 A1
Angepena, SA 157 E1
Angip, VIC 78 D3
Angledool, NSW 33 F3
Anglers Rest, VIC 82 A3
Anglesea, VIC 86 A4
Angorichina
  Roadhouse, SA 157 E2
Angurugu, NT 209 A6
Anketell, WA 187 E6
Anna Creek, SA..............152 B5
Anna Plains, WA............184 C5

Annalara, NSW..................37 H1
Annean, WA 186 D5
Anningie, NT 215 G6
Annitowa, NT 217 E5
Annuello, VIC....................77 F5
Ansons Bay, TAS..............238 D3
Antarrengeny, NT............216 C5
Anthony Lagoon, NT 212 D6
Antil Ponds, TAS..............241 E1
Antwerp, VIC....................78 C4
Apollo Bay, VIC................85 G5
Appila, SA........................157 E5
Appin, NSW......................40 C6
Appin, VIC 79 H3
Apsley, TAS......................241 E2
Apsley, VIC 78 A6
Arabella, QLD..................124 A1
Arajoel, NSW..................44 B2
Arakoon, NSW 41 F1
Araluen, NSW 45 F3
Aramac, QLD 119 H3
Arapunya, NT 216 D6
Ararat, VIC 85 F1
Arawerr, NT 216 C6
Arbuckle Junction, VIC 87 G1
Arcadia, QLD 118 A1
Arcadia, VIC......................80 C4
Archdale, VIC....................79 G5
Archer River
  Roadhouse, QLD 117 B4
Archies Creek, VIC............86 D4
Arckaringa, SA 151 H3
Arcoona, SA 156 C2
Ardath, WA 179 F6
Ardlethan, NSW 44 B1
Ardmore, QLD 118 B2
Ardno, VIC........................84 A2
Ardoch, QLD 123 F2
Ardrossan, SA..................158 D1
Areegra, VIC 79 E4
Areyonga, NT 219 F3
Argadargada, NT............217 E5
Argyle, VIC 80 B5
Ariah Park, NSW 39 E6
Arizona, QLD 115 E6
Arkaroola, SA 157 F1
Arkona, VIC 78 C4
Arlparra Store, NT............216 C6
Armagh, QLD 120 A4
Armatree, NSW 39 G1
Armidale, NSW..................34 D6
Armidale, WA 180 C2
Armraynald, QLD 114 C4
Armstrong, VIC 85 F1
Armuna, QLD 120 C1
Armytage, VIC 85 H4
Arno, QLD 119 G5
Arno Bay, SA 156 B6
Arnold, VIC 79 H5
Aroona, SA 157 H4
Arrabury, QLD 122 C2
Arrara, QLD 119 G1
Arrawarra, NSW 35 G5
Arrilalah, QLD................119 G4
Arrino, WA 178 B2
Arthur River, TAS............236 B3
Arthur River, WA 180 D4

Arthurton, SA..................156 D6
Arthurville, NSW 39 G3
Arubiddy, WA 189 B3
Arumpo, NSW..................37 F5
Ascot Vale, NSW 36 D3
Ashbourne, SA..................159 E2
Ashburton Downs, WA....186 C3
Ashens, VIC......................79 E5
Ashford, NSW 34 D4
Ashley, NSW 34 B4
Ashmont, NSW..................37 F3
Ashover, QLD 118 C2
Ashton, QLD 119 H2
Ashville, SA......................159 F2
Aston, NSW 37 E5
Atartinga, NT 220 B1
Atherton, QLD 116 A3
Atley, WA 187 E6
Atnarpa, NT 220 C2
Atneltyey, NT 216 C6
Attunga, NSW 34 C6
Atula, NT 221 E2
Auburn, SA 157 E6
Augathella, QLD 124 A1
Augusta, WA 180 B5
Augustus Downs, QLD....114 C5
Aurukun, QLD 117 A4
Auski Roadhouse, WA......186 D2
Austral Downs, NT..........217 G4
Australind, WA 180 B3
Authoringa, QLD 124 A2
Auvergne, NT 210 C3
Avalon, NSW 38 D3
Avenel, VIC 80 C5
Avenue, SA 159 G4
Avington, QLD 119 H5
Avoca, TAS 238 B5
Avoca, VIC........................79 G6
Avoca Downs, WA 182 C4
Avon Downs, NT 217 F3
Avon Downs, QLD 120 B2
Avondale, NSW 32 A5
Avondale, QLD 121 G6
Avondale, SA 157 E1
Avonmore, VIC 80 B4
Axedale, VIC 80 A5
Ayr, QLD..........................116 C6
Ayrford, VIC 85 F4
Ayton, QLD 116 A2

Baan Baa, NSW 34 B6
Babbiloora, QLD 120 B6
Babinda, NSW..................38 D2
Babinda, QLD..................116 A4
Bacchus Marsh, VIC 86 A2
Back Creek, NSW 39 F5
Backwater, NSW 35 E5
Badalia, QLD..................118 B3
Baddaginnie, VIC..............81 E4
Baden, TAS 241 F2
Baden Park, NSW............37 H2
Badgebup, WA 181 E4
Badgingarra, WA 178 B4
Badja, WA 178 D1
Bael Bael, VIC 79 G2
Baerami, NSW 40 B3
Baerami Creek, NSW 40 B3

Bagdad, TAS 241 E2
Bagshot, VIC 80 A5
Bailieston, VIC 80 C5
Baird Bay, SA 155 H5
Bairnsdale, VIC 82 B6
Bajool, QLD....................121 F4
Bakers Creek, QLD 120 D2
Bakers Hill, WA 178 C5
Baking Board, QLD..........125 E2
Balah, SA 157 F6
Balaka, NSW 37 F3
Balaklava, SA 157 E6
Balaree, NSW 33 E6
Balbirini, NT 212 D4
Balcanoona
  (N.P. H.Q.), SA 157 F1
Bald Hill, VIC 86 B1
Bald Rock, VIC 80 A3
Baldry, NSW 39 G4
Balfes Creek, QLD...........120 A1
Balfour Downs, WA 187 F2
Balgo, WA 185 G6
Balgowan, SA 158 D1
Balhannah, SA 159 E2
Balingup, WA 180 C4
Balladonia, WA 189 A4
Balladonia, WA 189 A4
Balladoran, NSW 39 G2
Ballan, VIC 86 A2
Ballandean, QLD.............125 F4
Ballarat, VIC 85 H2
Ballaying, WA 181 E3
Ballbank, NSW 43 E3
Balldale, NSW 44 A3
Ballendella, VIC 80 B4
Balliang, VIC 86 A2
Balliang East, VIC...........86 A2
Ballidu, WA 178 D4
Ballina, NSW 35 G3
Ballindalloch, QLD 119 G1
Ballyrogan, VIC..............85 F1
Balmattum, VIC 80 D5
Balmoral, VIC 84 C1
Balnarring, VIC 86 C4
Balook, QLD...................120 D2
Balook, VIC 87 F4
Bamaga, QLD.................117 B1
Bambaroo, QLD 116 B5
Bambill, VIC 76 B4
Bambilla, NSW 37 H3
Bamboo Creek
  Mine, WA 187 E1
Bambra, VIC 85 H4
Ban Ban Springs, NT 207 E5
Ban Ban Springs, QLD....125 F1
Banana, QLD 121 F6
Bancroft, QLD 121 F6
Banda, WA 187 G6
Bandiana, VIC 81 G3
Bang Bang, QLD.............114 D5
Bangalow, NSW 35 G3
Bangerang, VIC 79 E3
Bangham, SA 159 G4
Bangor, TAS...................238 A3
Banjawarn, WA 187 F6
Banjeroop, VIC 79 H1
Banjoura, QLD 119 G2
Banka Banka, NT 216 B1
Bannerton, VIC...............77 F5
Bannister, WA................180 C3

Bannockburn, QLD 119 H2
Bannockburn, VIC 86 A3
Banyan, VIC 79 E2
Banyena, VIC 79 E4
Barabon, QLD 119 F1
Baradine, NSW 33 H6
Barakula, QLD 125 E2
Baralba, QLD 121 E5
Barataria, QLD 119 F3
Baratta, SA 157 F3
Barcaldine, QLD 119 H4
Barcaldine Downs, QLD 119 H4
Bardoc, WA 182 B4
Barellan, NSW 38 D6
Barfold, VIC 80 A6
Barford, QLD..................120 A6
Bargara, QLD 121 G6
Bargo, NSW 40 B6
Barham, NSW 43 E3
Baring, VIC 78 C1
Baringhup, VIC 79 H6
Barjarg, VIC 81 E5
Barkly, VIC 79 F5
Barkly Downs, QLD 118 A1
Barkly Homestead
  Roadhouse, NT 216 D3
Barmah, VIC 80 C3
Barmedman, NSW 39 E6
Barmera, SA 159 G1
Barnadown, VIC 80 B5
Barnato, NSW 38 B2
Barnawartha, VIC 81 G3
Barnawartha South, VIC....81 G3
Barnes Bay, TAS 241 E4
Barnong, WA 178 C1
Barooga, NSW 43 H3
Barooga, VIC 80 D3
Baroondah, QLD 124 C1
Baroota, SA 156 D4
Barpinba, VIC 85 G3
Barraba, NSW 34 C5
Barradeen, QLD 124 A1
Barramunga, VIC 85 H4
Barraport, VIC 79 G3
Barraroo, NSW 37 F3
Barratta, QLD 116 C6
Barrington, NSW 41 E2
Barrington, QLD 120 A1
Barrington, TAS 237 F4
Barringun, NSW 32 C3
Barrow Creek
  Roadhouse, NT 216 B5
Barry, NSW 39 H5
Barry, NSW 40 D2
Barrys Reef, VIC 86 A1
Barton, VIC 85 E1
Barunduda, VIC 81 G3
Barunga, NT 211 G1
Barwidgee, WA 187 F5
Barwon, VIC 85 H4
Barwon Heads, VIC 86 A4
Baryulgil, NSW 35 F4
Basalt Creek, QLD 120 D5
Bass, VIC 86 D4
Batavia Downs, QLD 117 B3
Batchelor, NT 206 D4
Batchica, VIC 78 D3
Batehaven, NSW 45 F3
Batemans Bay, NSW 45 F3
Bathurst, NSW 40 A5

Batlow, NSW 44 C3
Batten Point, NT.............213 E3
Battery, QLD 116 A6
Bauhinia Downs, NT 212 D3
Bauhinia Downs, QLD 115 E6
Bauhinia Downs, QLD 120 D5
Baulkamaugh
  North, VIC 80 D3
Bawley Point, NSW 45 G3
Baxter, VIC 86 C3
Baykool, QLD 120 A6
Bayles, VIC 86 D3
Baynton, VIC 80 B6
Bayulu, WA 185 F5
Beachport, SA 159 F5
Beacon, WA 179 E4
Beaconsfield, TAS 237 G3
Beaconsfield Upper, VIC 86 D3
Beagle Bay, WA 184 D4
Bealiba, VIC 79 G5
Beardmore, VIC 87 F2
Bearii, VIC....................80 C3
Bears Lagoon, VIC...........79 H4
Beaudesert, QLD 118 D2
Beaudesert, QLD 125 G3
Beaufort, VIC 85 G1
Beaumaris, TAS 238 D4
Beauty Point, TAS 237 G3
Beazleys Br., VIC 79 F5
Beckom, NSW 39 E6
Bedford Downs, WA 185 G4
Bedgerebong, NSW 39 F5
Bedourie, QLD 118 B5
Bedourie, QLD 120 D6
Bedunburru, WA 184 D4
Beeac, VIC 85 G3
Beebyn, WA 186 D5
Beech Forest, VIC 85 G5
Beechford, TAS 237 H3
Beechworth, VIC 81 G4
Beelbangera, NSW 38 C6
Beenleigh, QLD 125 G3
Beerwah, QLD 125 G2
Beetaloo, NT 212 A5
Beete, WA 183 B3
Bega, NSW 45 F5
Beilpajah, NSW 37 G4
Beilpajah, NSW 37 G4
Belah, NSW 32 B6
Belarabon, NSW 38 B2
Belele, WA 186 D5
Belgrave, VIC 86 C3
Belingeramble, NSW 38 B5
Belka, WA 179 F5
Bell, NSW 40 B5
Bell, QLD 125 F2
Bell Bay, TAS 237 H3
Bellalie, QLD 123 E2
Bellangry, NSW 41 F1
Bellarwi, NSW 39 E6
Bellata, NSW 34 A5
Bellbird, NSW 40 D4
Bellbridge, VIC 81 H3
Bellbrook, NSW 35 F6
Bellbuoy Beach, TAS 237 G3
Bellellen, VIC 79 E6
Bellevue, QLD 115 H3
Bellfield, QLD 115 F6
Bellingen, NSW 35 F6
Bellingham, TAS 238 A3

Belltrees, NSW 40 C2
Belmont, NSW 40 D4
Beloka, NSW 44 D4
Beltana, SA 157 E2
Beltana Roadhouse, SA 157 E2
Belton, SA 157 E4
Belyando
  Crossing, QLD 120 B2
Belyuen, NT 206 D4
Bembah Point, NSW 41 E3
Bemboka, NSW 45 E4
Bemm River, VIC 83 E6
Ben Bullen, NSW 40 B4
Ben Lomond, NSW 34 D5
Bena, VIC 86 D4
Benalla, VIC 81 E4
Benambra, VIC 82 B3
Benanee, NSW 42 C1
Benarca, NSW 43 F3
Benayeo, VIC 78 A6
Bencubbin, WA 179 E4
Benda Park, SA 157 G4
Bendemeer, NSW 34 C6
Benderring, WA 181 F2
Bendick Murrell, NSW 39 G6
Bendigo, SA 157 F5
Bendigo, VIC 80 A5
Bendleby, SA 157 E4
Bendoc, VIC 83 E4
Bendolba, NSW 40 D3
Benetook, VIC 76 D4
Bengerang, NSW 34 A3
Bengworden, VIC 82 A6
Benlidi, QLD 119 H5
Benmara, NT 213 F6
Bentley, NSW 35 G3
Benwerrin, VIC 85 H4
Berajondo, QLD...............121 G5
Berangabah, NSW 38 A3
Berendebba, NSW 39 F6
Beresford, QLD 120 B3
Beresford (Ruin), SA........152 C5
Bergallia, NSW 45 F3
Beringarra, WA 186 C5
Bermagui, NSW 45 F4
Bermagui South, NSW 45 F4
Berri, SA 159 G1
Berrigan, NSW 43 H3
Berrima, NSW 45 G1
Berringa, VIC 85 G2
Berriwillock, VIC.............79 F2
Berrook, VIC 76 A5
Berry, NSW 45 G1
Berry Springs, NT 206 D4
Berrybank, VIC 85 G3
Berrys Creek, VIC 87 E4
Bertiehaugh, QLD 117 B3
Berwick, VIC 86 C3
Bessiebelle, VIC 84 C3
Beswick, NT 211 G1
Bet Bet, VIC 79 H5
Beta, QLD 120 A4
Bete Bolong, VIC 82 C5
Bethanga, VIC 81 H3
Bethungra, NSW 44 C1
Betoota, QLD 118 D6
Beulah, VIC 78 D3
Beulah East, VIC.............79 E3
Beulah West, VIC 78 D3
Bevendale, NSW 45 E1

Beverford, VIC 77 G6
Beveridge, VIC 86 C1
Beverley, WA 180 D2
Beverley Springs, WA 185 F3
Bews, SA 159 G2
Beyondie, WA 187 E4
Biala, NSW 45 E1
Bibbenluke, NSW 45 E5
Biboohra, QLD 116 A3
Bibyadanga
  (Lagrange), WA 184 C5
Bicheno, TAS 238 D6
Biddon, NSW 39 G2
Bidgeemia, NSW 44 A2
Bidgemia, WA 186 B4
Bidura, NSW 37 G6
Bierbank, QLD 123 G2
Big Billy, VIC 78 B2
Bigga, NSW 39 H6
Biggara, VIC 82 C1
Biggenden, QLD 125 F1
Bijerkerno, NSW 36 D2
Bilbarin, WA 181 E2
Billa Kalina, SA 152 B6
Billabalong, WA 186 C6
Billengarrah, NT 212 D3
Billilla, NSW 37 F2
Billiluna, WA 185 G5
Billimari, NSW 39 G5
Billinooka, WA 187 F2
Billybingbone, NSW 33 E5
Biloela, QLD 121 F5
Bilpa, NSW 37 G2
Bilpin, NSW 40 B5
Bilyana, QLD 116 A4
Bimbam, QLD 121 E4
Bimbi, NSW 39 F6
Bimbijy, WA 179 E3
Bimbowrie, SA 157 G3
Bimerah, QLD 119 F5
Binalong, NSW 44 D1
Binalong Bay, TAS 238 D4
Binamoor, NSW 37 F2
Binbee, QLD 120 C1
Binda, NSW 37 G5
Binda, NSW 39 H6
Binda, QLD 124 A3
Bindango, QLD 124 C2
Bindarra, NSW 37 E4
Bindi, NSW 38 B2
Bindi, VIC 82 B4
Bindi Bindi, WA 178 C4
Bindoon, WA 178 C5
Bing Bong, NT 213 E3
Bingara, NSW 34 C5
Bingera, QLD 121 G6
Binginwarri, VIC 87 F4
Biniguy, NSW 34 B4
Binnaway, NSW 40 A2
Binningup Beach, WA 180 B3
Binnu, WA 186 B6
Binnum, SA 159 G4
Binya, NSW 38 D6
Birchip, VIC 79 F3
Birdsville, QLD 122 A1
Birdwood, NSW 41 E1
Birdwoodton, VIC 76 D3
Birralee, QLD 120 C1
Birralee, TAS 237 G4
Birrego, NSW 44 A2

Birregurra, VIC 85 H4
Birricannia, QLD 119 H2
Birrimba, NT 211 F4
Birrindudu, NT 214 B1
Birriwa, NSW 40 A3
Bishopsbourne, TAS 237 H5
Black Flag, WA 182 B4
Black Hill, WA 187 E6
Black Mountain, NSW 34 D5
Black Point
  (Ranger Stn), NT 207 F2
Black Range, WA 187 E6
Black River, TAS 236 C2
Black Rock, SA 157 E4
Black Springs, NSW 40 A6
Blackall, QLD 119 H5
Blackbraes, QLD 115 G6
Blackbull, QLD 115 E4
Blackbutt, QLD 125 F2
Blackdown, QLD 115 G3
Blackfellows, NSW 37 F4
Blackfellows Caves, SA   159 G6
Blackheath, NSW 40 B5
Blackmans Bay, TAS 241 E4
Blackville, NSW 40 B2
Blackwater, QLD 120 D4
Blackwell, NSW 36 D4
Blackwood, VIC 86 A1
Blackwood Creek, TAS   237 H5
Bladensburg, QLD 119 F3
Blairmore, QLD 123 H3
Blampied, VIC 85 H1
Blanchetown, SA 159 F1
Blanchewater (Ruin), SA 153 F6
Blandford, NSW 40 C2
Blantyre, NSW 37 F3
Blaxland, NSW 40 B5
Blayney, NSW 39 H5
Blessington, TAS 238 B4
Blighty, NSW 43 G3
Blina, WA 185 E4
Blinman, SA 157 E2
Bloomfield, NSW 38 B2
Bloomfield, QLD 119 H5
Bloomsbury, QLD 120 D1
Blow Clear, NSW 39 F4
Blue Cow
  Mountain, NSW   44 D4
Blue Hills, NSW 39 H1
Blue Rocks, TAS 247 C6
Blue Water Springs
  Roadhouse, QLD 116 A6
Bluff, QLD 120 D4
Bluff Beach, SA 158 D1
Bluff Downs, QLD 116 A6
Blumont, TAS 238 A3
Blyth, SA 157 E6
Blythdale, QLD 124 C2
Boat Harbour, TAS 236 D2
Boatman, QLD 124 A2
Bobadah, NSW 38 D3
Bobawaba, QLD 116 C6
Bodalla, NSW 45 F4
Bodallin, WA 179 G5
Boddington, WA 180 C3
Bogan Gate, NSW 39 F4
Bogantugan, QLD 120 B4
Bogee, NSW 40 B4
Bogewong, NSW 33 F5

Boggabilla, NSW 34 B2
Boggabri, NSW 34 B6
Bogolo, NSW 38 D4
Bogolong Creek, NSW 39 F5
Bogong, VIC 81 H5
Boigbeat, VIC 79 E2
Boinka, VIC 76 C6
Boisdale, VIC 87 G3
Bolgart, WA 178 C5
Bolingbroke, QLD 120 D2
Bollards Lagoon, SA 153 H5
Bollon, QLD 124 B3
Bolton, VIC 77 F5
Bolwarra, QLD 115 G4
Bolwarra, VIC 84 C4
Bomaderry, NSW 45 G1
Bombala, NSW 45 E5
Bomera, NSW 40 A2
Bon Bon, SA 156 A1
Bonalbo, NSW 35 F3
Bonang, VIC 82 D4
Bond Springs, NT 220 B2
Bonegilla, VIC 81 G3
Boneo, VIC 86 B4
Bongaree, QLD 125 G2
Bonnie Doon, VIC 81 E6
Bonnie Downs, WA 187 E2
Bonnie Rock, WA 179 F4
Bonnie Vale, WA 182 B4
Bonny Hills, NSW 41 F2
Bono, NSW 37 E3
Bonrook, NT 207 F5
Bonshaw, NSW 34 D3
Bonton, NSW 37 H4
Bonus Downs, QLD 124 B2
Bonview, NSW 37 H1
Booberoi, NSW 38 D4
Booborowie, SA 157 E5
Boodarie, WA 184 A6
Boogardie, WA 186 D6
Bookabie, SA 155 F3
Bookaloo, SA 156 C3
Bookar, VIC 85 F3
Bookham, NSW 44 D1
Bookin, QLD 118 D1
Boola Boolka, NSW 37 F3
Boolardy, WA 186 C5
Boolarra, VIC 87 F4
Boolba, QLD 124 B3
Boolbanna, QLD 123 F2
Boolcoomta, SA 157 G3
Booleroo Centre, SA 157 E4
Booligal, NSW 38 B6
Boolite, VIC 79 E4
Boologooro, WA 186 A4
Boomarra, QLD 114 C6
Boomi, NSW 34 A3
Boomley, NSW 39 H2
Boompa, QLD 125 F1
Boonah, QLD 125 G3
Boonarga, QLD 125 E2
Boondandilla, QLD 125 E3
Boondara, NSW 38 A5
Boonderoo, QLD 119 G1
Boongoondoo, QLD 120 A3
Boonoo Boonoo, NSW 35 E3
Booraan, WA 179 F5
Boorabbin, WA 179 H5
Booral, NSW 41 E3
Boorara, QLD 123 F4

Boorhaman, VIC 81 F3
Booroolite, VIC 81 E6
Boorooma, NSW 38 D1
Booroopki, VIC 78 B5
Booroorban, NSW 43 F2
Boorowa, NSW 44 D1
Boort, VIC 79 G3
Boort East, VIC 79 H3
Boorungie, NSW 37 E2
Boothulla, QLD 123 G1
Booyal, QLD 121 G6
Booylgoo Spring, WA 187 E6
Boppy Mount, NSW 38 D2
Borambil, NSW 40 B2
Borden, WA 181 F5
Border Downs, NSW 30 C5
Border Village, SA 154 A3
Bordertown, SA 159 G4
Boree, NSW 39 G4
Boree, QLD 119 G1
Boree Creek, NSW 44 A2
Boree Plains, NSW 37 G5
Borenore, NSW 39 H4
Bororen, QLD 121 G5
Borrika, SA 159 G2
Borroloola, NT 213 E3
Borung, VIC 79 H4
Bosworth, SA 156 D2
Bothwell, TAS 240 D1
Bouldercombe, QLD 121 F4
Boulia, QLD 118 C3
Boundary Bend, NSW 42 D1
Boundary Bend, VIC 77 G5
Bourbah, NSW 39 G1
Bourke, NSW 32 C5
Bow Bridge, WA 180 D6
Bow Hill, SA 159 F2
Bow River, WA 185 H4
Bowelling, WA 180 C4
Bowen, QLD 116 D6
Bowen Downs, QLD 119 H3
Bowenville, QLD 125 F3
Bower, SA 157 F6
Boweya, VIC 81 E4
Bowgada, WA 178 C2
Bowie, QLD 120 A2
Bowna, NSW 44 B3
Bowning, NSW 44 D1
Bowral, NSW 45 G1
Bowraville, NSW 35 F6
Bowser, VIC 81 F4
Bowthorn, QLD 114 A4
Box Tank, NSW 37 E3
Box Valley, NSW 37 H3
Boxwood Hill, WA 181 F5
Boyanup, WA 180 B4
Boyeo, VIC 78 B4
Boyer, TAS 241 E3
Boynedale, QLD 121 F5
Boyup Brook, WA 180 C4
Brachina, SA 157 E2
Brackenburgh, QLD 118 D3
Brackendale, NSW 40 D1
Bracknell, TAS 237 H5
Bradshaw, NT 210 C2
Bradvale, VIC 85 G2
Braemar, SA 157 F5
Braeside, QLD 120 D2
Braidwood, NSW 45 F2
Braidwood, QLD 119 F5

Bramfield, SA 156 A5
Bramston Beach, QLD....116 B4
Bramwell, QLD 117 B3
Brandon, QLD 116 C6
Brandy Creek, VIC 87 E3
Bransby, QLD 122 D3
Branxholm, TAS 238 B3
Branxholme, VIC 84 C3
Branxton, NSW.................40 D4
Brawlin, NSW 44 C1
Brayton, NSW 45 F1
Breadalbane, NSW 45 E1
Breadalbane, QLD...........118 B4
Breadalbane, TAS 238 A4
Break O Day, VIC 86 C1
Bream Creek, TAS 241 G3
Breamlea, VIC 86 A4
Bredbo, NSW 45 E3
Breeza, NSW 40 B1
Bremer Bay, WA 181 G5
Brenda Gate, QLD 124 A4
Brentwood, SA 158 D1
Brentwood, VIC 78 D3
Breona, TAS.....................237 G5
Bretti, NSW 41 E2
Brewarrina, NSW 32 D5
Briagolong, VIC 87 G2
Bribbaree, NSW 39 F6
Bridge Creek, VIC 81 E6
Bridgenorth, TAS 237 H4
Bridgetown, WA 180 C4
Bridgewater, SA 157 E4
Bridgewater, TAS............241 E3
Bridgewater, VIC 79 H5
Bridport, TAS 238 A3
Brigalow, QLD 125 E2
Bright, VIC 81 G5
Brighton, TAS 241 E3
Brim, VIC 78 D3
Brimbago, SA 159 G3
Brimpaen, VIC 78 D6
Brinard, QLD 114 D6
Brindabella, NSW 44 D2
Brindiwilpa, NSW.............31 E5
Bringalbert, VIC 78 A5
Brinkworth, SA 157 E6
Brisbane, QLD 125 G3
Brit Brit, VIC....................84 C1
Brittania, QLD 120 B1
Brittons Swamp, TAS 236 B2
Brixton, QLD....................119 H4
Broad Arrow, WA 182 B4
Broadford, VIC 80 C6
Broadmarsh, TAS 241 E2
Broadmere, NT................212 C4
Broadwater, VIC 84 D3
Brocklehurst, NSW 39 G3
Brocklesby, NSW 44 A3
Brodribb River, VIC.........82 D5
Brogo, NSW 45 F4
Broke, NSW 40 C4
Broken Hill, NSW.............36 D2
Brolgan, NSW 39 F4
Bronte, QLD.....................123 G1
Bronte Park, TAS 240 C1
Bronzewing, VIC 77 E6
Brooksby, VIC 78 C6
Brookstead, QLD..............125 E3
Brookton, WA 180 D2
Brooman, NSW 45 G3

Broome, WA 184 C4
Broomehill, WA 181 E4
Brooms Head, NSW 35 G4
Brooweena, QLD 125 G1
Broughton, VIC 78 B3
Broula, NSW 39 G6
Broulee, NSW 45 F3
Brovinia, QLD...................125 E1
Bruce, SA 156 D4
Bruce Rock, WA 181 F1
Brucedale, QLD 124 C2
Brucknell, VIC..................85 F4
Bruinbun, NSW 40 A4
Brunchilly, NT 216 B2
Brundah, NSW 39 G6
Brunette Downs, NT 216 D1
Brunswick Heads, NSW....35 G3
Brunswick
  Junction, WA 180 C3
Brushwood, NSW 44 B1
Bruthen, VIC 82 B5
Bryah, WA 187 E4
Buangor, VIC 85 F1
Bubialo, QLD 120 D1
Bucasia, QLD 120 D2
Buchan, VIC.....................82 C5
Buchan South, VIC 82 C5
Bucheen Creek, VIC 82 A2
Buckalow, NSW 36 D4
Buckenderra, NSW 44 D4
*Buckingham
Downs,* QLD 118 C2
Buckinguy, NSW 39 E1
Buckland, TAS 241 F2
Buckland, VIC 81 G5
Buckland Junction, VIC....81 G5
Buckleboo, SA 156 B4
Buckleboo, SA 156 B4
Buckley, VIC 85 H4
Buckrabanyule, VIC 79 G4
Budda, NSW 37 H1
Buddabadah, NSW............39 E2
Buddigower, NSW 39 E6
Budgee Budgee, NSW.......40 A3
Budgeree, NSW 36 D4
Budgerygar, QLD..............119 G6
Budgewoi, NSW 40 D5
Buffalo, VIC 87 E5
Buffalo River, VIC 81 G5
Bugaldie, NSW 39 H1
Bugilbone, NSW 33 G5
Bukkulla, NSW 34 D4
Bulahdelah, NSW.............41 E3
Bulga, NSW......................40 C4
Bulga Downs, WA 179 H1
Bulgamurra, NSW.............37 F4
Bulgandramine, NSW 39 F3
Bulgandry, NSW 44 A3
Bulgary, NSW 44 B2
Bulgroo, QLD 123 F1
Bulgunnia, SA 151 H6
Bulgunnia, SA 155 H1
Bulimba, QLD 115 G3
Bulla, VIC 86 B2
Bulla Bulling, WA.............182 A4
Bullara, WA 186 A2
Bullaring, WA 181 E2
Bullaroo, NSW 32 C4
Bullarto, VIC 86 A1
Bullecourt, QLD 118 A1

Bullenbung, NSW 44 B2
Bullengarook, VIC 86 B1
Bullfinch, WA...................179 G4
Bullhead Creek, VIC 82 A2
Bulli, NSW 45 H1
Bullioh, VIC 82 A1
Bullita, NT 210 D3
Bullo River, NT 210 C2
Bulloo Creek, SA.............157 G4
Bulloo Downs, QLD.........123 E4
Bulloo Downs, WA 187 E3
Bullsbrook, WA................178 C5
Bulman, NT 208 B5
Bulumwaal, VIC 82 A5
Bumberry, NSW 39 G4
Bunarthue, SA 156 D4
Bunbury, WA 180 B4
Bunda, NT.......................210 B6
Bunda Bunda, QLD.........115 E6
Bundaberg, QLD 121 G6
Bundaburrah, NSW 39 F5
Bundalagauh, VIC 87 G3
Bundaleer, QLD 124 A4
Bundalong, VIC 81 E3
Bundalong South, VIC......81 E3
Bundanoon, NSW 45 G1
Bundarra, NSW 34 C5
Bundeena, QLD 123 E2
Bundella, NSW 40 B2
Bundoon Belah, NSW 38 B2
Bundoora, QLD 123 G3
Bundure, NSW 38 C4
Bundure, NSW 43 H2
Bundycoola, NSW 38 B2
Bung Bong, VIC 79 G6
Bungal, VIC 86 A2
Bungeet, VIC 81 E4
Bungendore, NSW 45 E2
Bungeworgorai, VIC 124 C2
Bungil, VIC 82 A1
Bungobine, QLD 120 B2
Bungonia, NSW 45 F1
Bungunya, QLD 124 D4
Bungwahl, NSW...............41 E3
Buniche, WA 181 F3
Buninyong, VIC 85 H2
Bunjl, WA 178 C2
Bunna Bunna, NSW 34 A4
Bunnaloo, NSW 43 F3
Bunnan, NSW 40 C2
Bunnawarra, WA 178 C1
Buntine, WA 178 C3
Bunyan, NSW...................45 E4
Bunyip, VIC 86 D3
Burabadji, WA 178 D5
Buradji, WA 178 D5
Burakin, WA 178 D4
Buralyang, NSW 38 D6
Burambil, QLD 123 H4
Burcher, NSW 39 E5
Burekup, WA 180 C3
Burgooney, NSW 38 D5
Burkan, QLD 121 E4
Burke & Wills
  Roadhouse, QLD 114 C5
Burketown, QLD 114 C4
Burleigh, QLD 119 F1
Burnabinmah, WA 179 E1
Burnamwood, NSW 38 A1
Burndoo, NSW 37 G3

Burngrove, QLD 120 D4
Burngup, WA 181 F3
Burnie, TAS 237 E3
Burns, WA 178 B5
Burns Creek, TAS............238 B4
Burnside, QLD 119 G2
Burra, QLD 119 H1
Burra, SA 157 E6
Burraboi, NSW.................43 F2
Burracoppin, WA 179 F5
Burraga, NSW 40 A6
Burragate, NSW 45 F5
Burramine, VIC 81 E3
Burrandana, NSW 44 B2
Burrapine, NSW 35 F6
Burrawantie, NSW 32 B3
Burren Junction, NSW 33 H5
Burrereo, VIC 79 E4
Burrill Lake, NSW 45 G2
Burringurrah, WA 186 C4
Burrinjuck, NSW 44 D2
Burrowye, NSW................82 B1
Burrum Heads, QLD 121 H6
Burrumbeet, VIC 85 G1
Burrumbuttock, NSW 44 A3
Burrundie, NT..................207 E5
Burslem, QLD 119 G2
Burta, NSW 36 C3
Burthong, NSW................38 D3
Burtundy, NSW................37 E5
Burtundy, NSW................37 G3
Burunga, QLD 124 D1
Bushfield, VIC 85 E4
Bushy Park, NT...............220 B2
Bushy Park, TAS 240 D3
Busselton, WA 180 B4
Busthinia, QLD 120 A4
Butchers Ridge, VIC 82 C4
Bute, SA 156 D6
Butmaroo, NSW...............45 E2
Buxton, NSW 40 B6
Buxton, VIC 86 D1
Byabarra, NSW 41 F2
Byaduk, VIC 84 C3
Byaduk North, VIC 84 C3
Byfield, QLD 121 F4
Byford, WA 180 C2
Bylong, NSW....................40 B3
Bylong, QLD 119 F1
Byrnedale, NSW 37 E3
Byrnestown, QLD.............121 G6
Byrnestown, QLD.............125 F1
Byrneville, VIC 78 D4
Byro, WA 186 C5
Byrock, NSW 32 D6
Byron Bay, NSW 35 H3

C Lake, NSW 37 G4
Cabanandra, VIC 82 D4
Cabbage Tree Creek, VIC 82 D5
Caboolture, QLD..............125 G2
Cabramurra, NSW 44 D3
Cacoory (Ruin), QLD.......118 B6
Cadelga (Ruin), SA 153 H1
Cadell, SA 157 F6
Cadney Homestead
  (Roadhouse), SA 151 G3
Cadney Park, SA 151 G3
Cadoux, WA 178 D4
Caiguna, WA 189 B4

Cairns, QLD 116 A3
Cairns, QLD 123 H1
Caiwarro, QLD 123 G4
Cal Lal, NSW 36 D6
Calca, SA 155 H5
Calcium, QLD 116 B6
Calder, TAS 236 D3
Caldervale, QLD 120 B6
Caldwell, NSW 43 F3
Caledonia, QLD 119 H3
Calen, QLD 120 D1
Calingiri, WA 178 C5
Calivil, VIC 79 H4
Callabonna (Ruin), SA 153 G6
Callagiddy, WA 186 A4
Callandoon North, QLD 124 D4
Callanna, SA 152 D6
Callanna (Ruin), SA 152 D6
Callawa, WA 184 B6
Callawadda, VIC 79 E5
Callide, QLD 121 E5
Callide Mine, QLD 121 F5
Callindary, NSW 31 E5
Callington, SA 159 E2
Calliope, QLD 121 F5
Callytharra Springs, WA 186 B4
Caloundra, QLD 125 G2
Calrossie, VIC 87 G4
Calton Hills, QLD 114 B6
Caltowie, SA 157 E5
Calulu, VIC 82 A6
Calvert Hills, NT 213 F5
Camballin, WA 185 E4
Cambeela, QLD 119 E3
Camberville, VIC 87 E2
Camberwell, NSW 40 C3
Cambooya, QLD 125 F3
Cambrai, SA 159 F1
Cambridge, TAS 241 E3
Camdale, TAS 237 E3
Camden, NSW 40 C6
Camel Creek, QLD 116 A5
Camena, TAS 237 E3
Cameron Downs, QLD 119 G2
Camfield, NT 211 E4
Camooweal, QLD 114 A6
Camp Creek, NT 206 D4
Campania, TAS 241 E2
Campbell Town, TAS 238 B6
Campbells Bridge, VIC......79 E5
Campbells River, NSW......40 A6
Campbelltown, NSW........40 C6
Campbelltown, VIC 79 H6
Camperdown, VIC 85 F4
Canary Island, VIC 79 H3
Canaway Downs, QLD....123 F1
Canbelego, NSW 38 D2
Canberra, NSW 45 E2
Candelo, NSW 45 F5
Cane River, WA 186 B2
Canegrass, SA 157 G5
Caniambo, VIC 80 D4
Cann River, VIC 83 E5
Canna, WA 178 C1
Cannawigara, SA 159 G3
Cannie, VIC 79 G2
Cannington, QLD 118 D2
Canobie, QLD 114 D6
Canonba, NSW 39 E1
Canopus, SA 157 G5

Canowindra, NSW..............39 G5
Canteen Creek, NT 216 D4
Canterbury, QLD 119 E6
Cape Barren Island, TAS 247 C7
Cape Bridgewater, VIC 84 B4
Cape Clear, VIC..................85 G2
Cape Crawford
  Roadhouse, NT 212 D4
Cape Jervis, SA 158 D2
Cape Paterson, VIC 86 D5
Cape River, QLD 120 A1
Capel, WA 180 B4
Capella, QLD 120 C4
Capels Crossing, VIC 79 H2
Capertee, NSW 40 B4
Capon, NSW 37 G2
Capricorn
  Roadhouse, WA 187 E3
Capricorn Roadhouse
  Fuel Dump, WA 187 G2
Captain Billy
  Landing, QLD................117 B2
Captains Flat, NSW 45 E3
Carabost, NSW 44 C3
Caradoc, NSW 31 F6
Caragabal, NSW 39 F5
Caralue, SA 156 B5
Caralulup, VIC 79 G6
Caramut, VIC 85 E3
Carandotta, QLD 118 A2
Carapooee, VIC 79 G5
Carapook, VIC 84 B2
Carawa, SA 155 H4
Carbeen Park, NT..............211 F1
Carbine, WA 182 A4
Carbla, WA 186 B5
Carboor, VIC 81 F4
Carboor Upper, VIC 81 F5
Carbunup River, WA 180 B4
Carcoar, NSW 39 H5
Cardigan Village, VIC........85 H2
Cardinia, VIC 86 D3
Cardross, VIC 76 D4
Cardstone, QLD................116 A4
Cardwell, QLD 116 A4
Carey Downs, WA 186 B4
Cargerie, VIC 85 H2
Cargo, NSW 39 G5
Cariewerloo, SA 156 C4
Carina, VIC 76 B6
Carina, VIC 78 A1
Carinda, NSW 33 F5
Carisbrook, VIC 79 H6
Carisbrooke, QLD 119 E3
Carlachy, NSW 39 F4
Carlindie, WA 184 A6
Carlisle River, VIC..............85 G4
Carlo, QLD 118 B4
Carlsruhe, VIC 86 A1
Carlton, NSW 39 E1
Carlton Hill, WA 185 H3
Carmala, NSW 37 F2
Carmila, QLD 121 E3
Carmor Plains, NT 207 F3
Carnamah, WA 178 C3
Carnarvon, QLD..............120 C5
Carnarvon, WA 186 A4
Carnes, SA 155 H1
Carnnegie, WA 187 G4
Caroda, NSW......................34 B5
Caron, WA 178 C2

Caroona, NSW 40 B1
Caroona, SA 157 F5
Carpendeit, VIC 85 F4
Carpentaria
  Downs, QLD 115 H5
Carpenter Rocks, SA 159 G6
Carrabin, WA 179 F5
Carrajung, VIC 87 G4
Carranballac, VIC..............85 F2
Carranya, QLD 119 E6
Carrarang, WA 186 A5
Carrathool, NSW 43 G1
Carrick, TAS 237 H4
Carrieton, SA 157 E4
Carroll, NSW 40 B1
Carron, VIC 79 E4
Carrum, QLD 119 E1
Carrum, VIC 86 C3
Carrum Downs, VIC 86 C3
Carse O Gowrie, QLD 120 B1
Carwarp, VIC 76 D4
Carwell, QLD 120 B5
Cascade, WA 183 B4
Cashmere Downs, WA 179 G1
Cashmere West, QLD 124 C3
Cashmore, VIC 84 B4
Casino, NSW 35 G3
Cassilis, NSW 40 B2
Cassilis, VIC 82 B4
Casterton, VIC 84 B2
Castle Forbes Bay, TAS ..240 D4
Castle Rock, NSW 40 C3
Castleburn, VIC 87 H2
Castlemaine, VIC 80 A6
Castlevale, QLD 120 B5
Cataby Roadhouse, WA 178 B4
Catamaran, TAS 240 D5
Cathcart, NSW 45 E5
Cathedral Hill, QLD 119 E2
Cattle Creek, NT 211 E5
Catumnal, VIC 79 G3
Caulfield, VIC 86 C3
Caveat, VIC 80 D6
Cavendish, VIC 84 D2
Caverton, SA 159 G6
Caveside, TAS 237 F5
Cawkers Well, NSW 37 F2
Cecil Plains, QLD 125 E3
Cedar Point, NSW 35 G3
Ceduna, SA 155 G3
Central Tilba, NSW 45 F4
Ceradotus, QLD................121 F6
Ceres, VIC 86 A3
Cervantes, WA 178 B4
Cessnock, NSW 40 D4
Chaffey, SA 157 G6
Chain of Lagoons, TAS   238 D5
Chalky Well, NSW 37 E4
Challa, WA 179 F1
Challambra, VIC 79 E4
Chandada, SA 155 H4
Chandler, SA 151 F2
Chandlers Creek, VIC 83 E5
Chandos, SA 159 G2
Charam, VIC 78 B6
Charleville, QLD 123 H1
Charleyong, NSW 45 F2
Charlotte Pass, NSW 44 D4
Charlotte Waters
  (Ruin), NT 220 C6

Charlton, VIC 79 G4
Charters Towers, QLD 116 B6
Chatham, QLD 120 A6
Chatsworth, QLD..............118 C2
Chatsworth, VIC 85 E3
Cheepie, QLD 123 G2
Cherbourg, QLD 125 F2
Cherrabun, WA 185 F5
Cherrypool, VIC 78 D6
Cheshunt, VIC 81 F5
Cheshunt South, VIC 81 F5
Chesney, VIC 81 E4
Cheshunt, SA 157 E4
Chetwynd, VIC 84 B1
Chewton, VIC 80 A6
Chidna, QLD 114 C6
Chifley, WA 182 D5
Childers, QLD 121 G6
Chilla Well O.S., NT 214 D5
Chillagoe, QLD 115 H3
Chillingollah, VIC 79 F1
Chilpanunda, SA 155 H4
Chiltern, VIC 81 F3
Chiltern Hills, QLD 118 D3
Chinaman Flat, VIC 78 C3
Chinchilla, QLD 125 E2
Chinkapook, VIC 77 F6
Chinside, QLD 120 C4
Chirnside, QLD 120 C4
Chorregon, QLD 119 F3
Chowey, QLD 121 G6
Christmas Hills, TAS 236 C2
Chudleigh, TAS 237 F5
Churchill, VIC 87 F4
Churinga, NSW 37 F2
Chute, VIC 85 G1
Clackline, WA 178 C5
Clanagh, QLD 119 G3
Clandulla, NSW 40 B4
Claraville, NT 220 C2
Claraville, QLD 115 E5
Clare, NSW 37 H5
Clare, QLD 116 C6
Clare, SA..........................157 E6
Claremont, VIC 81 F5
Clarence Point, TAS 237 G3
Clarencetown, NSW..........40 D3
Clarina, QLD 114 D4
Clarke River, QLD 116 A5
Clarkefield, VIC 86 B1
Claude Road, TAS 237 F4
Claverton, QLD 123 H2
Clayton, SA 153 E5
Clear Lake, VIC 78 C6
Clear Ridge, NSW 39 E5
Cleary, WA 179 E4
Clermont, QLD 120 C3
Cleve, SA 156 B6
Cleveland, TAS 238 A5
Clifford Creek, WA 186 C3
Clifton, QLD 119 F6
Clifton, QLD 125 F3
Clifton Beach, QLD 116 A3
Clifton Beach, TAS 241 F4
Clifton Hills, SA 153 F2
Clifton Springs, VIC 86 B3
Clio, QLD 119 F2
Clonagh, QLD 114 D6
Cloncurry, QLD 118 C1
Clouds Creek, NSW 35 F5
Clover Hills, QLD 119 H4
Cloyna, QLD 125 F1

Club Terrace, VIC 83 E5
Clunes, VIC 85 H1
Clybucca, NSW......................41 F1
Clyde, VIC 86 C3
Clydebank, VIC......................87 H3
Coalbrook, QLD 115 G6
Coaldale, NSW 35 F4
Cobains, VIC 87 H3
Cobar, NSW 38 C1
Cobargo, NSW 45 F4
Cobaw, VIC 86 B1
Cobbadah, NSW 34 C5
Cobba-da-mana, QLD...125 E4
Cobbannah, VIC......................87 H2
Cobbora, NSW 39 H4
Cobbrum, QLD 123 H3
Cobden, VIC 85 F4
Cobera, SA 159 G1
Cobra, WA 186 C3
Cobram, VIC 80 D3
Cobrico, VIC...........................85 F4
Cobrilla, NSW 37 G1
Cobungra, VIC 82 A4
Coburg, VIC 86 C2
Coburn, WA 186 B5
Cocamba, VIC 77 F6
Cochranes Creek, VIC 79 G5
Cockaleechie, SA 156 B6
Cockatoo, QLD 124 D1
Cockatoo, VIC 86 D3
Cockburn, SA 157 H3
Cockle Creek, TAS...........240 D6
Cocklebiddy, WA..................189 C4
Codrington, VIC 84 D4
Coffin Bay, SA 158 A1
Coffs Harbour, NSW 35 G5
Coghills Creek, VIC 85 H1
Cogla Downs, WA 187 E5
Cohuna, VIC 80 A2
Cokum, VIC 79 F2
Colac, VIC 85 G4
Colac Colac, VIC 82 B1
Colbinabbin, VIC...................80 B4
Coldstream, VIC 86 D2
Coleambally, NSW 43 H1
Colebrook, TAS 241 E2
Coleraine, QLD 119 F2
Coleraine, VIC 84 C2
Coles Bay, TAS 241 H1
Colignan, VIC 77 E4
Collarenebri, NSW 33 G4
Collector, NSW 45 E2
Collerina, NSW 32 D4
Colley, SA............................155 H5
Collie, NSW 39 G2
Collie, WA 180 C4
Collingullie, NSW 44 B2
Collingwood, QLD............124 D1
Collinsvale, TAS 241 E3
Collinsville, QLD 120 C1
Colly Blue, NSW 40 B1
Colo, NSW 40 C5
Colton, QLD 125 G1
Colton, SA 155 H5
Comara, NSW 35 E6
Comarto, NSW 37 F2
Combaning, NSW 44 C1
Combanning, QLD 123 H1
Combara, NSW......................39 G1
Combienbar, VIC 83 E5

Comboyne, NSW 41 E2
Come By Chance, NSW 33 G5
Comet, QLD 120 D4
Commodore, SA 157 E2
Commonwealth Hill, SA 151 G6
Comobella, NSW 39 H3
Comongin, QLD 123 F1
Compton Downs, QLD....119 F1
Conara, TAS.........................238 A5
Conargo, NSW 43 G2
Concongella, VIC 79 E6
Condah, VIC 84 C3
Condamine, QLD 124 D2
Condobolin, NSW 39 E4
Congelin, WA 180 D3
Congie, QLD 123 F2
Congupna, VIC 80 D4
Coniston, NT 215 F6
Conlea, NSW 32 A5
Conn, QLD............................116 B5
Connemarra, NSW 40 A2
Connemarra, QLD............119 E5
Conoble, NSW 38 A4
Consuelo, QLD 120 C5
Conway, QLD 120 C1
Conway, QLD 120 D1
Coober Pedy, SA 151 H5
Coobowie, SA 158 D2
Coodardy, WA 186 D5
Cooee, TAS 237 E3
Cooinda, QLD 119 F2
Coojar, VIC 84 C1
Cook, SA 154 C1
Cookamidgera, NSW...39 G4
Cookardinia, NSW 44 B3
Cooke Plains, SA 159 F2
Cooktown, QLD...................116 A2
Cookville, TAS....................241 E5
Coolabah, NSW 38 D1
Coolabri, QLD....................120 B6
Coolac, NSW 44 C2
Cooladdi, QLD 123 H2
Coolah, NSW 40 A2
Coolamon, NSW 44 B1
Coolanie, SA 156 C5
Coolatai, NSW 34 C4
Coolawanyah, WA............186 D2
Coolbinga, QLD 123 G2
Coolcalalya, WA...............186 B6
Coolgardie, WA 182 B4
Coolibah, NT 210 D2
Coolimba, WA 178 A3
Coolongolook, NSW 41 E3
Cooloola Village, QLD....125 G1
Coolullah, QLD.................114 C6
Coolup, WA 180 C3
Cooma, NSW 45 E4
Coomaba, SA 156 A6
Coomandook, SA 159 F2
Coomba, NSW 41 E3
Coombah
  Roadhouse, NSW 36 D4
Coombe, SA 159 G3
Coomberdale, WA 178 C4
Coombie, NSW 38 B4
Coomburrah, QLD...........124 A4
Coomeratta, NSW 38 A2
Coomoora, VIC.....................86 A1
Coomrith, QLD 124 D3
Coomunga, SA 158 A1

Coonabarabran, NSW 39 H1
Coonalpyn, SA 159 F3
Coonamble, NSW 33 G6
Coonana, WA 182 D5
Coonawarra, SA 159 G5
Coondambo, SA...............156 B2
Coondarra, QLD...............125 E1
Coonewirrecoo, VIC 84 B1
Coongan, WA 187 E1
Coongie (Ruin), SA 153 G3
Coongoo, QLD......................123 H3
Coonong, NSW 43 H2
Coonooer Bridge, VIC 79 F4
Coopernook, NSW 41 F2
Coorabie, SA 155 E3
Coorabulka, QLD..............118 C4
Cooralya, WA....................186 A4
Cooranbong, NSW 40 D4
Cooranga North, QLD....125 F2
Coordewandy, WA............186 C4
Cooriemungle, VIC 85 F4
Coorow, WA 178 C3
Cooroy, QLD 125 G2
Cootamundra, NSW 44 C1
Coothalla, QLD 123 H2
Cootra, SA.........................156 B5
Cope Cope, VIC 79 F4
Copley, SA 157 E1
Copmanhurst, NSW 35 F4
Coppabella, QLD 120 D2
Copper Hill, SA 151 H3
Copperfield, WA 182 A2
Copping, TAS 241 F3
Cora Lynn, VIC 86 D3
Corack East, VIC 79 F3
Coraguiac, VIC 85 G4
Coraki, NSW 35 G3
Coral Bay, WA 186 A3
Coralie, QLD 115 E4
Coramba, NSW 35 F5
Cordalba, QLD......................121 G6
Cordillo Downs, SA 153 H2
Corea Plains, QLD 120 A1
Coree South, NSW 43 G2
Coreen, NSW 44 A3
Corella, SA 157 H4
Corfield, QLD 119 F2
Corfu, QLD 124 A3
Corinda, QLD 119 H2
Corinda (ruin), QLD 114 B4
Corindi, NSW 35 G5
Corindi Beach, NSW..........35 G5
Corinella, VIC 86 D4
Corinna, TAS 236 C5
Corio, VIC 86 A3
Cork, QLD 119 E3
Cornwall, QLD 124 C1
Cornwall, TAS......................238 C5
Corny Point, SA 158 C1
Corobimilla, NSW 44 A1
Coromby, VIC 79 E4
Corona, NSW......................36 D1
Coronet Bay, VIC 86 D4
Coronga Downs, NSW 38 C1
Corop, VIC 80 B4
Cororooke, VIC 85 G4
Corowa, NSW 44 A3
Corowa, VIC..........................81 G3
Corraberra, SA 156 D4
Corrigin, WA 181 E2

Corringle, NSW 39 E5
Corryong, VIC 82 B1
Corunna, SA 156 C4
Corunna Downs, WA 187 E1
Cosgrove, VIC 80 D4
Cosgrove South, VIC 80 D4
Cosmo Newberry, WA....187 G6
Cosmos, QLD 120 D3
Cossack, WA......................186 C1
Costerfield, VIC 80 B5
Cotabena, SA 156 D3
Cotabena, SA 157 E3
Coulta, SA 158 A1
Countegany, NSW...............45 E4
Country Downs, WA 184 D4
Couta Rocks, TAS 236 B3
Coutts Crossing, NSW 35 F5
Cowan, NSW 40 C5
Cowan Downs, QLD 114 D5
Cowangie, VIC 78 B1
Cowangla, NSW 35 G3
Coward Springs
  (Ruin), SA........................152 C5
Cowarie, SA 153 E3
Cowell, SA 156 C6
Cowes, VIC 86 C4
Cowled Landing, SA 156 C5
Cowper, NSW 35 G4
Cowra, NSW 39 G5
Cowwarr, VIC 87 G3
Cracow, QLD 121 E6
Cradle Valley, TAS 237 E5
Cradoc, TAS 240 D4
Cradock, SA 157 E3
Craigie, NSW........................45 E5
Craigieburn, VIC 86 B2
Craiglie, QLD 116 A3
Cramenton, VIC 77 E5
Cramphorne, WA 179 F6
Cramps, TAS 237 G6
Cranbourne, VIC 86 C3
Cranbrook, TAS 238 C6
Cranbrook, WA 181 E5
Craven, NSW 41 E3
Cravensville, VIC 82 B2
Crayfish Creek, TAS 236 D2
Credo, WA 182 A4
Creeper Gate, NSW 38 D2
Cremorne, TAS 241 F3
Crendon, QLD 119 E2
Crescent Head, NSW 41 F1
Cresswell Downs, NT 212 D6
Cressy, TAS 237 H5
Cressy, VIC...........................85 G3
Creswick, VIC 85 H1
Crew, QLD 120 D4
Crib Point, VIC 86 C4
Cromarty, QLD.....................116 C6
Crooble, NSW 34 B4
Crookwell, NSW...................45 E1
Croppa Creek, NSW 34 B3
Crowdy Head, NSW 41 F2
Crowlands, VIC....................79 F6
Crows Nest, QLD...............125 F3
Crowther, NSW 39 G6
Croxton East, VIC...............84 D2
Croydon, QLD 115 E4
Croydon, QLD 120 D3
Cryon, NSW..........................33 G5

Crystal Brook, SA 156 D5
Crystalbrook, QLD...........120 C6
Cuballing, WA 180 D3
Cubba, NSW 38 B1
Cubbaroo, NSW.................33 H5
Cudal, NSW 39 G5
Cuddapan, QLD................118 D6
Cudgee, VIC.......................85 E4
Cudgewa, VIC....................82 B1
Cudgewa North, VIC 82 B1
Cue, WA 186 D5
Culburra, NSW 45 G2
Culburra, SA 159 F3
Culcairn, NSW 44 B3
Culfearne, VIC...................79 H2
Culgoa, VIC........................79 F2
Culgoora, NSW 34 A5
Cullen Bullen, NSW 40 B5
Culloden, VIC.....................87 H2
Cullulleraine, VIC..............76 C4
Culpataroo, NSW 38 A5
Culpaullin, NSW 37 G2
Culston, SA 159 G4
Cultana, SA 157 G4
Cultowa, NSW 37 H2
Cumborah, NSW 33 F4
Cummins, SA 156 A6
Cumnock, NSW 39 G4
Cundare, VIC......................85 G3
Cundeelee, WA 189 A3
Cunderdin, WA 178 D5
Cundumbul, NSW..............39 H4
Cungelella, QLD...............120 B5
Cungena, SA 155 H4
Cunnamulla, QLD.............123 H3
Cunningham, QLD...........125 F4
Cunyu, WA 187 E4
Cuprona, TAS 237 E3
Curban, NSW 39 G2
Curbur, WA 186 C5
Curdie Vale, VIC...............85 F4
Curdimurka (Ruin), SA   152 C5
Curlewis, NSW 40 B1
Curnamona, SA 157 F3
Currabubula, NSW 40 C1
Curragh Mine, QLD 120 D4
Curramulka, SA 158 D1
Currarong, NSW................45 G2
Currawarna, NSW 44 B2
Currawilla, QLD...............118 D6
Currie, TAS.......................247 C2
Curtin Springs
  Roadhouse, NT 219 F5
Curyo, VIC..........................79 E3
Cuthero, NSW 37 E4
Cygnet, TAS......................241 E4
Cygnet River, SA 158 D3

Dadswells Bridge, VIC 79 E5
Daguragu, NT 210 D5
Dagworth, QLD 115 G4
Dagworth, QLD 119 E2
Dahwilly, NSW...................43 F2
Daintree, QLD 116 A2
Dajarra, QLD.....................118 B2
Dalberg, QLD 120 C1
Dalby, QLD 125 E2
Dalgaranga, WA 186 D6
Dalgety, NSW 44 D4
Dalgety Downs, WA 186 C4

Dalhousie (Ruin), SA........152 A1
Dalmeny, NSW 45 F4
Dalmore, QLD..................119 G4
Dalmorton, NSW................35 F5
Dalton, NSW 45 E1
Dalveen, QLD....................125 F4
Dalwallinu, WA 178 D3
Daly River
  (Police Stn), NT 206 D5
Daly Waters, NT................211 H3
Dalyston, VIC 86 D4
Dalyup, WA 183 B4
Damperwah, WA 178 D2
Dampier, WA 186 C1
Dampier Downs, WA 184 D5
Dandaloo, NSW 39 F3
Dandaraga, WA 187 E6
Dandaragan, WA..............178 B4
Dandenong, VIC.................86 C3
Dandongadale, VIC 81 G5
Dangin, WA 181 E2
Danyo, VIC 78 B1
Dapto, NSW........................45 G1
Dardanup, WA 180 C4
Dareton, NSW.....................37 E6
Dargo, VIC..........................87 H1
Darke Peak, SA 156 B5
Darkin, WA 180 D4
Darlington, VIC 85 F3
Darlington Point, NSW 43 H1
Darlu Darlu, WA...............185 H4
Darnick, NSW 37 G4
Darnum, VIC......................87 E3
Daroobalgie, NSW 39 F5
Darr, QLD 119 G4
Darraweit Guim, VIC 86 B1
Darriman, VIC...................87 G4
Darrine, WA......................179 H4
Dartmoor, VIC...................84 B3
Dartmouth, QLD..............119 H4
Dartmouth, VIC.................82 A2
Darwin, NT 206 D3
Daubeny, NSW 37 F1
Davenport Downs, QLD 118 D5
Davyhurst (Ruins), WA   182 A3
Dawesville, WA 180 B3
Dawson, SA 157 E4
Dawson Park, QLD 121 E6
Dayboro, QLD 125 G3
Daylesford, VIC.................86 A1
Daymar, QLD 124 C4
Daysdale, NSW..................44 A3
De Grey, WA 184 A6
Dean, VIC...........................85 H1
Deans Marsh, VIC.............85 H4
Deddick, VIC......................82 D4
Deddington, TAS 238 A5
Dederang, VIC 81 G4
Dee, TAS...........................240 C1
Deep Lead, VIC.................79 E6
Deep Well, NT 220 B3
Deepwater, NSW...............35 E4
Deer Park, VIC..................86 B2
Deeragun, QLD................116 B6
Deeral, QLD 116 A3
Delamere, NT 211 E3
Delburn, VIC......................87 E4
Delegate, NSW...................45 E5
Delmore Downs, NT 220 C1
Delny, NT 220 C1

Deloraine, TAS 237 G4
Delungra, NSW 34 C4
Denham, WA 186 A5
Denial Bay, SA 155 G3
Denilcull Creek, VIC 85 F1
Deniliquin, NSW 43 G3
Denison, VIC......................87 G3
Denman, NSW....................40 C3
Denmark, WA 181 E6
Dennes Point, TAS 241 E4
Dennington, VIC................85 E4
Denver, VIC........................86 A1
Depot Springs, WA 187 E6
Derain, NSW.......................44 B1
Derby, TAS 238 B3
Derby, VIC..........................79 H5
Derby, WA 184 D4
Dereel, VIC.........................85 H2
Dergholm, VIC...................84 B1
Deringulla, NSW................40 A1
Deroora, QLD 119 H4
Derrinal, VIC......................80 B5
Derrinallum, VIC...............85 F3
Derriwong, NSW................39 E4
Derry Downs, NT 216 C6
Derwent, NT 219 F2
Derwent Bridge, TAS 240 B1
Devenish, VIC....................81 E4
Deviot, TAS 237 H3
Devonborough
  Downs, SA 157 G4
Devoncourt, QLD..............118 C2
Devonport, TAS................237 F3
Devonshire, QLD 119 G4
Dhuragoon, NSW...............43 E2
Dhurringile, VIC................80 C4
Diamantina Lakes, QLD 118 D4
Diamond Well, WA 187 E5
Diapur, VIC........................78 B4
Didoot, QLD 125 F1
Diemals, WA 179 G2
Digby, VIC 84 B3
Diggers Rest, VIC.............86 B2
Diggora West, VIC 80 A4
Dillalah, QLD 123 H2
Dillcar, QLD 119 F3
Dilpurra, NSW....................43 E2
Dilston, TAS 237 H4
Dimboola, VIC 78 C4
Dimbulah, QLD 116 A3
Dingee, VIC........................80 A4
Dingo, QLD 120 D4
Dingwall, VIC.....................79 H2
Dinner Plain, VIC..............81 H6
Dinninup, WA....................180 D4
Dinyarrak, VIC...................78 A4
Diranbandi, QLD..............124 B4
Dirk Hartog, WA..............186 A5
Dirnaseer, NSW.................44 C1
Dirrung, NSW.....................38 B5
Disney, QLD......................120 B2
Dixie, QLD 117 C6
Dixie, VIC...........................85 F4
Dixons Creek, VIC.............86 D2
Dneiper, NT 220 C1
Docker, VIC........................81 F4
Doctors Flat, VIC...............82 B4
Dodges Ferry, TAS 241 F3
Dollar, VIC..........................87 E4
Dolomite, QLD..................118 C1

Don, QLD 114 A6
Donald, VIC.........................79 F4
Doncaster, QLD 119 F1
Dongara, WA 178 A2
Dongon Plains, QLD 124 B4
Donnybrook, WA 180 C4
Donors Hills, QLD 114 D5
Doobibla, QLD..................123 H2
Dooboobetic, VIC...............79 F4
Doodlakine, WA 179 E5
Dooen, VIC.........................78 D5
Dookie, VIC........................80 D4
Dooley Downs, WA 186 C3
Doolgunna, WA................187 E4
Doomadgee, QLD 114 B4
Doongmabulla, QLD 120 A3
Doorawarrah, WA 186 B4
Dorisvale, NT....................211 E1
Dorodong, VIC...................84 A1
Dorrigo, NSW.....................35 F5
Dorunda, QLD..................115 E3
Dotswood, QLD................116 B6
Double Yards, NSW 37 E4
Doubtful Creek, NSW 35 F3
Doughboy, NSW.................45 F2
Douglas, NT 207 E5
Douglas, VIC......................78 C6
Douglas Experimental
  Farm, NT........................207 E5
Dowerin, WA 178 D5
Drake, NSW........................35 F3
Dreeite, VIC........................85 G3
Drekurni, SA 156 B5
Driffield, VIC......................87 F4
Drik Drik, VIC....................84 B3
Drillham, QLD 124 D2
Dromana, VIC....................86 C4
Dromedary, TAS 241 E3
Dronfield, QLD 118 C2
Drouin, VIC 87 E3
Drumborg, VIC..................84 C3
Drumduff, QLD.................115 F2
Drumlion, QLD.................119 G3
Drummartin, VIC...............80 A4
Drummond, QLD 120 B4
Drummond, VIC.................80 A6
Drummond Cove, WA.......178 A1
Drung Drung, VIC 78 D5
Dry River, NT 211 F2
Drysdale, VIC.....................86 B3
Drysdale River, WA 185 F3
Duaringa, QLD...................121 E4
Dubbo, NSW.......................39 G3
Dublin, SA 159 E1
Duchess, QLD 118 C2
Duck Creek, WA 186 C2
Ducklo, QLD 125 E3
Duddo, VIC 76 B6
Duff Creek (Ruin), SA 152 B4
Dulacca, QLD 124 D2
Dulbydilla, QLD................124 B1
Dulkaninna, SA 153 E5
Dulthara, QLD 115 G6
Dululu, QLD 121 E5
Dumbalk, VIC.....................87 E4
Dumbalk North, VIC..........87 E4
Dumbleyung, WA 181 E3
Dumosa, VIC......................79 F3
Dunach, VIC.......................85 H1
Dunalley, TAS 241 F3

Dunbar, QLD.................115 F2
Dundee, QLD 119 F2
Dundee Beach, NT..........206 C4
Dundinin, WA................181 E3
Dundonnell, VIC 85 F3
Dundoo, QLD................123 G3
Dunedoo, NSW 39 H2
Dungarvon, NSW.............32 A4
Dungog, NSW 40 D3
Dungowan, NSW 40 C1
Dungowan, NT..............211 F4
Dunkeld, NSW 40 A5
Dunkeld, VIC 84 D2
Dunluce, QLD 119 G1
Dunmarra
  Roadhouse, NT..........211 H4
Dunolly, VIC...................79 H5
Dunorlan, TAS...............237 G4
Dunrobin, QLD...............120 A3
Dunrobin, VIC.................84 B2
Dunsborough, WA 180 B4
Duntroon, NSW...............37 F1
Dunwinnie, QLD.............124 C4
Durabrook, QLD 120 B5
Durack River
  Roadhouse, WA...........185 G3
Duramana, NSW.............40 A5
Durdidwarrah, VIC 86 A2
Durham Downs, QLD......122 D2
Durham Downs, QLD......124 C1
Durham Ox, VIC...............79 H3
Duri, NSW 40 C1
Durong South, QLD.......125 E2
Durras, NSW 45 G3
Durri, QLD...................118 C6
Dutson, VIC 87 H3
Dutton River, QLD 119 G1
Dwellingup, WA 180 C3
Dynevor Downs, QLD......123 F3
Dysart, QLD..................120 C3
Dysart, TAS 241 E2

Eagle Bay, WA 180 B4
Eagle Point, VIC 82 B6
Eaglehawk, VIC................80 A5
Eaglehawk Neck, TAS 241 G4
Earaheedy, WA..............187 F4
Earlando, QLD 120 D1
Earlston, VIC...................80 D4
East Gresford, NSW 40 D3
East Sassafras, TAS 237 G4
Eastern View, VIC............85 H4
Eastlake, NSW...............34 D6
Eastmere, QLD...............120 A3
Eastville, VIC...................79 H5
Ebden, VIC 81 G3
Ebor, NSW 35 E6
Eccleston, NSW 40 D3
Echo Hills, QLD.............120 B5
Echo Point, VIC...............87 E1
Echuca, VIC 80 B3
Ecklin South, VIC 85 F4
Eddington, VIC................79 H5
Eden, NSW 45 F5
Eden Creek, NSW 35 F3
Eden Vale O.S., QLD 115 F4
Edenhope, VIC 78 B6
Edgeroi, NSW.................34 A5
Edi, VIC.........................81 F5

Edillilie, SA....................158 A1
Edith, NSW 40 A5
Edith Creek, TAS 236 C3
Edith Downs, QLD 119 E1
Edithburgh, SA...............158 D2
Edithvale, VIC..................86 C3
Edmonton, QLD 116 A3
Edmund, WA.................186 C3
Edron, NSW....................45 F5
Edsgee, WA..................186 B4
Edungalba, QLD 121 E4
Edwards Creek
  (Ruin), SA...................152 B4
Egg Lagoon, TAS............247 C1
Eginbah, WA.................187 E1
Ehlma, QLD...................125 C2
Eidsvold, QLD 121 F6
Eidsvold, QLD 125 E1
Eildon, VIC.....................87 E1
Eildon Park, QLD 119 E4
Einasleigh, QLD.............115 G5
Ejanding, WA 178 D4
El Arish, QLD 116 A4
El Questro, WA..............185 G3
El Trune, NSW 38 D1
Elaine, VIC.....................85 H2
Elalie, QLD...................121 E3
Elands, NSW 41 E2
Elbow Hill, SA................156 C6
Elderslie, TAS.................241 E2
Eldorado, VIC.................81 F4
Electrona, TAS................241 E4
Elgin Vale, QLD 125 F2
Elginbah, NSW................43 G1
Elizabeth Beach, NSW......41 E2
Elizabeth Downs, NT 206 D5
Elizabeth Town, TAS........237 G4
Elkedra, NT...................216 D5
Ella Vale, NSW................32 B4
Ella Valla, WA...............186 B4
Ellam, VIC......................78 C3
Ellenborough, NSW 41 E2
Ellenbrae, WA...............185 G3
Ellendale, TAS................240 D2
Ellendale, WA................185 E4
Ellerslie, VIC...................85 E3
Ellerston, NSW 40 D2
Ellinbank, VIC.................87 E4
Ellinminyt, VIC................85 G4
Elliott, NT......................211 H5
Elliott, QLD...................121 G6
Elliott, TAS....................237 G4
Elliott Heads, QLD..........121 G6
Elliston, SA....................155 H5
Elmhurst, VIC.................79 F6
Elmina, QLD.................124 A2
Elmore, VIC....................80 B4
Elong Elong, NSW..........39 H3
Elphinstone, QLD..........120 C2
Elphinstone, VIC 80 A6
Elsey, NT......................211 H2
Elsmore, NSW................34 D4
Elvo, QLD....................119 E4
Emby, NSW..................39 F1
Emerald, QLD................120 C4
Emerald, VIC..................86 D3
Emerald Beach, NSW.......35 G5
Emerald Hill, NSW..........34 B6
Emerald Springs
  Roadhouse, NT 207 E5

Emita, TAS....................247 B6
Emmaville, NSW.............34 D4
Emmdale
  Roadhouse, NSW 37 H2
Emmet, QLD..................119 G5
Emu, VIC.......................79 G5
Emu Flat, VIC..................80 B6
Emu Junction
  (Ruin), SA...................151 E4
Emu Park, QLD...............121 F4
Enarra, QLD..................124 D3
Eneabba, WA.................178 B3
Eneby, QLD..................116 B6
Enfield, VIC....................85 H2
Englefield, VIC................84 C1
Enmore, NSW................36 D3
Enngonia, NSW 32 C4
Ennuin, WA....................179 G4
Enryb Downs, QLD 119 F2
Ensay, VIC.....................82 B4
Epala, QLD....................121 F5
Epenarra, NT..................216 C4
Epping Forest, TAS..........238 A5
Epsilon, QLD.................122 C3
Epsom, VIC....................80 A5
Eriaba, QLD..................120 C1
Eribung, NSW.................39 F3
Eriba, QLD....................120 C1
Erigolia, NSW.................38 D5
Erica, VIC......................87 F3
Eringa (Ruin), SA...........151 H1
Eringa Park, SA..............157 G4
Erinundra, VIC................83 E5
Erldunda, NT................219 G5
Erldunda
  Roadhouse, NT..........219 G5
Erlistoun, WA................182 C1
Eromanga, QLD..............123 E2
Erong, WA.....................186 C4
Errabiddy, WA...............186 C4
Erong, WA.....................186 C4
Erudina, SA....................157 F3
Esk, QLD.......................125 F3
Eskdale, QLD.................119 G3
Eskdale, VIC...................81 H4
Esmeralda, QLD.............115 F5
Esperance, WA................183 C4
Essendon, VIC.................86 B2
Essex Downs, QLD 119 F1
Etadunna, SA................153 E5
Eton, QLD......................120 D2
Euabalong, NSW 38 D4
Euabalong West, NSW......38 D4
Eucareena, NSW 39 H4
Eucumbene, NSW............44 D4
Eudamullah, WA............186 B3
Eudunda, SA..................157 E6
Eugowra, NSW................39 G5
Eulca, WA......................189 D3
Eulo, NSW....................37 F5
Eulo, QLD......................123 G3
Eumundi, QLD................125 G2
Eumungerie, NSW 39 G2
Eungai Creek, NSW 35 F6
Eungella, QLD.................120 D2
Eurabba, NSW................39 F6
Eurack, VIC....................85 H3
Eurardy, WA..................186 B6
Euratha, NSW.................38 D6
Eurelia, SA.....................157 E4
Euroa, VIC......................80 D5
Eurobin, VIC..................81 G5

Eurobodalla, NSW.............45 F4
Eurolie, NSW..................43 G1
Eurongilly, NSW...............44 C2
Euston, NSW...................42 C1
Eva Downs, NT...............212 C6
Evandale, TAS.................238 A5
Evans Head, NSW 35 G3
Evansford, VIC 79 G6
Evelyn Downs, SA 151 H4
Evengy, QLD..................119 F5
Everton, VIC....................81 F4
Evesham, QLD................119 G3
Evora, QLD....................119 H5
Ewan, QLD.....................116 A5
Exeter, NSW....................45 G1
Exeter, TAS....................237 H4
Exford, VIC.....................86 B2
Exmoor, QLD..................119 F2
Exmouth, WA..................186 A2
Exmouth Gulf, WA...........186 A2
Exton, TAS.....................237 G4

Failford, NSW 41 E3
Fairfield, WA..................185 E4
Fairhill, QLD...................120 D4
Fairholme, NSW...............39 E4
Fairlight, QLD.................115 G2
Fairview, NSW 38 D4
Fairview, NSW 39 F3
Fairview, QLD.................115 H2
Falls Creek, NSW.............45 G2
Falls Creek, VIC...............81 H5
Falmouth, TAS................238 D4
Fanning River, QLD 116 B6
Faraday, VIC...................80 A6
Faraway Hill, SA..............157 F5
Farina (Ruin), SA.............153 E6
Fawcett, VIC...................80 D6
Federal (Ruin), SA...........152 A1
Fentonbury, TAS.............240 D2
Fentons Creek, VIC 79 G4
Ferguson, SA..................155 H2
Ferguson, VIC.................85 G5
Fermoy, QLD..................119 F4
Fern Tree, TAS.................241 E3
Fernbank, VIC.................87 H3
Fernihurst, VIC................79 H4
Fernlees, QLD.................120 C4
Fernshaw, VIC.................86 D2
Fernvale, QLD.................125 G3
Finch Hatton, QLD 120 D2
Fingal, TAS....................238 C5
Finger Post, NSW 39 H3
Finke (Aptula), NT 220 B5
Finley, NSW....................43 G3
Finniss River, NT.............206 D4
Finniss Springs, SA 152 D6
Fish Creek, VIC................87 E5
Fish Point, VIC................79 G1
Fitfield, NSW...................39 E4
Fitzgerald, TAS................240 C3
Fitzroy, NT.....................210 D2
Fitzroy Crossing, WA 185 F5
Five Corners, NSW 39 E3
Fleetwood, QLD..............120 A3
Flinders, VIC...................86 C4
Flintstone, TAS................237 G6
Flodden Hills, QLD..........119 E5
Flora Valley, WA..............185 H5
Floraville, QLD 114 C4

Florida, NSW 38 D2
Florina, NT 211 E1
Flowerdale, TAS...............236 D3
Flowerdale, VIC 86 C1
Fluorspar, QLD.................115 H3
Flying Fish Point, QLD ..116 B4
Flynn, QLD 118 C2
Flynn, VIC 87 G3
Flynns Creek Upper, VIC 87 F4
Fog Creek, QLD 115 F5
Fog Dam, NT 207 E4
Foleyvale, QLD.................121 E4
Forbes, NSW 39 F5
Forbesdale, NSW...............41 E3
Forcett, TAS........................241 F3
Fords Bridge, NSW 32 B4
Fords Lagoon, SA..............157 F5
Forest, TAS.........................236 C2
Forest Hill, NSW.................44 B2
Forest Vale, QLD...............124 B1
Forester, TAS......................238 B3
Forrest, VIC 85 H4
Forrest, WA 189 D3
Forrester, QLD...................120 B3
Forsayth, QLD 115 G5
Forster, NSW......................41 E3
Fort Constantine, QLD ...118 C1
Fortescue River
  Roadhouse, WA.............186 C1
Forth, TAS...........................237 F3
Fortland, QLD 124 A2
Fortuna, QLD 120 A3
Fossil Downs, WA..............185 F4
Fossilbrook Creek, QLD 115 H4
Foster, VIC 87 E5
Four Brothers, SA 157 F4
Four Corners, NSW.............38 D3
Four Mile Creek, TAS......238 D5
Fowlers Bay, SA 155 E3
Fowlers Gap, NSW 36 D1
Foxhow, VIC 85 G3
Framlingham, VIC 85 E4
Frampton, NSW..................44 C1
Frances, SA 159 G4
Frances Creek, NT 207 F5
Frankfield, QLD 120 B3
Frankford, TAS 237 G4
Frankland, WA 180 D5
Franklin, TAS.....................240 D4
Franklyn, SA 157 F5
Frankston, VIC 86 C3
Fraser Range, WA..............183 D2
Frazier Downs, WA 184 C5
Frederickton, NSW 41 F1
Freeburgh, VIC 81 G5
Freemans
  Waterhole, NSW 40 D4
Fregon Community, SA 151 E2
Fremantle, WA 180 B2
Freshwater Creek, VIC 86 A4
Frewhurst, QLD 115 H4
Frogmore, NSW...................39 G6
Frome Downs, SA 157 F2
Fulham, VIC 87 G3
Fumina South, VIC 87 E3
Furner, SA 159 G5
Fyans Creek, VIC 79 E6

Gabalong, WA 178 C4
Gabbin, WA.......................179 E4

Gabyon, WA 186 C6
Gaffneys Creek, VIC 87 E1
Galah, VIC 76 D6
Galaquil, VIC 78 D3
Galaquil East, VIC 79 E3
Galbraith, QLD 115 E2
Galiwinku, NT...................208 D3
Gallipoli, NT 217 G2
Galong, NSW 44 D1
Galore, NSW 44 A2
Galway Downs, QLD 119 F6
Gama, VIC 79 E2
Gamboola, QLD...............115 G3
Ganmain, NSW...................44 B1
Gannawarra, VIC 80 A2
Gapstead, VIC 81 G4
Gapuwiyak, NT.................208 D4
Garah, NSW 34 A3
Garden I. Creek, TAS........241 E4
Garema, NSW 39 F5
Garfield, QLD 120 A4
Garfield, VIC 86 D3
Gargett, QLD 120 D2
Garland, NSW 39 H5
Garrawin, QLD 123 G4
Gartmore, QLD..................120 A5
Garvoc, VIC 85 E4
Gascoyne Junction, WA 186 B4
Gatton, QLD 125 F3
Gatum, VIC 84 C1
Gawler, SA 159 E1
Gawler, TAS........................237 F3
Gayndah, QLD 125 F1
Geegeela, SA 159 G4
Geelong, VIC 86 A3
Geera, QLD 119 H4
Geeveston, TAS.................240 D4
Gelantipy, VIC 82 C4
Gelaro, QLD 115 H4
Gellibrand, VIC 85 G4
Gembrook, VIC...................86 D3
Gemoka, QLD 119 F1
Genoa, VIC 83 F5
George Town, TAS 237 G3
Georgetown, QLD 115 G4
Georgetown, SA 157 E5
Georgina, NT 217 G5
Geraden, NSW 39 G5
Geraldton, WA 178 A1
Gerang Gerung, VIC 78 C4
Geranium, SA 159 G2
Gerara, NSW 32 D3
German Creek
  Mine, QLD......................120 D4
Germantown, VIC 81 G5
Gerogery, NSW 44 B3
Gerringong, NSW 45 G1
Gerroa, NSW......................45 G1
Geurie, NSW 39 G3
Gheringhap, VIC 86 A3
Ghinghinda, QLD 121 E6
Gibb River, WA 185 F3
Gibson, WA 183 C4
Gidgealpa, SA 153 G3
Gidgee, NSW 38 B1
Gidgee, WA 187 E5
Gidginbung, NSW.............39 E6
Giffard, VIC..........................87 G4
Gilbert River, QLD 115 F4
Gilderoy, VIC 86 D2

Gilgai, NSW 34 D5
Gilgai, NSW 38 D2
Gilgandra, NSW 39 G2
Gilgooma, NSW 33 G6
Gilgunnia, NSW 38 C3
Giligulgul, QLD 124 D2
Gilliat, QLD 118 D1
Gilmore, NSW.....................44 C2
Gilmore, QLD 119 H6
Gilroyd, WA 186 B4
Gin Gin, NSW 39 F2
Gin Gin, QLD 121 G6
Gina, SA 151 H6
Gindalbie, WA 182 C3
Gindie, QLD 120 C4
Gingin, WA 178 C5
Gipsy Point, VIC 83 F5
Giralia, WA 186 A2
Girgarre, VIC 80 C4
Girragulang, NSW.............40 A2
Girral, NSW 39 E5
Giru, QLD...........................116 C6
Girvan, NSW 41 E3
Gisborne, VIC 86 B1
Gladfield, VIC 79 H3
Gladstone, NSW 41 F1
Gladstone, QLD 121 F5
Gladstone, SA 157 E5
Gladstone, TAS.................238 C3
Gladysdale, VIC 86 D2
Gleeson, QLD 114 C6
Glen, WA 186 D5
Glen Albyn, NSW 37 G3
Glen Alice, NSW................40 B4
Glen Aplin, QLD 125 F4
Glen Avon, QLD 120 B5
Glen Boree, SA 155 E3
Glen Creek, VIC 81 G4
Glen Davis, NSW 40 B4
Glen Gailic, NSW 40 C3
Glen Geddes, QLD 121 E4
Glen Helen, NT 219 F2
Glen Hill, WA 185 H3
Glen Huon, TAS 240 D4
Glen Ora, NSW 37 G3
Glen Ruth, QLD 116 A4
Glen Valley, VIC 82 A3
Glenaire, VIC 85 G5
Glenaladale, VIC 87 H2
Glenalbyn, VIC 79 H4
Glenample, QLD 119 H3
Glenariff, NSW 32 D6
Glenaroua, VIC...................80 C6
Glenayle, WA 187 G4
Glenbervie, QLD...............119 E2
Glenbrook, NSW................40 C5
Glenburgh, WA 186 C4
Glenburn, VIC 86 D1
Glencoe, NSW 34 D5
Glencoe, QLD 115 E3
Glencoe, SA 159 G5
Glendambo, SA 156 B2
Glendara, NSW 31 G5
Glenden, QLD 120 C2
Glendevie, TAS..................240 D4
Glendilla, QLD 123 H3
Glengarland, QLD 117 C5
Glengarry, NSW 38 D2
Glengarry, TAS..................237 H4
Glengarry, VIC 87 F3

Glengower, VIC 85 H1
Glengyle, QLD 118 B5
Glenhaughton, QLD 120 D6
Glenhope, NSW.................31 H3
Glenhope, NSW.................38 D1
Glenhope, VIC....................80 B6
Glenisla, VIC 84 D1
Glenlee, VIC 78 C4
Glenlofty, VIC 79 F6
Glenloth, VIC.......................79 G3
Glenlyon, QLD 119 F2
Glenlyon, VIC 86 A1
Glenmaggie, VIC 87 G3
Glenmore, QLD 124 C3
Glenmorgan, QLD 124 D2
Glenora, NSW 32 A5
Glenora, QLD 115 F5
Glenora, TAS......................240 D3
Glenorchy, VIC 79 E5
Glenore, QLD 114 D4
Glenore, TAS......................237 H5
Glenormiston, QLD 118 B3
Glenormiston
  North, VIC 85 F3
Glenorn, WA 182 C2
Glenreagh, NSW 35 F5
Glenrowan, VIC 81 F4
Glenroy, QLD......................121 E4
Glenroy, WA 185 F4
Glenstuart, QLD 119 H5
Glenthompson, VIC 85 E2
Glenusk, QLD 120 A5
Glenvale, VIC 86 C1
Glossop, SA 159 G1
Gloucester, NSW 41 E3
Gnaraloo, WA 186 A3
Gnarwarre, VIC 86 A3
Gnotuk, VIC 85 F3
Gnowangerup, WA...........181 E4
Gobondery, NSW 39 F4
Gobur, VIC 80 D6
Gocup, NSW 44 D2
Gogango, QLD...................121 E4
Gol Gol, NSW 37 E6
Gol Gol, NSW 37 G5
Golconda, TAS...................238 A3
Golden Bay, WA 180 B2
Golden Beach, VIC 87 H3
Golden Gate, QLD 115 E4
Golden Valley, TAS 237 G5
Golembil, QLD 121 F5
Gollan, NSW 39 H3
Golspie, NSW 40 A6
Goode, SA 151 H6
Goodooga, NSW................33 E3
Goolgowi, NSW.................38 C6
Goolma, NSW.....................39 H3
Gooloogong, NSW 39 G5
Goolwa, SA 159 E2
Goomalibee, VIC 81 E4
Goomalling, WA 178 D5
Goomally, QLD..................120 D5
Goombi, QLD 125 E2
Goombungee, QLD 125 F3
Goomeri, QLD 125 F2
Goon Nure, VIC 82 A6
Goonalga, NSW 37 G2
Goondiwindi, NSW...........34 B2
Goondiwindi, QLD 124 D4
Goondooloo, NT 211 H1

Goomalling, WA 178 D5
Goomally, QLD............120 D5
Goombi, QLD.................125 E2
Goombungee, QLD 125 F3
Goomeri, QLD 125 F2
Goon Nure, VIC 82 A6
Goonalga, NSW 37 G2
Goondiwindi, NSW...........34 B2
Goondiwindi, QLD...........124 D4
Goondooloo, NT 211 H1
Goondoon, QLD 121 G6
Goonery, NSW...................32 B5
Goongarrie, WA...............182 B3
Goongarrie, WA...............182 B3
Goongee, VIC.....................76 B6
Goongerah, VIC.................82 D4
Goonoolchrach, NSW 37 G2
Goonumbla, NSW..............39 F4
Goonyella Mine, QLD 120 C2
Gooram, VIC......................80 D5
Goorambat, VIC.................81 E4
Goorawin, NSW..................38 C5
Gooray, QLD....................124 D4
Goornong, VIC..................80 A5
Gooroc, VIC........................79 F4
Gooyea, QLD 119 G6
Gorae, VIC..........................84 C4
Gorae West, VIC.................84 B4
Goranba, QLD..................125 E3
Gordon, TAS.....................241 E4
Gordon, VIC.......................86 A2
Gordon (Ruin), SA 157 E3
Gordon Downs, WA.........185 H5
Gordonvale, QLD 116 A4
Gore, QLD........................125 E4
Gormandale, VIC...............87 G4
Goroke, VIC.......................78 B5
Gorrie, NT.......................211 G2
Goschen, VIC.....................79 G1
Gosford, NSW...................40 D5
Gosses, SA......................156 A1
Goughs Bay, VIC 81 E6
Goulburn, NSW.................45 F1
Goulburn Weir, VIC..........80 C5
Goulds Country, TAS 238 C4
Gowanford, VIC.................79 F1
Gowar East, VIC.................79 G4
Gowrie, QLD....................125 F3
Gowrie Park, TAS.............237 F4
Goyura, VIC.......................78 D2
Grabben Gullen, NSW......45 E1
Gracemere, QLD 121 F4
Gracetown, WA 180 B4
Gradgery, NSW.................39 F1
Gradule, QLD 124 C4
Grafton, NSW...................35 F4
Graman, NSW....................34 C4
Granada, QLD 114 C6
Grandchester, QLD 125 G3
Granite, NT.....................207 F6
Granite Downs, SA 151 G2
Granite Flat, VIC................82 A2
Granite Peak, WA.............187 F4
Grantham, QLD................125 F3
Grantleigh, QLD 121 E4
Granton, QLD..................118 C3
Granton, TAS 241 E3
Grantville, VIC...................86 D4
Granville Harbour,
  TAS 236 C5

Granya, VIC 81 H3
Grass Patch, WA 183 B3
Grass Valley, WA...............180 D1
Grassdale, VIC...................84 C2
Grassmere, NSW...............37 F1
Grassmere, VIC..................85 E4
Grassy, TAS......................247 C3
Grattai, NSW......................40 A3
Gravelly Beach, TAS 237 H4
Gravesend, NSW...............34 B4
Gray, TAS.........................238 D5
Graysholme, QLD 125 E4
Graytown, VIC...................80 C5
Great Western, VIC............79 E6
Gredgwin, VIC...................79 G3
Green Creek, QLD 115 E4
Green Head, WA...............178 A3
Green Lake, VIC.................78 D5
Greenbank, NT................213 F3
Greenbushes, WA.............180 C4
Greendale, VIC..................86 A2
Greenethorpe, NSW..........39 G6
Greenhill, QLD.................121 E2
Greenhills, WA..................180 D1
Greenmount, QLD 125 F3
Greenmount, VIC..............87 G4
Greenough, WA................178 A2
Greens Beach, TAS 237 G3
Greens Creek, VIC.............79 F6
Greenvale, QLD 115 H5
Greenwald, VIC.................84 B3
Greenways, SA..................159 F5
Greenwell Point, NSW......45 G2
Gregory, WA 186 B6
Gregory Downs, QLD 114 B5
Gregory Mine, QLD 120 C4
Gregory Springs, QLD......115 H6
Gregra, NSW......................39 G4
Grenfell, NSW....................39 F6
Grenville, VIC....................85 H2
Greta, NSW........................40 D4
Greta, VIC..........................81 F4
Greta South, VIC...............81 F5
Greta West, VIC.................81 F4
Gretna, TAS......................240 D2
Griffith, NSW.....................38 C6
Gringegalgona, VIC 84 C1
Grogan, NSW.....................39 F6
Grong Grong, NSW 44 A1
Grove, TAS.......................241 E3
Gubbata, NSW...................38 D5
Guilderton, WA 178 B5
Guildford, TAS.................236 D4
Guildford, VIC...................80 A6
Gular, NSW........................39 G1
Gulargambone, NSW........39 G1
Gulgong, NSW...................40 A3
Gulmarrad, NSW...............35 G4
Gulnare, SA......................157 E5
Gulpa, NSW.......................43 F3
Guluguba, QLD................124 D1
Gum Flat, NSW..................34 C4
Gum Lake, NSW.................37 F4
Gum Vale, NSW.................30 D4
Gumbalie, NSW.................32 B5
Gumbardo, QLD 123 G1
Gumbo, NSW....................31 H3
Gumlu, QLD......................116 C6
Gunalda, QLD..................125 G1
Gunana, QLD....................114 B3

Gunbar, NSW 38 B6
Gunbower, VIC..................80 A3
Gundagai, NSW.................44 C2
Gundagai, NT 207 F6
Gundaroo, NSW................45 E2
Gundiah, QLD 125 G1
Gundibindyal, NSW..........44 C1
Gundowring, VIC..............81 H4
Gundowring Upper,
  VIC...............................81 H4
Gundy, NSW......................40 C2
Gunebang, NSW................38 D4
Gungal, NSW.....................40 B3
Gunn, NSW........................38 D6
Gunnary, NSW..................39 G6
Gunnawarra, QLD............116 A4
Gunnawarra, QLD............124 A2
Gunnedah, NSW...............40 B1
Gunnewin, QLD...............124 C1
Gunniguldrie, NSW 38 C4
Gunning, NSW..................45 E1
Gunningbland, NSW 39 F4
Gunns Plains, TAS............237 E4
Gunyidi, WA 178 C3
Gurley, NSW......................34 A4
Gurulmundi, QLD............124 D2
Gutha, WA........................178 C2
Guthalungra, QLD 116 C6
Guthega, NSW..................44 D4
Guys Forest, VIC...............82 B1
Gwabegar, NSW................33 H6
Gwambegwing, QLD........121 E6
Gymbowen, VIC................78 B5
Gympie, QLD 125 G2
Gypsum, VIC.....................78 D1
Gypsum Palace, NSW........37 H3
Gypsy Downs, QLD 118 D1

Haasts Bluff
  (Kunparrka), NT............219 F2
Habana, QLD 120 D2
Haddon, VIC.....................85 H2
Haddon Rig, NSW.............39 F1
Hadspen, TAS..................237 H4
Hagley, TAS......................237 H4
Halfway Creek, NSW 35 G5
Half-Way Mill
  Roadhouse, WA............178 B3
Halidon, SA......................159 G2
Halifax, QLD.....................116 B5
Hall, NSW..........................45 E2
Hallett, SA........................157 E5
Hallidays Point, NSW........41 F3
Halls Creek, WA................185 G5
Halls Gap, VIC...................79 E6
Hallston, VIC.....................87 E4
Hamelin, WA....................186 B5
Hamelin Bay, WA..............180 B5
Hamersley, WA.................186 D2
Hamilton, SA....................152 A2
Hamilton, TAS..................240 D2
Hamilton, VIC...................84 D2
Hamilton Downs, NT 219 H2
Hamley Bridge, SA 159 E1
Hammond, SA..................157 E4
Hammond Downs,
  QLD..............................119 F6
Hampshire, TAS...............237 E4
Hampton, NSW.................40 B5
Hampton Hill, WA............182 C4

Hann River
  Roadhouse, QLD 117 C6
Hannaford, QLD 124 D3
Hannams Gap, QLD..........120 B4
Hannan, NSW....................38 D5
Hanson, SA......................157 E6
Hanwood, NSW.................38 C6
Hanwood, NSW.................43 H1
Happy Valley, QLD 119 F3
Harcourt, NSW.................37 E4
Harcourt, VIC....................80 A6
Harden, NSW.....................44 D1
Hardington, QLD.............119 H3
Hardwicke Bay, SA 158 C1
Harefield, NSW..................44 C2
Harford, TAS....................237 G3
Hargraves, NSW................39 H4
Harrietville, VIC.................81 G5
Harrington, NSW...............41 F2
Harrismith, WA.................181 E3
Harrisville, QLD................125 G3
Harrow, VIC.......................78 C6
Hartley, NSW.....................40 B5
Harts Range
  (Police Stn), NT.............220 C2
Hartwood, NSW................38 D2
Harvest Home, QLD..........120 B1
Harvey, WA 180 C3
Harwood, NSW.................35 G4
Haslam, SA......................155 H4
Hastings, TAS..................240 D5
Hastings, VIC....................86 C4
Hat Head, NSW.................41 F1
Hatfield, NSW....................37 G6
Hatfield, QLD...................120 D2
Hatherleigh, SA................159 G5
Hattah, VIC.......................76 D5
Haughton Valley, QLD ..116 B6
Havelock, VIC....................79 H6
Havilah, VIC......................81 G5
Havillah, QLD...................120 C2
Hawker, SA......................157 E3
Hawkesdale, VIC...............84 D3
Hawks Nest, NSW 41 E4
Hawley Beach, TAS..........237 G3
Hawston, QLD..................124 C4
Hay, NSW..........................43 F1
Haydon, QLD 115 E4
Hayes Creek
  Roadhouse, NT 207 E5
Haysdale, VIC...................77 G5
Haythorpe, NSW...............37 E3
Hazel Vale, NSW...............37 E2
Hazelbrook, NSW 40 B5
Hazeldene, VIC..................86 C1
Headingly, QLD 118 A2
Healesville, VIC.................86 D2
Hearson, WA....................186 C1
Heathcote, VIC..................80 B5
Heathcote Junction,
  VIC...............................86 C1
Heathmere, VIC.................84 C4
Hebel, QLD 124 B4
Hedley, VIC.......................87 F5
Heidelberg, QLD 120 C1
Heidelberg, VIC.................86 C2
Heka, TAS.........................237 E4
Helen, QLD.......................121 F5
Helen Springs, NT 216 B1
Helenvale, QLD................116 A2
Helidon, QLD 125 F3

Hermidale, NSW 38 D2
Herons Creek, NSW 41 F2
Herrick, TAS....................238 C3
Hervey Bay, QLD 121 H6
Hesso, SA 156 D3
Hexham, NSW 40 D4
Hexham, VIC.....................85 E3
Heybridge, TAS 237 E3
Heyfield, VIC.....................87 G3
Heywood, VIC...................84 C3
Hiamdale, VIC...................87 G4
Hidden Valley, NT 211 G4
Hidden Valley, QLD 116 A5
Hideaway Bay, QLD 120 B6
Higginsville, WA 182 B6
Highbury, QLD 115 F2
Highbury, WA 180 D3
Highclere, TAS.................237 E3
Highcroft, TAS.................241 F4
Highland Plains, QLD......114 A5
Highlands, QLD 119 G6
Highlands, VIC..................80 D6
Hill End, NSW 39 H4
Hill End, VIC.....................87 E3
Hill Springs, WA 186 B3
Hillgrove, NSW 35 E6
Hillgrove, QLD 116 A6
Hillside, QLD 118 C1
Hillside, QLD 124 B1
Hillside, WA 187 E1
Hillston, NSW 38 B5
Hilltown, SA 157 E6
Hillview, NSW 38 C2
Hiltaba, SA 156 A3
Hines Hill, WA 179 E5
Hinnomunjie, VIC 82 B3
Hivesville, QLD 125 F1
Hi-Way Inn
  Roadhouse, NT 212 A3
Hobart, TAS.....................241 E3
Hobartville, QLD 120 B4
Hobbys Yards, NSW 40 A5
Hodgson, QLD..................124 C2
Hodgson River, NT 212 B2
Holbrook, NSW 40 B3
Holbrook, NSW 44 B3
Hollands Landing, VIC.......87 H3
Hollow Tree, TAS 240 D2
Holowilena, SA................157 E3
Holroyd, QLD 117 B5
Holwell, TAS....................237 G4
Home Hill, QLD 116 C6
Home Valley, WA 185 G3
Homeboin, QLD................124 B3
Homerton, VIC..................84 C3
Homestead, QLD 120 A1
Homewood, VIC................80 C6
Hookina (ruin), SA 157 E3
Hooley, WA 186 D2
Hopefield, NSW 44 A3
Hopelands, NSW 32 A5
Hopetoun, VIC 78 D2
Hopetoun, WA 181 H4
Hopetoun West, VIC..........78 D2
Hopevale, QLD 116 A1
Hopevale, VIC 78 D2
Hordern Vale, VIC 85 G5
Hornsby, NSW 40 C5
Horrocks, WA 178 A1
Horse Lake, NSW..............37 E3

Horseshoe Bend, NT 220 B5
Horsham, VIC...................78 D5
Hotham Heights, VIC........81 H6
Hotspur, VIC.....................84 B3
Howard, QLD 121 G6
Howard Springs, NT 206 D3
Howden, TAS 241 E4
Howes Valley, NSW...........40 C4
Howlong, NSW..................44 A3
Howqua, VIC.....................81 E6
Howth, TAS 237 E3
Huckitta, NT 220 D1
Hughenden, QLD 119 G1
Humbert River
  (Ranger Stn), NT.............210 D4
Humeburn, QLD 123 G2
Humphrey, QLD 125 F1
Humpty Doo, NT 207 E4
Humula, NSW 44 C2
Hungerford, NSW 31 H3
Hungerford, QLD 123 F4
Hunter, VIC......................80 A4
Huntingfield, NSW 36 D5
Huntly, VIC.......................80 A5
Huon, VIC.........................81 H3
Huonville, NSW.................36 D3
Huonville, TAS 240 D4
Hurricane, QLD 115 H3
Hurstbridge, VIC...............86 C2
Huskisson, NSW...............45 G2
Hyden, WA 181 F2
Hynam, SA 159 G4
Hypurna, SA 157 H5

Iandra, NSW 39 G6
Icy Creek, VIC...................87 E3
Ida Bay, TAS....................240 D5
Ida Valley, WA 182 A1
Idracowra, NT 220 A4
Iffley, QLD 114 D5
Iffley, QLD 120 D3
Ilford, NSW 40 A4
Ilfracombe, QLD 119 G4
Illabarook, VIC.................85 G2
Illabo, NSW 44 C1
Illawarra, VIC...................79 E6
Illeroo, SA 156 D4
Iluka, NSW 35 G4
Imanpa, NT 219 G5
Imbergee, NSW 33 E3
Imbil, QLD 125 G2
Imintji, WA.......................185 F4
Impadna Siding, NT........220 A5
Indee, WA........................186 D1
Indiana, NT 220 D2
Indigo Upper, VIC 81 G3
Indulkana (Iwantja), SA 151 F2
Ingebyra, NSW..................44 D4
Ingham, QLD 116 B5
Inglewood, QLD 125 E4
Inglewood, VIC.................79 H4
Ingomar, SA 151 H6
Ingsdon, QLD...................120 C3
Injinoo, QLD 117 B1
Injune, QLD 124 C1
Inkerman, QLD.................115 E2
Inkerman, SA 156 D6
Inkster, SA 155 H4
Innamincka, SA 153 H3
Innesowen, NSW..............38 A1

Inneston, SA 158 C2
Innesvale, NT 211 E2
Innisfail, QLD 116 B4
Innouendy, WA 186 C4
Interlaken, TAS................241 E1
Inveralochy, NSW 45 F2
Inverell, NSW 34 D4
Invergordon, VIC 80 D3
Inverleigh, QLD 114 D4
Inverleigh, VIC.................85 H3
Inverloch, VIC..................86 D5
Inverway, NT 210 C6
Inyarinya
  (Kenmore Park), SA 151 E1
Iona, NSW 37 G6
Iowabah, NSW 38 D2
Ipswich, QLD 125 G3
Iris Vale, NSW..................38 D3
Irishtown, TAS.................236 C2
Iron Baron, SA 156 C5
Iron Knob, SA 156 C4
Ironhurst, QLD 115 G4
Irrapatana (Ruin), SA 152 B5
Irrewarra, VIC 85 G4
Irrewillipe, VIC.................85 G4
Irrwelty, NT 216 C6
Irvinebank, QLD 116 A4
Irwin, WA 178 A2
Isabel Downs, QLD 119 E1
Isisford, QLD 119 G5
Islay Plains, QLD 120 B4
Ivandale, NSW 38 A4
Ivanhoe, NSW..................38 A4
Ivy Tank Motel, SA 154 D2
Iwupataka, NT 219 H3

Jabiru, NT 207 G4
Jabuk, SA 159 F2
Jackadgery, NSW 35 F4
Jackeys Marsh, TAS 237 G5
Jackson, QLD 124 D2
Jallukar, VIC....................85 E1
Jallumba, VIC...................78 C6
Jamberoo, NSW................45 G1
Jamestown, SA 157 E5
Jamieson, VIC..................87 E1
Jan Juc, VIC.....................86 A4
Jancourt East, VIC 85 F4
Jandowae, QLD................125 E2
Jardine Valley, QLD 119 G1
Jarklin, VIC......................79 H4
Jarradale, WA 180 C2
Jarrahmond, VIC 82 C5
Jaurdi, WA 179 H4
Jeedamya, WA 182 B2
Jeeralang Junction, VIC 87 F4
Jeffcott North, VIC 79 F4
Jennacubbine, WA 178 D5
Jennapullin, WA 178 D5
Jenolan Caves, NSW.........40 B5
Jeogla, NSW 35 E6
Jeparit, VIC 78 C3
Jerangle, NSW 45 E3
Jericho, QLD....................120 A4
Jericho, TAS....................241 E1
Jerilderie, NSW................43 H2
Jerramungup, WA 181 G4
Jerrys Plains, NSW 40 C3
Jervis Bay, NSW 45 G2
Jervois, NT 221 E2
Jetsonville, TAS 238 B3

Jigalong, WA 187 F3
Jil Jil, VIC..........................79 F2
Jimaringle, NSW 43 F2
Jimboomba, QLD 125 G3
Jimbour, QLD 125 E2
Jimna, QLD 125 G2
Jindabyne, NSW 44 D4
Jindalee, NSW 44 C1
Jindare, NT 207 E6
Jindera, NSW 44 B3
Jindivick, VIC...................87 E3
Jingellic, NSW..................44 C3
Jingemarra, WA 186 C6
Jinka, NT 220 D1
Jitarning, WA 181 E3
Joel, VIC...........................79 F6
Joel South, VIC 79 F6
Johanna, VIC....................85 G5
Johnburgh, SA 157 E4
Johnsonville, VIC..............82 B6
Jondaryan, QLD 125 F3
Jooro, QLD 121 E5
Joyces Creek, VIC 79 H6
Jubilee Downs, WA 185 E5
Judbury, TAS....................240 D4
Jugiong, NSW...................44 D1
Julatten, QLD 116 A3
Julia Creek, QLD 119 E1
Jumbuk, VIC.....................87 F4
Juna Downs, WA 186 D2
Jundah, QLD 119 F5
Jundee, WA 187 F5
Junee, NSW 44 C1
Junee, QLD 120 D4
Junee Reefs, NSW 44 C1
Jung, VIC..........................78 D5
Jurema, QLD 120 C4
Jurien, WA 178 A3

Kaarimba, VIC..................80 C3
Kabelbarra, QLD 120 C4
Kabra, QLD 121 E4
Kadina, SA 156 D6
Kadji Kadji, WA 178 C2
Kadnook, VIC...................78 B6
Kadungle, NSW 39 F4
Kaimkillenbun, QLD 125 F2
Kajabbi, QLD 114 C6
Kajuligah, NSW................38 A3
Kalabity, SA 157 G3
Kalala, NT 211 H3
Kalamia, QLD 116 C6
Kalamurina, SA 153 E3
Kalanbi, SA 155 G3
Kalang, NSW 35 F6
Kalangadoo, SA...............159 G5
Kalannie, WA 178 D3
Kalarka, QLD 121 E3
Kalbar, QLD.....................125 G3
Kalbarri, WA 186 B6
Kaldow, SA 156 A6
Kaleeda, WA 185 E5
Kaleentha Loop, NSW 37 F3
Kaleno, NSW 38 B2
Kalgan, WA 181 E6
Kalgoorlie
  /Boulder, WA 182 B4
Kalimna, VIC....................82 B6
Kalinga, QLD 115 G1
Kalinjarri, NT...................216 B4

Kalkadoon, QLD 119 E3
Kalkallo, VIC 86 C2
Kalkarindji
  (Police Stn), NT 210 D5
Kalkaroo, NSW 37 H1
Kalkaroo, SA 157 G3
Kalkee, VIC 78 D4
Kallala, QLD 118 B2
Kalli, WA 186 D5
Kalpienung, VIC...............79 F2
Kalpowar, QLD..............117 D5
Kalpowar, QLD.................121 F6
Kaltukatjara
  (Docker River), NT 218 B4
Kalumburu, WA 185 G2
Kaluwiri, WA 187 E6
Kamarah, NSW 38 D6
Kamarooka, VIC 80 A4
Kamarooka East, VIC 80 A4
Kambalda, WA 182 B5
Kambalda West, WA 182 B5
Kamballup, WA 181 E5
Kameruka, NSW................45 F5
Kamileroi, QLD 114 C6
Kammel, QLD 120 C4
Kanagulk, VIC 78 C6
Kanandah, WA 189 B3
Kanawarrji, WA 188 A2
Kancoona, VIC 81 G4
Kandanga, QLD................125 G2
Kandos, NSW 40 B4
Kangan, WA 186 D1
Kangaroo Flat, VIC 80 A5
Kangaroo Valley, NSW......45 G1
Kangaroo Well, SA 156 A3
Kangawall, VIC 78 B5
Kangiara, NSW 44 D1
Kaniva, VIC 78 B4
Kanowna, WA 182 B4
Kantappa, NSW 36 C1
Kanumbra, VIC 80 D6
Kanya, VIC 79 F5
Kanyaka, SA 157 E3
Kanyapella, VIC 80 B3
Kapaldo, QLD 121 F6
Kapinnie, SA 156 A6
Kapooka, NSW 44 B2
Kapunda, SA 159 E1
Karabeal, VIC...................84 D2
Karalundi, WA 186 D5
Karara, QLD 125 F4
Karara, WA 178 D2
Karbar, WA 186 D5
Karcultaby, SA 156 A4
Kareela, QLD 120 C5
Kariah, VIC......................85 F3
Karin, QLD 120 C3
Karkoo, SA 156 A6
Karlgarin, WA 181 F2
Karmona, QLD 122 D2
Karnak, VIC 78 B5
Karonie, WA 182 D4
Karoo, NSW 32 B6
Karoola, NSW 37 E4
Karoonda, SA 159 F2
Karpa Kora, NSW 37 F4
Karratha, WA 186 C1
Karratha, WA 186 C1
Karratha
  Roadhouse, WA.............186 C1

Karridale, WA 180 B5
Kars, NSW 37 E3
Kars Springs, NSW 40 C2
Karte, SA 159 G2
Karuah, NSW 41 E4
Karumba, QLD 114 D4
Karunjie, WA 185 G3
Karwarn, NSW 38 B3
Karween, VIC 76 B4
Katamatite, VIC 80 D3
Katandra, QLD 119 G2
Katandra West, VIC 80 D3
Katanning, WA 181 E4
Katherine, NT 211 F1
Katoomba, NSW 40 B5
Katunga, VIC 80 D3
Katyil, VIC 78 D4
Kawana, QLD 179 G3
Kawarren, VIC 85 G3
Kayrunnera, NSW 31 E6
Keeroongooloo, QLD 123 E1
Keewong, NSW 38 B3
Keith, SA 159 G3
Kellalac, VIC 78 D4
Kellerberrin, WA 179 E5
Kelpum, QLD 120 B5
Kelso, TAS 237 G3
Kelvin, NSW 34 B6
Kelvin View, VIC 80 D5
Kempsey, NSW 41 F1
Kempton, TAS 241 E2
Kendall, NSW 41 F2
Kendenup, WA................181 E5
Kenebri, NSW 33 H6
Kenilworth, QLD 125 G2
Kenley, VIC 77 G5
Kenmare, VIC 78 D3
Kennedy, QLD 116 A4
Kennedys Creek, VIC 85 G5
Kennett River, VIC 85 H5
*Kensington
  Downs*, QLD 119 G3
Kentbruck, VIC 84 B3
Kentucky, NSW 34 D6
Keppel Sands, QLD 121 F4
Keppoch, SA....................159 G4
Kerang, VIC 79 H2
Kerang South, VIC............79 H2
Kerein Hills, NSW 39 E3
Kergunyah, VIC 81 G4
Kergunyah South, VIC 81 G4
Kerrabee, NSW.................40 B3
Kerrisdale, VIC 80 C6
Kerrs Creek, NSW 39 H4
Kersbrook, SA 159 E1
Ketchowla, SA................157 F5
Kettering, TAS 241 E4
Kevington, VIC 87 E1
Kewell, VIC 78 D4
Kewell East, NSW 37 H2
Kewell, QLD 120 B5
Keysbrook, WA 180 C2
Khancoban, NSW 44 C4
Ki Ki, SA 159 F2
Kia Ora, NSW 33 E5
Kia Ora, SA 157 F5
Kiacatoo, NSW.................38 D4
Kiama, NSW 38 B3
Kiama, NSW 45 G1
Kiana, NT 213 E5

Kiandool, NSW 34 A5
Kiandra, NSW 44 D3
Kiaora, NSW 38 B2
Kiata, VIC 78 C4
Kidman Springs, NT 210 D3
Kidston, QLD 115 G5
Kiewa, VIC 81 G4
Kihee, QLD....................123 E2
Kikoira, NSW 38 D5
Kilberry, QLD 119 E1
Kilcowera, QLD...............123 F4
Kilcoy, QLD 125 G2
Kilcunda, VIC 86 D4
Kilferra, VIC 81 E5
Kilkivan, QLD 125 F1
Killara, WA 187 E5
Killarney, NT 211 E3
Killarney, QLD 115 G1
Killarney, QLD 115 H6
Killarney, QLD 125 F4
Killarney, VIC 84 D4
Killawarra, VIC 81 F3
Killiecrankie, TAS.............247 B5
Kilmany, VIC 87 G3
Kilmany South, VIC 87 G3
Kilmore, VIC 86 C1
Kilmore East, VIC 86 C1
Kilto, WA 184 D4
Kimba, QLD 115 G2
Kimba, SA 156 B5
Kimberley, NSW 36 C4
Kimberley, TAS................237 G4
Kimberley Downs, WA 185 E4
Kimbriki, NSW 33 E6
Kimburra, QLD.................120 A1
Kinalung, NSW 37 E3
Kinchenga, NSW 37 E3
Kindred, TAS 237 F3
*King Edward River
  (Doongan)*, WA 185 F3
King Junction, QLD...........115 G2
King River, NT 211 G1
King River, WA 181 E6
King Valley, VIC 81 F5
Kingaroy, QLD 125 F2
Kinglake, VIC 86 C2
Kinglake Central, VIC 86 C1
Kinglake West, VIC 86 C1
Kingoonya, SA 156 A2
Kingower, VIC 79 H5
Kingscliff, NSW 35 G2
Kingscote, SA 158 D2
Kingsdale, NSW 45 F1
Kingston, TAS 241 E3
Kingston
  South East, SA 159 F4
Kingston-
  On-Murray, SA 159 G1
Kingstown, NSW 34 C6
Kinimakatka, VIC 78 B4
Kinnabulla, VIC 79 E3
Kinrola Mine, QLD 120 D4
Kintore, NT 218 B2
Kinypanial South, VIC 79 H4
Kioloa, NSW 45 G3
Kirkalocka, WA 179 E1
Kirkimbie, NT 210 B5
Kirkstall, VIC 84 D4
Kirup, WA 180 C4
Kirwan, WA 178 D4

Kiwirrkurra, WA 188 C2
Knockwood, VIC 87 F1
Knowsley, VIC 80 B5
Koah, QLD 116 A3
Kodj Kodjin, WA 179 E5
Koetong, VIC 82 A1
Kogan, QLD 125 E2
Kojonup, WA 180 D4
Kokatha, SA 156 A2
Kokotunga, QLD 121 E5
Kolendo, SA 156 B4
Kondinin, WA 181 F2
Kondoolka, SA 155 H3
Kondut, WA 178 D4
Kongorong, SA 159 G6
Kongwak, VIC 86 D4
Konnongorring, WA..........178 D4
Konupa, QLD 119 G5
Kooemba, QLD 121 E5
Koojan, WA 178 C4
Kookynie, WA 182 B2
Kookynie, WA 182 B2
Koolan, WA 184 D3
Koolanooka, WA 178 C2
Koolatah, QLD 115 F2
Koolburra, QLD 115 G1
Kooline, WA 186 C2
Kooloonong, VIC 77 G5
Kooltandra, QLD 121 E3
Koolunga, SA 157 E5
Koolyanobbling, WA 179 G4
Koombooloomba, QLD 116 A4
Koomooloo, SA 157 F5
Koonadgin, WA 179 F5
Koonalda, SA 154 B3
Koonamore, SA 157 F3
Koonandan, NSW 44 A1
Koonawarra, NSW 37 E1
Koonda, VIC 80 D4
Koondrook, VIC 80 A2
Koongawa, SA 156 B5
Koongie Park, WA 185 G5
Koonibba, SA 155 G3
Koonkool, QLD 121 E5
Koonmarra, WA 186 D5
Koonoomoo, VIC 80 D2
Koonwarra, VIC 87 E4
Koorawatha, NSW............39 G6
Koorda, WA 179 E4
Koordarrie, WA 186 B2
Kooreh, VIC 79 G5
Koorilgah Mine, QLD........120 D4
Koorkab, VIC 77 F5
Koorlong, VIC 76 D4
Koorongara, QLD 125 E3
Koota, QLD 121 E2
Kootaberra, SA 156 D3
Koothney, NSW 33 G5
Kootingal, NSW 40 C1
Koo-Wee-Rup, VIC...........86 D3
Kopi, SA 156 A5
Koppio, SA 158 B1
Korbel, WA 179 F5
Korbelka, WA 179 F5
Koriella, VIC 80 D6
Koroit, VIC 84 D4
Korong Vale, VIC 79 G4
Koroop, VIC 79 H2
Korrine, VIC 86 D4
Korumburra, VIC 87 E4

Kotta, VIC 80 B3
Kotupna, VIC 80 C3
Koumala, QLD 120 D2
Kowanyama, QLD...........115 E2
Kowguran, QLD...............124 D2
Koyuga, VIC.......................80 B3
Krambach, NSW 41 E3
Krongart, SA....................159 G5
Krowera, VIC.....................86 D4
Kubill, QLD 123 H3
Kudardup, WA.................180 B5
Kudgee, NSW....................36 D4
Kuender, WA....................181 F3
Kukerin, WA.....................181 E3
Kulde, SA 159 F2
Kulgera
 Roadhouse, NT 219 H5
Kulgera Siding, NT 219 H6
Kulin, WA 181 F3
Kulja, WA 178 D4
Kulkami, SA.....................159 G2
Kulkyne, VIC 77 E4
Kulnura, NSW 40 C5
Kulpara, SA 156 D6
Kulpi, QLD 125 F2
Kultanaby, SA..................156 A2
Kulwin, VIC 77 E6
Kulwyne, VIC.....................77 F6
Kumarina
 Roadhouse, WA............187 E4
Kumbarilla, QLD 125 E3
Kumbia, QLD 125 F2
Kunat, VIC 79 G2
Kundabung, NSW............41 F1
Kungala, NSW 35 F5
Kununoppin, WA 179 E5
Kununurra, WA 185 H3
Kunwarara, QLD 121 E4
Kupunn, QLD 125 E3
Kuranda, QLD 116 A3
Kurbayia, QLD 118 B1
Kuri Bay, WA 185 E3
Kuridala, QLD..................118 C2
Kurnell, NSW....................40 C6
Kurnwill, VIC.....................76 B4
Kurrajong, NSW 40 C5
Kurri Kurri, NSW...............40 D4
Kurting, VIC 79 H4
Kurukan, QLD 116 B5
Kurumbul, QLD 125 E4
Kurundi, NT 216 C4
Kuttabul, QLD 120 D2
Kwinana, WA 180 C2
Kwolyin, WA.....................181 E1
Kyabra, QLD 123 E1
Kyabram, VIC....................80 C4
Kyalite, NSW 42 D2
Kyancutta, SA..................156 A5
Kybeyan, NSW 45 E4
Kybybolite, SA 159 G4
Kyeamba, NSW 44 C2
Kyena, QLD 124 B4
Kyneton, VIC.....................86 A1
Kynuna, QLD 119 E2
Kyogle, NSW 35 G3
Kyong, QLD 120 A2
Kyvalley, VIC.....................80 C4
Kywong, NSW...................44 A2
Kywong, QLD 119 F3

La Perouse, NSW 40 C6
Laanecoorie, VIC 79 H5

Laang, VIC 85 E4
Laceby, VIC 81 F4
Lachlan Downs, NSW 38 C3
Lady Barron, TAS.............247 D7
Lady's Pass, VIC 80 B5
Ladysmith, NSW 44 C2
Laen East, VIC 79 E4
Lagaven, QLD...................118 D1
Laggan, NSW 45 F1
Laglan, QLD 120 B3
Lah, VIC 78 D3
Laharum, VIC 78 D6
Laidley, QLD 125 F3
Lajamanu
 (Police Stn), NT 210 D6
Lake Argyle Village, WA 185 H3
Lake Barlee, WA 179 G2
Lake Bathurst, NSW 45 F2
Lake Boga, VIC..................79 G1
Lake Bolac, VIC.................85 E2
Lake Cargelligo, NSW 38 D5
Lake Cathie, NSW 41 F2
Lake Charm, VIC 79 H2
Lake Conjola, NSW 45 G2
Lake Cowal, NSW 39 E5
Lake Dunn, QLD...............120 A3
Lake Everard, SA 156 A3
Lake Goldsmith, VIC.........85 G2
Lake Grace, WA 181 F3
Lake Harry (Ruin), SA 153 E5
Lake Illawarra, NSW 45 G1
Lake Julia, WA 179 G4
Lake King, WA 181 H3
Lake Leake, TAS...............238 B6
Lake Marmal, VIC.............79 G3
Lake Mundi, VIC...............84 A2
Lake Nash, NT 217 G4
Lake Nerramyne, WA 186 B6
Lake Rowan, VIC...............81 E4
Lake Stewart, NSW 30 C4
Lake Tabourie, NSW 45 G2
Lake Torrens, SA..............156 D3
Lake Tyers, VIC..................82 C6
Lake Victoria, NSW 36 D6
Lake Violet, WA................187 F5
Lake Wallace, NSW 30 D5
Lake Way, WA 187 F5
Lakeland, QLD 115 H2
Lakes Entrance, VIC..........82 C6
Lal Lal, VIC 85 H2
Lalbert, VIC 79 G2
Lalbert Rd, VIC 79 G2
Lalguli, QLD 124 D4
Lalla, TAS 238 A4
Lalla Rookh, WA...............187 E1
Lambina, SA 151 G2
Lamboo, WA 185 G5
Lameroo, SA 159 G2
Lammermoor, QLD...........119 H2
Lana, QLD 119 F2
Lancefield, VIC 86 B1
Lancelin, WA.....................178 B4
Lancevale, QLD 120 A4
Landor, WA 186 C4
Landridge, QLD 124 B3
Landsborough, QLD 125 G2
Landsborough, VIC 79 F6
Landwreath, QLD 124 B1
Lanena, TAS 237 H4
Lang Lang, VIC..................86 D4

Langawirra, NSW...............37 E2
Langhorne Creek, SA 159 E2
Langi Logan, VIC 85 F1
Langidoon, NSW................37 E2
Langkoop, VIC 78 A6
Langley, VIC.......................80 A6
Langton, QLD 120 C3
Langtree, NSW 38 C5
Langville, VIC 79 H2
Langwell, NSW..................36 D3
Lansdale, NSW 39 E3
Lansdown, NSW.................32 B5
Lansdowne, NSW 41 F2
Lansdowne, QLD 120 A6
Lansdowne, WA................185 G4
Lapoinya, TAS...................236 D3
Lappa, QLD 115 H4
Lara, QLD 115 E6
Lara, VIC 86 A3
Lara Lake, VIC 86 A3
Laramba, NT 219 G1
Larloona, NSW...................37 E3
Larnook, NSW 35 G3
Larpent, VIC 85 G4
Larras Lee, NSW 39 G4
Larrimah, NT.....................211 G2
Lascelles, VIC 79 E2
Latham, WA 178 C3
Latrobe, TAS 237 F3
Lauderdale, TAS 241 F3
Launceston, TAS 237 H4
Launching Place, VIC 86 D2
Laura, QLD 115 H2
Laura, SA 157 E5
Laura Bay, SA 155 G4
Lauradale, NSW.................32 C4
Laurel Hill, NSW 44 C3
Laurelvale, NSW................31 G6
Laurieton, NSW.................41 F2
Lavers Hill, VIC..................85 G5
Laverton, VIC 86 B2
Laverton, WA 182 D1
Laverton Downs, WA 182 D1
Lavington, NSW 44 B3
Lawler, VIC 79 E4
Lawloit, VIC 78 B4
Lawn Hill, QLD 114 B5
Lawrence, NSW 35 G4
Lawrenny, TAS..................240 D2
Lawson, NSW.....................40 B5
Leadville, NSW 40 A2
Leaghur, VIC 79 H3
Learmonth, VIC 85 H1
Learmonth, WA 186 A2
Lebrina, TAS 238 A3
Ledge Point, WA 178 B5
Leeman, WA 178 A3
Leeton, NSW......................44 A1
Lefroy, TAS 237 H3
Legana, TAS 237 H4
Legerwood, TAS................238 B3
Legume, NSW 35 F2
Legune, NT 210 B2
Legunia, TAS 238 C4
Leigh Creek, SA 157 E1
Leigh Creek, SA................157 E1
Leinster, WA 187 F6
Leinster Downs, WA 187 F6
Leitchville, VIC...................80 A3

Leith, TAS 237 F3
Lemon Tree
 Passage, NSW.................41 E4
Lemont, TAS 241 F1
Leneva, VIC........................81 G3
Lennox Head, NSW 35 G3
Leongatha, VIC..................87 E4
Leongatha South, VIC 87 E4
Leonora, WA 182 B1
Leonora Downs, NSW........37 E3
Leopold, VIC 86 A3
Leopold Downs, WA 185 F4
Lerida, NSW.......................38 C2
Lethbridge, VIC 86 A3
Lethere, NSW.....................37 E5
Levendale, TAS 241 F2
Lewisham, TAS..................241 F3
Lexton, VIC 85 G1
Leyburn, QLD....................125 F3
Liawenee, TAS 237 G6
Licola, VIC 87 F2
Liena, TAS 237 F5
Lietinna, TAS.....................238 B3
Liffey, TAS 237 G5
Lightning Ridge, NSW.......33 F4
Likkaparta, NT 216 B2
Lileah, TAS 236 C3
Lilla Creek, NT 220 B5
Lillimur, VIC 78 A4
Lillimur South, VIC 78 A4
Lilliput, VIC 81 F3
Lilydale, SA 157 G5
Lilydale, TAS.....................238 A4
Lilydale, VIC 86 C2
Lilyvale, QLD 117 C5
Lima South, VIC 81 E5
Limbla, NT 220 C3
Limbri, NSW 40 D1
Limbunya, NT 210 C3
Lincoln, NSW 39 H3
Lincoln Gap, SA................156 D4
Linda Downs, QLD 118 B3
Lindenow, VIC 82 A6
Lindenow South, VIC........82 A6
Lindfield, QLD 119 E1
Lindon, SA 153 H5
Lindsay, VIC 84 A2
Linga, VIC 76 C6
Linton, VIC 85 G2
Linville, QLD 125 F2
Lipson, SA 156 B6
Lismore, NSW....................35 G3
Lismore, VIC 85 G3
Lissadell, WA 185 H3
Listowel Downs, QLD 119 H6
Litchfield, NT 206 D5
Litchfield, VIC 79 E4
Lithgow, NSW....................40 B5
Little Billabong, NSW........44 C3
Little River, VIC 86 B3
Little Swanport, TAS 241 G1
Little Topar
 Roadhouse, NSW 37 E2
Littlemore, QLD................121 F5
Liverpool, NSW 40 C6
Llanelly, VIC 79 H5
Llangothlin, NSW 34 D5
Llorac, QLD 119 G3
Loch, VIC............................86 D4
Loch Sport, VIC 82 B6

Loch Valley, VIC 87 E2
Lochada, WA.....................178 C2
Lochinvar, NSW 40 D4
Lochmead, QLD 120 C4
Lochnagar, QLD 120 A4
Lock, SA............................156 A5
Lockhart, NSW 44 A2
Lockhart River, QLD........117 C3
Lockiel, SA........................156 D6
Lockington, VIC 80 B4
Locksley, VIC 80 C5
Lockwood, VIC 80 A5
Lockwood South, VIC 80 A5
Loddon, QLD 123 H2
Loddon Vale, VIC 79 H3
Logan, VIC 79 G5
Lombardina
  (Djarindjin), WA.............184 D3
Long Flat, NSW 41 E2
Long Plains, VIC 79 E1
Longerenong, VIC 78 D5
Longford, TAS 237 H5
Longford, VIC 87 G3
Longford Creek, QLD 120 D1
Longley, TAS 241 E3
Longreach, QLD 119 G4
Longton, QLD 120 A1
Longwood, VIC 80 D5
Lonnanvale, TAS 240 D3
Looma, WA 185 E4
Loomberah, NSW 40 C1
Loongana, TAS.................237 E4
Loongana, WA 189 C3
Loorana, TAS 247 C2
Lords Well, SA 157 G5
Lorella Springs, NT 212 D3
Lorna Glen, WA 187 F5
Lorne, NSW 41 F2
Lorne, QLD........................119 H5
Lorne, QLD........................120 B6
Lorne, VIC 85 H4
Lornvale, QLD 115 G5
Lorquon, VIC 78 C3
Lorraine, QLD 114 C5
Lorrinna, TAS 237 F4
Lotus Vale, QLD 115 E3
Louisa Downs, WA 185 F5
Louisville, TAS 241 G2
Louth, NSW 32 B6
Louth Bay, SA...................158 B1
Low Head, TAS.................237 G3
Lower Barrington, TAS   237 F4
Lower Boro, NSW 45 F2
Lower Norton, VIC 78 D5
Lower Turners
  Marsh, TAS.....................237 H3
Lowesdale, NSW 44 A3
Lowlands, NSW 38 B4
Lowmead, QLD 121 G5
Lowood, QLD....................125 G3
Loxton, SA........................159 G1
Lubeck, VIC 79 E5
Lucinda, QLD 116 B5
Lucindale, SA 159 G4
Lucknow, NSW 39 H5
Lucknow, QLD 118 D3
Lucky Bay, SA...................156 C6
Lucky Downs, QLD 115 H5
Lucky Downs, QLD 124 D1
Lucy Creek, NT 221 E1

Lucyvale, VIC....................82 B1
Lue, NSW 40 A4
Luina, TAS 236 D4
Lukies Farm, NT 207 E6
Lulworth, TAS...................237 H3
Lumeah, QLD 120 A6
Lunawanna, TAS..............241 E5
Lundayra, QLD 124 D3
Lune River, TAS 240 D5
Lurg, VIC 81 E4
Lurnea, QLD 124 A1
Lymwood, TAS 247 C3
Lynchford, TAS.................239 D1
Lyndavale, NT 219 G5
Lyndbrook, QLD 115 H4
Lyndhurst, NSW................39 H5
Lyndhurst, QLD 115 H5
Lyndhurst, SA...................157 E1
Lyndon, WA 186 B3
Lynwood, NSW 38 B1
Lyons River, WA 186 B4
Lyonville, VIC 86 A1

Mabel Creek, SA 151 H5
Mabel Downs, WA 185 H4
Macalister, QLD 125 E2
McAllister, QLD 114 D4
Macarthur, VIC 84 D3
McArthur River, NT 212 D4
McCoys Well, SA 157 F4
McDouall Peak, SA 151 H6
McDougalls Well, NSW.....36 C1
Macedon, VIC 86 B1
McIntyre, VIC 79 G5
Mackay, QLD 120 D2
McKenzie Creek, VIC 78 D5
Mackillop Bridge, VIC 82 D4
McKinlay, QLD 118 D2
Macknade, QLD 116 B5
Macksville, NSW 35 F6
Mackunda Downs, QLD ..118 D3
McLachlan, SA 156 A5
McLaren Vale, SA 159 E2
Maclean, NSW 35 G4
McLoughlins Beach, VIC 87 G5
McMahons Creek, VIC 87 E2
McMaster, QLD 119 G3
McNaughton, QLD...........120 C1
Macrossan, QLD 116 B6
Macumba, SA 152 A2
Madoonga, WA 186 D5
Madoonia Downs, WA 182 C5
Madora, WA 180 B2
Madura, WA 189 C4
Madura, WA 189 C4
Maffra, NSW 45 E4
Maffra, VIC 87 G3
Maggea, SA 159 G1
Maggieville, QLD 114 D4
Magowra, QLD 114 D4
Magrath Flat, SA 159 F3
Mahanewo, SA 156 B3
Maidenwell, QLD 125 F2
Mailapunyah, NT..............212 D4
Mailer Flat, VIC 85 E4
Maimuru, NSW 39 G6
Maindample, VIC..............81 E6
Mainoru, NT 208 B6
Maitland, NSW 40 D4
Maitland, SA 158 D1
Maitland Downs, QLD 115 H2

Majors Creek, NSW..........45 F3
Makowata, QLD 121 G5
Malabar, NSW 33 F4
Malacura, QLD 115 F5
Malagarga, QLD 122 D1
Malanda, QLD 116 A4
Malbina, TAS.....................241 E3
Malbon, QLD 118 C1
Malbooma, SA 155 G1
Malcolm
  (Abandoned), WA..........182 B1
Maldon, VIC 79 H6
Maldorkey, SA..................157 G4
Malebo, NSW 44 B2
Maleny, QLD 125 G2
Malinns, VIC 82 D5
Mallacoota, VIC 83 G5
Mallala, SA 159 E1
Mallanganee, NSW...........35 F3
Mallina, WA 186 D1
Malmsbury, VIC 80 A6
Malta, QLD 120 B6
Maltee, SA 155 G3
Malverton, QLD 119 H5
Mamboo, QLD 120 B4
Mambray Creek, SA 156 D4
Manangatang, VIC 77 F6
Manangoora, NT 213 F3
Manara, NSW 37 G4
Manara Mine, NSW 37 G4
Manberry, WA 186 A3
Mandagery, NSW 39 G4
Mandelman, NSW 37 G5
Mandora, WA 184 B6
Mandorah, NT 206 D2
Mandurah, WA 180 B2
Mandurama, NSW 39 H5
Mandurang, VIC 80 A5
Maneroo, QLD 119 G4
Manfred, NSW 37 G5
Mangalo, SA 156 C5
Mangalore, QLD 123 H2
Mangalore, TAS................241 E2
Mangalore, VIC 80 C5
Mangana, TAS 238 C5
Mangaroon, WA 186 B3
Mangoplah, NSW 44 B2
Manguri, SA 151 H5
Manildra, NSW 39 G4
Manilla, NSW 34 C6
Manilla, NSW 37 E5
Maningrida
  (Police Stn.), NT..............208 B3
Manjimup, WA 180 C5
Manly, NSW 40 C6
Manmanning, WA 178 D4
Mannahill, SA 157 G4
Mannanarie, SA................157 E5
Manners Creek, NT 217 G6
Manning Point, NSW 41 F2
Manns Beach, VIC 87 G5
Mannum, SA 159 F2
Mannus, NSW 44 C3
Manoora, SA 157 E6
Mansfield, VIC...................81 E6
Mantamaru, WA 188 C4
Mantuan Downs, QLD 120 B5
Mantung, SA 159 G1
Manuka, NSW 38 C3
Manunda, SA 157 F4

Many Peaks, QLD 121 F5
Manyallaluk, NT 207 G6
Manypeaks, WA 181 F6
Mapoon, QLD 117 A2
Maralinga, SA 154 D1
Marama, SA 159 G2
Maranalgo, WA 179 E2
Maranboy
  (Police Stn), NT 211 G1
Marandoo, WA 186 D2
Marathon, QLD 119 G1
Marble Bar, WA 187 E1
March, NSW 39 H4
Marchagee, WA 178 C3
Marcorna, VIC 79 H3
Marcus Hill, VIC 86 B4
Mardan, VIC 87 E4
Mardathuna, WA 186 B4
Mardie, WA 186 B1
Mareeba, QLD 116 A3
Marfield, NSW 37 H3
Margaret River, WA 180 B4
Margaret River, WA 185 G5
Margate, TAS 241 E4
Marillana, WA 187 E2
Marimo, QLD 118 C1
Marion, QLD 120 D2
Marion Bay, SA 158 C2
Marion Downs, QLD 118 B4
Marita Downs, QLD 119 G3
Markwood, VIC 81 F4
Marla, SA 151 G3
Marlborough, QLD 121 E3
Marlo, VIC.........................82 D6
Marma, VIC 79 E5
Marmor, QLD 121 F4
Marnoo, VIC 79 E5
Marnoo East, VIC 79 F5
Marona, NSW 37 G5
Maronan, QLD 118 D1
Marong, NSW 38 C6
Marong, VIC 79 H5
Maroochydore, QLD 125 G2
Maroomba, QLD 119 G3
Maroona, VIC 85 E1
Maroonah, WA 186 B3
Marqua, NT 221 F1
Marrabel, SA 157 E6
Marradong, WA 180 C3
Marrar, NSW 44 B1
Marrawah, TAS.................236 B2
Marraweeny, VIC 80 D5
Marree, SA 152 D6
Marrilla, WA 186 B3
Marron, WA 186 B4
Marryat, SA 151 F1
Marsden, NSW 39 E5
Martins Well, SA 157 F3
Marulan, NSW 45 F1
Marungi, VIC 80 D3
Marvell Loch, WA 179 G5
Mary River, NT 207 F5
Mary River
  Roadhouse, NT 207 F5
Mary Springs, WA 186 B6
Mary Valley, QLD 117 C6
Maryborough, QLD 125 G1
Maryborough, VIC 79 H6
Maryfield, NT 211 H3
Marymia, WA 187 E4

Marysville, VIC 86 D1
Maryvale, NSW 39 H3
Maryvale, QLD 116 A6
Maryvale, QLD 118 C3
Massey, VIC 79 E4
Matakana, NSW 38 C4
Mataranka, NT 211 G2
Mathiesons, VIC 80 B4
Mathinna, TAS 238 C4
Mathoura, NSW 43 F3
Matlock, VIC 87 F2
Matong, NSW 44 B1
Maude, NSW 43 F1
Maude, VIC 86 A3
Mawbanna, TAS 236 C3
Mawson, WA 180 D2
Maxwellton, QLD 119 F1
May Downs, QLD 120 D3
Maya, WA 178 C3
Mayberry, TAS 237 F5
Maydena, TAS 240 C3
Mayneside, QLD 119 E4
Mayrung, NSW 43 G2
Maytown, QLD 115 H2
Mazar, NSW 36 C4
Mead, VIC 80 A2
Meadow, WA 186 B5
Meadow Glen, NSW 38 B2
Meadowbank, QLD 115 H4
Meandarra, QLD 124 D3
Meander, TAS 237 G5
Meatian, VIC 79 F2
Meckering, WA 178 D5
Meda, WA 185 E4
Meeberrie, WA 186 C5
Meedo, WA 186 B4
Meekatharra, WA 186 D5
Meeleebee, QLD 124 C1
Meeline, WA 179 F1
Meena Murtee, NSW 37 F1
Meeniyan, VIC 87 E4
Meeragoolia, WA 186 B4
Meerlieu, VIC 82 A6
Megan, NSW 35 F5
Megine, QLD 124 C2
Meka, WA 186 C6
Mekaree, QLD 119 H5
Melaleuca, NT 207 E3
Melba Flats, TAS 236 D6
Melbourne, VIC 86 C2
Melita, WA 182 B2
Mellenbye, WA 178 C1
Mellish Park, QLD 114 B5
Melrose, SA 156 D4
Melrose, WA 187 F6
Melton, SA 156 D6
Melton, SA 157 F4
Melton, VIC 86 B2
Melton Mowbray, TAS 241 E2
Melville Forest, VIC 84 C2
Memana, TAS 247 C6
Memerambi, QLD 125 F2
Menangina, WA 182 C3
Mendleyarri, WA 182 B3
Mendooran, NSW 39 H2
Mengha, TAS 236 C2
Menindee, NSW 37 E3
Meningie, SA 159 F3
Menzies, WA 182 B3
Mepunga East, VIC 85 E4

Mepunga West, VIC 85 E4
Merah North, NSW 34 A5
Merapah, QLD 117 B4
Merbein, VIC 76 D3
Merbein South, VIC 76 D3
Mercunda, SA 159 F1
Meredith, VIC 85 H2
Meribah, SA 159 G1
Merimbula, NSW 45 F5
Merinda, QLD 116 D6
Meringur, VIC 76 B4
Meringur North, VIC 76 B4
Merino, VIC 84 B2
Merivale, QLD 120 C6
Merluna, QLD 117 B4
Mern Merna, SA 157 E3
Mernda, VIC 86 C2
Merolia, WA 182 D1
Merredin, WA 179 F5
Merri Merrigal, NSW 38 C5
Merriang, VIC 86 C1
Merricks, VIC 86 C4
Merrigum, VIC 80 C4
Merrijig, VIC 81 F6
Merrinee, VIC 76 C4
Merriton, SA 156 D5
Merriwa, NSW 40 B3
Merriwagga, NSW 38 C5
Merrygoen, NSW 39 H2
Merrywinebone, NSW 33 H4
Merseylea, TAS 237 F4
Merton, VIC 80 D6
Merty Merty, SA 153 G4
Meryula, NSW 38 C1
Metcalfe, VIC 80 A6
Metford, NSW 37 E2
Metung, VIC 82 B6
Meunna, TAS 236 D3
Mia Mia, VIC 80 B6
Mia Mia, WA 186 B3
Miami, NSW 38 D4
Miandetta, NSW 39 E2
Mica Creek, QLD 118 B1
Michelago, NSW 45 E3
Middalya, WA 186 B3
Middle Park, QLD 115 G6
Middle Point, NT 207 E4
Middlefield, NSW 39 F3
Middlemount, QLD 120 D3
Middleton, QLD 118 D3
Middleton, TAS 241 E4
Midgee, SA 156 C5
Midland, WA 180 C1
Midway Point, TAS 241 F3
Miena, TAS 237 G6
Miepoll, VIC 80 D4
Miga Lake, VIC 78 C6
Mihi, NSW 34 D6
Mila, NSW 45 E5
Milabena, TAS 236 D3
Milang, SA 159 E2
Milawa, VIC 81 F4
Mildura, VIC 76 D3
Miles, QLD 124 D2
Mileura, WA 186 D5
Milgarra, QLD 114 D4
Milgun, WA 186 D4
Milguy, NSW 34 B4
Milikapiti, NT 206 D2
Milingimbi, NT 208 C3

Millaa Milla, QLD 116 A4
Millaroo, QLD 116 C6
Millbank, NSW 41 F1
Mil-Lel, SA 159 G6
Millers Creek, SA 152 B6
Millfield, NSW 40 D4
Millgrove, VIC 86 D2
Millicent, SA 159 G5
Millie, NSW 34 A4
Milling, WA 178 C4
Millmerran, QLD 125 E3
Milloo, VIC 80 A4
Millpillbury, NSW 37 H1
Millrose, WA 187 F5
Millthorpe, NSW 39 H5
Milltown, VIC 84 C3
Millungera, QLD 115 E6
Milly Milly, WA 186 C5
Milo, QLD 119 G6
Milparinka, NSW 30 D4
Milray, QLD 120 A1
Milton, NSW 45 G2
Milton Park, NT 219 G2
Milvale, NSW 39 F6
Milyakburra, NT 209 A5
Mimili, SA 151 F2
Mimong, QLD 119 E2
Minara, WA 182 C1
Minburra, SA 157 E4
Mincha, VIC 79 H3
Mindarie, SA 159 G1
Minderoo, WA 186 B2
Mindi, QLD 120 D2
Minemoorong, NSW 39 E3
Miners Rest, VIC 85 H1
Minetta, NSW 32 A4
Mingah Springs, WA 187 E4
Mingary, SA 157 H4
Mingay, VIC 85 G2
Mingela, QLD 116 B6
Mingenew, WA 178 B2
Minhamite, VIC 84 D3
Minilya
  Roadhouse, WA 186 A3
Minimay, VIC 78 A5
Mininer, WA 186 D3
Mininera, VIC 85 F2
Miniyeri, NT 212 B2
Minjilang, NT 207 G2
Minlaton, SA 158 D1
Minmindie, VIC 79 H3
Minnamoolka, QLD 116 A4
Minnie Creek, WA 186 B3
Minnie Downs, QLD 120 A6
Minnie Water, NSW 35 G5
Minnies O.S., QLD 115 F4
Minnipa, SA 156 A4
Minnivale, WA 178 D5
Minore, NSW 39 G3
Mintabie, SA 151 F3
Mintaro, SA 157 E6
Minto, VIC 80 A4
Minyip, VIC 79 E4
Miralie, VIC 77 G6
Miram, VIC 78 B4
Miram South, VIC 78 B4
Miranda, NSW 43 F2
Miranda Downs, QLD 115 E3
Mirani, QLD 120 D2
Mirboo, VIC 87 E4

Mirboo North, VIC 87 E4
Miriam Vale, QLD 121 G5
Mirimbah, VIC 81 F6
Mirool, NSW 39 E6
Mirrabooka, NSW 38 C3
Mirrabooka, QLD 123 H2
Mirri, QLD 118 C2
Mirtna, QLD 120 A2
Missabotti, NSW 35 F6
Mission Beach, QLD........116 B4
Mistake Creek, NT 210 B5
Mitakoodi, QLD................118 C1
Mitchell, QLD 124 B2
Mitchellstown, VIC 80 C5
Mitchellville, SA................156 C5
Mitiamo, VIC 80 A3
Mitre, VIC 78 C5
Mitta Mitta, VIC 82 A2
Mittagong, NSW 45 G1
Mittagong, QLD 115 E5
Mittebah, NT 217 F1
Mittyack, VIC 77 E6
Moama, NSW 43 F4
Moble, QLD 123 F2
Mockinyah, VIC 78 D6
Moe, VIC 87 F3
Mogal Plain, NSW 39 E3
Moglonemby, VIC 80 D5
Mogo, NSW 45 F3
Mogongong, NSW 39 G6
Mogriguy, NSW 39 G2
Mogumber, WA 178 C4
Moina, TAS 237 G4
Mokepilly, VIC 79 E6
Mole Creek, TAS 237 F5
Molesworth, TAS 241 E3
Molesworth, VIC 80 D6
Moliagul, VIC 79 G5
Molka, VIC 80 D5
Mollerin, WA 179 E4
Mollongghip, VIC 85 H1
Molong, NSW 39 G4
Moltema, TAS 237 G4
Momba, NSW 37 G1
Mona Vale, NSW 40 C5
Mona Vale, QLD 123 G1
Monak, NSW 37 E6
Monak, NSW 42 C1
Monegeetta, VIC 86 B1
Monia Gap, NSW 38 C5
Monivea, NSW 37 H4
Monkey Mia, WA 186 A5
Monkira, QLD 118 C5
Monomie, NSW 39 F4
Monstraven, QLD 114 D6
Montague, TAS 236 B2
Montana, TAS 237 G5
Monteagle, NSW 39 G6
Montejinni, NT 211 F4
Montgomery, VIC 87 G3
Monto, QLD 121 F6
Montumana, TAS 236 D2
Moockra, SA 157 E4
Moodiarrup, WA 180 D4
Moogara, TAS 240 D3
Moojeeba, QLD 117 C5
Mooka, WA 186 B4
Mookarra, QLD 120 C1
Moola Bulla, WA 185 G5
Moolah, NSW 38 B3

Moolawatana, SA 153 F6
Moolbong, NSW 38 B5
Mooleulooloo, SA 157 G3
Mooloo Downs, WA 186 C4
Mooloogool, WA 187 E5
Mooloolerie, NSW 37 F4
Moolooloo O.S., NT 211 E3
Moolort, VIC 79 H6
Moomba (Private), SA....153 G4
Moonambel, VIC 79 G6
Moonan Flat, NSW 40 D2
Moonaree, SA 156 B3
Moonbi, NSW 40 C1
Moonbria, NSW 43 G2
Moondarra, VIC 87 F3
Moondene, NSW 38 A4
Moonee Beach, NSW.......35 G5
Moonera, WA 189 C3
Moonie, QLD 124 D3
Moonijin, WA 178 D4
Moonta, SA 156 D6
Moonya, QLD 119 H4
Moonyoonooka, WA 178 A1
Moora, WA 178 C4
Moorabbin, VIC 86 C3
Mooraberree, QLD 118 D6
Moorak, QLD 124 A1
Mooramanna, QLD 124 C3
Moorara, NSW 37 E5
Moorarie, WA 186 D4
Moore, NSW 40 C1
Moore, QLD 125 F2
Moore Park, QLD 121 G6
Mooren, NSW 39 H2
Mooreville, TAS 237 E3
Moorine Rock, WA 179 G5
Moorland, NSW 41 F2
Moorna, NSW 36 D6
Moorna, VIC 76 C3
Moorngag, VIC 81 E5
Moorook, SA 159 G1
Mooroopna, VIC 80 C4
Mooroopna North, VIC 80 C4
Mootwingee, NSW...........37 E1
Moppin, NSW 34 A3
Morago, NSW 43 F2
Moralana, SA 157 E3
Moralla, VIC 84 D1
Moranbah, QLD 120 C3
Morangarell, NSW...........39 F6
Morapoi, WA 182 B2
Morawa, WA 178 C2
Moray Downs, QLD.........120 B2
Morchard, SA 157 E4
Mordialloc, VIC 86 C3
Morea, VIC 78 B5
Moree, NSW 34 B4
Morella, QLD 119 G3
Morgan, SA 157 F6
Morgan Vale, SA 157 G5
Moriac, VIC 86 A4
Morialpa, SA 157 G4
Moriarty, TAS 237 F3
Morisset, NSW 40 D4
Morkalla, VIC 76 B4
Morney, QLD 118 D6
Morning Side, NSW 38 A4
Mornington, VIC 86 C3
Mornington, WA 185 F4
Moroak, NT 212 A1

Moroco, NSW 43 G3
Morongla Creek, NSW......39 G6
Morri Morri, VIC 79 F5
Morrisons, VIC 86 A2
Morstone Downs, QLD....114 A6
Mortlake, VIC 85 E3
Morton Plains, VIC 79 E3
Morundah, NSW 44 A2
Moruya, NSW 45 F3
Moruya Head, NSW 45 F3
Morven, QLD 124 A1
Morwell, VIC 87 F3
Moselle, QLD 119 F1
Moss Vale, NSW 45 G1
Mossgiel, NSW 38 A4
Mossman, QLD 116 A3
Mossy Point, NSW 45 F3
Moulamein, NSW 43 E2
Moulyinning, WA 181 E3
Mt Amhurst, WA..............185 G5
Mount Arrowsmith, NSW 30 D5
Mount Barker, SA 159 E2
Mount Barker, WA 181 E5
Mt Barnett
  Roadhouse, WA..............185 F3
Mount Barry, SA................152 A4
Mt Baw Baw
  Alpine Village, VIC 87 F2
Mount Beauty, VIC 81 H5
Mt Beckworth, VIC 85 G1
Mt Brockman
  Mine, WA 186 C2
Mount Bryan, SA............157 E5
Mt Buffalo, VIC 81 G5
Mt Buller
  Alpine Village, VIC 81 F6
Mt Bundy, NT 207 E4
Mt Burges, WA 182 B4
Mount Burr, SA 159 G5
Mount Carbine, QLD 116 A3
Mt Carnage, WA 182 B3
Mount Cavenagh, NT......219 G6
Mt Celia, WA 182 D2
Mount Clarence, SA 151 H5
Mt Clere, WA 186 D4
Mt Coolon, QLD 120 B2
Mount Cooper, QLD 120 B1
Mount Damper, SA 156 A5
Mount Dare, SA 152 A1
Mt Denison, NT 215 F6
Mt Direction, TAS 237 H3
Mt Divide, WA 187 F2
Mount Doris, NSW 38 A2
Mt Duneed, VIC 86 A4
Mount Eba, SA 152 A6
Mount Eba, SA 156 A1
Mount Ebenezer
  Roadhouse, NT 219 G5
Mt Edgar, WA 187 E1
Mt Elgin, VIC 78 B4
Mt Eliza, VIC 86 C3
Mt Elizabeth, WA 185 F3
Mt Elvire, WA 179 G2
Mt Emu, VIC 85 G2
Mount Emu Plains, QLD 115 H6
Mt Fairy, NSW 45 F2
Mt Fitton (Ruin), SA 153 F6
Mt Florance, WA 186 D2
Mount Gambier, SA 159 G6
Mount Gap, NSW 38 B1

Mount Garnet, QLD........116 A4
Mount George, NSW 41 E2
Mt Gibson, WA 179 E2
Mount Gipps, NSW 36 D2
Mount Gipps, NSW...........36 D2
Mt Gould, WA 186 D4
Mount Gunson, SA 156 C2
Mt Hart, WA 185 E4
Mount Hector, QLD.........120 D1
Mount Helen, VIC 85 H2
Mount Hill, SA 156 B6
Mount Hope, NSW 38 C4
Mount Hope, SA 156 A6
Mt Hopeless, SA 153 G6
Mt Horeb, NSW 44 C2
Mt House, WA 185 F4
Mount Howitt, QLD 122 D1
Mt Ida (Ruins), WA 182 A2
Mount Isa, QLD 118 B1
Mount Ive, SA 156 B4
Mt Jackson, WA 179 G3
Mt James, WA 186 C4
Mt Keith, WA 187 F5
Mount Kew, NSW 37 H2
Mount Kokeby, WA 180 D2
Mount Larcom, QLD 121 F5
Mt Lawless, QLD 125 F1
Mount Leonard, QLD 118 D6
Mount Lewis, NSW 38 D2
Mt Liebig, NT 219 E2
Mt Lloyd, TAS 240 D3
Mt Lonarch, VIC 85 G1
Mt Lyndhurst, SA 157 E1
Mt Macedon, VIC 86 B1
Mt McLaren, QLD 120 C3
Mt Magnet, WA 186 D6
Mount Manara, NSW 37 H3
Mount Margaret, QLD 123 E2
Mt Margaret, WA............187 G6
Mount Marlow, QLD........119 G5
Mt Martha, VIC 86 C4
Mount Mary, SA 157 F6
Mt Minnie, WA 186 B2
Mount Molloy, QLD 116 A3
Mt Monger, WA 182 C4
Mount Morgan, QLD......121 E4
Mt Moriac, VIC 86 A3
Mt Morris, QLD 123 H1
Mount Mulgrave, QLD 115 G2
Mount Mulligan, QLD 115 H3
Mt Murchison, NSW 37 G1
Mt Narryer, WA 186 C5
Mt Nebo, QLD 125 G3
Mount Norman, QLD 115 F6
Mount Ossa, QLD 120 D2
Mt Padbury, WA 186 D4
Mt Perry, QLD 121 G6
Mt Phillips, WA 186 C3
Mount Pleasant, SA 159 E1
Mt Remarkable, WA 182 C2
Mt Richmond, VIC............84 B4
Mt Riddock, NT 220 C2
Mt Ringwood, NT 207 E4
Mt Sandiman, WA 186 B4
Mt Sanford, NT 210 D4
Mount Sarah, SA 152 A2
Mt Satirist, WA 186 D1
Mount Seaview, NSW 41 E1
Mt Selwyn, NSW 44 D3

Mt Seymour, TAS.............241 F2
Mount Shannon, NSW 30 D5
Mt Skinner, NT 216 B6
Mt Sturt, NSW 30 D4
Mount Surprise, QLD 115 H4
Mount Swan, NT 220 C1
Mt Tabor, QLD 120 B6
Mt Taylor, VIC 82 B6
Mt Tenandra, NSW...........39 G1
Mount Torrens, SA 159 E1
Mt Vernon, WA 186 D3
Mt Vetters, WA 182 B4
Mt Victor, SA 157 F3
Mt Victoria, NSW 40 B5
Mt View, WA 186 B6
Mount Vivian, SA 156 A1
Mt Wallace, VIC 86 A2
Mount Wedge, NT 219 F1
Mount Wedge, SA 156 A5
Mt Weld, WA 182 D1
Mount Westwood, NSW....36 D1
Mount Willoughby, SA 151 G3
Mt Windsor, QLD 119 E4
Mt Wittenoom, WA 186 C5
Mount Woowoolahra,
  NSW...........................36 C1
Mountain Valley, NT 208 A6
Moura, QLD 121 E5
Mourilyan, QLD 116 B4
Mouroubra, WA 179 E3
Mowanjum, WA 184 D4
Mowla Bluff, WA 184 D5
Moyhu, VIC 81 F4
Moyston, VIC 85 E1
Muccan, WA 184 B6
Muchea, WA 178 C5
Muckadilla, QLD 124 C2
Muckatah, VIC 80 D3
Muckaty, NT 216 B1
Mudamuckla, SA 155 G3
Muddal, NSW 39 E2
Mudgeacca, QLD.............118 C3
Mudgee, NSW 40 A3
Mudgeegonga, VIC 81 G4
Mudludja, WA 185 F4
Mudg, WA 186 B5
Mukinbudin, WA 179 F4
Mulan, WA 185 G6
Mulbring, NSW 40 D4
Mulcra, VIC 76 B6
Mulcra, VIC 78 A1
Mulga Downs, WA...........186 D2
Mulga Park, NT 219 E6
Mulga View, SA 157 F2
Mulgaria, SA 152 D6
Mulgathing, SA 155 G1
Mulgildie, QLD 121 F6
Mulgrave, QLD 119 H5
Mulgul, WA 186 D4
Mulka, SA 153 E4
Mullaley, NSW 40 B1
Mullengandra, NSW.........44 B3
Mullengudgery, NSW 39 E2
Mullewa, WA 178 B1
Mullion Creek, NSW.........39 H4
Mullumbimby, NSW.........35 G3
Muloorina, SA 152 D5
Mulwala, NSW 43 H3
Mulyandry, NSW 39 F5
Mulyungarie, SA 157 H3

Mumbannar, VIC 84 B3
Mumbil, NSW 39 H4
Mumblebone, NSW 39 F1
Mummballup, WA 180 C4
Mummulgum, NSW 35 F3
Mumu, QLD 119 G1
Mundabullangana, WA 186 D1
Mundaring, WA 180 C1
Munderoo, NSW 44 C3
Mundijong, WA 180 C2
Mundiwindi, WA 187 E3
Mundoora, SA 156 D5
Mundowdna, SA 153 E6
Mundowney, NSW 34 C6
Mundrabilla, WA 189 D4
Mundubbera, QLD 125 E1
Mundulla, SA 159 G4
Mungabroom, NT 212 B5
Mungallala, QLD 124 B1
Mungana, QLD 115 H3
Mungar, QLD 125 G1
Mungerannie
  Roadhouse, SA 153 E4
Mungeribah, NSW 39 F3
Mungindi, NSW 33 H3
Mungkarta, NT 216 B4
Munglinup, WA 183 A4
Mungo, NSW 37 F5
Mungunburra, QLD 120 A1
Mungungo, QLD..............121 F6
Munna, NSW......................40 A3
Munro, VIC........................82 A6
Muntadgin, WA 179 F5
Muradup, WA 180 D4
Muralgarra, WA 178 D1
Murchison, VIC.................80 C5
Murchison Downs, WA....187 E5
Murchison East, VIC 80 C5
Murchison
  Roadhouse, WA..............186 C5
Murdinga, SA 156 A6
Murdong, WA...................181 E4
Murdunna, TAS 241 G3
Murgenella
  (Ranger Stn.), NT 207 G2
Murgheboluc, VIC.............86 A3
Murgon, QLD 125 F2
Murgoo, WA 186 C6
Muriel, NSW....................38 D2
Murkaby, SA 157 F5
Murmungee, VIC...............81 G4
Murnpeowie, SA...............153 F6
Murphys Creek, VIC.........79 H5
Murra Murra, QLD...........124 A3
Murra Warra, VIC.............78 D4
Murrabit, VIC....................79 H2
Murrami, NSW..................38 D6
Murranji, NT 211 G4
Murrawal, NSW 39 H1
Murray Bridge, SA 159 F2
Murray Downs, NT 216 C4
Murray Town, SA..............156 D5
Murrayville, VIC................78 A1
Murrindal, VIC 82 C5
Murrindindi, VIC 86 D1
Murringo, NSW 39 G6
Murroon Downs, VIC 85 H4
Murrumbateman, NSW ..45 E2
Murrumburrah, NSW........44 D1
Murrungowar, VIC.............82 D5

Murrurundi, NSW 40 C2
Murweh, QLD 123 H2
Murwillumbah, NSW 35 G2
Musgrave, QLD 117 C5
Muskerry East, VIC 80 B5
Muswellbrook, NSW 40 C3
Mutarnee, QLD 116 B5
Mutchilba, QLD 116 A3
Mutijulu, NT 219 E5
Mutooroo, SA 157 H4
Muttaburra, QLD 119 G3
Muttama, NSW 44 C1
Mutton Hole, QLD 114 D4
Myall, VIC 79 H2
Myall Creek, SA 156 C4
Myalla, TAS 236 D3
Myally, QLD 114 C5
Myalup, WA.....................180 B3
Myamyn, VIC....................84 C3
Myendett, QLD 123 H2
Myola, VIC 80 B5
Mypolonga, SA 159 F2
Myponga, SA 159 E2
Myria, SA 159 G1
Myrniong, VIC..................86 A2
Myrrhee, VIC.....................81 F5
Myrtle Springs, SA 157 E1
Myrtleford, VIC.................81 G4
Mysia, VIC........................79 H4
Mystic Park, VIC...............79 G2
Myuna, NSW 32 D4

Nabageena, TAS 236 C3
Nabawa, WA 178 A1
Nabiac, NSW 41 E3
Nabowla, TAS 238 A3
Nackara, SA.....................157 F4
Nagaela, NSW 36 D4
Nagambie, VIC 80 C5
Nagoorin, QLD 121 F5
Nalbarra, WA 179 E1
Nalinga, VIC.....................80 D4
Nallan, WA......................186 D5
Nambi, WA 182 C1
Nambour, QLD.................125 G2
Nambrok, VIC...................87 G3
Nambucca Heads, NSW 35 F6
Nanambinia, WA..............189 A4
Nanami, NSW 39 G5
Nanango, QLD.................125 F2
Nandaly, VIC 79 E1
Nandi, QLD 125 E2
Nanga Bay, WA 186 A5
Nangerybone, NSW...........38 D3
Nangiloc, VIC 77 E4
Nangus, NSW 44 C2
Nangwarry, SA.................159 G5
Nanneella, VIC 80 B4
Nannup, WA....................180 C4
Nantawarra, SA................156 D6
Nantawarrina, SA 157 F2
Nanutarra, WA 186 B2
Nanutarra
  Roadhouse, WA..............186 B2
Nanya, QLD.....................120 C4
Nap Nap, NSW 43 E1
Napier Downs, WA 185 E4
Napoleon, QLD................123 G2
Napoleons, VIC.................85 H2
Nappa Merrie, QLD..........122 C3

Napperby, NT 215 G6
Napperby, NT 219 G1
Napperby, SA 156 D5
Napranumo, QLD 117 A3
Napunyah, NSW 31 H6
Naracoopa, TAS 247 D2
Naracoorte, SA 159 G4
Naradhan, NSW 38 D5
Narbethong, VIC...............86 D2
Nardoo, NSW 31 H4
Nardoo, QLD 114 C5
Nardoo, QLD 123 H3
Nareen, VIC......................84 B1
Narembeen, WA...............181 F2
Nariel, QLD 124 C4
Nariel, VIC........................82 B2
Nariel Creek, VIC..............82 B2
Naringal, VIC....................85 E4
Narndee, WA 179 F1
Narooma, NSW 45 F4
Narrabri, NSW 34 A5
Narrandera, NSW 44 A1
Narraport, VIC..................79 F3
Narraway, NSW 33 F6
Narrawong, VIC................84 C4
Narre Warren, VIC............86 C3
Narrewillock, VIC..............79 G3
Narriah, NSW 38 D6
Narridy, SA 157 E5
Narrikup, WA...................181 E6
Narrina, SA 157 E2
Narrogin, WA 180 D3
Narromine, NSW 39 G3
Narwietooma, NT 219 G2
Narwonah, NSW 39 F3
Naryilco, QLD 122 D4
Nashdale, NSW 39 H5
Nathalia, VIC....................80 C3
Nathan River, NT 212 D2
Natimuk, VIC....................78 C5
National Park, TAS 240 D3
Natone, TAS 237 E3
Natte Yallock, VIC............79 G6
Natya, VIC........................77 G5
Navarre, VIC.....................79 F5
Nea, NSW 40 B1
Nebo, QLD 120 D2
Nectar Brook, SA..............156 D4
Neds Creek, WA 187 E4
Needles, TAS....................237 G5
Neerim, VIC......................87 E3
Neerim Junct., VIC 87 E3
Neerim South, VIC 87 E3
Neeworra, NSW 33 H3
Neilrex, NSW....................39 H2
Neilrex, NSW....................40 A2
Nelia, QLD 119 E1
Nelia Gaan, NSW 37 F3
Nelia Outstation, NSW 37 F4
Nelligen, NSW..................45 F3
Nelson, VIC......................84 A3
Nelson Bay, NSW.............41 E4
Nelson Springs, NT 210 B5
Nelungaloo, NSW 39 F4
Nembudding, WA.............179 E5
Nemingha, NSW 40 C1
Nepabunna, SA 157 F1
Nerang, QLD....................125 G3
Nereena, QLD 119 G4
Nerren Nerren, WA 186 B5

Nerrena, VIC.....................87 E4
Nerriga, NSW 45 F2
Nerrigundah, NSW 45 F4
Nerrima, WA 185 E5
Nerrin Nerrin, VIC.............85 F2
Netallie, NSW 37 F2
Netherby, VIC...................78 B3
Netley, NSW 36 D4
Netley Gap, SA 157 G4
Neuarpurr, VIC.................78 A5
Neumayer Valley, QLD 114 C5
Neurea, NSW 39 H4
Neuroodla, SA 156 D3
Neutral Junction, NT........216 B5
Nevertire, NSW 39 F2
New Chum, NSW 32 A6
New Crown, NT 220 C5
New Forest, WA 186 C6
*New Macdonald
  Downs, NT* 220 C1
New Mollyan, NSW 39 H2
New Norcia, WA 178 C4
New Park, NSW................44 A2
Newbridge, NSW..............40 A5
Newbridge, VIC 79 H5
Newbury, VIC 86 A1
Newcastle, NSW...............40 D4
Newcastle Waters, NT 211 H5
Newdegate, WA 181 G3
Newell, QLD 116 A3
Newfield, VIC....................85 F4
Newham, VIC....................86 B1
Newhaven, NT 219 E1
Newhaven, VIC.................86 C4
Newlands Mine, QLD 120 C2
Newlyn, VIC......................85 H1
Newman, WA...................187 E3
Newmerella, VIC...............82 C6
Newnes, NSW 40 B4
Newry, NT 210 B3
Newry, VIC........................87 G3
Newstead, VIC..................79 H6
Newton Boyd, NSW 35 E5
Ngalangkati, WA...............185 F5
Ngangganawili, WA.........187 F5
Nguiu (Police Stn), NT....206 D2
Ngukurr
  (Police Stn), NT 212 C1
Nhill, VIC..........................78 C4
Nhulunbuy, NT 209 B3
Niangala, NSW 40 D1
Nicholas Rivulet, TAS......241 E4
Nicholson, VIC..................82 B6
Nicholson, WA 185 H4
Nickavilla, QLD 123 F1
Niermur, NSW...................43 E2
Nietta, TAS.......................237 E4
Nildottie, SA.....................159 F1
Nile, TAS..........................238 A5
Nillahcootie, VIC 81 E6
Nilma, VIC........................87 E3
Nilpena, SA 157 E2
Nilpinna, SA 152 B4
Nimaru, QLD....................123 H2
Nimbin, NSW....................35 G3
Nimingarra, WA 184 B6
Nimmitabel, NSW 45 E4
Ninda, VIC 79 E1
Nindigully, QLD................124 C4
Nine Mile Cowal, NSW 39 F3

Ningaloo, WA 186 A2
Ninghan, WA 178 D2
Ninyeunook, VIC 79 G3
Nipan, QLD 121 E6
Nirranda, VIC......................85 E4
Nirranda East, VIC 85 F4
Nita Downs, WA 184 C5
Noarlunga, SA 159 E2
Nobby, QLD 125 F3
Nockatunga, QLD 123 E3
Noella, QLD 120 A6
Nome, QLD 116 B6
Nonda, QLD 119 E1
Nonning, SA 156 B4
Noojee, VIC 87 E3
Nookawarra, WA 186 C5
Noona, NSW 38 B2
Noonama, NSW 31 G5
Noonamah, NT 206 D4
Noondale, QLD 124 C4
Noondoo, QLD 124 C4
Noondoonia, WA 189 A4
Noongal, WA......................186 C6
Noonkanbah, WA 185 E5
Noorama, QLD 123 H4
Noorat, VIC 85 F3
Noorinbee, VIC..................83 E5
Noorinbee North, VIC 83 E5
Noorongong, VIC 81 H4
Noosa Heads, QLD 125 G2
Nooyeah Downs, QLD 123 F3
Noradjuha, VIC..................78 C5
Noranside, QLD 118 C3
Noreena Downs, WA 187 E2
Norfolk, QLD......................114 A5
Norley, QLD 123 F3
Normanby, QLD................115 H1
Normans Lake, WA............181 E3
Normanton, QLD 114 D4
Normanville, SA 158 D2
Normanville, VIC 79 G2
Nornalup, WA 180 D6
Norseman, WA..................183 C2
North Bannister, WA 180 C2
North Bourke, NSW 32 C5
North Condobolin, NSW 39 E4
North Dandalup, WA......180 C2
North Dorrigo, NSW..........35 F5
North Haven, NSW 41 F2
North Head, QLD..............115 F5
North Melbergen, NSW 38 C5
North Moolooloo, SA 157 E1
North Motton, TAS..........237 E3
North Mulga, SA 157 F1
North Peake (Ruin), SA 152 B4
North Scotsdale, TAS......238 B3
North Shields, SA 158 B1
North Star, NSW 34 B3
North Well, SA 156 A2
Northam, WA 178 D5
Northampton, WA............178 A1
Northcliffe, WA 180 C5
Northdown, TAS................237 F3
Northern Gully, WA 178 A1
Norwich Park
  Mine, QLD......................120 D3
Notts Well, SA 159 F1
Nowa Nowa, VIC................82 C6
Nowendoc, NSW 40 D2
Nowie North, VIC 77 G6

Nowingi, VIC........................76 D4
Nowra, NSW 45 G2
Nturiya, NT 215 H6
Nubeena, TAS....................241 F4
Nubingerie, NSW 39 G3
Nuccundra Hotel, QLD 123 E3
Nugadong, WA..................178 D3
Nugent, TAS 241 F3
Nukarni, WA 179 F5
Nula, QLD 124 D4
Nullagine, WA 187 E2
Nullamanna, NSW 34 D4
Nullan, VIC 79 E4
Nullarbor, SA 154 C3
Nullawarre, VIC..................85 E4
Nullawil, VIC 79 F2
Nulty, NSW 32 C5
Numbulwar, NT................208 D6
Numeralla, NSW 45 E4
Numery, NT 220 D3
Numurkah, VIC....................80 D3
Nunamara, TAS 238 A4
Nundle, NSW 40 C2
Nundroo, SA 155 E3
Nunga, VIC..........................77 E6
Nungarin, WA 179 F5
Nunjikompita, SA 155 H4
Nuntherungie, NSW 31 E6
Nuriootpa, SA 159 E1
Nurrabiel, VIC....................78 D5
Nurrungar, SA 156 C2
Nutwood Downs, NT 212 B3
Nyabing, WA......................181 F4
Nyah, VIC 77 G6
Nyah West, VIC 79 G1
Nyamup, WA 180 C5
Nyang, WA 186 B3
Nyarrin, VIC 79 E1
Nychum, QLD 115 H3
Nyirripi, NT 218 D1
Nymagee, NSW 38 D2
Nymboida, NSW 35 F5
Nyngan, NSW 39 E2
Nyngynderry, NSW 37 G3
Nyora, NSW 43 H3
Nyora, VIC............................86 D4
Nypo, VIC 78 C2

O.T. Downs, NT................212 C4
O.T.C. Station, SA..............155 G3
Oak Hills, QLD 116 A5
Oak Park, QLD 115 G5
Oak Vale, QLD 120 C6
Oakbank, SA 157 G5
Oakdale, NSW 40 B6
Oakden Hills, SA..............156 C3
Oakey, QLD........................125 F3
Oakey Creek
  Mine, QLD......................120 D4
Oakham, QLD 119 F6
Oakland Park, QLD..........115 E4
Oaklands, NSW 43 H3
Oakleigh, QLD 123 H1
Oakley, QLD 119 H1
Oakvale, SA 157 H5
Oakvale, VIC........................79 G3
Oakwood, NSW 34 C4
Oakwood, TAS 241 G4
Oasis Roadhouse, QLD 115 H5
Oatlands, TAS....................241 E1
Oban, QLD 118 B2

Oberon, NSW 40 A5
Obley, NSW 39 G4
Ocean Beach, WA 181 E6
Ocean Grove, VIC 86 B4
Ocean Shores, NSW 35 G2
Oenpelli
  (Police Stn), NT 207 G3
Offham, QLD 123 H3
Officer, VIC 86 D3
Ogmore, QLD....................121 E3
Olary, SA 157 G4
Old Andado, NT 220 D5
Old Bar, NSW 41 F2
Old Baratta (Ruin), SA 157 F3
Old Beach, TAS 241 E3
Old Bonalbo, NSW 35 F3
Old Burren, NSW 33 H5
Old Delamere, NT 211 E3
Old Halls Creek
  (Ruin), WA 185 G5
Old Herbert Vale, QLD 114 A5
Old Junee, NSW..................44 C1
Old Laura (Ruin), QLD 115 H1
Old Linda Downs, QLD 118 A3
Old May Downs
  (Ruin), QLD 118 B1
Old Moolawatana
  (Ruin), SA 157 G1
Old Quinyambie, SA 157 H1
Old Tallangatta, VIC 81 H3
Old Warrah, NSW 40 C2
Old Wooroona, QLD........118 A1
Oldina, TAS 236 D3
Olinda, NSW 40 B4
Olio, QLD 119 F2
Olive Downs, NSW 30 D3
Olive Downs, QLD 119 F1
Olive Vale, QLD................115 H2
Olorah Downs, SA 157 G4
Olympic Dam, SA 156 C1
Oma, QLD 119 G5
Omeo, VIC............................82 B4
Omicron, QLD 122 C4
Ondit, VIC............................85 G4
One Arm Point
  (Bardi), WA 184 D3
One Tree, NSW 38 A6
Ongerup, WA 181 F4
Onslow, WA 186 B2
Oobagooma, WA..............185 E4
Oodla Wirra, SA 157 E4
Oodnadatta, SA 152 A3
Ooldea, SA 155 E1
Oolloo, NT 207 E5
Oombulgurri, WA 185 G2
Oonah, TAS 236 D3
Oondooroo, QLD 119 F3
Oonoomurra, QLD 118 D1
Ooratippra, NT 217 G6
Oorindi, QLD 118 D1
Ootann, QLD 115 H4
Ootha, NSW 39 E4
Opalton, QLD 119 F4
Ophir, NSW 39 H4
Opium Creek, NT 207 E4
Opossum Bay, TAS 241 E4
Ora Banda, WA 182 B4
Orana, NSW........................37 H4
Orange, NSW 39 H5
Orange Creek, NT 219 H4
Orbost, VIC..........................82 D5

Orford, TAS 241 G2
Orford, VIC 84 D4
Orielton, TAS 241 F3
Orient, QLD 123 E3
Orientos, QLD 122 D3
Oriners, QLD 115 F1
Orkabie, QLD 121 E2
Ormley, TAS 238 B5
Orroroo, SA 157 E4
Orrtipa-Thurra, NT 221 E1
Ortona, QLD 115 G5
Osborne Flat, VIC 81 G4
Osborne Well, NSW 43 H3
Osterley, TAS......................240 D1
Osterley Downs, NSW 38 C2
Oudabunna, WA 179 E2
Oulnina Park, SA..............157 F4
Ouse, TAS 240 D2
Outalpa, SA 157 G4
Ouyen, VIC 77 E6
Ovens, VIC 81 G4
Overflow, NSW 38 D3
Overlander
  Roadhouse, WA............186 B5
Overnewton, NSW 37 G4
Owen, SA 157 E6
Owen Springs, NT 220 A3
Oxley, NSW 37 H6
Oxley, VIC............................81 F4
Ozenkadnook, VIC 78 B5

Paaratte, VIC 85 F4
Paddington, NSW 38 B3
Padthaway, SA 159 G4
Pakenham, VIC....................86 D3
Palana, TAS 247 B5
Palgarup, WA 180 C5
Pallamallawa, NSW 34 B4
Pallamana, SA 159 F2
Pallarenda, QLD 116 B5
Palm Island, QLD 116 B5
Palmer River
  Roadhouse, QLD 115 H2
Palmer Valley, NT 219 H4
Palmerville, QLD 115 G2
Palparara, QLD 118 D5
Paluma, QLD 116 B5
Palumpa, NT 206 C6
Pambula, NSW 45 F5
Panban, NSW 37 G5
Pandanus Creek, QLD 115 H6
Pandie Pandie, SA 153 F1
Pandora Park, QLD 119 G5
Paney, SA 156 A4
Panitya, VIC 78 A1
Panmure, VIC......................85 E4
Pannawonica, WA............186 C2
Pantijan, WA 185 E3
Panton Hill, VIC..................86 C2
Pappinbarra, NSW 41 E1
Papulankutja, WA 188 C4
Papunya, NT 219 F2
Paraburdoo, WA 186 D3
Parachilna, SA 157 E2
Paradise, TAS 237 F4
Paradise, VIC 79 F5
Parakylia, SA 156 B1
Paraparap, VIC 86 A4
Paratoo, SA 157 F4
Parattah, TAS 241 E1

Pardoo, WA 184 B6
Pardoo Roadhouse, WA 184 B6
Parenna, TAS 247 C2
Parilla, SA............................159 G2
Paringa, NSW 36 D2
Paringa, SA..........................157 G6
Parkes, NSW 39 F4
Parkham, TAS 237 G4
Parkside, TAS 238 D4
Parkville, NSW 40 C2
Parndana, SA 158 C3
Parnella, TAS.....................238 D4
Parnngurr
 (Cotton Ck), WA 187 G2
Paroo, WA 187 E5
Parrakie, SA........................159 G2
Parramatta, NSW.................40 C5
Parry Beach, WA 180 D6
Paruna, SA..........................159 G1
Parwan, VIC..........................86 A2
Paschendale, VIC................84 C2
Pasha, QLD........................120 C2
Paskeville, SA 156 D6
Pata, SA 159 G1
Patchewollock, VIC............78 D1
Pateena, TAS......................237 H5
Paterson, NSW.....................40 D4
Patersonia, TAS 238 A4
Patho, VIC.............................80 A3
Pathungra, QLD................118 C3
Pawleena, TAS 241 F3
Pawtella, TAS 241 F1
Payne, QLD 119 G4
Paynes Find, WA 179 E2
Paynesville, VIC...................82 B6
Paynters, NSW 44 A1
Peaceful Bay, WA 180 D6
Peak Downs Mine, QLD 120 C3
Peak Hill, NSW 30 D5
Peak Hill, NSW......................39 F4
Peak Vale, QLD..................120 B4
Peake, SA...........................152 B4
Peake, SA.............................159 F2
Peakview, NSW 45 E3
Pearcedale, VIC 86 C3
Pearlah, SA 158 A1
Pearshape, TAS 247 C3
Pedirka (Ruin), SA.............152 A2
Peebinga, SA 159 H2
Peechelba, VIC.....................81 F3
Peedamulla, WA 186 B2
Peel, NSW 40 A5
Peelwood, NSW 40 A6
Pegarah, TAS 247 C3
Pekina, SA 157 E4
Pelham, QLD......................115 F6
Pelham, TAS 240 D2
Pella, VIC..............................78 C3
Pelverata, TAS 241 E4
Pemberton, WA..................180 C5
Pembrooke, NSW 41 F2
Penarie, NSW 43 E1
Pencil Pine, TAS 237 E5
Pender, WA 184 D3
Peneena, NSW 37 G4
Penguin, TAS 237 E3
Penneshaw, SA 158 D3
Penola, SA 159 G5
Penong, SA 155 F3
Penrith, NSW 40 C5

Penshurst, VIC 84 D3
Pentland, QLD 120 A1
Penzance, TAS 241 G4
Peppermint Grove
 Beach, WA.......................180 B4
Peppers Plains, VIC............78 D3
Peppimenarti, NT 206 C6
Perekerten, NSW 43 E2
Perenjori, WA 178 C2
Perenna, VIC.........................78 C3
Perisher Village, NSW 44 D4
Perkolilli, WA 182 B4
Perlta, VIC.............................76 C4
Pernatty, SA......................156 D2
Peron, WA 186 A5
Perponda, SA 159 F2
Perrinvale, WA 179 H2
Perry Bridge, VIC 87 H3
Perth, TAS 237 H5
Perth, WA 180 C2
Perthville, NSW....................40 A5
Peterborough, SA...............157 E5
Peterborough, VIC..............85 F5
Petford, QLD......................115 H4
Petina, SA 155 H4
Petita, NSW 31 F5
Petrie, QLD 125 G3
Phillip Creek, NT 216 B2
Phillpott, QLD....................123 H3
Pialah, QLD.......................115 F6
Piallamore, NSW.................40 C1
Piallaway, NSW....................40 C1
Piamble, VIC.........................77 G5
Piambra, NSW 40 A2
Piangil, VIC...........................77 G6
Piawaning, WA 178 C4
Pickanjinnie, QLD.............124 C3
Pickertaramoor, NT 206 D2
Picola, VIC............................80 C3
Picton, NSW.........................40 B6
Pier Millan, VIC....................77 E6
Pigeon Hole, NT 211 E4
Pigeon Ponds, VIC 84 C1
Pikedale, QLD 125 F4
Pilgrim, QLD......................118 C2
Pillana, SA 158 A1
Pillar Valley, NSW...............35 G5
Pilliga, NSW........................33 H5
Pimba, SA 156 C2
Pimbaacia, SA 155 H4
Pimbee, WA 186 B4
Pimpara Lake, NSW...........30 D6
Pimpinio, VIC.......................78 D5
Pindabunna, WA 179 F2
Pindar, WA 178 B1
Pine Camp, NSW 36 C6
Pine Clump, NSW 39 F1
Pine Creek, NT 207 F5
Pine Creek, SA..................157 F5
Pine Gap, NT 220 A3
Pine Grove, VIC 80 A3
Pine Hill, QLD....................120 B4
Pine Lodge, VIC...................80 D4
Pine Point, NSW 36 D3
Pine Point, SA 158 D1
Pine Ridge, NSW 38 B2
Pine Ridge, NSW 40 B2
Pine Valley, SA 157 G5
Pine View, NSW 39 G2
Pinecliffe, NSW...................39 G4

Pinegrove, WA 186 C6
Piney Range, NSW 39 F5
Pingandy, WA 186 D3
Pingaring, WA 181 F3
Pingelly, WA 180 D2
Pingine, QLD.....................123 G1
Pingrup, WA 181 F4
Pinjarra, WA 180 C2
Pinjin, WA...........................182 D3
Pinkilla, QLD......................123 F1
Pinnacles, WA 187 F6
Pinnaroo, SA......................159 H2
Pintharuka, WA 178 C2
Pioneer, QLD 116 C6
Pioneer, TAS 238 C3
Pioneer, WA 183 B2
Piora, NSW...........................35 F3
Pipalyatjara, SA 150 A1
Pipers Brook, TAS 238 A3
Pipers River, TAS 237 H3
Pira, VIC................................77 G6
Piries, VIC.............................81 E6
Pirron Yallock, VIC.............85 G4
Pitfield, VIC..........................85 G2
Pithara, WA 178 D4
Pittong, VIC..........................85 G2
Pittsworth, QLD 125 F3
Planet Downs, QLD..........114 B5
Planet Downs, QLD..........120 D5
Planet Downs O.S., QLD 122 C1
Platina, NSW.......................39 E4
Pleasant Hills, NSW 44 A2
Plenty, TAS 240 D3
Plevna Downs, QLD 123 E2
Plumbago, SA....................157 G3
Pmara Jutunta, NT 215 H6
Poatina, TAS 237 H5
Point Cook, VIC...................86 B3
Point Lonsdale, VIC...........86 B4
Point Lookout, QLD..........125 H3
Point Samson, WA 186 C1
Poldinna, SA 156 A4
Polelle, WA 187 E5
Police Point, TAS 240 D4
Policemans Point, SA 159 F3
Pollygammon, QLD 118 C3
Polocara, NSW 31 H6
Pomborneit, VIC 85 G4
Pomborneit North, VIC 85 G4
Pomona, QLD 125 G2
Pomonal, VIC.......................85 E1
Pondana, WA 189 B3
Pontville, TAS 241 E2
Pony Hills, QLD.................124 C1
Poochera, SA 155 H4
Poolaigelo, VIC...................84 A1
Poole, TAS 238 D2
Pooncarie, NSW 37 F5
Poonindie, SA 158 B1
Pootilla, VIC.........................85 H2
Pootnoura, SA 151 G4
Poowong, VIC......................86 D4
Popanyinning, WA 180 D3
Popiltah, NSW....................36 D5
Poplar Grove, NSW 39 E2
Porepunkah, VIC 81 G5
Pormpuraaw, QLD 117 A5
Porongurup, WA 181 E5
Port Albert, VIC...................87 G5
Port Alma, QLD 121 F4

Port Arthur, TAS................241 G4
Port Augusta, SA 156 D4
Port Bonython, SA 156 D5
Port Broughton, SA........156 D5
Port Campbell, VIC.............85 F5
Port Clinton, SA.................156 D6
Port Davis, SA 156 D5
Port Denison, WA 178 A2
Port Douglas, QLD 116 A3
Port Elliott, SA 159 E2
Port Fairy, VIC 84 D4
Port Franklin, VIC...............87 F5
Port Germein, SA 156 D5
Port Gibbon, SA 156 C6
Port Headland, WA..........184 A6
Port Huon, TAS 240 D4
Port Julia, SA 158 D1
Port Kembla, NSW 45 H1
Port Kenny, SA...................155 H5
Port Latta, TAS 236 D2
Port Lincoln, SA.................158 B1
Port Macdonnell, SA 159 G6
Port Macquarie, NSW 41 F2
Port Neill, SA 156 B6
Port Pirie, SA 156 D5
Port Rickaby, SA 158 D1
Port Roper, NT 212 D1
Port Sorell, TAS 237 G3
Port Victoria, SA 158 D1
Port Vincent, SA 158 D1
Port Wakefield, SA 156 D6
Port Welshpool, VIC..........87 F5
Portarlington, VIC 86 B3
Porters Retreat, NSW........40 A6
Portland, NSW 40 B5
Portland, VIC......................84 C4
Portland Downs, QLD 119 G5
Portland Roads, QLD......117 C3
Portsea, VIC........................86 B4
Potato Point, NSW 45 F4
Pottsville Beach, NSW 35 G2
Pound Creek, VIC 87 E5
Powell Creek, NT 212 A6
Powelltown, VIC.................86 D2
Powers Creek, VIC.............84 B1
Prairie, QLD........................119 H1
Prairie, QLD 123 F3
Prairie, VIC..........................80 A4
Prairie Downs, WA............187 E3
Premaydena, TAS 241 F4
Premer, NSW.......................40 B1
Premier Downs, WA 189 B3
Prenti Downs, WA 187 G5
Preolenna, TAS..................236 D3
Preston, TAS 237 E4
Preston Beach, WA............180 B3
Prevelly, WA 180 B4
Price, SA 156 D6
Primrose Sands, TAS 241 F3
Princetown, VIC...................85 F5
Princhester, QLD...............121 E4
Pring, QLD 116 D6
Priory, TAS 238 D4
Prooinga, VIC......................77 F5
Proserpine, QLD 120 D1
Prospect, QLD...................115 E5
Proston, QLD 125 F1
Prubi, QLD..........................119 F2
Prungle, NSW 37 F6
Prungle, NSW 42 D1

Pucawan, NSW..................39 E6
Pucawan, NSW..................44 B1
Puckapunyal, VIC 80 C6
Puggoon, NSW 40 A3
Pukatja (Ernabella), SA 151 E1
Pularumpi, NT 206 D2
Pulgamurtie, NSW 31 E5
Pull Pulla, NSW 38 B1
Pullabooka, NSW 39 F5
Pullagaroo, WA 179 E2
Pullut, VIC 78 C3
Pungalina, NT...................213 F4
Punjaub, QLD 114 B4
Punmu, WA 187 G2
Puntabie, SA 155 G3
Pura Pura, VIC 85 F2
Puralka, VIC 84 A3
Purfleet, NSW 41 E2
Purlewaugh, NSW..............40 A1
Purnamoota, NSW 36 D2
Purnango, NSW 31 G6
Purnawilla, NSW 37 G1
Purnim, VIC 85 E4
Purnong, SA 159 F1
Purple Downs, SA 156 C2
Puttapa, SA 157 E1
Putty, NSW........................40 C4
Pyalong, VIC 80 B6
Pyengana, TAS..................238 C4
Pygery, SA 156 A5
Pymurra, QLD 118 D1
Pyramid, WA 186 C1
Pyramid Hill, VIC 79 H3

Quaama, NSW 45 F4
Quairading, WA 181 E2
Quambatook, VIC 79 G2
Quambetook, QLD 119 E2
Quambone, NSW 33 F6
Quamby, QLD 118 C1
Quamby Brook, TAS........237 G5
Quandary, NSW 39 E6
Quandialla, NSW 39 F6
Quandong Vale, SA..........157 G5
Quantong, VIC 78 C5
Quarrells, QLD 119 E1
Quarry Hill, NSW 37 E3
Quartz Hill, NT 220 C2
Queanbeyan, NSW 45 E2
Queenscliff, VIC 86 B4
Queenstown, TAS 236 D6
Questa Park, NSW 31 F5
Quilberry, QLD..................123 F1
Quilpie, QLD.....................123 F2
Quinalow, QLD 125 F2
Quindanning, WA.............180 D3
Quinninup, WA 180 C5
Quinns Rock, WA 178 B5
Quinyambie, SA 157 H2
Quirindi, NSW....................40 C2
Quobba, WA 186 A4
Quondong, NSW 39 F6
Quorn, SA 156 D4

Rabbit Flat
 Roadhouse, NT 214 C3
Raglan, QLD 121 F4
Raglan, VIC 85 G4
Railton, TAS......................237 F4
Rainbow, VIC 78 C3
Rainbow Beach, QLD 125 G1

Raleigh, NSW 35 F6
Ramingining, NT............208 C3
Ranceby, VIC 87 E4
Rand, NSW.........................44 A3
Ranelagh, TAS 240 D4
Ranga, TAS 247 C6
Rangelands, QLD 119 F3
Rangers Valley, QLD 120 A3
Ranken, NT 217 F3
Rankins Springs, NSW......38 D5
Rannes, QLD.....................121 E5
Rapid Bay, SA 158 D2
Rappville, NSW 35 F3
Rathdowney, QLD 125 G4
Rathgar, NSW 32 A3
Rathscar, VIC 79 G6
Ravendale, NSW 37 E1
Ravenshoe, QLD 116 A4
Ravensthorpe, WA 181 H4
Ravenswood, QLD 120 B1
Ravenswood, VIC 80 A5
Ravenswood, WA 180 C2
Ravensworth, NSW...........40 C3
Ravensworth, NSW 43 F1
Rawlinna, WA 189 B3
Rawson, VIC 87 F3
Ray, QLD 123 F1
Raymond Terrace, NSW   40 D4
Raywood, VIC 80 A4
Red Bluff, VIC 81 H4
Red Cap Creek, VIC...........84 B2
Red Cliffs, VIC 76 D4
Red Hill, WA 186 C1
Red Mountain, QLD........120 C3
Red Range, VIC 35 E4
Red Rock, NSW 35 G5
Redbank, QLD 121 F6
Redbank, VIC 79 G5
Redcliffe, QLD.................121 E5
Redcliffe, QLD..................125 G3
Redcliffe, SA 157 F6
Redesdale, VIC 80 B6
Redford, QLD 124 B1
Redhill, SA 156 D5
Redmond, WA 181 E6
Redpa, TAS 236 B2
Reedy, WA 186 D5
Reedy Corner, NSW 39 E1
Reedy Creek, QLD 120 D6
Reedy Creek, SA 159 F4
Reedy Creek, VIC 86 C1
Reedy Dam, VIC 79 E3
Reedy Spring, QLD 115 H6
Reefton, NSW 39 E6
Reekara, TAS.....................247 C2
Reid River, QLD 116 B6
Reids Flat, NSW 39 H6
Relbia, TAS.......................238 A4
Remine, TAS 236 C6
Remlap, WA.....................179 E3
Renison Bell, TAS 236 D5
Renmark, SA 157 G6
Renmark North, SA 157 G6
Renner Springs
 Roadhouse, NT 212 A6
Rennie, NSW 43 H3
Retreat, NSW 34 C6
Retreat, QLD 119 F6
Retro, QLD........................120 C4
Reynolds Neck, TAS 237 G6

Rheban, TAS 241 G2
Rheola, VIC 79 G5
Rhyll, VIC 86 C4
Rhyndaston, TAS.............241 E2
Riana, TAS 237 E3
Rich Avon, VIC 79 E4
Richmond, NSW 40 C5
Richmond, QLD...............119 F1
Richmond, TAS 241 E3
Riddells Creek, VIC 86 B1
Ridgelands, QLD 121 E4
Ridgelands, QLD 124 C1
Ridgley, TAS.....................237 E3
Rifle Creek, QLD 118 B1
Rimbanda, QLD...............119 G3
Ringarooma, TAS.............238 B4
Ringwood, NT 220 C3
Ringwood, VIC 86 C2
Risdon Vale, TAS 241 E3
Rita Island, QLD...............116 C6
River Heads, QLD 125 G1
Riveren, NT 210 C6
Riverina, WA 182 A3
Riverside, NSW 37 G2
Riverside, QLD 120 B5
Riverside Mine, QLD 120 C2
Riversleigh, QLD 114 B5
Riverton, SA 157 E6
Roach, NSW 44 A1
Robe, SA 159 F5
Robertson, NSW 45 G1
Robertson Range, WA 187 F3
Robertstown, SA..............157 E6
Robinhood, QLD 115 G5
Robinson River, NT.........213 F4
Rocherlea, TAS.................238 A4
Rochester, VIC 80 B4
Rochford Rock, VIC 86 B1
Rock Flat, NSW 45 E4
Rockbank, VIC 86 B2
Rockhampton, QLD........121 F4
*Rockhampton
 Downs, NT* 216 C2
Rockingham, WA 180 B2
Rocklands, QLD 114 A6
Rocklea, WA 186 D2
Rockley, NSW 40 A5
Rockton, NSW 45 E5
Rockvale, QLD 119 E1
Rockview, NSW 44 B1
Rockwood, QLD 119 G2
Rocky Cape, TAS 236 D2
Rocky Glen, NSW 38 B1
Rocky Glen, NSW 40 A1
Rocky Gully, WA 180 D5
Rocky River, NSW 34 D6
Rocky River, SA 158 C3
Roebourne, WA 186 C1
Roebuck Plains, WA 184 D4
Roebuck
 Roadhouse, WA.............184 D4
Roger River, TAS 236 C3
Rokeby, TAS 241 E3
Rokeby, VIC 87 E3
Rokewood, VIC 85 H3
Roland, TAS......................237 F4
Rollands Plains, NSW........41 F1
Rolleston, QLD 120 D5
Rollingston, QLD 116 B5
Roma, QLD 124 C2

Romani, NSW 38 C3
Romsey, VIC 86 B1
Rookwood, QLD..............115 H3
Roopena, SA 156 D4
Roper Bar, NT 212 B1
Roper Valley, NT 212 B2
Roseberth, QLD 118 B6
Rosebery, TAS 236 D5
Rosebery, VIC 78 D2
Rosebery East, VIC 79 E2
Rosebrook, VIC..................84 D4
Rosebud, VIC 86 B4
Rosedale, QLD 121 G6
Rosedale, VIC 87 G3
Rosegarland, TAS 240 D3
Rosella Plains, QLD 115 H5
Rosemount, QLD 120 A4
Rosevale, QLD 119 E2
Rosevale, TAS 237 H4
Rosevears, TAS 237 H4
Rosewhite, VIC 81 G4
Rosewood, NSW................44 C3
Rosewood, NT 210 B4
Rosewood, QLD 125 G3
Roslyn, NSW 45 F1
Roslynmead, VIC 80 A3
Ross, TAS 238 B6
Ross Creek, VIC 85 H2
Rossarden, TAS................238 B5
Rossbridge, VIC 85 E2
Rosscommon, NSW 33 E4
Rosslyn, QLD 121 F6
Rossville, QLD 116 A2
Rostron, VIC 79 F5
Roto, NSW 38 B4
Rowella, TAS 237 H3
Rowena, NSW 33 H4
Rowsley, VIC 86 A2
Rowville, VIC 86 C3
*Roxborough
 Downs, QLD* 118 B3
Roxburgh, NSW 40 C3
Roxby Downs, SA 156 C1
Roxby Downs, SA 156 C1
Roy Hill, WA 187 E2
Royal George, TAS 238 C5
Rubicon, VIC 87 E1
Ruby Downs, WA 185 G5
Rubyvale, QLD.................120 C4
Rudall, SA 156 B6
Ruffy, VIC 80 D6
Rugby, NSW 45 E1
Rum Jungle, NT................206 D4
Running Creek, VIC 81 G4
Running Stream, NSW 40 A4
Runnymede, QLD 119 F1
Runnymede, QLD 124 A3
Runnymede, TAS.............241 F2
Runnymede, VIC 80 B4
Rupanyup, VIC 79 E5
Rupanyup North, VIC.......79 E4
Rupanyup South, VIC 79 E5
Rushworth, VIC 80 C4
Russells, NSW 37 H1
Rutchillo, QLD* 118 D1
Rutherglen, VIC 81 F3
Ruthven, QLD 119 G5
Rye, VIC 86 B4
Rye Park, NSW 45 E1
Rylstone, NSW 40 B4

Ryton, VIC 87 F4
Rywung, QLD....................125 E2

Saddleworth, SA............157 E6
St Albans, NSW 40 C5
St Andrews, VIC 86 C2
St Arnaud, VIC 79 F5
St Arnaud East, VIC.........79 G5
St Evins, VIC......................78 C6
St Fillans, VIC....................86 D2
St George, QLD 124 C3
St Germains, VIC 80 C3
St Helens, TAS 238 D4
St Helens Plains, VIC 78 D5
St James, VIC......................81 E4
St Kilda, VIC.......................86 C3
St Lawrence, QLD............121 E3
St Leonards, TAS 238 A4
St Leonards, VIC...............86 B3
St Marys, TAS 238 D5
St Patricks River, TAS 238 A4
St Pauls, QLD 117 B1
Sale, VIC.............................87 G3
Salisbury, NSW..................40 D3
Salisbury, VIC....................78 C4
Salisbury Downs, NSW 31 F5
Salisbury West, VIC...........79 H4
Salmon Gums, WA 183 B3
Salt Creek, SA...................159 F3
Saltern, QLD 119 H4
Saltwater River, TAS 241 F4
Samaria, VIC.......................81 E5
Samford, QLD 125 G3
San Marino, SA.................151 H3
San Remo, VIC...................86 D4
Sandalwood, SA 159 G2
Sandfire
  Roadhouse, WA...............184 C6
Sandfly, TAS 241 E4
Sandford, VIC....................84 B2
Sandhill Lake, VIC 79 G2
Sandigo, NSW 44 A2
Sandilands, SA.................158 D1
Sandon, VIC......................79 H6
Sandon, VIC......................85 H1
Sandringham, QLD..........118 B4
Sandringham, VIC............86 C3
Sandsmere, VIC 78 B4
Sandstone, WA 187 E6
Sandy Camp, NSW 33 F6
Sandy Creek, VIC 81 H4
Sandy Hollow, NSW 40 C3
Sandy Point, VIC...............87 E5
Sangar, NSW 43 H3
Sangar, NSW 44 A3
Sanpah, NSW....................30 C6
Santa Teresa, NT 220 B3
Santos, QLD 122 D3
Sapphire, QLD 120 C4
Sapphire Beach, NSW 35 G5
Saraji Mine, QLD 120 C3
Sarina, QLD.......................120 D2
Sarsfield, VIC 82 B6
Sassafras, TAS...................237 G4
Sassafras Gap, VIC............82 B2
Sassafrass, NSW................45 G2
Saunders Beach, QLD......116 B5
Savage River, TAS 236 C4
Savannah Downs, QLD 115 E6
Savernake, NSW 43 H3
Sawtell, NSW 35 G6

Saxby Downs, QLD 115 F6
Sayers Lake, NSW 37 G4
Scaddan, WA 183 B4
Scamander, TAS................238 D4
Scarsdale, VIC....................85 G2
Scartwater, QLD 120 B2
Sceale Bay, SA 155 G5
Scone, NSW........................40 C3
Scotsburn, VIC...................85 H2
Scotsdale, TAS 238 B3
Scott Creek, NT 211 F1
Scotts Creek, VIC...............85 F4
Scotts Head, NSW 35 F6
Sea Elephant, TAS............247 C2
Sea Lake, VIC......................79 E2
Seabird, WA 178 B5
Seacombe, VIC...................87 H3
Seaforth, QLD 120 D1
Seal Rocks, NSW 41 E3
Seaspray, VIC.....................87 H4
Seaton, VIC.........................87 F3
Sebastian, VIC....................80 A4
Sebastopol, NSW 44 C1
Sedan, SA 159 F1
Sedan Dip, QLD................114 D6
Sedgeford, QLD 120 B4
Sedgwick, VIC....................80 A5
Seemore Downs, WA 189 B3
Seisia, QLD 117 B1
Sellheim, QLD 116 B6
Selwyn, QLD......................118 C2
Serpentine, VIC 79 H4
Serpentine, WA 180 C2
Serviceton, VIC..................78 A4
Sesbania, QLD 119 F2
Seven Emu, NT 213 F3
Seven Mile Beach, TAS   241 F3
Seventeen
  Seventy, QLD 121 G5
Seville, VIC..........................86 D2
Seymour, TAS 238 D5
Seymour, VIC 80 C6
Shackleton, WA 179 E6
Shadforth, NSW.................39 H5
Shannons Flat, NSW..........45 E3
Sheans Creek, VIC.............80 D5
Sheep Hills, VIC 79 E4
Sheffield, TAS....................237 F4
Shelbourne, VIC.................79 H5
Shelburne, QLD 117 B2
Shelford, VIC......................85 H3
Shelley, VIC........................82 B1
Shellharbour, NSW 45 G1
Shenandoah, NT 211 H4
Shepherds, NSW................44 B2
Shepparton, VIC................80 D4
Sheringa, SA......................156 A6
Sherlock, SA......................159 F2
Sherlock, WA 186 D1
Sherwood, NSW 41 F1
Shoalhaven
  Heads, NSW 45 G1
Shoreham, VIC...................86 C4
Shutehaven, QLD 120 D1
Siam, SA 156 C4
Sidmouth, TAS..................237 H3
Silent Grove, WA 185 A4
Silkwood, QLD..................116 B4
Silverton, NSW..................36 C2
Simmie, VIC.......................80 B4

Simpson, VIC.....................85 F4
Singleton, NSW 40 C3
Singleton, NT 216 B4
Singleton, WA 180 B2
Sisters Beach, TAS............236 D2
Sisters Creek, TAS 236 D3
Skenes Creek, VIC.............85 H5
Skipton, VIC.......................85 G2
Skye, QLD.........................120 B5
Slade Point, QLD...............120 D2
Slashes Creek, QLD 118 D3
Slaty Creek, VIC 79 F4
Smeaton, VIC.....................85 H1
Smiggin Holes, NSW 44 D4
Smithfield, QLD.................116 A3
Smithton, TAS...................236 C2
Smithtown, NSW...............41 F1
Smithville, SA 159 G2
Smoko, VIC.........................81 G5
Smoky Bay, SA..................155 G4
Smythesdale, VIC..............85 G2
Snake Valley, VIC..............85 G2
Snobs Creek, VIC...............87 E1
Snowtown, SA...................156 D6
Snug, TAS...........................241 E4
Sofala, NSW........................40 A4
Somerby, QLD 120 D5
Somers, VIC........................86 C4
Somerset, QLD 117 B1
Somerset, TAS...................237 E3
Somerton, NSW.................34 C6
Somerton, VIC...................86 B2
Somerville, VIC..................86 C3
Sommariva, QLD 124 A1
Sorell, TAS 241 F3
Sorrento, VIC.....................86 B4
Soudan, NT 217 F3
South Arm, TAS 241 E4
South Blackwater
  Mine, QLD........................120 D5
South Forest, TAS 236 C2
South Franklin, TAS 240 D4
South Galway, QLD 119 E6
South Gap, SA 156 D3
South Grafton, NSW 35 F4
South Hedland, WA 184 A6
South Ita, NSW 36 D4
South Johnston, QLD 116 A4
South Kilkerran, SA 158 D1
South Kumminin, WA 181 F2
South Nietta, SA 237 E4
South Preston, TAS 237 E4
South Riana, TAS...............237 E3
South Springfield, TAS   238 B3
South West Rocks, NSW   41 F1
Southend, SA 159 F5
Southern Brook, WA 178 D5
Southern Cross, QLD......120 A1
Southern Cross, WA........179 G5
Southern Hills, WA...........183 D2
Southport, TAS 240 D5
Spalding, SA 157 E5
Spargo Creek, VIC.............86 A1
Speed, VIC..........................78 D1
Speewa, VIC.......................77 G6
Spirit Hills, NT 210 B2
Split Rock, QLD.................114 B6
Spoonbill, QLD 114 D6
Sprent, TAS........................237 F4
Spreyton, TAS....................237 F3

Spring Beach, TAS 241 G2
Spring Creek, NT 213 E4
Spring Creek, QLD 115 H5
Spring Creek, WA 185 H4
Spring Hill, NSW 39 H5
Spring Hill, NT 207 E5
Spring Hill, WA.................178 D5
Spring Ridge, NSW 40 B1
Springdale, NSW 44 C1
Springfield, QLD 115 H4
Springfield, QLD 124 B2
Springfield, TAS................238 B3
Springhurst, VIC................81 F3
Springsure, QLD 120 C5
Springton, SA....................159 E1
Springvale, QLD 117 D6
Springvale, QLD 118 D4
Springvale, QLD 120 A4
Springvale, QLD 120 B3
Springvale, WA 185 G4
Springwood, NSW 40 B5
Springwood, QLD 120 C5
Squirrel Hills, QLD 118 D2
Staghorn Flat, VIC 81 G4
Stamford, QLD..................119 G2
Stanage, QLD....................121 E3
Stanbroke, QLD 118 C2
Stanhope, VIC....................80 C4
Stanifords, NSW 38 C3
Stanley, TAS 236 C2
Stanley, VIC.......................81 G4
Stannifer, NSW 34 D5
Stansbury, SA....................158 D1
Stanthorpe, QLD...............125 F4
Stanwell, QLD...................121 E4
Stanwell Park, NSW 40 C6
Starke, QLD 116 A1
Staughton Vale, VIC 86 A2
Stawell, VIC 79 E6
Steiglitz, VIC.......................86 A3
Stenhouse Bay, SA 158 C2
Stephens Creek, NSW 36 D2
Steppes, TAS.....................237 H6
Stewart, WA 182 A4
Stieglitz, TAS.....................238 D4
Stirling, NT 216 A5
Stirling, QLD 115 E3
Stirling, QLD 120 A4
Stirling, QLD 124 C1
Stirling North, SA 156 D4
Stockinbingal, NSW 44 C1
Stockmans Reward, VIC   87 E2
Stokes Bay, SA 158 C2
Stonehenge, QLD..............119 F5
Stoneyford, VIC.................85 G4
Stonor, TAS........................241 E2
Stony Crossing, NSW 43 E2
Storys Creek, TAS 238 B5
Stowport, TAS 237 E3
Stradbroke, VIC..................87 G4
Strahan, TAS 239 C1
Strangways Bore
  (Ruin), SA........................152 C5
Stratford, NSW...................41 E3
Stratford, VIC.....................87 G3
Strath Creek, VIC...............80 C6
Strathalbyn, SA 159 E2
Stratham, WA 180 B4
Strathaven, QLD 117 B5
Strathblane, TAS 240 D5

Strathbogie, VIC 80 D5
Strathburn, QLD 117 B5
Strathdownie, VIC 84 B2
Strathearn, SA 157 G3
Strathelbiss, QLD 118 C3
Strathfield, QLD 118 D2
Strathfieldsaye, VIC 80 A5
Strathgordon, QLD 117 B5
Strathgordon, TAS 240 B3
Strathkellar, VIC 84 D2
Strathleven, QLD 115 G2
Strathmay, QLD 117 B5
Strathmerton, VIC 80 D3
Strathmore, QLD 115 C4
Strathmore, QLD 120 C1
Strathpark, QLD 115 F6
Stratton, VIC 79 E1
Streaky Bay, SA 155 H4
Streatham, VIC 85 F2
Strelley, WA 184 A6
Strickland, TAS 240 C1
Stroud, NSW 41 E3
Stroud Road, NSW 41 E3
Struan, SA 159 G5
Strzelecki, VIC 87 E4
Stuart, QLD 116 B6
Stuart Creek, SA 152 C6
Stuart Mill, VIC 79 F5
Stuart Town, NSW.............39 H4
Stuarts Point, NSW 35 F6
Stuarts Well
  Roadhouse, NT 219 H3
Sturt Creek, WA 185 H5
Sturt Meadows, WA 182 B1
Sturt Vale, SA 157 G5
Sudley, QLD......................117 B3
Suggan Buggan, VIC 82 C3
Sujeewong, QLD 125 E1
Sullivan, WA 178 B1
Sulphur Creek, TAS 237 E3
Summerfield, VIC 80 A4
Summervale, QLD 119 H5
Sunbury, VIC 86 B2
Sunday Creek, NT 211 G3
Sunnyside, VIC 82 A3
Sunset Strip, NSW.............37 E3
Sunshine, VIC 86 B2
Supplejack, NT 214 C2
Surat, QLD.......................124 C2
Surfers Paradise, QLD 125 G3
Surges Bay, TAS 240 D4
Surveyors Lake, NSW 37 G3
Sussex, NSW.....................38 D1
Sussex Inlet, NSW 45 G2
Sutherland, NSW...............40 C6
Sutherland, VIC 79 F4
Sutherlands, SA...............157 F6
Sutton, NSW 45 E2
Sutton, VIC........................79 F2
Sutton Forest, NSW 45 G1
Sutton Grange, VIC...........80 A6
Swan Hill, VIC 79 G1
Swan Marsh, VIC 85 G4
Swan Reach, SA................159 F1
Swan Reach, VIC 82 B6
Swanpool, VIC 81 E5
Swansea, NSW 40 D4
Swansea, TAS 241 G4
Swanwater, VIC 79 F4
Swifts Creek, VIC 82 B4

Swim Creek, NT 207 F3
Sydenham, VIC 86 B2
Sydney, NSW.....................40 C6
Sylvania, WA 187 E3

Tabba Tabba, WA 184 A6
Tabberabbera, VIC 82 A5
Tabbita, NSW 38 C6
Tableland, WA 185 G4
Tabletop, QLD...................115 E4
Tabratong, NSW 39 E3
Tabulam, NSW 35 F3
Taggerty, VIC 86 D1
Tahara, VIC.......................84 C2
Tailem Bend, SA 159 F2
Takone, TAS.....................236 D3
Takone West, TAS 236 D3
Takura, QLD 121 H6
Talawa, TAS 238 B4
Talawanta, QLD 114 C5
Talbingo, NSW 44 D3
Talbot, VIC 79 G6
Taldra, SA........................159 G1
Taleeban, NSW 38 D6
Talgarno, VIC....................81 H3
Talia, SA 155 H5
Talisker, WA 186 B5
Tallalara, NSW 31 H6
Tallandoon, VIC 81 H4
Tallangatta, VIC 82 A1
Tallangatta Valley, VIC 82 A1
Tallarook, VIC 80 C6
Tallawang, NSW 40 A3
Tallebung, NSW 38 D4
Tallering, WA 178 B1
Tallygaroopna, VIC 80 D3
Talmalmo, NSW 44 B3
Talwood, QLD 124 D4
Tamala, WA......................186 A5
Tamarang, NSW 40 B1
Tambar Springs, NSW 40 A1
Tambellup, WA 181 E5
Tambo, QLD 120 A5
Tambo Crossing, VIC 82 B5
Tambo Upper, VIC.............82 B6
Tamboon, VIC...................83 E6
Tamborine
  Mountain, QLD 125 G3
Tambua, NSW 38 B1
Tamleugh, VIC 80 D4
Tamleugh North, VIC 80 D4
Tammin, WA 179 E5
Tamworth, NSW 40 C1
Tamworth, QLD.................119 G1
Tanami Downs, NT 214 C4
Tanbar, QLD.....................122 D1
Tandarra, VIC 80 A4
Tanderra, QLD 120 C5
Tangadee, WA 187 E3
Tangambalanga, VIC 81 G4
Tangorin, QLD 119 G2
Tanja, NSW 45 F4
Tanjil Bren, VIC 87 E2
Tanjil South, VIC 87 F3
Tankarooka, NSW 37 H1
Tannum Sands, QLD 121 F5
Tantanoola, SA.................159 G5
Tanumbirini, NT 212 C4
Tanunda, SA 159 E1
Tanwood, VIC 79 G6
Tanybryn, VIC...................85 H5

Taplan, SA 159 H1
Tara, NSW 32 A6
Tara, NSW 38 C2
Tara, NSW 38 D3
Tara, NT 216 B5
Tara, QLD.........................125 E3
Taradale, VIC 80 A6
Taragoola, QLD 121 F5
Taragoro, SA 156 B6
Taralga, NSW 45 F1
Tarana, NSW 40 A5
Taranna, TAS 241 G4
Tarbrax, QLD....................119 E1
Tarcombe, VIC 80 D6
Tarcoola, SA 155 H1
Tarcoon, NSW 32 D5
Tarcutta, NSW 44 C2
Tardie, WA 186 C6
Tardun, WA 178 B1
Taree, NSW 41 E2
Tarella, NSW 37 F1
Tarella, QLD 119 H2
Targa, TAS 238 A4
Tarin Rock, WA 181 F3
Taringo Downs, NSW 38 B3
Tariton Downs, NT 221 E1
Tarlee, SA 157 E6
Tarmoola, WA 182 B1
Tarnagulla, VIC 79 H5
Tarnook, VIC.....................81 E4
Taroborah, QLD................120 C4
Taroom, QLD 124 D1
Taroon, VIC 85 F4
Tarpeena, SA 159 G5
Tarragal, VIC.....................84 B4
Tarraleah, TAS 240 C1
Tarranginnie, VIC 78 B4
Tarrango, VIC...................76 C4
Tarranyurk, VIC 78 C4
Tarrawingee, VIC 81 F4
Tarrayoukyan, VIC 84 B1
Tarrington, VIC 84 D2
Tarvano, QLD 119 F2
Tarwin, VIC.......................87 E4
Tarwong, NSW 37 H6
Tasman, NSW 38 A3
Tathra, NSW 45 F5
Tatong, VIC 81 E5
Tatura, VIC 80 C4
Tatyoon, VIC 85 F2
Tatyoon North, VIC 85 F1
Tawallah, NT 212 D3
Tawarri, QLD 124 C4
Tawonga, VIC 81 H5
Taylors Arm, NSW 35 F6
Taylors Flat, NSW..............39 H6
Tea Gardens, NSW 41 E4
Teddywaddy, VIC 79 G3
Teddywaddy West, VIC 79 F3
Teds Beach, TAS 240 B3
Teesdale, VIC 85 H3
Telangatuk, VIC 78 C6
Telegraph Point, NSW 41 F1
Telfer Mine, WA 187 G1
Telford, VIC 81 E3
Telopea Downs, VIC..........78 A3
Temma, TAS 236 B3
Temora, NSW 44 C1

Tempe Downs, NT 219 F4
Tempy, VIC.......................78 D1
Tenango, NSW 40 A2
Tenham, QLD 119 F6
Tenham, QLD 123 E1
Tennant Creek, NT 216 B3
Tennant Creek, NT 216 B3
Tennyson, VIC 80 A4
Tent Hill, SA 156 D4
Tenterden, WA 181 E5
Tenterfield, NSW 35 E3
Tepco, SA 157 H4
Terang, VIC 85 F4
Teridgerie, NSW 33 H6
Terip Terip, VIC 80 D6
Terka, SA 156 D4
Termeil, NSW 45 G3
Terowie, SA 157 E5
Terrananya, NSW 36 D4
Terrick Terrick, QLD 119 H5
Terry Hie Hie, NSW 34 B4
Teryawynnia, NSW 37 G3
Teutonic, WA 182 B1
Teviot, QLD 119 F3
Tewantin, QLD 125 G2
Texas, QLD 125 E4
Texas Downs, WA 185 H4
Thalanga, QLD 120 A1
Thalia, VIC 79 F3
Thallon, QLD 124 C4
Thane, QLD 125 F4
Thangana, WA 184 C5
Thangool, QLD 121 F5
Tharbogang, NSW 38 C6
Thargomindah, QLD 123 F3
Tharwa, NSW 45 E3
The Avenue, NSW.............37 F1
The Bluff, NSW 38 C2
The Caves, QLD 121 F4
The Entrance, NSW...........40 D5
The Garden, NT 220 B2
The Gardens, TAS 238 D3
The Gums, SA 157 F6
The Gurdies, VIC 86 D4
The Heart, VIC 87 H3
The Lakes, WA 178 C6
The Lynd
  Junction, QLD 115 H5
The Monument, QLD 118 C2
The Oaks, NSW.................40 B6
The Oaks, SA 157 F5
The Rock, NSW.................44 B2
The Sisters, VIC 85 E3
The Strip, NSW 37 G2
The Troffs, NSW................39 F4
The Twins, SA 152 A6
The Yanko, NSW 43 H2
Theda, WA 185 F2
Theebine, QLD 125 G1
Thelangerin, NSW.............38 A6
Theldarpa, NSW 30 D4
Theodore, QLD 121 E6
Theresa Creek, NSW.........35 F3
Thinoomba, QLD 125 G1
Thirlmere, NSW 40 B6
Thirlstane, TAS 237 G3
Thologolong, VIC 81 H3
Thomby, QLD 124 C3
Thoona, VIC......................81 E4
Thoopara, QLD 120 D1

Thora, NSW 35 F6
Thornleigh, QLD 119 H5
Thorntonia, QLD 114 B6
Thorpdale, VIC.....................87 E4
Thowgla, VIC.......................82 B1
Thowgla Upper, VIC 82 B2
Thredbo Village, NSW 44 D4
Three Rivers, WA 187 E4
Three Springs, WA 178 B2
Three Ways
  Roadhouse, NT 216 B2
Thrungli, QLD 120 A5
Thuddungra, NSW 39 F6
Thulloo, NSW 38 D5
Thundelarra, WA 178 D1
Thurlga, SA 156 A4
Thurloo Downs, NSW 31 G4
Thurrulgoona, QLD..........123 H4
Thursday Island, QLD 117 B1
Thylungra, QLD 123 F1
Thyra, NSW 43 F3
Ti Tree Roadhouse, NT   215 H6
Tiaro, QLD 125 G1
Tiarra, NSW 38 B4
Tibarri, QLD 118 D1
Tibooburra, NSW 30 D4
Tichborne, NSW 39 F4
Tickera, SA 156 D6
Ticklara, QLD 122 D4
Tidal River, VIC 87 F6
Tielta, NSW 36 C1
Tieri, QLD 120 C4
Tieyon, SA 151 G1
Tilba Tilba, NSW 45 F4
Tilcha, SA 153 H6
Tilmouth
  Roadhouse, NT 219 G1
Tilpa, NSW 37 H1
Tiltagara, NSW 38 A2
Tiltagoonah, NSW 38 A1
Timbarra, VIC 82 C4
Timber Creek
  (Police Stn), NT 210 D3
Timberfield, WA 179 H4
Timberoo South, VIC 78 D1
Timbertop, VIC....................81 F6
Timboon, VIC......................85 F4
Timmering, VIC...................80 B4
Timor, NSW 40 C2
Timor, VIC............................79 G6
Timora, QLD 115 E4
Tin Can Bay, QLD 125 G1
Tinamba, VIC.......................87 G3
Tincurrin, WA 181 E3
Tindarey, NSW 38 C1
Tinderry, QLD 123 F2
Tindo, QLD 119 G1
Tingha, NSW 34 D5
Tingoora, QLD 125 F2
Tinnenburra, QLD 123 H4
Tintaldra, VIC......................82 B1
Tintinara, SA 159 F3
Tipperary, NT 206 D5
Tiranna, QLD 123 H1
Tirlta, NSW 37 E1
Tirranna
  Roadhouse, QLD 114 B4
Titjikala (Maryvale), NT 220 B4
Tittybong, VIC.....................79 G2
Tiverton, SA......................157 F4
Tjarramba, WA 184 D4

Tjukayirla
  Roadhouse, WA..............187 H5
Tjukurla, WA 188 D3
Tobermory, NT 217 G6
Tobermory, QLD................123 F2
Tocal, QLD.........................119 F4
Tocumwal, NSW 43 G3
Todd River, NT 220 B3
Todmorden, SA..................151 H2
Togari, TAS 236 B2
Tolga, QLD 116 A3
Tolmie, VIC..........................81 F5
Tom Price, WA 186 D2
Tomahawk, TAS 238 B2
Tomerong, NSW 45 G2
Tomingley, NSW 39 G3
Tomingley West, NSW 39 F3
Tomoo, QLD 124 A2
Tongala, VIC........................80 C4
Tonganah, TAS...................238 B3
Tongio, VIC..........................82 B4
Tongio West, VIC................82 B4
Tongy, QLD 124 A2
Tonimbuk, VIC.....................86 D3
Tonkoro, QLD 119 E4
Toobanna, QLD 116 B5
Toobeah, QLD 124 D4
Tooborac, VIC......................80 B6
Toodyay, WA 178 C5
Toogong, NSW 39 G5
Toogoolawah, QLD 125 F2
Toolakea, QLD 116 B5
Toolamba, VIC....................80 C4
Toolangi, VIC.......................86 D2
Toolebuc, QLD 118 D3
Toolern Vale, VIC...............86 B2
Tooleybuc, NSW 42 D2
Toolibin, WA 181 E3
Tooligie, SA 156 A6
Toolleen, VIC.......................80 B5
Toolondo, VIC......................78 C6
Tooloom, NSW 35 F3
Tooloombilla, QLD 124 B1
Tooma, NSW 44 C3
Toombullup, VIC 81 F5
Toompine Hotel, QLD....123 F2
Toongabbie, VIC 87 F3
Toora, VIC............................87 F5
Tooradin, VIC 86 D3
Toorale, NSW......................32 B5
Tooraweenah, NSW 39 H1
Tooronga, VIC......................87 E2
Toowoomba, QLD 125 F3
Top Hut, NSW 37 F5
Top Springs
  Roadhouse, NT 211 F4
Topar, NSW 37 E2
Torbanlea, QLD 121 H6
Torbay, WA 181 E6
Toronto, NSW 40 D4
Torquay, VIC........................86 A4
Torrens Creek, QLD 119 H1
Torrington, NSW 34 D4
Torrita, VIC..........................76 D6
Torrita, VIC..........................78 C1
Torrumbarry, VIC...............80 A3
Torwood, QLD 115 G3
Tottenham, NSW.................39 E3
Tottington, VIC....................79 F5
Toukley, NSW 40 D5

Towaninny, VIC 79 G2
Towaninny South, VIC 79 G3
Towera, WA 186 B3
Townson, QLD 125 F3
Townsville, QLD 116 B6
Towong, VIC.........................82 C1
Trafalgar, VIC......................87 E3
Tragowel, VIC......................79 H3
Trajere, NSW 39 G5
Trangie, NSW 39 F2
Traralgon, VIC.....................87 F3
Traralgon South, VIC 87 F4
Trawool, VIC........................80 C6
Trayning, WA 179 E5
Traynors Lagoon, VIC........79 F5
Trebonne, QLD 116 B5
Trelega, NSW 37 E5
Trentham, VIC......................86 A1
Tresco, VIC...........................79 G1
Trevallyn, NSW 37 H1
Trewalla, VIC.......................84 B4
Trewilga, NSW 39 G4
Triabunna, TAS...................241 G2
Trida, NSW 38 B4
Trillbar, WA 186 D4
Trinidad, QLD 119 G6
Trowutta, TAS......................236 C3
Trundle, NSW 39 F4
Trunkey Creek, NSW 40 A5
Truro, SA 159 E1
Tryphinia, QLD 121 E4
Tubbut, VIC..........................82 D4
Tucabia, NSW 35 G4
Tuckanarra, WA 186 D5
Tuena, NSW.........................39 H6
Tulendeena, TAS 238 B3
Tullah, TAS 236 D5
Tullamore, NSW 39 F3
Tullibigeal, NSW 38 D5
Tully, QLD 116 A4
Tulmur, QLD 119 E3
Tumbar, QLD 120 A5
Tumbarumba, NSW 44 C3
Tumblong, NSW 44 C2
Tumby Bay, SA...................158 B1
Tumorrama, NSW 44 D2
Tumut, NSW 44 D2
Tunart, VIC..........................76 B4
Tunbridge, TAS 241 E1
Tuncurry, NSW 41 E3
Tundulya, NSW 32 B6
Tungamah, VIC....................81 E3
Tunnack, TAS 241 F2
Tunney, WA 181 E5
Turee Creek, WA 186 D3
Turill, NSW 40 A3
Turlee, NSW 37 F6
Turlinjah, NSW 45 F3
Turners Beach, TAS 237 F3
Turners Marsh, TAS 237 H4
Tuross Heads, NSW 45 F3
Turrawan, NSW 34 B6
Turriff, VIC..........................78 D1
Tuttawa, NSW 33 F3
Tutye, VIC............................78 B1
Tweed Heads, NSW 35 G2
Twelve Mile, NSW 37 E5
Twin Peaks, WA 186 C6
Twin Wells, NSW 36 D4
Two Rivers, QLD 118 C3

Two Rocks, WA 178 B5
Two Wells, SA 159 E1
Tyaak, VIC............................80 C6
Tyabb, VIC...........................86 C4
Tyagong, NSW 39 G6
Tyalgum, NSW 35 G2
Tycannah, NSW 34 A4
Tyenna, TAS 240 C3
Tyers, VIC.............................87 F3
Tylden, VIC..........................86 A1
Tynedale, NSW 35 G4
Tynong, VIC.........................86 D3
Tyntynder Central, VIC 79 G1
Tyntynder South, VIC 79 G1
Tyrendarra, VIC...................84 C4
Tyrendarra East, VIC 84 C4
Tyringham, NSW 35 F5
Tyrrell Downs, VIC.............79 F1

Uanda, QLD 119 H2
Uarbry, NSW 40 A2
Uaroo, WA 186 B2
Ubobo, QLD 121 F5
Ucharonidge, NT 212 B5
Ucolta, SA 157 E5
Ulan, NSW 40 A3
Ularunda, QLD 124 A2
Ulimaroa, QLD 124 D2
Ulladulla, NSW 45 G2
Ullawarra, WA 186 C3
Ullina, VIC...........................85 H1
Ulmarra, NSW 35 G4
Ultima, VIC..........................79 F1
Ulverstone, TAS 237 F3
Umagico, QLD 117 B1
Umbakumba, NT 209 B5
Umbeara, NT 220 A5
Umberatana, SA 157 F1
Umolo, QLD 120 D4
Undera, VIC.........................80 C4
Underbool, VIC....................76 C6
Underwood, TAS.................238 A4
Undilla, QLD 114 B6
Undina, QLD.......................118 D1
Undoolya, NT 220 B3
Ungarie, NSW 39 E5
Ungarra, SA 156 B6
Ungo, QLD 119 G5
Uno, SA 156 C4
Uplands, VIC.......................82 B3
Upper Blessington, TAS 238 B4
Upper Castra, TAS............237 F4
Upper Esk, TAS..................238 B4
Upper Horton, NSW 34 B5
Upper Lansdowne, NSW 41 E2
Upper Maffra West, VIC....87 G3
Upper Manilla, NSW..........34 C6
Upper Natone, TAS 237 E3
Upper Stone, QLD 116 A5
Upper Yarra Dam, VIC 87 E2
Urala, WA............................186 B2
Uralla, NSW 34 D6
Urandangi, QLD 118 A2
Urangeline East, NSW 44 A2
Urania, SA 158 D1
Uranquinty, NSW 44 B2
Urapunga, NT....................212 B1
Urbenville, NSW 35 F2
Urisino, NSW......................31 G4
Urunga, NSW 35 F6

Useless Loop
  (Saltworks), WA 186 A5
Uteara, NSW 32 B5
Uxbridge, TAS 240 D3

Vacy, NSW 40 D3
Valencia Creek, VIC.........87 G2
Valla Beach, NSW 35 F6
Van Lee, QLD 115 G4
Vandyke, QLD 120 C5
Vanrook, QLD 115 E3
Vasey, VIC 84 C1
Vasse, WA 180 B4
Vaughan, VIC 80 A6
Vaughan Springs, NT 214 D6
Veitch, SA 159 G1
Vena Park, QLD 114 D5
Venus Bay, SA...................155 H5
Venus Bay, VIC 87 E5
Verdun Valley, QLD 119 E3
Verdure, QLD 115 H3
Vergemont, QLD 119 F4
Vermont Hill, NSW 38 D3
Verona Sands, TAS 241 E4
Verran, SA 156 B6
Vesper, VIC 87 E2
Victor Harbor, SA 159 E2
Victoria River
  Downs, NT 210 D4
Victoria River
  Roadhouse, NT 211 E2
Victoria Settlement, NT 207 F2
Victoria Valley, TAS 240 D1
Victoria Valley, VIC 84 D2
Victory Downs, NT...........219 G6
Victory Downs, SA...........151 F1
Viewmont, NSW 37 F3
Villafranca, QLD 120 C3
Vinifera, VIC 77 G6
Violet Town, VIC................80 D5
Violet Vale, QLD 117 C5
Virginia, SA 159 E1
Vite Vite, VIC 85 F3
Vivonne Bay, SA 158 C3
Volo, NSW 37 H2

Waaia, VIC 80 C3
Wabricoola, SA.................157 F4
Waddamana, TAS 240 D1
Waddi, NSW 43 H1
Waddikee, SA....................156 B5
Wadeye (Port Keats)
  (Police Stn), NT 206 B6
Wadnaminga, SA 157 G4
Wagant, VIC 77 E6
Wagga Wagga, NSW 44 B2
Waggarandall, VIC............81 E3
Wagon Flat, VIC 78 B3
Wahgunyah, VIC 81 F3
Wahroonga, WA 186 B4
Waikerie, SA 157 F6
Waiko, NSW 38 A4
Wail, VIC 78 D4
Wailki, WA 179 F4
Wairewa, VIC 82 C5
Wairuna, QLD 116 A5
Waitara, QLD 120 D2
Waitchie, VIC 79 F1
Waite River, NT 220 B1
Waka, NSW 30 C4
Wakes Lagoon, QLD 119 H6

Wakool, NSW 43 F2
Wal Wal, VIC 79 E5
Walbundrie, NSW 44 A3
Walcha, NSW 40 D1
Walcha Road, NSW 40 D1
Waldburg, WA 186 D4
Walebing, WA 178 C4
Walenda, NSW 38 A3
Walgett, NSW 33 F5
Walgra, QLD 118 A2
Walhalla, VIC 87 F3
Walhallow, NT 212 D5
Walkaway, WA 178 A1
Walkcege, QLD 119 G1
Walker Flat, SA.................159 F1
Walkers Hill, NSW.............38 D3
Walkerston, QLD..............120 D2
Walkerville, VIC 87 E5
Walla Walla, NSW 44 B3
Wallabadah, NSW 40 C2
Wallace, VIC.......................85 H2
Wallace Rockhole, NT 219 G3
Wallacia, NSW 40 C6
Wallal, QLD 123 H2
Wallal Downs, WA............184 B6
Wallaloo, VIC 79 F5
Wallan, VIC 86 C1
Wallan East, VIC 86 C1
Wallangarra, QLD 125 F4
Wallangra, NSW 34 C4
Wallareenya, WA 184 A6
Wallaroo, QLD 121 E4
Wallaroo, SA 156 D6
Wallatinna, SA 151 F3
Wallendbeen, NSW 44 C1
Wallerawang, NSW 40 B5
Wallerberdina, SA 156 D3
Walleroo, WA 182 A4
Wallinduc, VIC 85 G2
Walling Rock, WA 182 A2
Wallington, VIC 86 B3
Walloway (ruin), SA 157 E4
Wallumbilla, QLD 124 C2
Wallundry, NSW..................44 C1
Wallup, VIC 78 D4
Walmer, NSW 39 G3
Walpeup, VIC 76 D6
Walpole, WA 180 D6
Walton, QLD 120 D4
Walwa, VIC 82 B1
Wamberra, NSW 37 E6
Wamboyne, NSW 39 E5
Wammadoo, QLD 119 F4
Wammutta, QLD................118 C2
Wanaaring, NSW 31 H4
Wanalta, VIC 80 B4
Wanbi, SA 159 G1
Wandagee, WA.................186 B3
Wandana, SA 155 G3
Wandandian, NSW 45 G2
Wandering, WA 180 D3
Wandilo, SA 159 G5
Wando Bridge, VIC 84 B2
Wandoan, QLD 124 D1
Wandong, VIC....................86 C1
Wandovale, QLD 115 H6
Wandsworth, NSW 34 D3
Wandsworth, QLD 119 G6
Wanertown, SA 156 D5

Wanganella, NSW 43 F2
Wangangong, NSW 38 D4
Wangarabell, VIC 83 F5
Wangaratta, VIC..................81 F4
Wangary, SA 158 A1
Wangi, NT 206 D4
Wangkatjungka, WA 185 F5
Wanilla, SA 158 A1
Wanko, QLD 123 H2
Wanna, WA 186 C3
Wannarra, WA 178 D2
Wanneroo, WA 178 C6
Wannon, VIC 84 C2
Wannoo Billabong
  Roadhouse, WA..............186 B5
Wansey Downs, QLD 123 H1
Wantabadgery, NSW 44 C2
Wapet Camp, WA 186 B1
Warakurna, WA 188 C4
Warakurna
  Roadhouse, WA...............188 C4
Waratah, NSW 33 E5
Waratah, TAS 236 D4
Waratah Bay, VIC 87 E5
Waratah North, VIC 87 E5
Warbreccan, QLD 119 F5
Warburn, NSW 38 C6
Warburton, VIC 86 D2
Warburton, WA 188 B4
Warcowie, SA 157 E3
Wards River, NSW 41 E3
Wareek, VIC 79 G6
Wareo, QLD......................123 G2
Wargambegal, NSW..........38 D5
Warialda, NSW 34 C4
Warianna, QLD 119 G2
Warkworth, NSW...............40 C3
Warmun
  (Turkey Creek), WA 185 H4
Warnambool
  Downs, QLD 119 F3
Warncoort, VIC 85 H4
Warne, VIC 79 F2
Warooka, SA 158 C2
Waroona, WA 180 C3
Warra, QLD 118 C4
Warra, QLD 125 E2
Warrachie, SA 156 A5
Warracknabeal, VIC 78 D4
Warraderry, NSW 39 G5
Warragoon, NSW 43 H3
Warragul, VIC 87 E3
Warrak, VIC 85 F1
Warrakimbo, SA 156 D3
Warral, NSW 40 C1
Warralakin, WA 179 F4
Warrambine, VIC 85 H3
Warramboo, SA 156 A5
Warranangra, NSW...........36 D6
Warrandyte, VIC.................86 C2
Warrawagine, WA 187 F1
Warraweena, SA 157 E2
Warreah, QLD 119 H1
Warrell Creek, NSW 35 F6
Warren, NSW 39 F2
Warren Vale, QLD 114 D5
Warrenbayne, VIC 81 E5
Warriedar, WA 178 D2
Warrigal, NSW 39 E2
Warrigal, QLD....................119 H1
Warrina (Ruin), SA 152 B4

Warringa, TAS...................237 E4
Warrion, VIC 85 G4
Warrnambool, VIC 85 E4
Warrobil, NSW 40 A3
Warrong, QLD 120 C6
Warrong, VIC 84 D4
Warroo, NSW 39 F5
Warroora, WA 186 A3
Warrow, SA 158 A1
Warrumbungle, NSW........39 G1
Warruwi, NT 207 H2
Wartaka, SA 156 C4
Wartook, VIC 78 D4
Warwick, QLD 125 F4
Watalgan, QLD 121 G6
Watchem, VIC 79 E3
Watchupga, VIC 79 E2
Waterbag, NSW 37 E2
Waterbank, WA 184 C4
Waterford, VIC 87 H2
Waterloo, NT 210 B4
Waterloo, SA 157 E6
Waterloo, TAS 240 D4
Waterloo, VIC 85 G1
Watervale, SA 157 E6
Wathana, QLD 116 D6
Watheroo, WA 178 C3
Watsons Creek, NSW 34 C6
Watten, QLD 119 G1
Wattle Creek, VIC...............79 F6
Wattle Flat, NSW 40 A4
Wattle Hill, VIC 85 G5
Wattle Vale, NSW 31 F5
Waubra, VIC 85 G1
Wauchope, NSW 41 F2
Wauchope
  Roadhouse, NT 216 B4
Waukaringa (Ruin), SA 157 F4
Wave Hill, NSW 37 G2
Wave Hill, NT....................211 E5
Waverley, QLD 120 B6
Waverley Downs, NSW 31 G3
Waverney, QLD 119 E6
Wayatinah, TAS................240 C1
Weabonga, NSW 40 D1
Wearne, NSW 34 B3
Webbs, NSW 39 G3
Wedderburn, VIC 79 G4
Wedderburn
  Junction, VIC 79 G4
Wee Elwah, NSW 38 B4
Wee Jasper, NSW...............44 D2
Wee Waa, NSW...................34 A5
Weebo, WA 187 F6
Weedallion, NSW 39 F6
Weegena, TAS 237 G4
Weelamurra, QLD 123 H3
Weelarrana, WA 187 E3
Weemelah, NSW 34 A3
Weeragua, VIC 83 E5
Weerangourt, VIC 84 C3
Weerite, VIC 85 F4
Weetaliba, NSW 40 A2
Weethalle, NSW 38 D6
Weetulta, SA 156 D6
Weetulta, SA 158 D1
Wee-Wee-Rup, VIC 80 D2
Wehla, VIC 79 G5
Weilmoringle, NSW 33 E3
Weipa, QLD 117 A3

Weja, NSW 38 D5
Welaregang, NSW 44 C3
Welbourne Hill, SA 151 G3
Welbungin, WA 179 E4
Weldborough, TAS 238 C3
Wellclose, QLD 119 H6
Wellingrove, NSW 34 D4
Wellington, NSW 39 H3
Wellington, SA 159 F2
Wellshot, QLD 119 G4
Wellstead, WA 181 F5
Welltown, QLD 124 D4
Welltree, NT 206 D4
Welshmans Reef, VIC 79 H6
Welshpool, VIC 87 F5
Wemen, VIC 77 E5
Wenlock (ruin), QLD 117 B4
Wensley, QLD 119 E1
Wentworth, NSW 37 E6
Wentworth Falls, NSW 40 B5
Wepar, SA 159 G5
Weranga, QLD 125 E3
Werna, QLD 119 F2
Wernadinga, QLD 114 C4
Werneth, VIC 85 G3
Werribee, VIC 86 B3
Werribee South, VIC..........86 B3
Werrimull, VIC 76 C4
Werris Creek, NSW 40 C1
Wertaloona, SA 157 F1
Wesley Vale, TAS 237 F3
West Frankford, TAS........237 G4
West Kentish, TAS............237 F4
West Leichhardt, QLD 118 C1
West Montague, TAS 236 B2
West Pine, TAS 237 E3
West Ridgley, TAS 237 E3
West Scotsdale, TAS........238 A3
West Wyalong, NSW 39 E6
Westbury, TAS 237 G4
Westby, NSW 44 B3
Westby, VIC 79 H2
Westdale, NSW..................40 C1
Westdale, WA 180 D2
Western Creek, NT 211 G3
Western Creek, TAS 237 G5
Western Flat, SA 159 G4
Western Junction, TAS   238 A5
Westerton, QLD 119 F4
Westerway, TAS 240 D2
Westgate, QLD..................123 H2
Westgrove, QLD 120 C6
Westland, QLD 119 G4
Westmere, VIC 85 F2
Westmoreland, QLD 114 A3
Westonia, WA 179 F5
Westward Ho, QLD 118 C3
Westwood, QLD 121 E4
Westwood, TAS 237 H4
Wetherby, QLD 119 F2
Weymouth, TAS 237 H3
Wharminda, SA 156 B6
Wharparilla, VIC 80 B3
Wheeo, NSW......................45 E1
Whetstone, QLD 125 E4
Whim Creek, WA 186 D1
Whiporie, NSW....................35 F4
Whirily, VIC 79 F3
White Beach, TAS 241 F4
White Cliffs, NSW 31 F6

White Cliffs, WA 182 D1
White Flat, SA 158 B1
White Hills, TAS 238 A4
White Leeds, NSW 36 D3
White Wells, WA 178 D2
Whitefoord, TAS 241 F2
Whitemark, TAS................247 C6
Whitemore, TAS 237 H5
Whitewood, QLD 119 G2
Whitfield, VIC 81 F5
Whitlands, VIC 81 F5
Whittata, SA 156 D3
Whittlesea, VIC..................86 C1
Whitton, NSW....................43 H1
Whitwarta, SA 157 E6
Whorouly, VIC 81 F4
Whroo, VIC 80 C5
Whyalla, SA 156 D5
Whyte Yarcowie, SA 157 E5
Wiangaree, NSW 35 G2
Wickepin, WA 181 E3
Wickham, WA 186 C1
Wickliffe, VIC 85 E2
Widbury, QLD 121 F6
Widgee Downs, NSW 32 D3
Widgelli, NSW 38 C6
Widgelli, NSW 43 H1
Widgiemooltha, WA 182 B5
Widgiewa, NSW 43 H2
Widgiewa, NSW 44 A2
Wilangee, NSW 36 D2
Wilburville, TAS 237 H6
Wilby, VIC 81 E3
Wilcannia, NSW 37 G2
Wilga, NSW 37 H1
Wilga Downs, NSW 38 D1
Wilgareena, NSW 32 C6
Wilkatana, SA 156 D3
Wilkur, VIC 79 E3
Wilkur South, VIC 79 E3
Wilkurra, NSW 37 F4
Willa, VIC 78 D1
Willaba, NSW 37 E4
Willalooka, SA 159 G4
Willangie, VIC 79 E2
Willare Br.
  Roadhouse, WA............184 D4
Willatook, VIC 84 D3
Willaura, VIC 85 E2
Willawarrin, NSW 41 F1
Willbriggie, NSW 43 H1
Willenabrina, VIC 78 D3
Willeroo, NT 211 E2
William Creek, SA 152 B5
Williambury, WA 186 B3
Williams, WA....................180 D3
Williamsdale, NSW............45 E3
Williamsford, TAS 236 D5
Williamstown, SA 159 E1
Willippa, SA 157 E3
Willochra (Ruin), SA 156 D4
Willora, NT 216 A5
Willow Grove, VIC 87 E3
Willow Tree, NSW 40 C2
Willowie, SA 157 E4
Willowmavin, VIC 80 B6
Willowmavin, VIC 86 B1
Willowra, NT 215 G5
Willows, QLD 120 C4
Willung, VIC 87 G4

Willunga, SA 159 E2
Willurah, NSW 43 G2
Wilmington, QLD 116 D6
Wilmington, SA 156 D4
Wilmot, TAS 237 F4
Wilpena, SA 157 E3
Wilpoorinna, SA 153 E6
Wiltshire, TAS 236 C2
Wiluna, WA 187 F5
Wimbledon, NSW 40 A5
Winbin, QLD 123 G2
Winchelsea, VIC 85 H4
Windalle, NSW 37 F3
Windara, NSW 38 A1
Windera, NSW 38 C1
Winderie, WA 186 B4
Windeyer, NSW 40 A4
Windidda, WA 187 G5
Windimurra, WA 179 F1
Windmill
  Roadhouse, WA............178 B4
Windorah, QLD 119 F6
Windouran, NSW 43 E2
Windsor, NSW 40 C5
Wingeel, VIC 85 H3
Wingelinna, WA 188 D4
Wingello, NSW 45 F1
Wingen, NSW 40 C2
Wingham, NSW 41 E2
Winiam, VIC 78 C4
Winiam East, VIC 78 C4
Winjallok, VIC 79 F5
Winnaleah, TAS 238 C3
Winnambool, VIC 77 F5
Winnindoo, VIC 87 G3
Winninowie, SA 156 D4
Winslow, VIC 85 E4
Wintinna, SA 151 G3
Winton, NSW 40 C1
Winton, QLD 119 F3
Winton, VIC 81 E4
Wiragula, NSW 40 D3
Wirrabara, SA 156 D5
Wirraminna, SA 156 B2
Wirraminna, SA 156 B2
Wirrappa, SA 156 C2
Wirrealpa, SA 157 E2
Wirrega, SA 159 G3
Wirrida, SA 151 H6
Wirrilyerna, QLD 118 B3
Wirrinya, NSW 39 F5
Wirrulla, SA 155 H4
Wiseleigh, VIC 82 B5
Wisemans Ferry, NSW 40 C5
Witchcliffe, WA 180 B5
Witchelina, SA 152 D6
Witchitie, SA 157 E3
Withersfield, QLD 120 C4
Withywine, QLD 119 F4
Wittenburra, QLD 123 G3
Wittenoom, WA................186 D2
Wivenhoe, TAS 237 E3
Wodonga, VIC 81 G3
Wogarl, WA 181 F1
Wogarno, WA 179 E1
Wollar, NSW 40 B3
Wollombi, NSW 40 C4
Wollomombi, NSW 35 E6
Wollongong, NSW 45 G1
Wollun, NSW......................34 D6

Wolseley, SA 159 G4
Wolumia, NSW....................45 F5
Wolverton, QLD 117 B4
Womalilla, QLD 124 B2
Wombat, NSW 44 D1
Wombelano, VIC 78 C6
Womboota, NSW 43 F3
Wombungi, NT 210 D1
Won Wron, VIC 87 G4
Wonboyn, NSW 45 F6
Wondai, QLD 125 F2
Wondalga, NSW 44 C2
Wondinong, WA 186 D6
Wondoola, QLD 114 D5
Wonga, NSW 31 F4
Wonga, NSW 36 D3
Wonga Lilli, NSW 31 G5
Wongabinda, NSW 34 B4
Wongalara, NSW 37 H2
Wongalee, QLD 119 G1
Wongan Hills, WA 178 D4
Wonganoo, WA 187 F5
Wongarbon, NSW 39 G3
Wongarra, VIC 85 H5
Wongatoa, NSW 38 B6
Wongawol, WA 187 G4
Wongianna (Ruin), SA....152 D6
Wongulla, SA 159 F1
Wonthaggi, VIC 86 D5
Wonwondah East, VIC 78 D5
Wonwondah North, VIC 78 D5
Wonyip, VIC 87 F4
Wood Wood, VIC 77 G6
Woodanilling, WA............181 E4
Woodbourne, VIC 85 H2
Woodbourne, VIC 86 D1
Woodbridge, TAS 241 E4
Woodburn, NSW 35 G3
Woodbury, TAS 241 E1
Woodenbong, NSW 35 F2
Woodend, NSW 44 B2
Woodend, VIC 86 B1
Woodford, QLD 125 G2
Woodgate, QLD 121 H6
Woodie Woodie
  Mine, WA 187 F1
Woodlands, QLD 124 B2
Woodlands, WA 186 D4
Woodleigh, WA 186 B5
Woods Point, VIC..............87 F2
Woods Well, SA 159 F3
Woodsdale, TAS................241 F2
Woodside, SA 159 E2
Woodside, VIC 87 G4
Woodside Beach, VIC........87 G4
Woodstock, NSW 39 G5
Woodstock, QLD 115 F6
Woodstock, QLD..............116 B6
Woodstock, QLD 119 E3
Woodstock, VIC 79 H5
Woodstock, VIC 86 C2
Woodstock, WA 187 E1
Woodvale, VIC 80 A5
Woohlpooer, VIC 84 D1
Woolah, WA 185 H3
Woolamai, VIC 86 D4
Woolbrook, NSW 40 D1
Wooleen, WA 186 C5
Woolerina, QLD 124 B4
Woolgoolga, NSW 35 G5
Woolgorong, WA 186 C6

Jooli, NSW 35 G5
Joolibar, WA 182 B5
Joolla Downs, NT............216 A6
Joolner, NT 207 E3
Joolomin, NSW 40 C1
Joolooga, QLD.................125 G1
Joolshed Flat, SA 156 D4
Joolsthorpe, VIC 85 E3
Jooltana, SA 157 F1
Joomargama, NSW 44 B3
Joomelang, VIC 79 E2
Joomera, SA 156 C2
Joonigan, QLD 118 C1
Jooragee, VIC 81 G4
Joorak, VIC 78 C4
Jooramel
  Roadhouse, WA.............186 B4
Joorarra, VIC 87 F5
Joori Yallock, VIC 86 D2
Joorinen, VIC 79 G1
Joorlba, WA 189 A4
Joorndoo, VIC 85 E3
Jooroloo, WA 178 C6
Jooroona, QLD 118 A1
Jooroonook, VIC 79 F4
Joosang, VIC 79 G4
Jootton, NSW 41 E3
Jorsley Refinery, WA 180 C3
Jotonga, QLD...................120 C2
Jowan, QLD 121 E5
Joy Woy, NSW....................40 D5
Jrattonbully, SA..............159 G5
Jrightley, VIC 81 E5
Jrotham Park, QLD 115 G3
Jubagul, QLD....................124 D1
Jubin, WA 178 D3
Judinna, SA.......................156 A5
Jujal Wujal, QLD 116 A2
Juk Wuk, VIC 82 A6
Julgulmerang, VIC 82 C4
Jumalgi, QLD 121 E3
Jundowie, WA 178 C6
Junghnu, VIC 80 D3
Junkar, SA 159 G1
Jurankuwu, NT 206 C2
Jurruk, VIC 87 G3
Juttagoona, NSW 38 B1
Jutul, QLD 125 F2
Jyaga, QLD 125 E3
Jyalkatchem, WA 179 E5
Jyalong, NSW 39 E6
Jyan, NSW 35 F3
Jyandotte, QLD 115 H5
Jyandra, QLD 123 H2
Jyanga, NSW......................39 F3
Jyangala, NSW 39 H6
Jycarbah, QLD 121 E4
Jycheproof, VIC 79 F3
Jychitella, VIC 79 G4
Jycliffe Well
  Roadhouse, NT 216 B4
Jydgee, WA 179 E1
Jye River, VIC 85 H5
Jyee, NSW 40 D4
Jyeebo, VIC 82 A2
Jyelangta, VIC 85 G5
Jyerba, QLD 125 F4
Jyloo, WA 186 C2
Jyloona, VIC 37 H1
Jymah, NSW 44 B3
Jyndham, NSW 45 F5

Wyndham, WA...................185 H3
Wynyangoo, WA 186 D6
Wynyard, TAS 236 D3
Wyoming, NSW 38 B6
Wyong, NSW......................40 D5
Wyrra, NSW 39 E5
Wyseby, QLD.....................120 D6
Wyuna, VIC 80 C3

Yaamba, QLD 121 E4
Yaapeet, VIC 78 C2
Yabba North, VIC 80 D3
Yaboroo, QLD....................120 D1
Yabulu, QLD 116 B5
Yacka, SA 157 E5
Yackandandah, VIC 81 G4
Yadlamulka, SA 156 D3
Yakabindie, WA 187 F6
Yakara, QLD 123 F3
Yakka Munga, WA 184 D4
Yalamurra, QLD 123 G2
Yalardy, WA 186 B5
Yalata, SA 155 E3
Yalata Roadhouse, SA 155 E3
Yalbalgo, WA 186 B4
Yalbra, WA 186 C4
Yalgogrin, NSW 38 D5
Yallakool, NSW..................43 F3
Yallalong, WA 186 C6
Yallaroi, NSW 34 C3
Yalleen, WA 186 C2
Yalleroi, QLD 120 A5
Yallingup, WA 180 B4
Yalloch, NSW 38 A3
Yallook, VIC 80 A4
Yallourn North, VIC..........87 F3
Yallunda Flat, SA 156 B6
Yalpara, SA 157 E4
Yalwal, NSW 45 G2
Yalymboo, SA 156 C3
Yamala, QLD 120 C4
Yamarna, WA 187 H6
Yamba, NSW 31 G4
Yamba, NSW 35 G4
Yambacoona, TAS............247 C1
Yambah, NT 220 A2
Yamboyna, QLD 120 C4
Yambuk, VIC 84 D4
Yambutta, QLD 123 F2
Yan Yan, QLD 120 D4
Yan Yean, VIC 86 C2
Yanac, VIC 78 B3
Yanakie, VIC 87 E5
Yancannia, NSW 31 F5
Yanchep, WA 178 B5
Yanco, NSW........................44 A1
Yanco Glen, NSW 36 D2
Yandal, WA 187 F5
Yandamindra, WA 182 C2
Yandanooka, WA 178 B2
Yandaran, QLD 121 G6
Yandeyarra, WA 186 D1
Yandil, WA 187 E5
Yandilla, NSW 32 C6
Yandina, QLD 125 G2
Yando, VIC 79 H3
Yandoit, VIC 79 H6
Yanerbie Beach, SA 155 G4
Yanergee, NSW 40 B1
Yangalake, NSW................43 E1
Yangan, QLD 125 F4

Yaninee, SA 156 A4
Yankalilla, SA 159 E2
Yankaninna, SA 157 F1
Yanna, QLD 123 H2
Yannathan, VIC 86 D3
Yanrey, WA 186 B2
Yantabulla, NSW 32 B4
Yantanabie, SA 155 H4
Yara, NSW 38 C4
Yaraka, QLD 119 G5
Yarck, VIC 80 D2
Yardea, SA 156 A4
Yarding, WA 181 E1
Yaringa, WA 186 B5
Yarlarweelor, WA 186 D4
Yarloop, WA 180 C3
Yarmawl, NSW 38 D6
Yarra Creek, TAS 247 C3
Yarra Glen, VIC 86 D2
Yarra Junction, VIC 86 D2
Yarrabah, QLD 116 A3
Yarrabandai, NSW 39 F4
Yarraberk, VIC 79 H5
Yarrabubba, WA...............187 E5
Yarraby, VIC 77 G6
Yarraden, QLD 117 C5
Yarragon, VIC 87 E3
Yarralin, NT 210 D4
Yarraloola, WA 186 B1
Yarram, VIC 87 G4
Yarramalong, NSW 40 C5
Yarraman, NSW 40 B2
Yarraman, QLD 125 F2
Yarramba, SA 157 G3
Yarrara, VIC 76 B4
Yarras, NSW 41 E2
Yarrawalla, VIC 79 H3
Yarrawalla South, VIC 79 H3
Yarrawin, NSW 33 E5
Yarrawonga, QLD 124 A1
Yarrawonga, VIC 81 E3
Yarromere, QLD 120 A2
Yarronvale, QLD...............123 G2
Yarroweyah, VIC...............80 D3
Yarroweyah South, VIC 80 D3
Yarrowitch, NSW 41 E1
Yarrowyck, NSW 34 D6
Yarwun, QLD 121 F5
Yass, NSW...........................45 E1
Yatchaw, VIC 84 D2
Yathong, NSW 38 C3
Yathonga, NSW 32 A6
Yatpool, VIC 76 D4
Yea, VIC 80 D6
Yealering, WA 181 E2
Yearinan, NSW 39 H1
Yearinga, VIC 78 A4
Yednalue, SA 157 E3
Yednia, QLD 125 G2
Yeeda, WA 184 D4
Yeelanna, SA 156 A6
Yeelirrie, WA 187 E5
Yeerip, VIC 81 E3
Yelarbon, QLD 125 E4
Yelbeni, WA 179 E5
Yellowdine, WA 179 H5
Yelta, NSW 37 G3
Yeltacowie, SA 156 C2
Yelvertoft, QLD 114 B6
Yelvertoft, QLD 118 B1

Yenda, NSW 38 C6
Yenloora, QLD 123 F3
Yeo Yeo, NSW....................44 C1
Yeodene, VIC.....................85 H4
Yeoval, NSW 39 G4
Yeppoon, QLD 121 F4
Yerecoin, WA 178 C4
Yerelina, SA 153 F6
Yerelina, SA 157 F1
Yerilla, WA 182 C2
Yerong Creek, NSW 44 B2
Yerrinbool, NSW 43 F1
Yerrinbool, NSW 45 G1
Yethera, NSW 39 F3
Yetman, NSW 34 C3
Yeungroon, VIC 79 G4
Yiddah, NSW......................39 E6
Yilliminnung, WA 181 E3
Yin Barun, VIC 81 E5
Yindi, WA 182 D4
Yinnar, VIC 87 F4
Yinnetharra, WA 186 C4
Yirrkala, NT 209 B3
Yiyili, WA 185 G5
Yolla, TAS 236 D3
Yongala, SA 157 E5
Yoogali, NSW 38 C6
York, WA 180 D1
York Plains, TAS 241 F1
Yorketown, SA 158 D2
Yorkrakine, WA 179 E5
Yornaning, WA 180 D3
Yornup, WA 180 C5
Yoting, WA 181 E2
Youangarra, WA 179 F1
Youanmi Downs, WA 179 F1
Youanmite, VIC 80 D3
Young, NSW 39 G6
Youngerina, NSW 32 B4
Youngs, WA 181 E6
Yowah, QLD 123 G3
Yowergabbie, WA 186 D6
Yudnapinna, SA 156 C3
Yuelamu, NT 215 F6
Yuendumu
  (Police Stn), NT 215 F6
Yuimmery, WA 179 G1
Yuin, WA 186 C6
Yulara, NT 219 E5
Yulcarley, NSW 32 B4
Yuleba, QLD.......................124 D2
Yullundry, NSW 39 G4
Yuluma, NSW 44 A2
Yumali, SA 159 F2
Yuna, WA 178 A1
Yungaburra, QLD 116 A3
Yungera, VIC 77 F5
Yungundi, NSW 39 G2
Yunnerman, QLD..............124 A3
Yunta, SA 157 F4
Yuraraba, QLD 125 E4
Yuruga, QLD 116 B5
Yuulong, VIC 85 G5

Zamia, QLD........................120 C5
Zanthus, WA 189 A3
Zeehan, TAS 236 C6
Zenoni, QLD 123 F4
Zumstein, VIC 78 D6

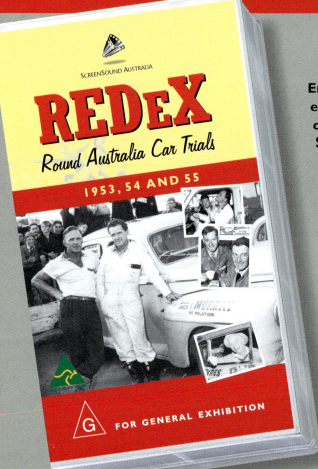